The English S

'Nothing to do but run

By

Anthony Randall

&

Doug Goddard

Jemmett Affection Publishing

First published in Great Britain 2004
Jemmett Affection
31 Hill View
Great Kimble
Aylesbury
Buck HP17 9TP

Kindle version worldwide 2014
Jemmett Affection

Text © Anthony Randall and Doug Goddard 2005

The moral right of Anthony Randall and Doug Goddard to be
Identified as authors for this work has been asserted in accordance
with the Copyright, Designs and patents act, 1988 and the duration
of Copyright and rights in Performances Regulations 1995.

All rights reserved. No part of this publication may be
Reproduced, stored in a retrieval system, or transmitted,
In any form or by ant means, electronic mechanical,
photocopying, recording or otherwise, without prior written
permission of the publisher and copyright owner, nor be
otherwise circulated in any form of binding or cover
other than that in which it is published and without a
similar condition including this condition being
imposed on the subsequent purchaser.

A CIP catalogue record for the hard copy of this book is
Available from the British Library

Paperback edition worldwide 2015
ISBN-10: 1516991168
ISBN-13: 978-1516991167

Cover concept by Kim Crawford
Photography by Jeremy Trew

Contents

Introduction 5

Chapter one: Left or right 6

Chapter two: The suits arrive 19

Chapter three: A thousand to one 32

Chapter four: Acceptance 41

Chapter five: The blessing 52

Chapter six: Kitted out 63

Chapter seven: The Chinese sting 74

Chapter eight: The meeting 92

Chapter nine: The alliance 113

Chapter ten: Reality bites 128

Chapter eleven: Nuevo cuisine 148

Chapter twelve: Hot head 160

Chapter thirteen: Walk before I can walk 176

Chapter fourteen: Unexpected presents 196

Chapter fifteen: The calling 220

Chapter sixteen: Helping hands 240

Chapter seventeen: All round friends 266

Chapter eighteen: Nothing to do but run 294

Song credits 320

The English Sombrero

is dedicated to the memory of Doug's mother Pat Shirt.

A day is not lost if a good memory is made.

Introduction

It's 1999 and time to meet Don Simmons, a self made businessman with a larger than life character, who is about to experience the greatest transformation ever. If you ever needed a kickstart to take up the battle for some 'waistline definition' or simply yearn to get more out of life than a nine-to-five existence, you've picked up the right book. Don's story contains inspiration, perspiration and self revelation with a healthy dose of humour and life observations along the way.

CHAPTER ONE
Left or right

"THREE OR FOUR EGGS on your Monty?"

"Actually you'd better make it four, I'm meeting the boys later so I'll need some soaking-up material," I hollered down to Ann.

"It'll be on the table in five minutes!" she replied, turning around and walking back up the hall into the kitchen. My wife had been shouting at me from the bottom of the stairs, trying to ascertain this morning's breakfast requirements, not that it was any deviation from the norm. Just like Field Marshall Bernard Montgomery, I always had the Full Monty at the start of each day.

"If I were a rich man, Yubby dibby dibby dibby dibby dibby dum."

"You're in fine voice today," said my sarcastic daughter as she passed the bathroom where I was finishing off my shave.

"Well what do you expect; it's a glorious Sunday morning?" I replied enthusiastically.

And what a splendid day it was, the kind of morning when the air smelt good and reminded you of some warm, safe far-off place that you can't quite put your finger on. Sunlight streamed in through the opaque glass window and sparkled on the water in the handbasin.

"What a handsome bastard," I told my reflection in the mirror. The irony would not have been necessary, were I not carrying an obsolete 13 stone of flab about my frame.

Thirty years ago I had been a truly good-looking man, fit, sharp as a blade and very ambitious. I'd left school with no grades and started as a car salesman at a prestigious Porsche dealership in town. Within a year, and blessed with the gift of the gab, I was outselling all the other salesmen by far. I admit that I was cheeky, but I was never rude. I had a vast knowledge of the cars that I was selling. It was for me a real passion.

More sales meant more money. More money meant classy suits, flash motors, better nightclubs, loads of women, but one woman in particular, Ann. She worked in a nearby jeweller's shop, and appreciated the finer things in life. She would often walk by the showroom on her lunch break to admire the Porsches, sit in one now and again and flirt with the idea of someday owning one; and I, being utterly smitten, would flirt with her. These days though I weighed in at a staggering twenty-five stone, thirteen and a half pounds. Well at least that's what the scales screamed at me last Tuesday!

The large oval plate, close to overflowing, had been placed at the head of our farmhouse kitchen table. Next to it another prepared place lay empty, waiting for its occupant to arrive. Les was always late, even for a Sunday morning fry-up. My son Mathew and his pal Ian, who had stayed over for the night, were busy tucking into their Coco Pops. June our youngest and her friend Jenny were gorging themselves on their second bowl of Sugar Puffs, in anticipation of this morning's riding lesson. Trish sat at the opposite end of the table, as far away from me as possible, her legs tucked underneath her, listening to her Walkman and texting some useless piece of information to one of her freaky mates.

"Another ten pence down the toilet," I spouted across the table. Trish looked up briefly, glared at me and then continued stabbing away at her phone keypad. Half a bowl of muesli sat idle in front of her.

"Aren't you going to finish your rabbit food?" I enquired.

Nothing!

I needed to get a response. "Do I live in a parallel universe to you lot?"

Still nothing.

There we have it then, I concluded. A cut and dried case of being worlds apart!

My family was growing up. No longer did the kids want to sit around the Sunday breakfast table and ask about the 'fabulous deals' their father was going to pull off — those days were truly over. Instead they would buzz around the table, barely noticing my existence. I shouldn't complain though, they were good kids. My thoughts were interrupted by Ann's soothing voice.

"You got enough there love?"

"Yes thanks petal, this should fill the gap for at least ..." I stopped mid-sentence, totally missing the sarcasm in Ann's question but noticing her look of displeasure. She had been disappointed to say the least when I had given up Weight Watchers, but knew wholeheartedly that once I had made my mind up there was no turning me. Years of gentle persuasion, persistent nagging or even blatant blackmail had failed to address my addictions. I was having none of it; I was as fit as a double bass and as I had always said, "The day that drinking starts to affect my work, I'll give up work!" My smooth-operator charm had sold me thousands of cars over the years, and this morning it had miraculously secured me another Full Monty!

On a points-scoring diet, a man of my stature would be allotted 38 points a day. The breakfast that lay before me, including two mugs of tea, bread and butter, and a pint of orange juice, would make up about 50 of those points. And this would only fill me up until I made it to the newsagents for a quick sugar fix of two Mars Bars, a family size bag of Liquorice Allsorts and a litre bottle of Coke to accompany me and Les on a business adventure. Some days I would even buy a paper.

I looked down and scoured the terrain of my platter with the enthusiasm of a man who had just been rescued from years of being chained to a wall.

"Any chance of some cutlery love?" I yelled across the kitchen, at the same time picking up a piece of fried bread and slamming it into an egg, scooping up the fat-rich yolk and shovelling it piping hot into my gob.

"How graceful," Ann sighed. She knew what I was like with me when it came to food and drink. I had little patience, and absolutely no self-control.

"Couldn't you have waited for these?" she enquired, handing me a knife and fork while shaking her head disapprovingly.

"What?" I replied.

"The picture of innocence," she said sardonically.

I had always been a big boy. On my wedding day 23 years ago, I'd weighed in at 18 stone, but I carried it well by being 6'2". Luckily, size had never been an issue for Ann. She loved me for the man that I was. In her words I was "kind, warm-hearted and clever," and of course she knew I'd go far! She'd picked a good 'un. These past two or three years, though, I was looking more like Doughboy than Don Boy, piling on the pounds quicker than a Saturday-night lottery machine. I'd truly bloated out of control; it was like my body and face had gone walkabout.

A couple of weeks ago Ann had gone behind my back and spoken to our family GP, Dr Amstone, who had treated our family ailments for the past two decades. Fortunately he hadn't had to deal with me much— I wasn't the kind to complain very often. Dr Amstone didn't favour breaking the ethical code, patient confidentiality and all that, but he was a family friend and he could see the strain that Ann was going through worrying about my body size. A couple of nights ago he'd popped round unannounced for a friendly discussion with the two of us.

"You know that Donald is suffering from cartilage trouble in both knees, don't you Ann?" he said.

I can still remember the evil look that Ann had cut me across the living room. "No, he kept that one to himself!"

"I shan't go into detail, but Don came in to see me recently about a possible operation. I told him …" Dr Amstone glanced over his specs as if to give me the opportunity to confess all to Ann. No chance, I'd leave that to the professional.

He went on, "I told him that a kinder and easier resolve would be to shed some weight. A man of your Don's height should average around 14 stone. This ideal weight would reduce the problem by 70 to 80 per cent!"

Ann said nothing, but slowly nodded. The worry on her face had been clearly visible, but nothing could have prepared me for the shit that was about to hit the fan.

"I have to admit that when I saw you recently in the newsagents, I was shocked by how much bigger you'd got. You need to slim down, Don. Come and see me at the surgery, please. I don't want to worry you but if the truth be known you're on the verge of a heart attack, or at the very least a stroke — either way an early grave!"

My line of thought was interrupted by a sudden burst of frantic barking from my German shepherd dogs, Buck and Ben, who were sounding the alarm bells for someone approaching the house. I let them have a free range of the grounds at the back of the property, to deter any unwanted visitors, but I could tell by their excited yelping that they had gotten a whiff of someone they knew. My suspicions were confirmed when I heard the gravel tones of my longest and oldest friend.

"'Ello pups, what's all the noise for, eh, eh?"

A large bone went flying past the kitchen window as Ann turned to the door. Les sneaked in and slammed the door shut before the dogs realised they'd been thrown a decoy.

"You having your normal, Les?" Ann asked. She had cooked as many breakfasts for Les as she'd rustled up for me, but suspiciously Leslie had remained a tad skinnier than I.

"Smashing, Ann," replied Les rubbing his hands together, "You alright Don?"

I had known Les most of my life. We had lived next door-but-one to each other on the council estate where we had both grown up. The houses that we lived in were built in the 1950s: fairly characterless, built to last, but the most redeeming features about them and the secret of my early rise to fortune, were the garages at the bottom of the garden. I'm lovingly fond of that damp oil-smelling little sanctuary and it feels just like yesterday that we were up to our elbows in grease restoring some pride to an old breaker. To drive to the garage you had to go round the block to the rear and into the cul-de-sac that served all the neighbouring gardens; on foot you could just negotiate a strip of cracked and weathered concrete that we called the garden path. Our friendship had been born from within these garages. It was an unlikely relationship because of the age difference. Les was 26-years-old when we met, twice my age, but we shared a common interest: motor cars.

It had become apparent to all at this early age, that I would become an entrepreneur. I had acquired a small fortune by using my dad's garage to buy, sell or fix pushbikes, motorbikes and their spares. My business soon expanded to such an extent that I had taken over the garden shed and our parking bay as well. My father hadn't been best pleased at the time, as it meant he'd had to buy road tax for his car for the first time ever, in order to park it out in the street. My ambition had always been to sell second-hand cars, but to do this I needed a few more things: a larger garage, a driveway and, of course, a driving licence. This is where Les had come up trumps. He not only had a full licence but the council, in its wisdom, had provided him with a double garage, perfect for my future plans.

Les was not a simple man, but he wasn't the brightest bulb on the Christmas tree either. Neither was he was an idle man, he just didn't have the resolve to push himself, and on the day that we cemented our friendship, he was conveniently in a state of 'looking for employment'. It had started off with an "Alright?" over the garden fence, and within a matter of weeks we were both under a bonnet and deep in conversation about classic cars, how the new model compared to the old or, in fact, how they didn't compare. By the time the year had finished, Les was chauffeuring me about and was on my payroll.

My eyes flicked towards Les for the briefest second and I managed to mouth, "Yeah fine mate, have a seat" before returning to my first love, the breakfast plate in front of me! My eyes bulged as I loaded another fork full of cholesterol into a black hole, sending bacon grease and mushroom juice abseiling over my tastebuds. I was in utopia and it took a while for me to realise that the family were squabbling over the tabloids. Our house was not on a paperboy's route, so Les had taken it upon himself to do the paper run each Sunday.

"Did you pick up the Classified on your way?" I asked through a mouthful of plum tomatoes.

"Certainly did, here you go," Les leant across the breakfast table and handed me the paper.

"Did you get me anything, Uncle Les?" June asked sweetly.

"Hmm, I got Horse and Pony, but you wouldn't want that, would you?" Les joked. June ran over and grabbed it, then scampered off, giggling down the hall with Jenny in tow. Ann cleared away the crockery, to allow me more room to spread the paper and get a better look at the motoring section.

When I'd first started dealing in prestigious cars, Les and I would take a couple of drivers and go into London in order to grab the first editions hot off the press. We'd then head to an all-night café, have some breakfast and start ringing around. It would piss off an awful lot of people who were hoping to have a Sunday lie-in, but it allowed me to muscle-in on some pretty good deals. I continued to do the same early morning run when I had built up the business to what it is today, having eight showrooms with more than 200 staff. Other private dealers thought I was mad, but just like my appetite for food and drink, making money was an obsession.

In the past decade the car trade had changed dramatically: snapping up bargains from out of a newspaper was a rare occurrence these days. Too many punters had become wise to the market and knew how to 'tonce up' a motor. What's more the Internet had put its oar in. All the major classified magazines now had websites that were updated daily, which meant that cars could be had at the click of a button, if you're that way inclined! Frankly, all that website malarkey is a foreign land to me. I admit it — I'm a complete technophobe. I leave all the computer stuff to my staff and crack on in the old-fashioned way: newspaper and telephone.

"'Ere's one that's 15 grand behind book," I said at length. For anyone not in the car trade, this was a good earner and required some immediate attention. I frantically picked up the telephone and started dialling. Five minutes later, I could tell that today was going to be a good day. The car was the right mileage, colour, had a full service history, the description was perfect and better still, no-one else was on to it! If I managed to pull off this little beauty, I'd be looking at a 25 grand profit. Not bad for a Sunday morning.

"Too late for that now, mate, we've no time." I said to Les who was looking longingly at his newly arrived breakfast. "Ann, stick it in a sandwich for him, he can have it on the way!"

Les managed to pop in a sausage and take a couple of swigs from his mug of tea while I lurched off to the safe to retrieve a couple of grand deposit.

"I've got the address. I know exactly where we're going: Golders Green. I told the owner we'd be there within an hour."

Bargain chasing was a delight from a bygone era. One particular Sunday some years ago, we'd managed to secure deals on ten prestigious cars, all before lunchtime. That day's roast dinner had been the finest meal that I had tasted all week.

"You ready Les?" I asked eagerly.

"Here you are Les. Shame you couldn't have sat down and enjoyed it properly," said Ann, as she handed him his packed breakfast.

She shot me a disapproving glare — time to go!

"Goodbye love, have a good day. I won't be too late."

Long Lane ran up from Wooburn Green village, parallel to Daws Hill Road for more than three miles, and then curved into Daws Hill itself. Our mock Tudor farmhouse nestled halfway along this lane in 12 acres of fields and woodland. To travel to London via the M40 motorway, we'd have to turn left out of our drive onto Long Lane, go up to Daws Hill Road, then left again up the Marlow Hill, which would bring us to the Handy Cross motorway junction, then east into London. Alternatively, we could turn right out of the drive, travel for about a mile, then turn left, go over the crossroads at Daws Hill, under the motorway bridge, down into Loudwater and pick up the A40, by turning right on to the London road.

"Left or right?" asked Les, interrupting my daydream in car-bargain heaven. The decision I was about to make would change my life forever. Blissfully ignorant of that knowledge, I made a swift choice: "Let's do the motorway."

I rarely drove these days. A combination of being eternally employed on the telephone and in a constant state of partial inebriation meant that the passenger seat was the appropriate place for me. My choice of transport these days was a Range Rover Vogue. It was less than a year old and roomy enough, but I had had the seat track changed to accommodate the larger gentleman. Naturally, its personalised number plate read 'DON 1'.

Approaching the T-junction at Daws Hill, I could see that two men in fluorescent jackets were cordoning off the road. I started to snatch feverishly for my redundant seatbelt, as one of them was clearly a policeman.

"Better buckle up ol' son," I muttered.

Les stopped the car and I lowered my window. The policeman walked over.

"What's all the hold up mate?" I enquired.

"It's the Wycombe Half-Marathon today. You could wait till it passes or you could try another route."

"OK mate, thanks." I gritted my teeth and smiled falsely at the policeman.

"Bloody hell, turn 'round Les, we'll go the A40."

I always kept three mobiles around me: two permanently in the car and one somewhere about my body. Apparently this was a pointless operation, with 'Call waiting' and 'Messaging services' I only needed one phone, but an old-fashioned boy's habits die hard. It had taken an unexpected Birthday present from my office staff for me to adapt to the mobile phone, but now they were a part of my persona. I was just about to use one of them, when we were suddenly confronted with yet another roadblock.

"For fuck's sake!" — I was never known for my airs and graces — "What the fuck's going on?"

Three cars were queued ahead of us and it looked certain we would get sandwiched in if more vehicles brought up the rear.

"Quick! Reverse up to that field gate and spin her round, Les."

Our only other option was via the village. Although Long Lane was a double-track road, it was very narrow in parts, especially if you met oncoming farm traffic. Shit hitting the fan as it was this morning; we had to get friendly with the hedge twice! We finally reached the village just as a policeman was unreeling red tape across the road.

"I don't fucking believe it!" I shouted, hitting the window button again.

"I don't suppose there's any chance of quickly letting us through, Officer? We're running pretty late." No sooner had I asked the question than a stream of athletes flew past and rounded the bend into Wooburn.

"Not now, Sir. The road will be closed for at least a couple of hours."

This time I couldn't force a smile. My annoyance apparent, I took in a huge breath, purse-lipped, and then let it out ever so slowly. "Is this a joke, a fucking ironic joke?"

Les stared ahead. "Shall we go back home or wait until it all passes?" He glanced over to me, and offered a third option. "Or we could just go back to the first roadblock, it'll be open soon."

"Yeah, do that Les. I'm not sitting here all day," I said moodily.

After a series of reverse manoeuvres and amid lots of horn blowing and colourful gesticulating to our fellow motorists, we finally made our way back up to the first cordon, to find that it had been abandoned long ago.

"For Christ's sake, put your foot down mate, we're well behind," I ordered.

Like a prat I had left the posh bird's phone number on the kitchen table. By the time we arrived at her house we were more than an hour late. On the drive stood the 'steal of the century', a Rolls Royce Corniche Convertible in pristine condition, with its promise of certain profit. But as quick as my heart had risen when I had seen the beautiful car, it plummeted to the depths of an abyss when I saw mouthy Ralph Stevens, the car's smug new owner, shaking hands with its satisfied seller. I was gutted. I'd been gazumped by one of my oldest competitors and cheated out of pocket by 25 grand, and all because of some stupid pathetic fucking fun-run.

"Keep driving, Les. I don't want that fucker thinking 'e's got one over on me!" I snarled.

We headed home in silence, dejected.

"Pub mate?" Les asked as we came off the M40.

"Yep, yep, I need a drink now."

Boisterous applause, hoots and childish cheers erupted from the far corner of The George, my local, where it seems I had been the subject of yet another bet placed by my drinking buddies. My time of arrival had been masterly predicted by James Woodall, a roofing contractor, who had just earned himself 40-odd quid, which I'm sure he had duly placed behind the bar for all to enjoy. Tom the pub landlord had received a phone call telling them that I would be late and so a wager as ever, could not be resisted.

"How fucking juvenile," I yelled in good humour as I waddled through the smoke-filled room. "Just get the fucking drinks in Jimmy."

Our 'drinking school', made up of car traders and assorted builders, had become a Sunday lunchtime tradition and ever since moving in up the road, I had rarely missed an occasion. Ann called this 17th-century country inn my second home, my first being the office of course. It boasted the most excellent menu, and many a Simmons family gathering had been held in this very corner of the pub that we were occupying today.

My poison had always been a strong bottled lager, with whisky chasers, but I occasionally slipped into a bitter mood, an ale that The

George prided itself in. My distinctive beer glass stood waiting at the end of the bar for me, keeping company with two cold bottles of uncapped lager and a double malt whisky.

"Where's Les?" asked Cathy the barmaid.

"Parking the motor," I replied. Les had dropped me off outside the front door; these days I never walked anywhere, not even the distance from the car park to the pub.

"There's two more in the stable for you both," Cathy announced. "The boys have been keeping you in."

Good lads, I thought to myself approvingly.

When Les arrived he picked up his half pint of bitter and mooched over to the rowdy bunch that had taken over half the pub. Les was the sort of bloke who was content just to sit there, listening to all the banter, offering an occasional quip and enjoying a roll-up or two. He always limited himself to one pint, so that he could drive his slobbering boss home. Today was no different as I had to get home for the family barbeque.

"Good timing Don!" Tom and his wife Sylvia were lining the bar with bowls of pickles, cheese and biscuits.

"That's nice of you, Tom, but I've had a heck of a morning. I think I need something a little more substantial, how about a bowl of roast spuds?"

"We don't want you wasting away, do we Don?' Tom laughed, "Be with you in five."

I devoured the potatoes in less time than it had taken them to arrive from the kitchen. Four bottles of lager were soon demolished and we were in full flow.

"My round I believe. Les, get 'em in mate!"

As ever, Les obliged without question.

For the next hour, this corner of the pub became a menagerie for raucous joke-telling, spoof playing and drunken idiots putting the world to right. I always took centre stage, distinctively attired in colourful braces, with a fat cigar and a drink in either hand. My jokes were a mixture of timeless favourites and sidesplitting real-life misadventures. There were only two rules in 'The School': you never drank and drove, and you were never late home for your dinner. The session normally tailed off at around a quarter past two and it was just coming up to two o'clock. The bar was still buzzing with punters eager to slip into the restaurant, when in walked Ray, my brother-in-law.

"Ah, there you are, I was just about to give you a bell!"

Ray had come over for the barbeque. I'd called him earlier this morning to arrange for Ann to drop him off at the pub for an appetiser, and while on the phone I couldn't help but mention the deal that I was intending to pull off. Ray was a 'Bitter' man and a pint of the oak-aged heaven was waiting for him on the bar. "How'd you get on this morning with the motor?" he asked, picking up the straight glass and offering it to his lips.

"I missed it, mate," I said gloomily, reflecting on the day's earlier fiasco. Ray stopped drinking mid-flow with a look of surprise.

"What happened?"

Normally I would have shrugged such a thing off, since I'm not one to cry over spilt milk; instead I would just look for the next deal and move on. Today's unbelievable set of events, though, from the ballsed-up journey, not to mention the huge profit loss and, of course, that bastard Ralph Stevens, drove me to tell him the whole sorry saga. I exaggerated my frustration, wading into great detail, as always, and labelling the runners 'wankers' and describing the half-marathon as a complete waste of everybody's time. I was just coming to the part of the story where I was about to get onto the motorway, when I had the sensation of having something fallen on my shoulder. My audience was no longer looking at me, but peering inquisitively behind me. I turned around to be confronted by a smartly dressed elderly gentleman with a full head of white hair and a raised cane in one hand. Evidently I'd been tapped.

"Can I help you?" I asked.

"Young man, I'd like an apology."

"An apology, I said confused, "For what?"

"For the two insulting remarks that you have just made about the half-marathon and its athletes!"

I was taken aback and bemused as to why the hell this old fart was getting on his high horse. What had it got to do with him? Ray looked perplexed and the boys who had been listening to the old fellow's affront were now hushed and waiting for the next move. It was like a scene from High Noon: two rivals taking up facing positions at a short distance apart, a silenced bar room, and each contender mentally sussing the other one out. The old boy must have been in his 80's, well turned out, fit for his age and obviously from good stock. I towered over him; my massive frame loomed like a landslide that had fallen into the passage between two tables blocking the stranger's path. Neither man was going to budge. A younger man in his early twenties stood behind the old gent. He was holding an empty bar tray, having just taken a round of drinks to their table. Clearly they'd taken offence to something I'd said during my conversation with Ray. So what? I was convinced I had all the ammunition I needed to win this fight.

"Sir, those runners and those sodding roadblocks cost me a very lucrative deal this morning, to the sum of £25,000, and I'd appreciate it if you'd mind your own bloody business!" With an air of smugness, I turned around to face Ray and picked up my malt glass. I was just about to take a well-deserved swig, when the cane fell upon my shoulder for a second time. I closed my bloodshot eyes, gritted my teeth, and then lumbered round to launch myself into Round Two. Staring the old git right in the face, I calmly said "Please don't keep hitting me with that thing, it's ruining my Sunday."

There was anger in the old boy's eyes. I could see by the obstinate determination in his face that he needed to make a point. Telling him to piss off wasn't going to do the trick, and I certainly was not going to apologise. The old boy stood rigid, like a stiff-upper lipped officer from the colonial days of the Raj. "My grandson ran in that race and completed it in less than an hour and a half! So is he a 'wanker' then?" demanded the old man, as he stiffened poker straight.

Bollocks, I thought, realising that I must have touched a raw nerve here. Taking up my defence, I decided to attempt reasoning with him. "Listen, I apologise for insulting your grandson. Nothing personal mate, but anybody who trained for long enough, could do exactly the same, easy!"

"You think so, do you?" retorted the old boy on the verge of combustion. "I certainly couldn't see you achieving it!" he sneered. "Eh?" and proceeded to tap my enormous stomach with the side of his cane.

I had to think fast. I wasn't about to let this old bloke make a twat out of me, especially in front of my mates. In a flash I saw the opportunity that would shut this old duffer up for good. "Alright then," I sneered, "a quarter of a million quid says that I could!"

"What? Run a half-marathon in less than an hour and a half? A man of your stature? Ha-ha!"

Now I was really pissed off.

"That's the deal grandad. Now either put up or shut up!" I said soberly.

Audible gasps were heard around the pub, as varying levels of disbelief raced through the punters' minds. I knew that my pals would know that I was only bluffing. Les, with a glint in his eye, merely drew another pull on his roll-up. As far I was concerned, my philosophy was simple: working on the basis that nobody could afford to actually lose a quarter of a million quid, it stood to reason therefore that no-one in their right mind would take up my bet.

Taking a business card from my jacket pocket, I handed it to my opponent, offering him an outstretched hand. To everyone's delight, the old man shook it, firmly. With an air of aloofness and an animal look of certain triumph that suddenly unnerved me, he went back to his table and sat down.

CHAPTER TWO
The suits arrive

THE HEALTH AND SAFTY ACT OF 1974 decrees that all places of work that include the presence of petroleum and petrol-powered vehicles shall be strictly 'no smoking areas'. It was a law that was heavily enforced on my premises and checked upon at regular intervals by the council health and safety officers. The consequences of any discrepancies of this act were clear — they could shut me down at a moment's notice, so I was fervent in its enforcement. I also knew that the time afforded by smokers to their habit would cost me many man-hours over a period of time, but being a puffer myself and a slave to the craving, I had erected some designated smoking shelters outside in the grounds and had christened them 'nico-teens'. My office was exempt of course, having no petrol or cars in it, and out of the ten people that were allowed into my inner sanctum, nine of them smoked. Testaments to this were three half-filled ashtrays that adorned my leather-topped desk.

Les sat at a coffee table trying to forecast this afternoon's winning geegees. While white paper bags ripped open and laid flat acted as makeshift plates for the dozen or so bacon, dog and fried egg rolls that he'd just brought in from the local café. They occupied every available square of empty desk space and filled my nostrils with delight. Eight coffee mugs of various designs accompanied the carnage; four of them stained and empty, four with a fresh brew inside. A large bottle of brown sauce took centre stage, nursing some heavy spillage down one side.

The informal breakfast meeting took place every Monday morning. The usual crowd in attendance were Les and I, Alan Telson and Simon Collins, both ex-salesmen who had risen to the board of directors; Richard Varsley, the company solicitor; my brother Charlie; and brother-in-law Ray, who ran my caravan and motorhome sales centre, the largest of its kind in Europe.

The head office was in Ruislip, my first-ever garage and the flagship of my fleet. It stood in the well-manicured grounds of nearly ten acres, and was by far the largest of my showrooms. Many changes had taken place since its inaugural days — building extensions, new workshops and landscaping — but a picture of the original forecourt hung in a large gilt frame on the wall behind my chair. Sentimental as it seemed, its function was actually more blatant. The picture served as a statement of pride and a stern reminder to everyone that perused it, of all the years of hard work, of shrewdness and of sheer cunning, through which I had become, it couldn't be denied, a very successful businessman. The showroom boasted a magnificent twin, double-storey glass dome entrance and had become just as much a landmark to city commuters on the A40 as the Hoover building. My office had been designed to overlook the number-one showroom, a view that gave me pride and offered me a vista soothing enough to contemplate new ideas or somewhere to lose myself in times of cosy reflection.

"I wonder who they are?" I whispered, suddenly distracted from gloating as two be suited strangers walked in through the dome entrance. Alan and Simon both looked up from their sandwiches towards the front door. It had been almost 30 years since I had sold my first Rolls Royce, and in that time I'd made one golden rule — a rule I had firmly installed into my sales force: Treat anyone that enters the showroom as a potential customer. The odd couple hovering around the Bentley were clearly appealing for attention, but there was something 'not right' about them. You get a rather mixed bag of clientele in the prestigious car market: pop stars who don't look like they have a pot to piss in; lottery winners; old-school company directors; movie luvvies; sports personalities; gangsters; and even Joe public, looking to upgrade his status on the block. This pair of city slickers had me foxed though. It was doubtful that they were officials, taxmen, Customs and Excise, or solicitors, because they would have parked in the visitors' car park and gone into the main office block, which dealt with all the administration. There again, they didn't come across as punters either. In their early thirties, immaculately dressed in well-tailored pinstriped suits, hers cut just above the knee and complimented by good legs and expensive shoes, the strangers smelled of the legal profession. Yet it didn't make sense that they would come direct to the showroom unless they wanted to buy a car. David, a young salesman, came out of his office to greet them and, as is customary at Simmons, offered them a hand. This gesture was met with a rebuttal and a mere business card in return, which left David quite perplexed. After a short exchange, he turned around and made his way directly to my office. I never saw anyone without an appointment, so these two must have made an impression.

The sheer grandeur of more than 50 Rolls Royce's and Bentleys, some nearly 90-years-old and all in pristine condition is usually a sight impressive enough to bowl anybody over, but these two didn't grace a single car with a second glance or admiring look. They kept their eyes transfixed to a point on the floor like a couple of automatons.

Meanwhile, it only took one look from me to Alan for him to reach for his phone. Like me, he had felt the hairs stand up on the back of his neck, something wasn't right about these two. Richard would be here in a couple of minutes to safeguard our interests.

David rapped on the door and then entered the office. "Sorry about this, Don. They insisted that I give you their card. They're briefs," he said.

"Davina B. Daylon, Practitioners in Law, Kensington, London," I read out loud. "Thank you, David, I'll deal with this."

David shot off to the showroom floor, assuring the pair that I would be with them shortly. Les snorted back some mucus that had been gathering at the back of his nose and returned to the Racing Post, nonplussed by the situation. It wasn't long before Richard Varsley arrived at the showroom. He rushed past the now ever-so-slightly impatient solicitors, offering them a cautionary nod as he did so. After giving the business card the once over, Richard brought his glasses back to rest in their usual position of dangling by a cord on his chest, and stood there chewing the inside of his cheek.

"Are you familiar with this firm?" I asked.

"Let me put it this way, Don. If you or your family were ever in the gravest of situations, you would definitely want these people to be on your side." That coming from Richard meant that this team of barristers must be in the premier league. As advised I kept schtum when Davina and her sidekick entered my office and let Richard do all the talking.

"Good morning. I'm Richard Varsley, Mr Simmons's legal advisor."

Neither visitor returned the courtesy of an introduction. Davina took centre stage and opened the proceedings. "We are acting on behalf of our client, Lord Belington," she announced, handing to Richard a cream-coloured sleeved folder with my name on it, which her associate had produced from a briefcase. No-one spoke while Richard read its contents, occasionally glancing my way, indicating that we could have a problem here. If this were the case it must be to do with the real-estate business. Our company bought and sold about 15 to 20 properties each month, and legal problems cropped up all the time. Thinking that this should be a detail for the admin department to sort out and that the pinstriped pair were in the wrong office, I decided my time would be better spent by quelling my concern with another mouthful of sausage sandwich. I bit in hard, causing an amalgamation of melted butter and brown sauce to ooze out from between the slices of bread and drop down with a heavy splat on a paper bag. A grimace of disgust at my behaviour preceded the slow apparition of a smug, lopsided grin from Ms Daylon. She not only looked like the cat who had got the cream, but also one who had eaten the cream, tortured a mouse and then curled up snugly on her master's lap in the warmth and serenity of a cosy cottage. An air of superiority surrounded her as she took in the contents of my office: the overfilled ashtrays, the abundance of greasy spoon fare, the vulgar array of malt whisky bottles in a glass-fronted cabinet, and the sheer size of her client's opponent. She felt comfortably aloof, and I could imagine her in the wine bar with her legal chums that evening, recounting this scene with scathing relish and quipping, "He was so keen to fill his face with his sandwich that he almost swallowed his own fingers, urgh gross!"

Once Richard had finished reading the contents of the file, he turned towards the solicitors, thanked them for coming and informed them that they would be hearing from him by correspondence within a week. This time they both accepted a loose handshake. Just before they left Davina turned to me and said, "Your company epitomises its motto perfectly." She managed a false smile before turning around sharply and leaving. The waft of her sweet perfume lingered in her wake, as though she had just marked her territory. I never replied to her comment, but was left pondered upon its meaning, which was soon to become apparent.

The lawyers were halfway across the showroom floor when Les broke the ice with a fart. "Pardon me!" he said, reaching across the table for another dog roll.

"Filthy fucker!" said Simon with a scowl. Alan opened the office door and began fanning the room. "Really, Les" he scolded.

Richard, openly aggrieved by the visit, turned to me with an air of inoffensive sarcasm and said "Busy weekend, was it Don?" His manner had changed. He was no longer the friendly company solicitor, more like a predatory courtroom barrister.

"Yes, I suppose it was in one way or another, quite eventful."

The mood in the office had deteriorated from being one of four men happily enjoying breakfast, a smoke and a chat, to one of downcast bewilderment, exemplified by the sour face of one company solicitor.

"Well?" he enquired.

Sensing that I needed to elaborate on my weekend's events, I attempted a summary. "On Saturday I viewed three properties, two commercial and one private, and made a bid for one of the commercials.

I went to both car warehouses, then over to Reading to see Ray, met some of the boys in The George, picked up an Indian and finally went home."

"And on Sunday?' asked Richard, determined to track down the information he needed.

"Don't talk to me about Sunday!" I despaired. "We should've made 25 grand profit on a Roller from Golders Green if it 'adn't 've got bollocksed up!" The bitterness returned to poison me and changed the tone in my voice.

"How come?"

"Bloody roadblocks set up in Long Lane and down in Wooburn Green, just to let a load of wanky runners run past for the half-fucking-marathon. It held us up for the best part of an hour!" Richard gestured that he wanted more, so I went on. "By the time we got to London, that cunt Ralph Stevens had sneaked in and stolen the Roller! I was so fucked off that we headed back to The George to console ourselves, didn't we Les?"

I looked over at Les for reinforcement as I could tell from Richard's glare that my answer had not been adequate.

"Is that all Don?" he probed deeper.

Suddenly I felt like a schoolboy being given the Inquisition by the headmaster, and a cold, dark shadow crept up my spine. "Well I did have a ruck with some old fart in the pub over the marathon, but then Ray came in and dragged me back to the house for the barbeque. I fell a kip about eight o'clock. Who's this Lord Belington anyway?" As the words slipped from my mouth the connection fell into place and a massive cloud of gloom engulfed me.

"Lord Belington," said Richard "is the old fart that you had an argument with in the pub. He's the old fart that you made a £250,000 bet with that you could run the half-marathon in an hour and a half! A quarter of a million pounds, Don! Are you out of your mind?"

I felt the blood drain from my face and gather somewhere near my shoes. "He was serious then?"

By now even Les was paying attention. It was all fitting into place. No wonder that pair of suits had been grinning like cartoon cats. They had come to witness the hopelessness of their opponent's predicament and it had obviously given them great satisfaction. There was no contest. To them, I was a dead-cert loser, an easy day.

"Marathon man! Don't they call them Snickers theses days?" Davina had said to her colleague on the way out of the showroom.

"He's fucking serious alright. He's brought in the best firm of lawyers in town just to issue you with a contract!'" Richard said, slightly losing his cool.

"Worth a few bob then, is he?" I asked awkwardly.

"Try around a million acres of land in Scotland, Wales and the Home Counties, and almost as much property in the City as the Duke of Westminster. Don, he's a billionaire! The sheer magnitude of the situation that I had got myself into was beginning to sink in and I slumped into my oversized recliner with a fast-creeping sense of dread. Simon, Alan, Les, Ray and about 20 others in the pub had all been witnesses to the bet. I had shook hands on it. Well, I'd believed in myself at the time. Yeah, at the time I was four parts pissed.

"It's only a handshake though, Richard, surely that's not legally binding?" Simon interjected.

"Technically, yes it is," said Richard, "although he'd have to take you to court to enforce it, and that could prove to be very expensive, perhaps costing more than the initial bet. The point is, Don, do you really want to lose your credibility as an honest businessman? That's what it might come to if you don't keep to your agreement. A case like this is meat and gravy to the British press. You'd better read this first before you decide what to do." Richard handed me the cream file, inside which were two items, a letter and a contract. The letter read:

Dear Mr Simmons,

On Sunday 25th of July 1999 a heated discussion took place, at The George Inn public house, Buckinghamshire, between you and our client Lord Belington. During this exchange a wager was put in place, to the effect that you could run the High Wycombe Half-Marathon 2000, within 90 minutes or less. You both accepted that the wager would be to the sum of £250,000 and, in front of much witness, shook hands upon this agreement.

Please find enclosed a contract for the said wager. It is for you to sign and return at your earliest convenience.

Yours sincerely

Davina B. Daylon

For and on behalf of Lord Belington

The contract said much the same thing only using all the legal jargon, to the effect that if I ran the race in more than one and a half hours I'd have to cough up more than my pride. What a mess: damned if I did, damned if I didn't. I passed the papers to Alan, who read them before passing them on to Simon who then passed them, surprisingly, to Les.

Well, Richard, what do you suggest?" I asked at length, holding my breath and waiting for the executioner's axe to fall. Richard was looking out through the glass panelling that encased the first-floor office; his eyes were following a sparrow that had got itself trapped in the showroom and was frantically trying for an escape route. After a pregnant pause he replied, "One. You pay him the money right now!"

"I'm not just giving him a quarter of a million quid. No fucking way!" I protested.

"Or two, let it go to court ..." Richard looked down his nose at me reprovingly before adding, "and get your arse kicked! Belington is a shrewd old sod. He knows that even if he loses the court battle, he'll have dragged your name through the dirt, portraying you through the media as a less honourable man than your reputation suggests. Your rivals will have a field day. Not to mention the stress that it would put on Ann and the children. Do they need this? That's what Davina meant when she referred to the company motto, 'Our word is our bond'. It's on every letterhead, every sign above every garage. Don, he's won already!"

I lifted my heavier-than-usual frame from out of the chair and joined Richard by the glass. "There is a third choice," I said solemnly.

"And what's that?" Richard asked, raising his eyebrows.

"I could run the race!" I said with a glint in my eye. It was something I had been toying with in my head for the past ten minutes. I was just surprised that no-one else had suggested it.

It seemed that everyone in the room had stopped breathing, immobilised by my lunatic proposal. Charlie eventually broke the silence, "Run the race, Don? You couldn't run to the door! You'd collapse, have a heart attack. I love you bruv, but what a stupid statement. You've lost it mate."

Alan pitched in, "You're fucking joking, right? Pulling my pisser? You're in no shape to run a fucking marathon."

"Half-marathon!" I retorted.

"Even so, Don," said Simon, "You'd kill yourself."

"I think that you'd better take some professional advice before you venture down that avenue," Richard said soberly.

"They're right, Donny. The old ticker won't take it, and what about your dodgy knee? That ain't gonna carry ya," added Les earnestly.

My mind was racing. All the old feelings were coming back to me, like when I chased a Sunday morning deal. The tingling in my loins, the butterflies in my stomach, and the glassy eyes as the adrenalin pumped through my veins. "Richard, you're right," I agreed. I picked up the phone to ring down to the restoration workshop. A row of baffled faces looked on, waiting so see what the crackpot was going to do next.

James Fox was a complete gent, a man in his early fifties with a meticulous work ethic and an expert with a spray gun. He'd been running my workshop for 18 years.

"James, it's Don ere. Could you get Terry for me please?"

"He's out the back having a Kit Kat," said James, "I'll go and get him."

"No, it's alright," I replied, "I'll come down; I could do with the exercise."

James didn't reply.

Twenty-six years ago, when I first bought the business, it had employed just five people: three mechanics, a paint sprayer and Terry, the panel beater. I had kept them all on. They had a fair if not good reputation, and I knew zip about restoration. Within a month all the lads apart from Terry had moved on. They couldn't take my relentless pace, whereas Terry recognised the challenge and rose to it, working seven days a week and sometimes nights. He personally oversaw the recruitment of staff and gradually month-by-month increased the workload. In less than five years we had on our hands one of the finest and best-known car restoration workshops in Britain. Having played a major part in achieving this status, Terry then asked to be dropped down a peg or two and return to being an ordinary panel beater working a nine-to-five existence. I thought this was odd at the time, but understood his need to spend more time with his young family and to pursue his own passion — marathon running. He'd raced in all the big ones: London, New York, Paris, Tokyo, and even across the Kalahari. Everybody knew him as 'Running Bear' and his eternal schemes for raising sponsorship money were legendary.

Terry's life and mine couldn't have been more different. I had never given marathon running a second thought, until now. Although we were at opposite ends of the scale, I had never forgotten the immense amount of work that Terry had put in at the start, to lift the business off the ground. Although his wage reflected my appreciation, I felt that I owed him, big time. We'd always remained chums, always confided in each other and even though we kept it in reserve, always had a great deal of respect for one another. If anybody could advise me about running it would be Terry, but how would I explain the happenstance that led up to the bet, without insulting a man who'd spent most of his spare time in tracksuits. I'd called the runners 'wankers' and ripped the sport to pieces, I wasn't going to be able to lie my way out of that one! All things considered, there was only one option: I'd have to apologise.

The restoration workshop was at the far end of the garage complex, a good 300 yards away. I couldn't recall the last time that I'd made this arduous journey. In fact, I couldn't remember walking that sort of distance for years, but if I was going to take on this running lark, I'd have to start with the first steps and they were down this flight of stairs. Just as I was about to leave, Les piped up "Shall we have Dettori or Fallon in the 3:30 at York, Don?"

I stood poised as if at the summit of a cloud-drenched mountain. "Let's take a chance on it, mate. Let's go for Fallon," I said. With that I took out my cigarette pack, removed all but two cigarettes and crumpled them into the bin at my feet. "I'm gonna do it boys, so these can go for a start," I announced assertively.

The lads, still in shock, were now taking a reality check and pinching themselves to make certain they weren't adrift in dreamland and that the real, waking day had yet to begin.

"You've been smoking for 30-odd years, Don, you can't just quit like that!" protested Alan.

"You'll need gum or patches or something," added Simon.

Only Les knew that I had been planning to quit for sometime, so this wasn't a snap decision; that seed had already been sown.

"We'll see," I said.

••▼••

The week previous, Les and I had been enjoying an early evening snifter in The George. We were puffing away merrily at the bar when Tom came over with his half pint of bitter to join us. As my fag had been nearing its end, I pulled another from the pack and lit it with the dog end of the previous one. "How many of them are you on a day?" Tom asked with some concern.

"Oh, about 30 or 40." (It was more like 50 or 60 and Les probably smoked about 60 including roll-ups).

In all the years I had known Tom he had never once brought up the subject of smoking and I wondered what had prompted him to do so that afternoon. Not realising that my foot was slowly working its way into my mouth, I went on to explain that the main reason for my smoking was to keep my weight down. Rounding off with my usual gag, I joked, "Without these little sticks, I could get rather chubby!"

Responding with nothing more than a polite smile, Tom pursued the subject. "You remember my old mate Jack Piely? I used to play golf every Thursday afternoon with him," he said.

I couldn't place him.

"Used to have half-a-dozen butcher's shops till he sold up," Tom added, to jog my memory.

"Oh yeah, yeah, I remember him now," I said.

"Well, he passed away last Monday, they're burying him tomorrow," he said with a heavy sigh.

"How old was he mate?" Les asked, his own remaining time on the planet suddenly giving him cause for concern.

"Just turned 60 Les." Tears were now welling up in Tom's eyes. "Lung cancer I'm afraid. That's the third mate I've lost to the …" he was just about to say 'deadly weed' then thought better of it. "Another drink, Don?" he suggested instead.

"Tell you what, Tom," I replied, "Let's all have a large one, alright for you Les?"

"Just one, I've gotta drive you home in' I."

I had always been fascinated by the way Tom mixed his own gin and tonic. He'd take a long tumbler and fill it with ice and a slice of lemon. Next he'd pour in less than an eighth of gin, top it up with Slimline tonic, and then put another eighth of gin on top of that. Another little quirk of his was not to charge full price to anyone who bought him a drink. Old-fashioned boy!

While Tom had been fixing the drinks, both Les and I chipped our fags in the ashtray and moved it along the bar, as a mark of respect. The publican noted our gesture and nodded in appreciation.

"You're lucky never to have picked up the habit Tom," I sighed. He looked up and smiled, then pointed towards a small shelf next to the till where the menus were kept. Stood upright was a packet of 20 Benson and Hedges with a Bic lighter bold by its side, I was puzzled. Tom had never once hinted that he'd been a smoker or even had a craving for a cigarette. He took the packet down from the shelf and brought it over to us: inside were just two cigarettes. "I'd better explain," he said. "When I first took on The George, I probably smoked around 60 fags a day and was hitting the old mother's ruin like there was no tomorrow. My life was turned around in an instant when I had a deathly wake-up call one day."

"Go on," I urged, intrigued by the revelation.

"I had to run after the draymen who had short-levied me in the cellar. By the time I had caught up with them — it had only been a run of about 20 yards — I had almost collapsed. I felt like my heart was going to bust through my ribcage and spoil a good shirt. When I caught sight of my reflection in a shop window, I was ashen grey. It shit the life out of me."

Les and I just listened attentively, breaking away only to take the occasional sip of whisky. Tom continued, "I knew then that it was either time to change my life or to prepare a will. It was Sylvia's dad that suggested I try this. It was how he had given up — his 'lifeboats' he called them. He kept just two fags in a packet; they were there for emergencies only."

At this point Les blurted out the question that I wanted to hear answered, "So what 'appens if the urge overpowers you and makes you smoke one?"

Tom was ready for this one, and replied with confidence. "Easy," he said, "You buy another packet of 20, take one out and throw the rest away."

"Fucking nuts if you ask me!" muttered Les, receiving a sharp elbow from me for his lack of decorum.

"Has it worked then Tom?" I asked tactfully.

"It worked for Sylvia's dad, till that car killed him, and so far it has worked for me!" he replied.

"How many packets of cigarettes have you bought over the last 20 years to replace that little emergency?" I asked. Tom knew exactly how many: 62 and he was proud of it.

"So in all that time you've only smoked 62 fags?" scoffed Les.

"Correct," replied Tom, straightening with pride.

Tom was the same age as Les, around the 61 mark, but not only did he look ten years younger, he also made me look old. Apart from a small paunch, which was in keeping with a man who offered one of the finest beer cellars in the south of England, he was a picture of health.

That had been a strange old afternoon. Les and I had driven home in silence, both deep in our own thoughts. I knew that I had to do something radical to change my lifestyle, but to force me into action it was going take a very large carrot at the end of a painfully long stick.

•• ▼ ••

As I made my way across the showroom, another sense of foreboding shuddered along my core. What the fuck was I doing? Giving up smoking, entertaining the idea of going running, and even contemplating the idea of giving up the odd meal or two? I almost turned around and walked right back to the office, but the thought of giving away the second dearest thing to my heart — a pile of cash — was all the incentive I needed to come out fighting.

Having come from an office where the air-conditioning was in full operation to combat the mid-morning heat of a smouldering July day, my sweat glands swung into action with immediate effect. I was only a minute into the walk, yet rivulets were forming on my face and as I waddled between the Rolls Royce's and Bentleys towards the glass front of the building. My leather-soled shoes slipped on the showroom carpet with every step I took, so I had to steady myself against the sides of the cars. My handkerchief had now become sodden from the frequent mopping of my brow and I was all too aware that this wasn't my best idea to date. This little walk showed me unequivocally what piss-poor shape I was in. What a ludicrous idea! What a loser! What a predicament: I couldn't turn back yet I could barely shuffle forward. I thought it best to have a sit down, so I made my way over to the low brick wall that snaked around the car park. It seemed an ideal resting place, being roughly halfway between the office and the workshop. I sat there for a full five minutes stressing the brick mortar to the max, but within that time David and at least two other salesmen had come over to ask me if I was alright. I'd assured them I was fine and blamed the weather for my meltdown. I was getting more and more paranoid by the minute, exacerbated by the more-than-average number of heads popping up at the main office windows to 'take a look at the boss'. My white cotton shirt displayed some interesting patterns from the cascades of sweat exiting from every pore. If it hadn't been for my Marks & Spencer vest, I would now look like some big old unit that had blagged her way into a wet T-shirt competition.

I looked a mess and felt ashamed of it, so with a great deal of effort I pushed myself off the wall, left my embarrassment behind and sashayed off in the direction of the workshop. As I crossed the car park exit, I was forced to a halt by a black BMW 7 series, which nearly took my legs with it. Inside were the smirking faces of Lord Belington's two mouthpieces who were finding the whole affair highly amusing. The affront had me seething. "Fucking pretentious pricks," I shouted after them, but they were way out of earshot and I could do no more than give them the bird. On the final leg over to see Terry, I boiled with resentment that these two fuckheads had made the point of coming to deliver their missive in person. They had obviously wanted to witness my gluttony, assure themselves of a winning hand and gloat over the certainty of their commission. It definitely looked as though the money was in the bag for Belington, but they hadn't counted on one thing: my bloody-minded determination. Once this big ball got rolling, there'd be no escape lane.

CHAPTER THREE
A thousand to one

A WHISPER OF A BREEZE just strong enough to bother the summer leaves, brief and frail, kissed me full in the face and like an elixir spurred me on for the last 20 feet. As I reached the corner of the brick-built restoration shop, I could see my old confidante perched on the edge of a Teak two seater garden bench. He was so engrossed in the Daily Mail crossword that he didn't even hear the wheezing jelly on approach.

"Alright Tel?" was all I could manage.

Startled, Terry spun around, open-mouthed, with a half-eaten sandwich in his hand. "Gawd blimey, Don, you made me jump!" he spluttered. "You look terrible mate, sit down quick!" He got up and helped me onto the bench. "You better undo your collar and loosen your tie mate. Whatcha been eating, chocolate sauce?"

"A… Oh it's probably a touch of Daddies," I puffed, "had a spot of brekkie in the office."

"What? Did you walk over here from the office?" he asked.

"Yep," I gasped, still trying to catch my breath.

"You on a suicide mission?" he queried, perplexed. "Must be important, you haven't walked round 'ere in two years."

I couldn't reply yet. I had only just got my breath back, and at one point had thought that I was going to be sick.

"You ain't 'arf gone white in the face mate, 'ere drink some of this." Terry unscrewed the cup from his Thermos flask and poured out some iced tea.

"Ta. Coke, is it?" I asked, swigging it back in one gulp but tasting enough of it to know that it was a new flavour on me. "Cor, what's that?"

"Lemon iced tea, mate. All natural, and it's brought the colour back to your face. Want some more?" offered Terry.

"Go on then," I sighed. I couldn't just launch into this sticky conversation cold. The mood needed to be jollied a little first, so I looked around for inspiration. "You know I'd forgotten what a tranquil place this was back here," I said, suddenly realising it to be true. The grounds were neat and tidy, laid to lawn with a smattering of flowering shrubs and trees that lined the perimeter fence of the neighbouring airbase. Not quite Kew Gardens, but then again this were only a garage complex. Around the back here, though, it was warm in the sun and nicely screened from the hubbub of daily life.

"My little sanctuary," said Terry proudly. "The only place I can get some solitude round 'ere, and some time to think. The other blokes use the fallout shelters for their breaks but you know what I'm like about smoking."

"Yeah, only too well," I laughed.

"I'll fetch you a towel from the washroom," he said, "won't be a minute."

While he was gone I sat and reflected on the past hour, and the traumatic turnout of the day's events. My brain felt like a huge ball of elastic thread, totally knotted and beyond unravelling. Terry's soothing and understanding nature was quite an asset to have on your side when the pressure is on, and I was grateful to have been on the receiving end. I had never drunk tea without sugar before. It was normally three heaped teaspoons, even a bit more in coffee, but this iced tea was one of the best drinks I'd ever tasted, so refreshing. "Where've you been all my life?" I asked my beverage, but it wasn't in the mood for talking to strangers. I looked down at Terry's plastic lunchbox. Through its transparency I could make out three pieces of fruit, some brown bread salad sandwiches and a piece of homemade flapjack. Where were the chocolate bars and crisps? The only time I ate fruit was when it was covered in pastry and baked in a pie.

Terry returned with a freshly laundered white towel. It smelled like a spring meadow and I held it to my face for longer than was necessary, just to breathe in and drift away momentarily to another dimension. After some time I took a long, deep breath, and began my opening speech. "You'd best sit down Tel, this is a toughie."

The panel beater, stout and formidable in his dark green one-piece overall, dutifully sat down beside me.

"First things first, I have to apologise to you, mate," I confessed.

"Apologise? What for Don?" he puzzled.

"How long have we been mates, 20 odd years? In all that time, have I ever slagged off the sport that you do once?" I asked.

"Don't think so," replied Terry, wondering where this was going.

"Well I did yesterday, big time!" I went on to tell him the whole sorry saga, apologising again for calling all runners 'wankers'.

Terry said nothing during my owning-up, and only turned away momentarily to fix himself some iced tea in a second cup and take the occasional sip.

"So I've decided to do the fucking half-marathon and have come round here for your advice," I said all in one breath.

Terry sat in stunned silence. The only time I had ever indulged in physical exercise was to raise things to my mouth or squeeze them out of my backside. I was bloody dreaming if I thought for one minute that I could even attempt a half-marathon. I had a feeling that Terry was about to list my shortcomings in precisely this order.

"If you want my advice, I'd pay Belington the money and hang on to ya life mate," Terry recommended.

"But I can't do that. It's not an option. I've seen the light!" I argued.

"Listen mate. We're not all 'wankers' you know. Some of us can recognise a lethal situation and know how to avoid it!" said Terry wryly.

"Yes, I'm sorry, I'm sorry. I was just angry at the time, I didn't consider you at all," I squirmed.

Running bear smiled. I couldn't recall ever hearing a swear word pass his lips before, so it came as quite a pleasant shock and cheered me up no end. The cream-coloured folder had been under my armpit the whole time and was now a soggy damp mess that the breeze was threatening to punch holes in. I gave it to Terry, who handled it with some disdain. "Read this," I insisted.

The letter and the contract appeared to have survived the sweaty onslaught and were duly digested, then without a word Terry took a notebook and pen from his rucksack and, wandered over to the perimeter fence. Although he had nothing but contempt for the idea of me becoming an athlete, his appetite for a challenge had been roused. He cast his gaze out over the airfield for quite some time, juggling the bare facts and wrestling for a conclusion, before starting to jot down some bravely outlandish ideas. I watched him nervously, waiting in anticipation, tapping my foot and biting my undernourished lip. It was nearly midday and a meal of just one thin lip wasn't going to satisfy my ever-grumbling stomach. If I had only known the monumental sacrifices that I would have to make to get into any kind of shape, the outright gruelling drudgery that long-distance runners put themselves through to achieve their personal bests, I wouldn't have been so quick-fired with my bravado in the pub yesterday.

After some time Terry ambled back over to me.

"Maybe, just maybe, and given a year, a man of your size could slim down to be agile enough to run," He said cautiously, "Maybe you could be trained to run properly, to pace yourself, to keep your heart in good shape. But to do it in less than an hour and a half, Don, I think that's impossible. Guys that have been competing in half-marathons for years only put in times of one-and-a-quarter hours. What you need is a miracle mate!"

"They've happened before, Tel. Now what 'ave you got in store for me?" I asked.

Terry sighed and looked decidedly concerned, but I kept faith. This man was methodical and always approached a problem from several different angles, a trait that I distinctly lacked and had always secretly envied.

"I've made some preliminary notes and whittled it down to four main issues that need to be discussed. One, what are the goals you'd have to achieve to even consider entering a half-marathon? Two, is the time limit even feasible? Three, do you have anything in your favour?"

That's a joke, I thought to myself.

"And four, my personal experience." Terry paused to let the harsh truths sink in. "For a start, in just one year Don, you'll have to lose at least half your bodyweight in order to run. Give up smoking ..."

"I already 'ave," I interrupted.

"When?" He asked gobsmacked.

I glanced down at my watch. "About an hour an' half ago," I said defiantly.

Terry tutted, he knew the size of my habit from time gone by and so had good reason to be sceptical. In the early days, when the lads would all jump in a motor to go pick up a deal from the auction rooms, there was always an argument about Les and me smoking. Terry hated the smell of tobacco smoke, to the point where he refused to even sit in the same car as either of us unless we kept our fags in our pockets until we reached the salesrooms. Les and I always found it a bit of a wind-up to promise faithfully only to spark up when we were halfway down the street. Finding himself held captive, Terry used to go berserk in the back of the car and subject us to long drawn-out arguments about the hazards of nicotine abuse. The window would be fully opened whatever the weather, expelling the sound of two big kids giggling our heads off through the haze of Old Holborn.

"This is no joke, Don," Terry's voice called me sharply back to the present. "If you're gonna do this, you'll have to change your entire perspective on the way you eat, drink and smoke. Your lifestyle has to totally change over the next year, big time. Read my lips, no alcohol!"

"Ok, ok, a crash diet I can handle, and as I've said I've chucked the fags already, really, but surely a drop of whisky won't do me any 'arm," I whinged. Tears found their way to my big puffy eyes at the thought of my pristine collection of malt whiskies, containing every delicious brand and strength that had ever been made. I'd probably amassed the finest hoard of the beloved stuff in the whole wide world. No way could I exist without whisky. My heart was starting to break.

"While you're in training, mate, not a drop. It not only kills your brain cells and dehydrates your body, it's also very fattening."

"Is it?" I said genuinely surprised.

"You checked out a mirror lately? The same goes for all the rest of that junk that you chuck down your neck," Terry paused and tightened up his lips. "But 'ere look at my notes." Next to where he'd written alcohol, there was a question mark and underneath that was written the word 'moderation'.

"Not one of my favourite words, Tel," I said, trying to crack a joke.

"I've noticed," he retorted. "To be honest the only thing you could possibly get away with would be a red wine, but in my opinion, you shouldn't have anything."

I was just about getting my head around being deprived of my heart and lungs, but this bit of news was a killer blow. My supposed friend was hell-bent on taking away my soul as well. Didn't he realise that I'd sooner slit my own throat than not douse it in amber liquid. As I sat there feeling as though a team of fullbacks had each taken it in turn to run up and kick me in the crotch, leaving my bollocks firmly lodged in my thorax. I really did want to throw up now.

A minute passed before Terry spoke, "You know what you've gotta do?"

"What's that?" I asked, expecting another smack.

"Take a year out mate."

"Take a year out? How the fuck am I gonna do that? I've got a business to run," I remonstrated.

"But you've got directors who can do that for you. You don't have to be 'ere," Terry pointed out. "Get yourself a personal trainer and get away for a year. Away from all your temptations, preferably to somewhere that has a hill, a bloody great hill."

"Why a hill?" I enquired.

"Because the Wycombe half has one! Its gradient is 1:10, that's steep enough for anyone," he assured me.

A year off was hard to swallow. I had never even liked taking a two-week holiday with the family. I could never relax, my mind would always be on the business; stressing out that I might be missing some major deal. I was the boss and needed to be there. Besides, I would miss the drinking club, the takeaway food and my right-hand man. A year out? It seemed impossible. My head was awash with conflicting scenarios, swilling around the pros and cons of each and trying to play out my immediate future. In truth, though, I knew that there was really only one choice and I was grudgingly edging towards its.

"What will Ann say? She doesn't even know about the bet. How will she cope without me here?" I said, at a loss as to how I was going to tackle this one.

"She'll probably enjoy it," joked Terry.

"True, she's been desperately trying to get me to lose a few pounds," I added. "The kids won't miss me at all, apart from little Junie. She'll miss the bouncy castle rides on Daddy's belly and the trips to Pizza Hut, McDonald's, Chan's and Victoria Wine — all quality time, you know."

"I reckon Ann'll be right behind you mate. If you can manage to pull this off, she'd be so proud of you. In fact, I can't see how anyone could fail to be impressed."

Sheepishly I asked "What odds do you think I have?"

"Oh, I'd say about 10,000 to 1."

"In my favour," I joked. "So it's possible then?"

"Maybe," said Terry gallantly, as the lines in his forehead suddenly deepened and etched concern on his face. He seemed quite surprised by my apparent joviality, but that was me all over: a true player who rarely showed his hand. My mind was made up. Ten thousand to one was an extremely long shot, but there it was, a chance. And if Terry believed in that glimmer of hope, then that was good enough for me.

"I'd have given you better odds if it weren't the Wycombe half you were attempting," said Terry.

"Why's that?"

"It's gotta be one of the toughest half-marathons in England. What with that hill at the beginning. Even well-seasoned runners find it hard. Belington's a cunning old goat, he's got things well sussed."

Great! The obstacles were piling up against me by the minute. Belington must be thinking this bet was like taking candy from a baby.

What I needed now was to tip the scales forcefully in the other direction. "So what have I got in my favour then, Tel?" I asked, as my friend poured me another cup of iced tea.

"Well you've given up smoking and taking sugar within the last hour. There's also the things that helped to shape you into one of Europe's wealthiest car dealers: ambition, determination and downright stubbornness!"

"Thanks for the analysis, but what I need right now is the luck of Foinavon."

"Who?" asked Terry.

"He was the 100/1 outsider, who won the Grand National in 1967. A stray, Po Pen Down, carved up the rest of the field at a fence and brought most of them down. Foinavon's jockey kept his cool, went around the outside of the main pack and managed to pootle on to the finish line," I beamed.

"You can't compare your situation to that horse race, Don. Even if all 2,000 runners fell over, failed to turn up or pulled out, there's still one contender that never stops and can never lose," said Terry.

"Introduce me to him, Tel, and I'll pay him off," I replied with a smile.

"Time Don, an hour-and-a-half's worth. That's approximately seven minutes per mile and with that hill…" Terry stopped for a few seconds. "Do you have a pound coin on you?" he asked.

"I've got a pocket full of them from that Sam, the sandwich bird, this morning."

"Here's an offer for you," said Terry as he pulled a couple of ten-pound notes out of his wallet. "I'll swap you these two for that pound coin."

I seized at the opportunity so quickly I nearly took Terry's hand off in the proceeds. "Is that a good business deal or what?" He said.

"Good for me, but rotten for you old chap," I said with relish. "Do you want another go?"

"No thanks mate. Look, what I'm trying to show you is this. Say that a pound represents a year: if you give one up, you'll gain another 20 on your current life expectancy. Just look at the state of you, Don. Even if this bet hadn't come along, you'd still 'ave 'ad to change your lifestyle. Hospitals are full of people who've abused their bodies."

Terry had touched a raw nerve; I didn't like being told the truth and leaped to my defence. "I've paid thousands if not millions of pounds in taxes over the years, I think I've got a right to a hospital bed."

"Yes, you may have the right to a bed, but are you happy to die 20 or 30 years before your time in one?" said a slightly irate Terry. "Besides, you owe it to the people who love you to stick around for a bit more. I'm telling you, mate. We'll lose you if you don't make some drastic changes even without this stupid bet." Terry went on to list some of the many illnesses associated with obesity: heart attack, stroke, diabetes, liver disease, gout, the list was endless. Finally he came to the problem with my knees.

"The knees, blimey, I'd forgotten about those. Have they been operated on yet?" he asked.

I admitted that they hadn't and repeated the information that Dr Amstone had given me, about how losing a substantial amount of weight would alleviate the problem.

I expected yet another shakedown from my pal, but instead Bear just pulled out his notebook and jotted something else down. "You're about 25 stone I reckon," he said, putting his pen in his mouth.

"More like 26, mate," I confessed.

"Right, so even before you attempt one stride as an athlete, you've gotta get down to 19 or even 18 stone."

"How am I gonna run a half-marathon if I can't train?" I asked.

"It'll be tight, but after you've lost the blubber, you'll have to train intensely. That means jogging, swimming, bike-riding, a few light weights." Terry was writing things down as he was talking, "You'll do more damage to those knees if you don't."

Having taken everything that Terry had told me on board, and understanding all the pitfalls and knowing the commitment needed to pull this off, I now accepted that I couldn't train on my home turf; there would be too many distractions. But where would I go and who would train me? I also needed a dietician. I looked over at Terry with little-boy-lost eyes, but before I could launch any appeals for assistance, he stopped me in my tracks. "No way, Don. You need somebody permanent, on hand day and night. I can't commit to that; I've too many responsibilities of my own. You'll have to look elsewhere mate. Sorry!"

"Too bad, too bad," I said, crushed by my fall at the first hurdle. "Do you know somebody that could help?"

"I'll talk to some running pals of mine. One of them owns a sports shop in Ruislip. He's got loads of contacts. I can pop in on my way home tonight," he offered, showing real enthusiasm at last.

"Thanks, Tel. I need all the help I can get."

He raised both eyebrows, which said it all.

I wasn't about to take the near-murderous route back to my office. The journey here had been like wading through treacle and had almost wiped me out. Besides, I had received about all the ridicule I could take for one day. Terry went back into the workshop and called up Les to pick me up in the car. My suit was now in need of a good dry clean and my body was in desperate need of a steam press. While we waited for Les, Terry said something that lifted my spirits a little. "You know, if you put as much energy and enthusiasm into this enterprise as you do into the car trade, then this time next year I might just increase your odds."

"Oh yeah, what to?"

"Ten thousand to two."

We both smiled but with trepidation, knowing that the task ahead ranked somewhere alongside the Alamo on the achievable scale. As I clambered into the car, I thanked Terry for his honesty and most of all for his advice. I handed back his 20 quid, assuring him that the moral of the story had hit home. In fact, this little chat may well have just saved my life.

CHAPTER FOUR
Acceptance

IN THE SHORT CAR RIDE FROM THE WORKSHOP TO THE OFFICE, I told Les of my intentions to take a year off. He didn't seem surprised about me taking up the challenge; Les knew me well enough to know that I'd never just hand over a quarter of a million pounds — that was an outrageous assumption — but what did scupper him was just how long I planned to be away.

"A year off? You sure? You can't even ave the afternoon off!"

"It's the only way, mate," I replied. "There are too many distractions round 'ere. I've gotta get out of it."

Les was looking lost at the very thought of it. He had only been away from my side less than a dozen times in the last 30 years and it clearly made him feel very jumpy. He bravely tried to mask his fear with a show of camaraderie. "Look mate, I'm right behind you," he said, showing me a cigarette packet with just two remaining snouts in it. "We'll both do a 'Tom'."

With the best intention in the world, Les had more chance of finding rocking-horse shit than giving up smoking. A few years back, we had both tried to cut down and decided that using roll-ups was the best way forward. I had struggled through half an ounce of Old Holborn before binning my Rizla's and returning to the ready-mades, whereas Les has turned what he found to be a most therapeutic hand-rolling practice into an art form and is never without one clinging to his bottom lip. He's probably consumed more tobacco smoke in his life than fresh air.

"Ok mate," I said with a wink, confident that I was totally alone on this one.

Walking back through the showroom Les said, "When you off then mate?"

I leant on a Bentley and took a deep breath. "Oh, either Wednesday or Thursday," I wheezed.

"Right then, 'ere's what I'll do, I won't 'ave a fag 'til after you leave. That'll 'elp, won't it?" said Les, reflecting on the length of time his selfless gesture was going to involve. Suddenly he added, "Couldn't you go on Wednesday not Thursday?" We both laughed and pressed on to the office.

"Les, can you keep an extra eye on Ann and the kids for me? She'll probably have her mum round quite a bit for company. But if you could keep up a presence …"

Les butted in, ever loyal, "good as done mate, good as done. 'Ow do you think she's gonna take to you having a year's holiday?" he asked, still baffled over this one himself.

"After what Terry's said, it's gonna be no fucking holiday, Les. Besides she's the one who's been nagging me for years to lose a bit of weight, so … I'm just taking her advice."

We reached the bottom of the stairs and took another breather.

"Tom's takings are gonna take a nose dive," Les said, "And the boys'll miss ya as well."

I squinted like I had just received a sudden sharp slap. "It's gonna feel like I've had me cock cut off, Les. But they are all part of the problem you see. I've been doing the same old routine for decades and if I don't make a clean sweep now, I ain't never gonna win this bet. And you know me Les, I ain't never gonna lose this bet!" I climbed my way up to my office, making each stair run creak with agony.

"I'm off down the paper shop to get some sweets to help with the 'ole wos' name, craving," said Les, "D'you want anything?"

"Yeah, get us some sugar-free chewing gum, mate will ya?" I replied. Just the mention of the word 'craving' made me ache for a cigarette, but my lifeboats were nestled warmly inside my jacket pocket and weren't ready to be launched just yet.

Since my first home was supposed to be my office, why not keep a wardrobe there? Many a time I had gone on a session with the lads straight from work. It was an indisputable fact that I needed to get rid of my crumpled, stinking fronds, just to make myself presentable, and today's need was point-critical. I surveyed my office with a smile. Les had indeed been a busy bee while I had been with Terry. Gone were the sandwich wrappings, the sauce bottles and the dirty coffee mugs; even the ashtrays had done a disappearing act. "How thoughtful," I said out loud. Someone had had the sensitivity to put up a 'No Smoking' sign and a Glade air freshener had been plugged into a socket. "Nice touch," I noted. Then panic set in and I spun around, with the all the grace of a hippo performing a pirouette, and lunged towards my drinks cabinet. The fear quickly waned as I found them, my precious whiskies, all present and correct. No-one had dared touch my sacred malt collection, not yet anyway. This treasure trove was the ultimate temptation and the number-one priority to be abstained from. With pangs of guilt shooting through me, I turned my back on them, aimed myself at the closet and dragged my heavy heart towards it. Once there, I grabbed a fresh suit, shirt, underwear and my toiletry bag, and headed for the men's room defiantly. Before leaving I sneaked one last sad glance at my beloved bottled friends.

I'd never been totally tackle-out in the bog before, so I locked the door to save everyone's embarrassment. The large mirror above the hand basins told a very sorry tale. Baggy bloodshot eyes took a pitiful tour around my torso. Below my chin the skin of my neck was positively reminiscent of a bullfrog's vocal sac and wobbled when I shook my head. Bingo wings of saggy skin drooped from under my upper arms, with all the beauty that only cellulite can provide. I had advanced 'moobs', which fell earthward and exaggerated my nipples so that they resembled burgundy jelly pendants. My gut had taken on its own persona, at least 12 inches beyond my chest at its peak and hanging like a thick fleshy lid over my private parts; how ironic that it shared the appearance of the bloated stomach of a malnourished child. It was red and pimply in places, with stretchmarks and large blue veins running in from the sides. It billowed down from where once a waist had been. Along with the flabby Michelin man love handles, my midsection hung from my anaemic body like a heavy drape curtain, overused and forever faded. The bits below my abdomen were relatively normal. I had the same bum I'd always had; only for the amount of food that I consumed these days should require two arseholes. My legs were more in keeping with a man of 12 stone and my feet, although large, had tiny toes. Probably my best feature, I thought, my fucking toes. I needed the mirror these days to view my most precious of crown jewels, and although most of me had outgrown to an enormous degree, this area, which could have done with some exaggeration, alas hadn't!

"You look like a fucking freak," I whispered. "A hundred years ago, they'd have put you in a street show." Images of bearded ladies and Siamese twins popped into my head. Ladies? That was a joke. Ann needed the lights off nowadays before she would side up to me and that wasn't very often. I knew all to well that lovemaking was done out of a sense of duty more than anything else, much more than desire. Sweat covered my entire body and glistened under the fluorescent light. The smell of it was making me ill. It had an odour unique to heavy drinkers; a blend of perspiration, alcohol and shit, and it seeped from every pore.

Most people would be jettisoned into the depths of depression when presented with this reflection. Not Don Simmons. It disgusted me for sure, made me feel like I had been deluding myself, made me feel like a total loser. Yet these realisations were the stuff that stirred my spirit, the stuff that fired up the resolve that has made me what I am today. They made me stronger. I had a moment of clarity and was suddenly even more determined to win. I drew in a huge breath and set about cleansing and deodorising myself. In 20 minutes I was transformed, fresh as a spring lettuce and wafting of Ralf Lauren. I gathered my rank pile of clothing into a bin bag and mopped up their drippings with some paper towel, washed my hands once more and headed back to my office.

From the showroom floor, I could see Richard standing with Keith Harper, the manager of my real estate business. Keith had most probably been filled in on this morning's debacle, but neither of them would have any idea about my intended sabbatical. A dedicated and enthusiastic employee for the past 15 years, Keith had long been due a seat on the board of directors and my imminent absence would give the perfect opportunity to present him with his just reward.

"Afternoon Keith, has Richard informed you of my little dilemma?" I asked with a slight saltiness.

"Yes Don," he replied, still not completely clear on the situation. He glanced up at the No Smoking sign. "Commencement underway is it?" he said.

Keith, like most of my crew, was a hefty smoker and clearly felt uneasy about not being aloud to spark up in the usually nicotine-friendly zone.

"Why the fuck not boys? Anyone for tea?" I said jauntily.

Richard and Keith both opted for coffee, so I buzzed through the request to my PA. At the same time, I asked her to arrange a board of directors' meeting for 10:30 a.m. the following morning.

"Right, this is the situation. I'm pissing off for a year to get my act together. Keith, I'm putting you on the board. You deserve it — it's well overdue. Richard, I'm making you Director-in-Chief. You'll have total command of day-to-day business. I'm at the end of a line, of course, should things go tits up, but I don't want to be bothered with the general agro. I know you can handle it Dick, I have total faith."

The newly promoted pair stood there, astonished. I, with my usual brash manner hadn't given them time to breathe, let alone think. "Of course you'll both get a better package. We'll sort the finer details out by the end of the week," I said, not even considering that they might not want the jobs. As the financial gains quickly registered in their minds, they exchanged looks and launched into a tirade of effusive thanks and gratitude for my confidence in them. I recited an abridged version of my reasons for going and my plan of action. From their cautious response, I could tell they were far from convinced that I could actually put it into practice, but I didn't let on.

"About the matter of a personal trainer Don, I think that I can help you there," said Richard. "My wife and I go to a gym owned by a couple called Tony and Chris. They've been talking about expanding into 'one-on-one' training, maybe they'll be interested."

"What are they like?" I asked.

"They're both really nice people, very helpful, fit as anything, not your average gym instructors at all," he replied.

"They're not a pair of iron hoofs, are they?" I said, at lightning speed.

"No," laughed Richard, "Not in the least."

"Good," I said, "I couldn't be seen going away with a bandit for a year, could I? People would talk." I knew that for the right price, anyone could be tempted away from Britain for a year. That wasn't the problem: getting the right person was the problem.

"Right, arrange a meeting for me, Richard, as soon as you can. I'll need someone on board straightaway," I said.

When the drinks arrived, Richard and Keith were both momentarily at a loss with their spoons. They were used to having to wait their turn for the sugar bowl, because I would always dive in first and shovel a mountain into my own coffee mug, leaving them with the dregs. Today, alien as it was, I had PG Tips, white with no sugar. At that moment Les arrived back from the sweet shop, tossing me my chewing gum. "Where's my tea then?" he asked.

"You've missed the order for beverages, old boy," I told him, "but I'm sure that you could catch up with Claire and beg your way into her teapot."

Les tutted and slipped out of the room.

In between slurps, I asked Richard if he could inform Lord Belington's solicitor of my intention to take on the wager and to gain, although I had no doubts, confirmation that his lordship could indeed afford such a sum. It was a petty dig but I just couldn't help myself.

The next two hurdles were big ones: telling Ann and finding the ideal place to train. Ann would have to wait until I got home from work. Ultimately I knew what the outcome would be after a bout with her. I always got my own way; she'd just have to understand that it was for my health's sake. It was going to happen and that was that! Only this time I was weighed down by the biggest guilt complex ever. I could see myself telling her but it felt as if pure deceit were rolling off my tongue, even though I had nothing to hide. It all sounded far too much like make-believe.

I have an urgency to get on with things — I had this morning already given up smoking, cut out sugar and taken my longest walk in two years — but I had little patience and needed to see things happening fast. I had the bit between my teeth and by Wednesday or Thursday I wanted to be fully embarked on a training programme elsewhere in a foreign country.

To some people life is pre-ordained; all mapped out for you to stumble through till you reach a ghastly end. I had always thought the opposite: that you carved your own destiny, made your own luck. After today's events, though, I was raising one eyebrow to the former idea. Belington had unwittingly done me a massive favour; he had altered the course of my life.

Each Monday morning Keith and I would put an hour aside to sift through a pile of new properties that had come on to the market and to review the ones currently on the books. This job was soon to be undertaken solely by Keith. The stack of faxes, catalogues and literature that sat idle on a corner of my desk had been largely disregarded. Until now, when I noticed a glossy picture of a sunny apartment block graced with a swimming pool, palm trees and what appeared to be mountains in the background.

"Where's that?" I asked, nodding my head at the top brochure.

Keith glanced down. "Oh that's the Dutchman's property in Spain," he said.

I turned down my mouth and shrugged, none the wiser. Richard leant over and looked at the glossy. "Yes, I gave Domingo's our estate agent over there the go-ahead to put it on the market yesterday," he said.

I held out my hand and Keith slipped the magazine off the top of the pile so I could have a closer look, while Richard explained how we'd come about owning it. Apparently it had been taken in part exchange for six stretched limousines. When the Dutchman couldn't come up with the full payment, Richard had done the necessary.

"Bless your arse, Dickey boy," I said. Studying the cover for a while, I then flicked through the catalogue. 'Luxury four-bed apartment near Pineda de Mar, Spain,' read the caption below its picture.

"Where's Pineda de Mar then?" I asked.

"It's in a region called Catalonia, on the Costa Brava between Barcelona and the French border," replied Richard. "Not too touristy. Has its own language, you know."

"What Spanish?"

"No Don" said Richard sardonically, "Catalan."

Studying the views of the area with growing enthusiasm, I could see that the foothills behind the apartment were ideal training ground for the Wycombe half-marathon, and a pool was exactly what Terry had suggested I use as exercise until I had lost at least seven stone. It was also close to a coastal road — perfect for cycling. Was it coincidence or just a stroke of luck? I couldn't contain myself. "Fucking hell," I murmured. "This is it boys."

"What?" they both chimed in unison.

"My destiny," I said at length, staring dreamily at the sun-drenched complex.

From the expressions on their faces, Richard and Keith were wondering if I'd completely lost my marbles. In my head I was there already, gliding through the crystal water like a dolphin on ecstasy. Of course, in reality, I hadn't been in a swimming pool since I was ten years old and that had been a truly awful experience. I had struggled halfway across the shallow end with a self-styled doggy paddle, only to be salvaged from drowning by someone's dad and brought to the side coughing and spluttering. I'd spent the rest of the session there, wrapped in a towel and shivering, more out of fear than cold. A mistrust of water had stayed with me ever since, and I had always used this as an excuse for not adding it to my whisky. That episode aside, swimming pools had never held an attraction for me. If I was honest, it was the shame that I carried around with me about my physique. Hopefully, the seclusion of the apartment would provide a shield for my embarrassment.

"The blurb on the apartment is written in English, Spanish and Catalan," said Keith.

"How different is Catalan from Spanish then, Keith?" I asked.

"I'm not sure, mate. It's probably about as different as Cornish is to English. I suppose they have their own words for things, my lover," he replied.

"As long as they speak English to me, we'll all get along fine." I was from the old-fashioned school of British abroad, who expected the whole world to be bilingual.

"This is gonna be a long learning curve," muttered Keith, but I was too nose-deep in the literature to detect the air of scepticism. By now, I was feeling all the more certain that I had stumbled on the perfect training ground. The apartment's four bedrooms each had ensuite bathrooms, with an extra guest bathroom in the hall; a 44 ft furnished lounge; a huge fully fitted kitchen; plus a very impressive terraced garden in typical Spanish style, expansively tiled and boasting many planters filled with agaves, palms and geraniums. The balcony boasted a little courtyard fountain, which gave an impression of welcome coolness. It all overlooked the idyllic aquamarine crushed velvet that was the Mediterranean Sea, and it beckoned me. Other features in the apartment blocks were two tennis courts and a security wall, which ran the entire perimeter, and a caretaker who lived onsite with his wife, who would apparently do the laundry if required. But its *piéce de resistance* for me was simple: the architect had designed just 17 apartments, deliberately placing quality before quantity, and that meant everything to me.

"Richard, you better inform that Spanish estate agent to take this property off the market pronto and get all the bills to be paid by direct debit. I don't want my training to be hindered by all that crap. I'm on a mission. You've got the keys haven't you?" I asked.

"We have two sets of keys, the caretaker has another set. He tends the gardens when no-one's around. I also have a map of how to find the place along with all the legal documents back at the office. I'll bring everything here tomorrow morning and inform Domingo's right away."

"Good old boy," I replied. It was all fitting into place. I buzzed through to my PA again. "Claire, could you cancel all of my mobile phone contracts for me? As of next Wednesday I won't need them any more. Cheers love."

Claire repeated my request back to me just to clarify that she had heard it correctly, and then replied with a slow "Ok" before shaking herself.

At two o'clock that afternoon, I decided to pack it in for the day and go home. An unprecedented move because normally at the end of the day I would have headed straight for The George for a top-up. But today was a day of epic change and these changes meant a new lifestyle. I was going to take the car, but Les pointed out that I might still be inebriated from the weekend's deluge. So my ever-faithful sidekick insisted on taking me home. It was the best idea in many ways because I had already been prosecuted on two previous occasions for driving while under the influence of alcohol, both times on the day after a massive session. A third court appearance would definitely see me losing my licence for good, and maybe a prison sentence to boot.

"Yeah, good thinking Les, the last thing I want is me collar felt," I said, popping a stick of gum into my mouth. As we drove along, both of us chewing, we exchanged little in the way of conversation. My head was full of monologue, trying to decide on the right opening line for delivering the bad news to my wife. I still hadn't come up with a blinder when we finally crunched to a halt on the gravel drive. Les obviously knew it was best to scoot off straightaway, so after checking whether I needed anything doing he took his leave.

"I'd like you to take the Vogue to the four-wheel drive centre in Oxford for a service. Eddie'll do it overnight if I give him a large one. Get 'em to take that bloody phone holder out as well. It'll get on me tits without a phone in it. 'Ere's a monkey, take a cab home and pick up the motor in the morning before you come and get me, that should cover it."

"You're not gonna take a phone with you to Spain?" queried Les, baffled.

Mobile phones had been essential accessories for me, like pistols to a gunslinger. "I won't be needing them for a while mate — excess baggage."

Les still hadn't quite got the gist of what was going on and it showed on his face. Like a dog rejected by his master he turned his head away as I got out of the car.

"You'll be glad to see the back of me," I said as I closed the door, but Les neither replied nor looked my way. He performed a short wheelspin as he applied too much force to the accelerator and sped off out of the drive. I decided to ask Ann to keep an eye on Les while I was away the old boy definitely wasn't himself.

Leaning on the doorframe between the hall and kitchen of my house, I stood unnoticed as I watched Ann down in the utility room take a load of laundry from out of the tumble dryer and place it on to the table, ready to be sorted into two piles, ironing and non. She suddenly felt a presence and looked up with a start. "Ooh you scared me! What are you doing home so early, everything alright?"

"Everything's fine,' I said, with a schoolboy smile. "Here's some more washing for you." I handed her my bin bag.

"Oh, thank you very much, just what I needed," she quipped and took the bag straight back into the utility room. Once Ann started to sort through that rank bundle of garments, questions would fill her head. In a flash I knew exactly what to do. I stripped down to my birthday suit, all bar my socks.

When Ann came back into the kitchen her jaw dropped two inches and she burst out laughing, putting her hands to her face in mock horror. Before she could utter a word I cut in. "What do you see?" I barked. Without waiting for her to return fire, I answered for her. "I'll tell you what you can see. 26 stone of shit! Twenty-six stone of shit that most definitely won't be standing here next year if I don't do something about it!" I paused, waiting for a response.

Having been cut short twice already, though, Ann simply sat down at the table and picked up her coffee mug. Still grinning with raised eyebrows she stared over her mug, waiting for my next move.

"I've got something to tell you, love," I said at length.

She reached across the table and threw me a warm pair of underpants and a vest.

While I wriggled into them, she got up and poured me a mug of coffee from the percolator. She was at the brink of shovelling sugar into it when I interjected.

"No sugar love, and just black," I said, sitting down.

Her head twitched a double-take as she again stared at me wide-eyed and notion less. Still silent, she handed me my drink and moved around to the back of my chair to massage my walrus-like neck and shoulders. She knew this treatment always unwound me and would ease out the words I'd been wrestling with all day, making them trickle from my tongue like honey from a spoon.

"I'm sorry Ann, for being so abrupt. It's just that I've been worrying myself silly over how to tell you this."

"The best way is just to tell me, isn't it?" she said, and lightly patted my shoulders.

So I began, and 15 minutes later I finished up by saying, "... So your husband's about to become the fattest half-marathon runner in history!"

Throughout my full confession, Ann never uttered a word. There was the odd facial expression from time to time, but otherwise she simply listened. When I had finished she rose and poured us both another coffee, quietly contemplating everything that she had heard. She knew that once I had made up my mind to do something, torturous wild Orcs from the Mines of Moria couldn't change my mind. She sat back at the table.

I was experiencing mixed waves of emotion. Joy, that my wife hadn't burst a blood vessel and laid into me like a cornered vixen (in fact, she was showing no anger at all.) and suspicion, that perhaps she was so sick of the sight of me these days that she was decidedly pleased that I was buggering off for a year. Whichever it was, I knew all too well that I wasn't going to be let off the hook that easily. She placed the coffee in front of me.

"I've put one sugar in it, as a sweetener," she said and winked. I smiled a weak smile and wondered what was coming.

"I'm laying down three conditions for you, Don Simmons."

"What are they?" I timidly enquired.

"First, the kids and I can come and visit whenever we want."

Floods of relief poured over me, dousing hot coals of concern.

"Of course, I intended that anyway," I said weakly.

"Second, you swear to me that you won't kill yourself in the proceeds."

I was gaining more control. "One of the reasons I'm doing this is so that I can live longer, my love," I pledged.

She interrupted. "I know the way that you approach things Don, all or nothing, you'll push yourself silly!"

I reminded her of Terry's conditions, that I shouldn't attempt any strenuous exercise at all until I had shed at least seven stone. So far Ann's requests hadn't been anywhere near demanding, but there was still one more to come. She looked at me square in the face. It was the same look she had given me at the altar 23 years ago, a look of nervous glee, hopefulness, fear and optimism all at once. Here it comes, I thought, the crushing blow.

"Don't bring one of those straw donkeys back home with you, will you? They're so 1970's!"

I leapt up from the table to grapple with her in pure delight. I tickled her so much she could hardly breathe and we collapsed onto the kitchen floor, laughing like children.

CHAPTER FIVE
The blessing

THE BACK DOOR FLEW OPEN and in tumbled two whirling dervishes, dishevelled and starving after another gruelling day at school. Mathew, like a locust, headed straight for the biscuit barrel, while June decided that a cuddle with the unusually home-early Daddy was in order. Just for a few seconds, of course, then she joined her brother in front of the TV for a bout of who owns the remote control. The clock on the wall said that it was 4:30 p.m. but for Ann and me, time had stood still this afternoon. We had been talking about the past 23 years of marriage, and come to the conclusion that we were closer together now than at any other time before in our marriage. Over a lengthy period of time together, our coupling had evolved into a new kind of beast; a oneness brought on by the melding of our souls. It doesn't suit everybody; some people actually resent it, describing such a relationship as 'taking each other for granted'. Is that always such a bad thing? Knowing each other's moods, moves and whereabouts can take the stress out of life. You know that you can rely on one another; at worst, this could be considered to be boring.

I was never boring. In truth, I was hardly ever at home, especially not at sociable hours. The one thing that I'd had to hold my hands up to was that I hadn't spent enough quality time with my family and it was heavily underlined during our conversation. I felt like I'd neglected them on a grand scale and I promised Ann that when this battle was over, I'd make it up to them big time. And my word was my bond. We joined the children in the sitting room, which brought about some curious exchanges from our siblings. The TV was put on mute so that I could address my audience with clarity.

I cleared my throat, "Kids, your dad's going to live in Spain for a year … and although it's going to break my heart to leave you all for so long, I want you to know that it's for the best … and that you can come and visit me any time you like."

Two faces stared up from the couch, about as vexed as game-show contestants. "You and mum getting divorced?" quizzed Mathew.

"No, not at all," I laughed. "I'm just going away to work."

"Oh," said Matt, then they both turned their heads back towards the box.

I was deeply disappointed by their lack of interest. I shrugged and looked to Ann with my arms held out and palms turned upwards, "What can you do?" I despaired.

"Ian and Jenny are coming round later. They've probably only got that on their minds, love," she assured me.

"Huh," I said disgruntled, and stomped off to the kitchen, closely followed by Ann.

"They're both becoming a little chubby, those two," I said.

"Here we go," Ann groaned, "the emergence of a reformed glutton."

It had never bothered me before. Why would it? I was blinkered to any weight problems. "We'll have to nip that right in the bud. Put them on a diet as of now," I ordered.

"I shouldn't have to. With you out the way there'll be no more fast food around here, I can tell you," she said, stamping her authority.

"Ah... Right," I said, reluctantly taking the blame.

Trish didn't have a weight problem at all; her strict vegetarian diet put paid to that. She wasn't particularly skinny either; in fact, the local lads would have called her 'well fit' if she had graced them with her presence, but she kept well away from the 'idiots' in town. The war between 'Scream'-ager and Dinosaur Dad was almost over now that her five-year reign of terror had used up most of its energy and she was mellowing into a more broadminded, sensitive type of human being. Of course, she'd also done the compulsory job of putting her mum through hell — at one point Ann must have been the most hated woman in Britain. Everybody was wrong about everything: meat was murder; cigarettes were drip-fed cancer; and cruelty to animals included putting spiders out in the cold. Funnily enough, marijuana and Ecstasy were 'cool' and so were the New Age travelling wastes of space that she presented as boyfriends. I would have barred all the lazy bastards if I'd had my way, but Ann declared that would only fuel the fire and that in time Trish would find level ground. She was right, of course. A mother's love includes a mountain of tolerance.

Six weeks' previous I had taken Trish shopping in Knightsbridge. I had bought her half-a-dozen designer bits from Harvey Nichols, Harrods and the Burberry shop. I then took her for a very expensive lunch and rounded the day off by presenting her with a top-spec convertible BMW. This indeed put a smile on her usually angst-ridden face, and had put us on an even keel. Sharing the same space in the house was now just about tolerable for her. It was the least I could do, after completely forgetting both her 18th and 19th birthdays, mostly due to absentmindedness, but with a tiny hint of spite thrown in, just because she'd been such a complete nightmare.

While Ann and I were talking, the urge for a smoke had been building up into to a blood-aching crescendo; I'd chewed my way through two packets of gum in the proceeds without even realising it. Ann had noticed but kept quiet. Now, with the added guilt of being responsible for the kids getting fat, I was starting to lose it. Ann sensed my anxiety coming to a boil. "You don't have to totally quit all at once you know. You can cut down a bit at a time," she said softly, trying to ease the pain.

"I know!" I snapped. "I know, love, but that's not my style is it? It's all or nothing for me. I'll do it Tom's way and be done with it. I've gotta be strong," I added, taking in a large breath and thrusting out my lips. "God, I need a drink," I sighed, and slumped into my chair. At this time of day I'd normally be getting my daily fix at The George, and I was turning glassy eyed at the deprivation. I hadn't gone a day without the embrace of alcohol gently caressing my lips since I was 18 and legally entitled. Today was going to be no exception.

A bottle of Gordon's gin gathering dust in the back of the cocktail cabinet gave me a brainwave. "Have we got any tonic water in the house, love?" I asked Ann.

"I think there's some Slimline in that cupboard with the Coke and squash. What have you got in mind?" she asked.

"We got any lemons?" I answered with a question.

"Yeah!"

"Ice?"

"Yes, in the freezer where it normally lives!"

"Right, we're having a Tom's Special," I said at last. Apparently she was joining me. Ann watched as I fixed us both a gin and tonic in a most peculiar fashion. "This'll sort me out," I said with relish. The liquid never touched the sides as it hurtled its way south and my glass was empty before Ann had even taken a sip. I fixed myself another, but at a more leisurely pace. It did the trick — convinced my nervous system that the storm was over in my veins and the fire was out. The frustration eased, for the time being anyway.

"Oh, while I think of it, can you get some iced tea in tomorrow? I've acquired a taste for it," I said staring lovingly at my empty glass.

"I'll do my best," she mused. "Now I've got to get the tea going, Don. What am I gonna do for you?" she asked.

Trish kept all of her food and drink in a separate cupboard and her own refrigerator so as to not 'contaminate' her stuff with any animal products. It was all veggie gear and exactly what I needed, but I didn't fancy any of it. "Tell you what I'll have, dear. A jacket spud with some beans on, no butter," I said. Heinz Baked Beans were my favourite, but I usually made the potato float on a sea of butter, so going without would be like devouring a bowl of cotton wool and sawdust sat at a table on the plains of Death Valley. But as long as I had a drink in my hand, I could tolerate any form of tyranny.

At that moment Trish poked her head around the door and asked Ann to pop some pasta on to boil while she took a shower. She was in her usual state of frantic wild abandonment and having no natural body clock or the conscience to endorse some kind of timekeeping device, she was also running late.

"Can I have a word with you, Trish?" I enquired. My very presence stopped her dead in her tracks and curiosity took hold.

"What are you doing home?" she asked with some astonishment.

Trish could feel a lecture coming on and was on the verge of making a swift exit so I pre-empted her getaway with a "Come and sit down, love."

She looked at her mum for support. Ann raised her eyebrows and nodded her approval at the request. I told her my tale and when I got to the bit about having to lose half my bodyweight, I paused and waited for her response. Everybody up until now had openly shown some concern at this point, but Trish in typical Trish-style just said "Your sex life's gonna improve ... without that extra person you're carrying around."

Ann went scarlet; I just frowned, coughed a little and then carried on. When I summed up my state of affairs, instead of being upset, she jumped up, kissed me on the cheek and said "Go for it Dad. I'm off for a shower."

We parents were astounded by her turnaround. Two months ago she'd have laughed in my face and given me the wanker sign behind my back before nonchalantly strolling off, not giving me a second thought. Now, it was like having a different girl in the house. What a joy it was! I had got my entire family's blessing and the freedom to launch my plan on full throttle. I couldn't bear the thought of watching other people eat the good stuff without joining in, so I fixed another G&T and slipped into the solitude of the garden to stare at the world, while Ann and the kids had their dinner.

Half an hour later and feeling much more positive, I strolled back into the house to eat my first healthy meal in 46 years. I then booked an early night as I had a very important day ahead of me. Tomorrow's meeting of directors was going to be short and sweet. Everybody in the room would have a clear picture of my intentions; I just had to rubber stamp it. I had phoned Terry and asked him to take the day off from the paint shop. He was to join us at around eleven o'clock in my office. I needed to clarify a few points — well, go over the whole bloody lot again really. I was in desperate need of some last-minute confidence, mostly due to nicotine withdrawal. Besides Terry's methodical approach put everything into perspective.

Les picked me up at 9:30 a.m. sharp. The Range Rover was purring like a happy kitten and the smell of Oxford leather and *Feu* Orange freshener greeted me as I opened the door. It hit me like a new experience as I took a nice long breath, I smiled; my sense of smell was being rekindled. The car as usual was immaculately clean, apart from the area around the driver's seat. Les was eating chocolate digestives like there was no tomorrow.

"What the fuck do you think you're doing?" I snapped.

"What?" said Les, his mouth full of biscuit.

"Look at the fucking mess you've made!" I said in a higher tone.

Les looked down at his lap. "I can't stop eating Don, it must be the wos' name," he said, nervously tapping his thumb on the steering wheel. "I'll clear it up when we get to the showroom, I promise. I'll get the Hoover out," he added.

"Fucking right you will. I can't drive to Spain with a packet of crumbs up my arse. I'll end up looking like a fucking cheesecake." I was in a particularly colourful mood this morning, compiled by the fact that I'd purposely missed breakfast. This, I would soon discover is not the best way to start off a diet.

Claire had spotted the Range Rover pulling into its parking bay and by the time I had puffed and panted my way up to the office, a cup of tea was waiting on my desk. Having been on the firm for 20 years, my PA was second-to-none and knew exactly what I wanted doing. She'd cleared my desk, leaving my teacup with two bunches of keys and the paperwork for the apartment in Spain as its only companions.

"Good girl, Claire," I said in my usual fatherly way. She knew I'd never patronize her; it was just my manner — besides, she was very tough-skinned! The office seemed different to me, not just because of the absence of a smoke haze or waft of fried food; it had a very sombre atmosphere, almost as if it was sad to see me go. Les hadn't helped to cheer the mood either. He had worn a longer face than Nijinsky all the way into work. It was understandable though. He was losing his best friend for a year. I had tried my utmost to occupy the man's time while I was to be away; I'd told him to carry on as normal, only to drive Richard around instead of me, and to take the newspapers and magazines to Ann on a Sunday morning and, of course to keep an extra eye on my whole family in my absence. All this would help, but Les would still miss his old mucker real bad. And I had to admit I would miss the old bugger too.

"Now that's better!" said Richard, as he strode into the office with a huge smile on his face. "One can breathe in here now," he added, still smiling, a briefcase in one hand and a cup of percolated coffee in the other. I perched, as best as an elephant seal could do, on the edge of my desk and just stared at my new director-in-chief, while chomping away on three sticks of chewing gum.

"Just tell me what you got," I said flatly. I was like a time bomb today and sarcastic comments would simply serve to wind me up.

"Oh right," said Richard, suddenly realising that addiction comedowns were agony to deal with and that he should be more sensitive. He put down his briefcase and coffee. "There's two things really before we, err, go into the meeting. One is that I've drafted a letter for Lord Belington's solicitor, as per your request, if you could sign that? And second, I called Tony and Chris last night and explained your situation. They're interested for at least one of them to go to Spain, and they'd be happy to come and see you at home tonight, say at around 6:30, if that's ok? I tried to phone you last night and this morning but your landlines were constantly engaged and your mobiles don't seem to be working."

"Turned the bloody things off, my programme started last night!" I interjected. "You'll have a job getting me on the home phone, the kids are constantly on the Internet," I added.

Richard closed his eyes and nodded, being a fellow sufferer.

"Have you got to call them back?" I asked.

"Yes. Is 6:30 ok then?" replied Richard.

"Make it six. I want to get the ball rolling as soon as."

"Right you are," agreed Richard. He polished off his coffee and we headed for the boardroom.

There were no airs or graces at our board meetings. The directors were all either friends or family and all in the drinking school. They had all been so pissed in one another's company that none of them had anything gracious left anyway. But today's meeting would be different. Absent was the informal breakfast and banished were the ashtrays. Gone was the childish banter of pranks and conquests and most definitely 'in' was a very serious bundle of anxiety that could quite easily take the life of somebody who even vaguely smelt of tobacco.

I plonked myself at the head of the table. "Morning lads," I said with a sigh. "You've all heard the rumours and they're all true. So I'd just like to welcome Keith on to the board and let you know that Richard's taking care of things in my absence. The business is in good shape and I know that you'll all keep it that way."

Just then Claire came into the room wielding a tray of drinks and set them in the centre of the table. Everyone's eyes lit up and they all reached for a glass. I stood up and they all followed suit. "To Simmons," I toasted.

"To Simmons," they replied and guzzled away at their beverages, with the most quizzical expressions, some stopping midway through a gulp to examine their glass. Richard then piped up. "I'd like to take this opportunity to wish Don all the luck in the world. If any man has the guts and determination to pull this off, it would be Don! To Don!" he said and raised his glass once more. Some people even took another swig. Then they all clapped and cheered their boss in genuine warm-hearted admiration. A tear was welling up in my eye. I quelled it by announcing that I would be gone as from tomorrow and that I didn't want to see their ugly faces for at least a year, by which time they wouldn't recognize me anyway, "so fuck off the lot of you."

Everybody cleared the room except Charlie and Ray. "You never do things by halves, do you bruv?" said Charlie, and he put his arm around some of me and laughed.

As we walked out Ray said, "What was that stuff you gave us to drink?"

"Lipton's finest old son," I replied, which left my brother-in-law none the wiser.

Terry, prompt as ever, was waiting back at my office and had been impressed by its fresh demeanour. "Morning Terry," I said with a smile. He gave me a wink in return. "I spoke to my running pals last night. We can trot over to their shop today and sort you out some trainers, if you like?" he said.

"I'm not trotting anywhere just yet," I joked, "We'll take the car."

••▼••

Two expansive walls, decked out top to bottom in space-age technological running shoes, stared down at me from a totally different universe. They made me feel extremely outside of my comfort zone and mocked me with their aloofness. My only experience with any kind of sports footwear was at school, and that was a pair of black elasticised plimsolls that stank to high heaven after a very short while. This lot were totally alien to me. I felt like a field mouse in a pet shop trying to choose the most ergonomic plastic cage to relocate to. I was blinded by brand names: Nike, Adidas, Reebok, Solomon, Saucony, Puma, North Face, and Walsh. The choice was endless, each one drenched in its own neon publicity, proclaiming its definite supremacy.

I was utterly at a loss where to start, so it was a great relief when Terry's friends Phil and Steve were introduced to me. The men were clearly very enthusiastic about long-distance running. They had, of course, both done the Wycombe-Half and many others with hill climbs. 'Meat grinders' they called them: Hastings, Snowdonia, Ben Nevis and The Boston Heartbreak. They spoke of the pleasures and pains of being out on your own against a mass of like-minded men, all aiming for the same goal — to be first to break that white tape in a time better than anything previous. They told of cross-country runs in freezing conditions with just a lightweight vest between you and the elements. They informed me of the downsides too. Jogger's nipple, where your shirt rubs non-stop on your nipples until they bleed; runners' trots, brought on by muscle fatigue, so much so that the bowels relax and before you know it you're sporting the latest line in brown squelchy shorts. Then there was the Wall, a barrier you come up against if you haven't taken on enough fluids (dehydration) or loaded up on carbohydrates, and this can cause vomiting and or cramps, as can indeed motion sickness.

Another hazard that can lead to nausea is when all of the body's glucose has been eaten up by the exertion of a run; energy is then obtained from the digestion of fat cells by the enzyme lipase, this in turn causes an irritation in the gastrointestinal tract and a response in the brain's higher CNS centre, which makes you feel like chucking up. Only a seasoned athlete can deal with this. If correct training is assumed from the outset, where the exercise is paced slowly and is not too intense, the body will burn up fat at a more congenial rate and will not enrage the appetite of the runner to an object-defeating level.

"That's why we're all so skinny," said Phil, and then coughed to hide his faux pas.

At first I thought these two jokers were taking the piss, but as I listened, I warmed to them and realized that they had genuine integrity. Even though my running career hadn't realized conception yet, Steve and Phil generously treated me as a fellow and offered wholeheartedly their expertise in choosing the right equipment for my training programme. "I think that we ought to start with the most important piece of kit first," suggested Steve, "yourself Don. You're certainly a lot bigger than the usual blokes that we have coming in here and without being patronizing, I hope that Terry has stressed the need to lose a few kilos before you start running?"

I nodded, visibly irritated. Talk about state the fucking obvious, I thought.

"Err, um, yes; well have you seen your GP? I mean is your heart ok?" Steve inquired tentatively.

"It fucking won't be if I carry on like this!" I joked.

They all laughed nervously. "Have you any other problems? Injuries, funny feet, fear of tarmac?" asked Phil.

"I've got a fear of kissing it Phil, but no, joking apart, my cartilage is playing up in both knees. The doctor seems to think that it will ease when I shed a couple of stone."

"It should help enormously, but I'd recommend wearing supports while you train. Anything else?" asked Steve.

"Yes," I said, "I'm short-sighted as well. I have trouble reading the bill in a restaurant."

"I can't see that interfering with your running," said Phil, "but you might want to buy a stopwatch with large numbers on it. We have them in stock."

I was only pulling their leg of course but these two seemed so eager to help that I went with the flow.

"Right, let's sort you out with some shoes," said Steve with authority.

I sat on a fitting bench while the two men brought over a selection of trainers. Terry, silent but ever mindful, perched beside me on the edge of his seat, arms locked forward. I hoped that my plates weren't too pungent this morning.

"Here you go, Don, try these. Adidas A3s. Well-suited to the larger runner, with the emphasis on rear-foot cushioning," enthused Steve.

"It's all French to me, Steve," I said as I slipped off my brogues. I was beginning to get a little hot under all the display lights and sweat droplets were making a keen appearance on my forehead. "Cor, these are comfy, not too flash either. What else you got?"

"Well, there are these bad boys. Nike Air Durhams. They have a full-length polyurethane midsole for maximum durability. The medial post has been extended two-thirds of the way down the shoe for better stability," added Phil on techno-jargon overload.

I turned my hands palm side-up and shrugged. "Steady!" I said, "You're talking to an old-fashioned boy here." I tried them on as well. "These are good 'n' all. It's like walking on cushions," I announced tramping up and down the sales floor.

After a few more pairs had been pranced about in, the sweat patches were becoming more apparent on my shirt. So I decided to call time on this particular exercise. We settled on a really comfortable shoe that suited me best for training. The Asics Gel Nimbus 4, or 'jelly shoes' as I put it, were just right. In fact I bought three pairs: one in my present shoe size and two in a size smaller, because my feet would most definitely shrink along with the rest of me, as my diet progressed. Steve also mentioned that after I'd broken them in, one pair of shoes would somehow feel more comfortable than the other. I should keep these specifically for the race day.

They then moved on to the watch counter, a glass case filled with a cacophony of exotic, ticking timepieces that left me bewildered. Just then a young man breezed into the shop smoking a cigarette. Phil looked up after getting a whiff and told him that smoking wasn't allowed on the premises. The man apologized and made his way out of the building. I got wind of the cigarette and my lungs filled with the most intoxicating aroma, I was drawn to it, like a bee to a honeysuckle bloom.

"You'll come to think of one of these as your best friends," said Phil waking me from my fantasy with a jolt. He carefully laid out a pair of high-tech stopwatches on the counter.

"What? Oh yeah," I replied, as I slid back into the land of retail. The usual problem occurred with me when trying on wristwatches: none of the straps would fasten and the elasticised ones were way too tight for my chubby arms. So I opted for a 'Polar Coach', a watch that I could wear around my neck or just keep in my pocket for now, and a Nike speed–distance monitor, that I could adorn my wrist with in the slimmer times ahead. "That'll be a great marker, the day I can slip this one on," I said with some anticipation. I was starting to believe in myself.

"That's what we like to hear — the power of positive thinking," said an over-eager Steve.

Plonker, I thought, he's read too many New Age books.

We all perused the aisles of designer sportswear. Phil and Steve were way out in front, while I waddled behind and Terry brought up the rear. He was clearly enjoying his day out, absorbing the pantomime as he strolled along with his arms crossed behind his back. Phil remarked that although they didn't have any clothing to match my size, everything in the shop could be ordered in XXXL, so I should go ahead and choose whatever I liked. I took a fancy to Ron Hill clothing, the coincidence being in the name of course; it wasn't the logo but the lightweight weatherproof material and plain styling that I liked, and besides blue was my favourite colour! I chose three pairs of everything in three decreasing sizes, working on the expectation that 'Large' was going to be the smallest stature that I'd ever reach.

I chose the multipurpose Active bike jacket, the Trackster running trousers with underfoot stirrups, the Marathon shorts, Marathon vests and Marathon S/S tee-shirts. On top of this I purchased 12 pairs of Thurlo running socks, a Nathan G-Trek bottle belt, a clip-on wallet, a multitude of knee and ankle supports in varying sizes and an Asics Teamline bag to put it all in. There wasn't much change from a grand and as I laid down a wad of fifties, Steve came over from the shoe section. "Here you go, Don. Have these on the house. Make them your lucky ones," he said and presented me with a pair of Asics Kayano. "I've got you a size ten. When you can get your feet into these, you know you're in with a chance!"

I'd spent a nice few quid with these boys, but it didn't really warrant a hundred pounds' worth of trainers as a free gift. The size of the gesture told me that it was a genuine gift from the heart, from someone who championed a trier and it bolstered my resolve. "What can I say lads? I'm very, very touched. Thank you," I said, swallowing hard.

"You're welcome," said Steve.

"Just do me two favours," added Phil. "Don't kill yourself trying to do this and love every minute that you're doing it."

"You sound like my wife," I said. "If you were as good looking as her I'd kiss you both!" I had to knock back a few tears as Terry and I walked back to the car and we barely spoke. The emotion of the camaraderie was a new experience for me and a hard one to deal with.

CHAPTER SIX
Kitted out

THE GENTLE SNORING that could be heard from outside of the Vogue was brought to an abrupt end as soon as the doors were wrenched open.

"Asleep at your post?" I said with a big cheery grin on my face. "That's a court marshal offense!"

"I was just resting my eyes Don. Didn't get much kip last night," said a very weary Les, wiping dribble from his chin, "where we off to?"

"Wycombe my man, Arthur's Cycles post haste," I said, and off we sped.

This bicycle shop was established in the 1940s and was run by eccentric father-and-son partnership who were definitely 'old school'. Although the façade had been modernized, the mechanics of salesmanship and ordering hadn't altered a drop since day one. The chaps knew every model of bicycle that had ever been manufactured and probably had every component for every machine available, neatly stacked within a warren of ancient shelving. I had been buying cycles and parts from Arthur's since I was seven and trusted their opinion implicitly.

As we entered the shop a brass bell tinkled above our heads and the smell of rubber and three-in-one oil flooded our senses. It took me back to my youth in an instant and a homely feeling swept over me. Terry and Les stopped by the window to admire the new mountain bikes and to tut-tut at the prices of them. Meanwhile I meandered to the back of the customerless shop, stopping at the service counter to look for one of the boys. Harold, dressed in his pristine khaki overalls, was on one knee and deeply engrossed in a tyre repair.

"Alright 'Arold?" I said, finally spotting the old man. Harold jerked upwards at my words and nutted the saddle of his charge, before turning to see one of his favourite customers leaning on his elbows at the counter, wincing with commiseration.

"Hello Donald! Haven't seen you in a while, you alright, are you?" he enquired, rubbing his head.

"I'm very well, thank you," I replied. "How's Sidney?"

"He's very well too, thank you," droned a voice from behind a wall of shelving. I could see Sid's shoes, but nothing more of the man.

Harold was very particular about the sale of a bicycle. He insisted that the recipient of the machine had to be present for a fitting before he would let any bike leave the premises, in case there should be any comebacks. "Whose turn is it today?" he asked, looking down the shop for one of my offspring.

"The bike's for me, 'Arold," I said, waiting for a reaction.

The old man wasn't outwardly fazed and kept his professional stance; after all, this was a paying customer and all channels of sales etiquette had to be observed. "The town and country section it is then," advised Harold as he headed for the back of the shop.

As we walked, we passed row upon row of modern racing bikes and lightweight chunky mountain bikes until we reached a small selection of sturdy 'proper' bikes.

"One of these should suit you, Don. I have a Peugeot myself," he said with an air of confidence. By this time, Terry and Les had caught up with us and Les eloquently informed me that one of those racing bike saddles would split his arse in two — a statement I chose to ignore.

At first I plumped for the Peugeot Country 200, but after several attempts at trying to mount the thing, knocking over a row of road bikes and having to be steadied by the boys in the process, I reassessed the situation and went for a Country 505. Although at first glance the lack of a crossbar gave it the appearance of a woman's bike, the 505 was in fact multigender. It was lighter than the 200 better equipped; it was also more expensive. The colour was a very prestigious-looking silver, and it was by far the better suited to my requirements. I didn't realize it at the time of course but this beast and I were gonna see plenty of action together.

While Terry and Les struggled outside trying to fit a bike rack to the back of the Range Rover, I settled the bill at the counter, adding a speedometer, air pump, puncture repair kit and pannier bags to the bundle.

"Now let's sort you out a helmet, Don. What size are you?" asked Harold.

I had always insisted on the kids wearing helmets, but knew that I'd feel a complete pillock in one myself, so I turned down the opportunity to buy one.

"You sure, Donald? A road usually wins in a fight you know," Harold reminded me.

"Usually wins a fight? Always does," said Sid's shoes.

"I'm sure lads, and thank you very much, but I don't intend to come off!"

"Happy cycling," said father and son in unison as I tinkled my way out of the shop.

Once the bike had been hitched to the rack, we sped off towards Ruislip, with Les at the wheel chewing the head off of a large fruit and nut chocolate bar, Terry munching on an organic honey and walnut flapjack and me biting my fingernails, substituting pain for nicotine.

"Nice bit of kit that," commented Running bear, between mouthfuls of rolled oats.

"Umm," I said, not really listening. We had just passed my favourite sandwich bar in Bridge Street; the most deliciously beautiful aroma of crispy fried bacon had seduced my senses and left me in a dreamy state of salivation.

"I've got to eat something, I'm fucking dying here," I said all of a sudden. "Les, pull over and run back to that shop. Get me a salad sandwich … and some iced tea if they've got it. I should have had fucking breakfast!"

He bought me two sandwiches and some peach tea. As we set off again, I demolished them like a ravenous bear emerging from hibernation; semi-content, I then sat back and contemplated the rest of the day.

By the time we arrived at the showroom, Richard had already left for the day, but Claire had passed on my goodbye to him. I did the rounds of the office block, the workshops and the showroom floor, shaking everybody's hand and wishing them well for the forthcoming year. They in turn wished me safe passage and the best of luck — I was wishing for a time machine! I gave Claire a kiss on the cheek and told her to carry on doing her magic. I knew that I could rely on her to keep the business afloat.

Terry had sat with Les all this time, reminiscing about near scrapes and dodgy moments in the motor trade; there had been a few. When I approached them to be taken home, Terry got up and held out his hand. "Well all the best, mate," he said. "You've got my number if you need it. Feel free to call me with any fears or worries, and I'll do my best to put you right."

"Thanks, Tel. You've been a real inspiration. I'll pay you back by running this race."

"You do that, Don! See ya on the start line." We shook hands with a firmer than usual grip and then parted.

It was almost five o'clock when we finally reached home and I was desperate for a G&T. The thought of it prompted me to give Les one last request for the day — I asked him to nip up to the cash and carry warehouse and buy three cases of Slimline tonic water, a case of Gordon's gin and a dozen lemons. If this was to be my only poison for the time being, I was going to stock up in case I couldn't get the ingredients over there. (I had yet to learn that Spain was a modern country and also Europe's largest producer of lemons!)

"Oh, you better get me four cases of iced tea while you're at it."

"Right-o boss, can I get myself some chocolate as well?" he asked.

"Knock yourself out mate," I replied. We unloaded the day's purchases and Les shot off in a cloud of gravel dust.

Ann hadn't been able to reach me all day. I'd either been out of the office or offline and so she'd been at a loss as to what to make me for dinner. She'd been to the supermarket and bought a selection of low-calorie ready-made meals and a ton of vegetables, but had no idea what I really fancied, so she'd put a couple of jacket potatoes in the oven just in case.

"Have you eaten anything today, love?" she asked as I walked in the back door.

"Just a wee sandwich," I said in a pathetic voice accompanied by a pained expression.

"You'll be hankering after some supper then," she said with a wry smile.

"A morsel of floor sweepings is all I need to continue living, missus," I replied in my best Oliver Twist.

"You won't be wanting these jacket potatoes then?" she jested.

"I'll fight you for 'em," I said showing my true colours.

She laughed. "That won't be necessary Mr Simmons, now get up off the floor."

By 6:05 p.m. I had taken a shower and listened to the evening news, and now I was back on the floor, this time on all fours in my underwear with my head in the oven trying to cut the potatoes in half so that they would cook quicker. The sound of the dogs barking made Ann check the security camera monitor, "looks like a VW Golf pulling in Don."

"Bugger me, is that the time?" I said. "That must be Tony and Chris, the fitness guys. Let me put some clothes on." With that, I disappeared upstairs, threw on some trousers and a shirt and was just buttoning up when Ann in walked the bedroom.

"Have you ever seen Tony and Chris before?" she enquired.

"No, why?" I quizzed.

"No reason," she said, her tongue firmly in cheek as she calmly walked away.

I cascaded down the stairs like an avalanche but was brought to an abrupt halt, followed by an embarrassing silence. In the sitting room sat two of the most attractive women I had ever laid eyes on. Beautiful fresh faces, simple natural hairstyles and bodies to die for.

"Hello, you must be Don," said Toni, and stretched out a hand.

I limply took hold of it.

"I'm Chris," said the other girl, and she too extended her heavenly hand.

I could sense Ann looking on and enjoying every moment. Of course there was no way on Earth that she would allow either of these two gorgeous women to live with me for a year. That was totally out of the question. How could I have made such a balls-up? Surely Richard knew the score? What was he playing at? Still, I'd have to go through the motions of interviewing them, just to be polite. After all, they had made the effort to come all the way out here. I gathered myself and went into business mode.

"Welcome to my home, ladies. Can I get you a drink of some sort?" I said with a smile.

"Diet Coke for me, please," said Chris.

"OJ if you've got it, please," said Toni.

"Certainly," said Ann, and was about to shoot off like a cheetah when I spoke up.

"Um, could I have the old …?" I gesticulated a drinking motion.

Ann nodded and was back in record time.

The girls' credentials were impeccable. They had great references, certificates in physiotherapy, physical training, weight training, as dieticians and as swimming instructors. They were perfect, in fact too perfect. I then had the uncomfortable job of explaining to the girls that I was in fact expecting men to show up tonight, and how stupid I felt over the mix-up. Although their talents were exactly what I needed, I just wouldn't feel comfortable with a female instructor sharing my apartment in Spain. I said that I was sorry for wasting their time and hoped that they didn't feel unfairly treated. I then thanked them for coming and wished them all the best. They seemed a little perturbed but fully understood my predicament. I offered them some petrol money which they absolutely refused and left in good spirits.

I closed the front door, turned around and leant against it, releasing a sigh of relief. I opened my eyes to see Ann smirking at me from the doorway.

"Jesus," I said. "I'll kill that fucking Richard!"

Ann burst out laughing and swanned off to the kitchen to rescue the jacket spuds. Within seconds I was on the phone to my deputy. "How bloody embarrassing, Richard. You might have told me that they were birds. I'd never get away with taking one of them abroad with me. They'd put me off the training anyway, I'd have a constant stalk on."

"Evening Don," said Richard joyously.

"Hell-fucking-o," I replied. "Now explain yourself, if you would be so kind."

"Sorry Don, my mistake. I thought that they'd be good for you, keep your spirits up," he said sheepishly.

"Keep me chopper up, more like. I suppose you thought Ann would be ok with this?"

"I thought that maybe you'd bring her round to your way of thinking. It was a daft thing to do, Don. I'm really sorry, how can I make it up to you?" he squirmed.

"Got any pictures of them in leotards?" I joked.

"I'll see what I can do," he replied with a laugh. We exchanged goodbyes and best wishes and then I trundled off to the kitchen to still my grumbling stomach.

Around the dinner table the only sound to be heard was the smacking of podgy lips as spoonfuls of veggie chilli and jacket potato were shovelled into a hollow cavern. Ann sat twirling a straw in her tall glass of spritzer and it was some time before she spoke. "You know what you ought to do?" she paused. "Go back and see Marion."

I winced in pain at the mere mention of that woman's name, "what for?" I asked bewildered. I sat back waiting for the explanation, with bits of kidney bean and sweetcorn stuck to my chin.

"She'll sort your diet out. Besides, you owe her an apology."

Fear and dread washed through me like a rinsing agent, but I quickly resigned myself to the fact that Ann was spot-on as usual. It was Tuesday night and Weight Watchers would be convening down at the village hall. If I got my skates on I'd just about make chucking-out time. "You're right, love. I'll go now, and with a bit of luck she won't brain me with her scales," I said, wiping my greasy face with a napkin. "See you in a bit."

I parked at the far end of the car park and watched as the dumplings rolled out. First to leave were the only two blokes in the class, who chatted for a while before departing. Then a steady stream of go-lightly ladies exited until just Marion was left, merrily loading her car boot with paraphernalia. I scrutinized each Weight Watcher intently, this time not with contempt and hilarity, but with interest and compassion, with the eye of a convert who'd suddenly become an expert in this field. I'd certainly changed my tune from last week. How could I have called these people fat, when I was clearly top of the pile when it came to bulk blubber?

I approached Marion from the shadows, nervous as hell and unsure of the outcome, but as my old dad used to say, "A job won't get done unless you start it!"

"Lovely night for it," I said from out of the dark.

Marion nearly dropped her box of books. She turned sharply with the look of a startled rabbit. When she realised that it was me, she pursed her lips in total disapproval.

"Let me take care of that," I said, taking the box from her and resting it in the boot of her car.

"What do you want, Mr Simmons?" she hissed.

"I need your help actually," I said, as sweet as a spring lamb.

Suspicion registered in her mind and her eyes narrowed. "You better come inside," she said, and with that closed the boot lid with a sharp click.

The musty old hall regained its nostalgic appeal and relaxed me a little, even though the floorboards seemed to be complaining louder than ever. We reached the stage end and the table where Marion's handbag stood like a heat-wilted soldier on guard duty.

"Now Mr Simmons, whatever could you want from me?" said the cougar, readying to pounce.

"I have to lose half my bodyweight by this time next year!" I said, getting straight to the point. From the expression on Marion's face, she suspected that a big health scare had brought me to this conclusion. My condition was obviously life threatening, but she needed to know what circumstance had brought me to admit it.

"And what makes you think that I would be willing to help?" she challenged.

"That's what you do isn't it, help people lose weight?" I said rising to the jibe.

"People that want to help themselves, yes. People that don't mock the system, people with integrity. Mr Simmons, you've shown nothing but contempt for my classes in the past, why the sudden change of heart?"

It wasn't going as well as I had expected and I hadn't even got to the part about the bet yet, so I tried a new tactic. "Look Marion, I know I've been a total waste of your time in the past and for that I absolutely apologize. I'll be honest with you, something has happened that has changed my world completely. I am without question a different man for it. I've quit smoking, cut right down on my food intake and almost totally given up drinking."

"Almost totally?" she repeated scathingly.

"I have to have a little gin and Slimline tonic, to keep the motor running, just for now. I'll kick it later."

"No more takeaways?" she asked.

"No way, honestly," I replied. The tide was turning.

"Mr Simmons…"

"Please, call me Don, Marion," I implored.

"So tell me, Don, what catastrophic event has brought all this on?"

"This might take a while Marion. Do you have the time?"

"Just a moment." she said, and then pulled out her mobile phone to tell her husband that she was running late.

I launched into the saga and she listened with furrowed brow, showing disapproval at the nature of the wager and gasping at the sum of money involved. At the end of the story she sat back in her chair, meditative yet drawn to my cause. She removed her glasses and rubbed her eyes. "It's a shame it has taken money to motivate you, Don, but it may be that this act of machismo in the pub has inadvertently saved your life. Your friend Terry is absolutely correct with his analysis. You owe him a favour!" She continued, "You do realise that to lose that amount of weight in one year can also be very damaging, don't you? If you want my honest opinion I'd say don't do it. But it doesn't seem like you have a choice, does it? Half your bodyweight?" she paused. "As I recall your weight at the last meeting was twenty-five stone, thirteen and a half pounds."

"Yes," I said, managing to get a word in. I was flabbergasted that she'd remembered my weight exactly. I must have made an impression.

"I'll have to go home to do some calculations and prepare a strategy for you. Can we arrange a meeting in the near future, Don?"

"No time Marion, I'm leaving for Spain tomorrow, so if you can manage it, a strategy will have to be worked out tonight!"

"What? Good God!" She looked panicked and turned her head away with one hand over her mouth. After a minute she said, "One plan we offer here at Weight Watchers is for 'housebound' clients. We loan them a set of scales, give them all the literature necessary, and they ring in once a week with their weight. I visit them once a month for a progress analysis. Obviously I couldn't commute to Spain once a month, but we could work something out along those lines." Marion was indifferent to my wealth and didn't show an ounce of surprise when I offered to fly her out each month. Driven by her keen work ethic, though, she politely turned me down.

Neither of us spoke for a while. Then I said, "Your meetings definitely work, those two chaps…"

"Steve and Rob," she interjected.

"Yes, they must have lost a couple of stone each since I've been coming."

"Well Don, I'm here to guide and offer advice, that's all. The rest is up to the individual," she proudly announced.

"Well, you do a good job, that's all I have to say," I said. This last sweetener did the trick and she smiled, revealing rare evidence of a softer nature. I felt smugly charming. We talked for a good deal longer and decided that the housebound strategy was definitely the way to go. I would weigh myself every Tuesday evening, phone her the next day with the results and discuss any problems that arose. She would use my last recorded weigh-in as my starting weight and begin the programme as of tonight.

"What time do you leave tomorrow?" she asked briskly, as her manner resumed the tone of schoolmistress.

"Three in the afternoon," I replied.

"I can come round to your house at about ten in the morning to give you everything you need. Will that suit you?"

"That'll be fine," I said.

"Do you have all your weekly booklets from the meetings?"

I could feel my cheeks turning red; I couldn't quite squeeze out the words. I had actually binned them all! I just shook my head.

"Never mind, I'll bring a full set along with me," she said.

"Until tomorrow then, and thanks for giving me a second chance," I blurted gratefully, as I rose from my much-relieved stacking chair.

"See you then," she said looking over the top of her glasses. She watched me sway down the aisle of the village hall until I disappeared out of the back door and into the night. I sailed away on that tender summer evening on a wave of confidence, the smell of the musty old hall behind me and the call of *Ambre Solaire* up ahead.

Next morning, Marion arrived as promised at ten on the dot. With her she had brought a set of scales, the replacement booklets and a list of non-perishable Weight Watchers goods for me to buy from a supermarket. I handed the list straight to Les, who puzzled over it as though it were written in a foreign tongue.

"Go and get that lot from Sainsbury's for me would you mate? 'Ere's a 50," I said. Les loved to shop, especially with someone else's money.

After handing Marion a cheque for the annual subscription and the cost of the scales, I tried to give her another one to the sum of £500, by way of a 'thank you', but she flatly refused. Her rebuttal was the act of a proud woman who, I realised, wasn't driven by money but by a sense of responsibility for the well-being of fellow men and women; she helped others from the kindness of her heart and I admired her for that.

Ann had made a pot of percolated coffee and brought it into the sitting room on a tray along with a few digestive biscuits. I had only eaten a grapefruit for breakfast and my stomach was doing cartwheels, so I was elated when Marion refused her share of the biscuits. The need for a cigarette was driving me nuts and I was sitting on the edge of the sofa tapping my fingers on my knees and biting my lip. I took my coffee black and sugarless, but devoured the biscuits in six consecutive mouthfuls. Marion roosted on the settee with a look of disdain on her face.

"Rich Tea would be much better for you, Don," she advised.

"Yes, of course. I just needed something to quell the hunger pangs," I whined. "As soon as Les gets back with the goods, I'll be strictly a Weight Watchers man."

We managed to keep up a conversation for a while, mostly about the year ahead, and then Marion rounded off her visit by unexpectedly saying, "You know, Ann, you won't recognize him in a year's time. Don't you find that rather exciting?"

"I do actually," Ann agreed. I knew just where she was coming from. It would be like having a new man in the house, hopefully one with plenty of stamina.

As I walked Marion to her car I thanked her again and said that I would look forward to our Wednesday chats. She wished me *bon voyage*, and implored me not to overdo it. "I'll see half of you next year!" she quipped, clearly proud of her 'witty' parting shot. She then slid into her Fiat and chugged away. A little cloud of blue exhaust smoke told me that she was running a bit rich and burning too much oil.

"Half of you next year," that last remark stayed on my mind for a few days, indelible like a sentence on a slow loop.

CHAPTER SEVEN
The Chinese sting

THREE THINGS OCCUPIED MY MIND as I tackled the M25 and eventually the featureless monotony that is the M20, lolling its way down towards the Channel Tunnel. On several occasions my thoughts almost caused me to have an accident, as I lost contact with the present through sheer boredom. A recurring vision of Ann and Trish outside the front door, arm-in-arm and waving goodbye was burned into my mind. I had held back the tears when I kissed them both, but cried uncontrollably once I had passed the gate. My bloodshot eyes still stung from the onslaught of the summer sun. Where had the last 19 years gone? The occasional shopping trip and the meals at McDonald's were poor compensation for an absent parent and the loss of quality time was heavily underlined on my amendments list and heavy on my mind. I hadn't stumbled on an antidote yet but I was committed to finding one.

Since that day when Lord Belington's lawyers had walked into my office and slapped me with an iron glove, my whole attitude towards life had begun to change. Could just three days of asceticism (overlooking the 24 bottles of gin in the back of the car) be making me feel so different, so responsive and so much more alive? I congratulated myself; it had only been three days but I was proud of my progress, just another 362 to go! As I popped a stick of gum into my mouth, a picture of Les sparking up a roll-up the moment that he opened his eyes this morning flashed into my head, and I chuckled for a while.

The third thing that kept circulating around my grey matter was Marion's parting comment. "I'll see half of you next year." Half of me — wouldn't that be freaky, if just the bottom half turned up? Perhaps what Marion had said might even come true? Maybe on my return journey I would be half the man, but hopefully a fitter, healthier half.

The first *péage* to confront me on the motorway outside Calais was UK-friendly. It carried a huge Union Jack flag above one booth and offered the comfort of a right-handed ticket machine, so it was no problem for travelling Brits to obtain a ticket from the driver's side. From thereon, though, the toll stations were merciless. I followed the A16 past Boulogne and on to Abbeville where I had to switch on to the A28 towards Rouen. This was where the fun started. I came to a grinding halt beside a glass-panelled pay point, and was duly presented with a blue-sleeved French arm and an outstretched hand, waiting in anticipation. The cashier, unpaid, nonchalantly took a quick glance before retracting his moustachioed face with well-rehearsed disdain. I took off my seatbelt and arched my back in order to rummage through my pocket for some francs, which I had bought at the bureau de change inside the shuttle terminal. I then grabbed the ticket off the dashboard, flopped down from my seat and stomped around to the cashier to show that I was somewhat put out. This was my induction to toll systems, and my first 40 miles inside the country had cost me 40 francs.

"Fuck this for a game of soldiers," I muttered to myself. At this rate I was going to have to take out mortgage just to cross France. I pulled the car over and studied my map. After Rouen I could stay mostly on the main roads until Chateauroux, midway through the country, then pick up the A20 motorway. From there, it would be auto routes all the way south and into Spain via the A9 past Perpignan. This would cut the cost down a bit: money was not a consideration, but I had taken umbrage at having to fork out every half an hour to use the motorways.

Two minutes down the road I had to stop again, this time to collect another ticket for the next segment of the motorway. The auto-ticket dispensers were conveniently at window height but infuriatingly on the wrong side of the car. A person of average build can cope with leaning across the passenger seat and snatching the chit without too much hassle, but not for this walrus of car dealership. I was going to have to unbuckle myself again and lumber around to the machine. Being unfamiliar with this procedure I had parked the Vogue much too close to the next booth along and my door would only open by two-thirds. I thought about reversing back and realigning myself but another car had pulled up tight behind me, so I had no choice. I would have to prise myself free.

Squeezing past the door panel ripped off four buttons from my shirt and made me curse aloud, much to the bemusement of the impatient French couple sitting behind. I gave them a little wave and mouthed 'Sorry', which registered zero on their sympathy meter. Feeling very steamy under the collar, I swayed around to the dispenser only to find it *en panne*. I didn't know what that meant, but pressing the green button half a dozen times failed to deliver a ticket, so I gathered it meant bollocksed. I was now getting the right hump, but restrained myself from giving the machine a good kicking. Besides, yet a third car had pulled up and it was beginning to get a little embarrassing. I would have to ask both of them to back up before we could all get on our merry way

— but saddled with a French vocabulary consisting of just six words, gesticulation was about to play a major role. They soon got the idea. All three cars gradually snaked back in reverse to a chorus of honking and verbal abuse from other motorists. The whole 'getting out of the seat to retrieve a ticket' scenario had to be repeated again and my sweat glands were on overdrive, making me even more irritable. My fellow travellers were now waving their arms at me in that continental manner typified by the passionate. I grabbed a ticket and responded to their primitive furore in true British fashion: next to 'Coca-Cola' the words 'fuck off' are internationally renowned and their use reliably achieves extemporary results.

It was a mild enough evening, but the fracas at the tollbooth had caused me to perspire so much that cress seeds could sprout on the surface of my now flapping, gaping shirt. It was time to find a service station and change my wrappings.

British motorway services offer a variety of fare sufficient for any traveller, but this French stop-shop overwhelmed me. It was more than a supermarket; it had every thing from wine to windscreen wipers, pornography to pastrami, *chocolat* to *chaussettes*. At one time you could only buy petrol and oil from a garage, but as I perused the aisles in starry eyed wonderment, I noticed that nine out of every ten customers had purchased some kind of goodie as well as their fuel. Maybe I should open up a supermarket in the showroom!

My mind drifted to this morning's breakfast. I had had porridge, not my usual bucketload made with whole milk and Carnation cream, laden with sugar to the point where it caramelised from the heat of the oats, but a leaner blend prepared by Ann using water and just a hint of brown sugar. She had stopped short of using salt. This was all that I had eaten that day and I was ravenous, so standing in the middle of a snack-lover's heaven was swiftly becoming perilous and not recommended practice for the dieting fraternity. I had cornered myself in temptation alley, the very place I had to steer clear of. What should I do? Have one last feast before the fast? Gorge myself sick in a final frenzy in the car park? A week ago I would have thought nothing of scooping up armfuls of munchies, crisps, chocolate and fizzy pop and downing the lot before I reached my next port of call. Biscuits were normally my best buddies and a tube of chocolate Hobnobs or Jaffa Cakes were lethal. I likened myself to a Ghurkha soldier: once a Ghurkha had unsheathed his knife, he had to draw blood; if there were no enemy around to puncture, he would nick his own thumb to satisfy tradition. For me, once I had opened a packet of biscuits, I had to scoff the lot!

I was getting giddy with the heady scent of it all. I should have brought a packed lunch, but hindsight is a wonderful thing and totally fucking useless in most situations. "Healthy eating," I reminded myself and looked around for something resembling low fat, sugar-free and tasteless. Pre-packed salads caught my eye but they were all drenched in oily salad dressings and sprinkled with croutons. "Ah, there we go, my saviours,' I said, spotting a selection of fruit segments. I picked up two packets, three bananas, two oranges, two litres of *eau minerale naturelle* and four packets of chewing gum, then made my getaway. At the pay point the female cashier eyed me with some suspicion, for I must have looked like I'd been brawling in the street and needed the vitamin C to recuperate. After paying for my goods and the diesel I took a night bag from the car and headed for the loo. Ducking into the nearest cubicle I was confronted by an unearthly sight. "What the fuck?" I gasped. It was my first introduction to a traditional French public toilet, so I regarded this porcelain hole in the ground, decorated with off-target missiles, to be taking the piss. Excuse the pun! I quickly exited and bundled into the next cubicle only to be presented with the same agenda. Surely not! I thought, Fucking weird this lot. My words echoed off the ceramics. I backed out of that one too and hurriedly changed my shirt in front of the mirror, spraying on copious amounts of Right Guard under my sweaty pits. Soon I was back on the road again and safe from the seduction of the boutiques.

I came off at the Rouen exit. Just a few hundred metres around a bend there loomed another *péage*. Its checkpoint overtones made me a bit uncomfortable, and I felt slightly like an undercover operative chancing his arm at a border crossing. I approached with some trepidation. This time I didn't want the palaver of extracting myself from the car so I tried a new tactic. I pulled as close to the tollbooth as I could judge from my side of the car and lowered the window.

"*Bonsoir*," said a pretty young thing from within.

"*Bonsoir* to you too, love," I replied and praised the Lord that she was young and healthy. She held out her hand and waited with a cute friendly smile. I put the Vogue into park and started my manoeuvre. Twisting my blubberous frame around so as to almost face her, I leant across the passenger seat taking extreme care not to crush my new all-fruit passengers. However, my overburdened hand slipped off the leather seat, causing me to smack my chin on the armrest of the passenger door. Quickly righting myself with an elbow I saw that the girl was doing her utmost not to laugh and was chewing her bottom lip in anticipation of my next blunder. I then realised that I hadn't taken any money out of my pocket yet, so lying in that position and shaking with the strain, I struggled into my now very tight trousers and pulled out a 50-franc note. I handed it to her, along with the slightly sodden ticket that had been in my mouth this whole time. The giggling girl leant out of her booth, stretched into the car, took the ticket and the money and processed it to reveal another 45 franc charge.

"*Quarante-cinq francs, monsieur, s'il vous plaît,*" she said through her barely stifled laughter.

I was struggling back to the driver's seat, but it was proving difficult. My belly had been reshaped into an inverted jelly mould by the gear stick, such that the impression of a Range Rover centre console was now forever embedded in my stomach. I finally slumped into my seat and gestured to the girl that she should keep the change. I was far too embarrassed to attempt retrieval. She raised the barrier with a '*merci, au revoir*' and smiled that smile again, which was somewhat reminiscent of a young Goldie Hawn. I put my foot down but my shoe had come off unnoticed in the fracas, hence I gave the pedal too much gas, exaggerating the engine noise because I hadn't put the thing into gear. She laughed again, this time raising a hand to her face. Now completely flummoxed, I yanked it into drive and wheel spun away, leaving rubber on the tarmac, and headed for town behind a cloud of exhaust smoke.

Once through the confusingly signposted streets of Rouen, I was out on the open road again and heading southwest on the A13 towards Paris. Only a minute had passed when the overwhelming urge to tuck into my fruit companions gripped me like a tractor beam on a marooned spacecraft, pulling my hand from the steering wheel towards the cellophane-wrapped containers. I grabbed a packet and hauled it to my mouth hoping to tear through the cellophane with my teeth, but it proved to be too tough. Dribble was hanging from my chin and the sharp edge of the container kept poking up my left nostril; my frantic gnawing and getting nowhere was really beginning to piss me off. What's more, keeping control of the car had taken second place and I was wandering across lanes. Finally I ripped through the packaging only for the fruit juice inside to spurt out in an orgasmic thrust of energy and coat the interior of the car with sticky sweet liquid. Dashboard, windscreen and yours truly were all subjected to decoration. My fresh shirt now sported a contemporary orange motif, my crotch offered signs of incontinence and my hands were dripping with the syrupy stuff.

I pulled over and sat there for a while contemplating my sorry state. "Am I ever gonna get out of fucking France?" I snarled, dumping the packaging on the passenger seat and shaking my hands out of the window. Wiping them on my shirt I got out and went to the rear door where I fished around inside my overnight bag again for some new togs. The only things to hand were my sky-blue pyjamas and a pair of belted Hawaiian shorts. I couldn't be arsed to unpack my suitcases, so these would have to do. Given the very light traffic on this road, I decided it would be OK to debag there and then, and proceeded to put on the pyjama top and shorts. I realised I had neglected to pack any sandals, so I had to step back into put my Trader boots, making me look a complete prat. I decided that no-one would see me if I steered clear of any amenities but I was forgetting fuel stops. I bundled the clothes back into my holdall and clambered into the car. This time before setting off I was going to prepare myself. I pierced through the second pack of fruit and peeled back the film, positioned the container so that it wouldn't slide off the seat, opened a bottle of water and placed it in the door pocket. I then started the engine and was off again, ready for the road.

As I drove along, the last rays of the dying sun filtered through orange sorbet clouds, lifting my spirits to mingle with the gorgeous warm air that billowed in through the open window. I devoured the small segments of mango, pear, melon and strawberry with apprehension at first and then with relish, as I found to my delight that each fruit was a delicious new taste sensation pirouetting on the surface of my tongue. I was in my element again, eating. I licked my sticky fingers clean after each mouthful and thought about the last time that I'd eaten fruit. I still adored bananas, albeit liberally coated with sugar between thickly buttered slices of bread, a banana-sandwich habit from my childhood. This was the first time that I had tried them solo. Someone had once told me that if you had to survive on just one food alone, then bananas would be it. They contained just about the right balance of nutrients and fibre to give the human body a meagre existence. Malt whisky alas doesn't offer the same prospects.

I couldn't remember the last apple that I had scoffed and I had never even tasted an orange before, although Ann found pleasure in reminding me that I had come home from The George one Christmas Eve and demolished 20 Satsuma's before falling asleep in front of the telly, festooned in curly peel. But I have no memory of this!

Five hours and a couple of tolls later I had to stop for diesel. I'd eaten all the fruit segments and the bananas, and had drunk both bottles of water, that rendered me to stop at the side of the road twice already to relieve my aching bladder. There was no-one on the forecourt so I didn't feel too ridiculous at the pump, but my slow waddle to the shop was an agonising walk of shame. The mere noise that I made walking seemed unnecessarily loud; the ruffle of my clothing, the flapping of my boots, it seemed that my entire being was a luminescent apparition against the dark night. Worse still, the world appeared to have stood still to take a look; even tiny creatures busy in the surrounding trees stopped to take note. The cashier's gaze was fixed in wonderment; I swallowed hard and pressed on through the front door. Being English I kept all my chins up and paraded through the aisles as though nothing was amiss. I purchased two more bottles of water and another three bananas, wished the goggle-eyed attendant *'Bon soirée'* and thundered back to the Range Rover with a face as red as a baboon's arse. Safe again in my cocoon, I took to the road.

At around one o'clock in the morning, a further urination was required and although having to stop was irritating, I convinced myself that all the water I was drinking was detoxing my system. Considering the alcohol intake I had endured over the years, it would need the contents of Loch Ness to cleanse this particular structure.

Four-thirty, French time, the sky was just beginning to show signs of a new dawn. I had driven all through the night and considering all the hold-ups *en route* I had made pretty good time, but once more I had to pull over for a leak. I steered into a pretty little *aire* on the other side of Toulouse and strode over to a laurel bush to irrigate it liberally. Staring up at the really bright stars and enjoying the languid night air I forgot about the direction of my aim, until my shin felt unnaturally warm. I recoiled with the speed of a startled cobra, lost my balance backwards off the kerb and landed flat on my backside, causing a mini dust storm and a wet patch on my shorts. "Fucking bollocks," I shouted out in frustration. I wallowed there for a few seconds. Then heaving my soiled mass to an upright position, I dusted myself down and headed for the car feeling rather dejected. I opened the driver's door causing the courtesy light to illuminate a pair of oranges on the passenger seat like two tiny suns radiating enchantment. It was like seeing an orange for the very first time; the orbs spoke of promise and dared me inside to taste their soft, sweet juice. I pounced on one, ripped through its rind and peeled off a segment. I held it to the sky and made a toast, "To all things new," then stuffed it into my mouth like a feasting barbarian. "Beautiful," I murmured, "Really refreshing and tasty, my virgin orange."

For a man that ate for a pastime, who ate anything and everything in copious amounts, it seemed outrageous that I had avoided oranges. The exclusion from my diet stemmed from a childhood observation that a bowl of fruit in someone's house usually meant that they were ill. The association had kept me citrus-light for all these years, but yet again I was being enlightened. I plonked myself back into the car and set off for another three hours' worth of motorway, slavering over the rest of the orange and a couple of bananas along the way. Eating the fruit reminded me of the poster displayed at Marion's Weight Watchers meetings: 'Eat fruit for a sweeter life'. I had always wanted to insert the word 'pastilles' after 'fruit'; it seemed to me a blundering omission by the graphic designer.

••▼••

It was Ann who had insisted I should sign up to Weight Watchers. They convened once a week at the old church village hall, and although I had originally been appalled by the prospect, I ended up going along just to keep the peace. I love that distinctive musty smell that old wooden buildings inherit, a blend of dust, rotting books and floor polish. It gave me a cushion and reminded me of humble things from my youth like jumble sales, bric-a-brac fairs and Women's Institute ladies selling tea and homemade cakes beside a large stainless steel Burco boiler. The meeting was predominantly all female, with the exception of Steve and Rob, a couple of chaps in their early 30's who were around 16 stone apiece. I remember discussing bodyweight with them on my induction day, and had told them that in my opinion they were wasting their time. To my amazement, I then found out that they had been coming since January and had lost more than eight stone between them.

The classes started at 7:30 in the evening. I would pay my subscription fee, which entitled me to suffer the embarrassment of being weighed on their scales, never at home, and then I was expected to listen to a lengthy speech by Marion, but I must admit I never stayed for the 'talking to'. I had always managed to rustle up some excuse. By my sixth week I had still only shed half a pound; for a man of my size, this was seen as an extremely poor effort. Marion 'the headmistress' had been itching for a showdown with me, so this particular Tuesday she made sure she had the attention of the whole class when she cornered me, and insisted that I stayed for the duration. Feeling everyone's eyes burning into the back of my big head, I shrank back into my plastic chair, like a naughty schoolboy waiting to be hauled in front of the assembly by the ear to be given a ruler across the palm of my hand. I sat there with my eyes closed, waiting for a roasting; the incessant chatter from a hall full of diet heads blended into one indistinguishable noise. The noise tailed off to a whisper as Marion negotiated the steps that took her to the stage. Her eyes tightened as they focused on me and her lips pursed tight as though she had just bitten into a lemon. "She'll 'ave you now," warned Steve.

"Mr Simmons." Her voice sent a shiver down my spine. "I do not allow smoking in my meetings." The flame from my gold Ronson lighter had not yet touched the tip of my cigar. It flickered blue while I froze for a second before snapping its lid shut. Nonchalantly I put it back into my pocket and returned the cigar to its pack.

"Thank you," she said disdainfully.

"Sarcastic bitch," I had muttered to myself, mind you, looking back at it now I acknowledge it was very inconsiderate of me, especially in that health-conscious environment. Although I understood that cigarette smoke bothered some people, I certainly had not expected to be publicly reprimanded for it. I felt embarrassed and narked. Who the fuck did she think she was?

Marion now turned her attention from me to address the whole class with her evening's talk. "First, I would like to say what an excellent turnout we've had this evening. And what a superb overall weight loss has been achieved by all." The word 'all' had fallen in my direction as she peered over the top of her glasses. I had successfully managed to gain half a pound this week and was definitely not in her good books. Marion continued to ramble on for another 15 minutes about a new slimming product that had just come on the market 'radically changing lives' — yeah right, I had thought to myself. After that she congratulated another member for reaching her 'gold weight' and the class gave up a round of applause. Marion asked if anyone had any questions or problems, pointedly looking in my direction. One lady reported difficulties in finding a particular brand of soup that had been recommended, while another commented that the casserole recipe Marion had given the previous week had turned out rather well. After another half a dozen or so mind-numbing exchanges, I was beside myself with boredom and getting extremely agitated. I had some paperwork to do at home and a bottle of whisky was whispering my name.

"Any questions from you, gentlemen?"

When none of us spoke, Marion grabbed her opportunity. "Mr Simmons, has coming here on a regular basis helped you to lose weight?" This was showdown time. There was a distinct clash of personalities, fuelled by my lack of enthusiasm and bad attitude of course. To be fair, I had been wasting her time as well as my own but I wasn't about to be humiliated. Thirty-three years in the secondhand car trade had taught me one important lesson: sell yourself first. Once the customer has you on board you can sell ice to an Eskimo, or in this case, bullshit to a cow!

To the headmistress' surprise, I stood up resolutely and spoke. "Marion, ladies and gentlemen, I have a confession to make. I've been coming here for six weeks now and haven't managed to shed a drop of fat. In fact, I've gained! I'm a failure, but in no way am I going to give up. You see my two biggest enemies are takeaway food — Chinese and Indian especially — and alcohol, in copious amounts." I glanced across at Marion for her glare of disapproval. "My first week at Weight Watchers was the toughest. I managed to stick to the plan and leave my demons alone, but it was hell. I had good intentions of staying on track, but one business meeting after another, usually in a restaurant or pub, and I'm right back where I started. However, I will not let this beat me. As from today I'm walking out of here a determined man." There was a small round of applause from my audience. How easy they had been to reel in! Of course I had absolutely no intention of ever coming back.

Only Marion knew what a feeble attempt I had made towards losing weight, but thankfully the club's confidentiality rules held her back from revealing a client's failings. Her fixed stare almost burnt holes in my skin, but I didn't give a toss. The audience had bought my story, so rounding the sale off I made a pledge that from then on I would be giving 100 per cent effort to achieving my goal weight. This got a second, even louder applause. Rob and Steve both shook my hand. A heavy-jowled lady in front turned round and told me to "stick with it mate". It seemed that from all around the hall, fellow members were offering me words and gestures of encouragement. From within my bubble of deception, I began to feel really uncomfortable and started wishing that I were somewhere else, when Marion shouted above the din, "May I help you young man?" She was addressing somebody who had just appeared at the back of the hall. All heads bar mine turned in perfect unison towards the new arrival. I thought better of it, as the spindly legs of my stacking chair were under enough pressure from my bulk as it was.

"Mr Don, prease" said a voice from the back of the hall.

The blood fell from my face as I closed my eyes in horrible resignation.

"Chan you fucking idiot!"

I wanted the ground to swallow me up, but the hall floor wasn't hungry tonight. I glanced down at my watch: 8 fucking 15! I had stayed too long. All eyes were now back on me, deception over, it was time to escape.

I had been a regular at Low Chan's for more than 30 years. He was like an uncle to me. In that time, Chan had managed to put his four children through university and they were prime examples of today's well-educated multicultural society. He himself, alas, had only mastered the basics of 'Engrish'. Missing every other word out of a sentence almost made one feel pity for the man, until he hit you with the price of your meal in a perfect Bucks accent.

Now, takeaway food had become a way of life in the Simmons household, a far cry from the days of fish 'n' chips on a Friday night. And even though Ann was a wizard in the kitchen, four or five nights a week were fuelled by food brought to the door. Large amounts too, but always paid for with a decent tip for the poor drowned rat delivering on the doorstep. Keep the driver happy and he'll bend over backwards to keep the grub hot.

Tuesday night had always been Chinese night and it seemed the practical thing to do: pre-order the food, rush through the bare minimum required at Weight Watchers, then pop round the corner to Low's to pick up the order, swinging by the off-licence next door to grab a bottle of Pinot Gregio and a box of chocolates for Ann, sweets for the kids, beer and whisky for me and then home. Boom boom, no problem, right? The problem was Chan knew that I went to the village hall every Tuesday, but had no idea why. It seemed absurd to tell him that I was being weighed at a slimming club after ordering a huge meal. In fact it was a joke. I was only trying to appease Ann and had absolutely no intention of giving up food. I loved food — I wouldn't eat anything else! Not wishing to have an unsatisfied customer or miss out on the dosh, the ever-smiling Chan had brought the greasy seeping order into the hall.

"Are those bags for Mr Simmons?" enquired the Witchfinder General.

"Yes, orda Mr Don," replied Chan.

"May I ask what's in those bags?" asked Marion. It didn't take a fucking genius to work that one out. Brown paper bags, smell of sesame oil, Chinese bloke! Taking a gamble, I managed to twist round enough to catch Chan's eye and gestured politely for him to piss off, but I was too late. Marion had decided that it was payback time; she had taken it personally! "I'm sure that we are all very interested in finding out exactly what Mr Simmons will be eating for his supper tonight."

Chan still hadn't cottoned on to the fact that he was in the middle of a slimmer's' meeting, but sensed somehow that he was ever so slightly in the wrong. The smile began to fade from his face, "Ah, Mr Don, big orda." Chan was about to unknowingly play the devil's advocate and reveal me for the charlatan that I was. There was nothing I could do, except walk out there and then — but bad credibility wasn't in my dictionary. Though I didn't know anybody in the room personally, a few faces were familiar from PTA meetings, local shops and the like. Whatever, this was gonna be awful.

Like a tennis match crowd in synchronised motion, row upon row of Weight Watchers' heads swivelled from one end of the hall to the other: from Chan to me; from me to Chan. With each dish revealed like an expert stroke of a racquet, there came gasps of astonishment.

"Peking spare ribs, pancake loll, wan ton with sweet 'n' sour sauce, satay-fried steak on skewer, butterfry kling pawn, an' main course."

(Even bigger gasp.)

"Aromatic clispy duck, chricken ginger and pincapplc, bee' in oyster sauce, bee' an' brack pepper sauce, chilli prork Szechwan style, sweet 'n' sour pork ball, oh an' egg-flied lice." Silence followed and I thought that Chan had finished, his charges read out, but no; "Ah yes," he added innocently, "Me faget, flee blags plawn clackers."

Tumbleweed rolled silently down the centre aisle, along with it a ghostly wind, only to disappear beneath the stage. Beads of sweat glistened on my forehead, lit up by bare fluorescent tubes in dire need of replacement, but I refused to mop my brow — a show of weakness that would give Marion great delight.

"And in the yellow bags?" she sang with raised eyebrows.

Oh for fuck's sake, I thought, he's only gone and collected the 'offy' stuff as well. This had gone on for long enough; I had to come up with a blinder to dig myself out of a crater. "Marion, I can explain …"

"Young man, is Mr Simmons a regular at your shop?" Why did she keep calling Chan a young man? He was at least 60! I was a regular, I practically had fucking shares in the place. When my mates and I had been about 10 or 11, we would end up in Chan's every night. We had even invented our own addition to the menu, the 'D' set meal for four persons: two bags of chunky chips, two bags of prawn crackers, two cups of sweet and sour sauce and four cans of Coke. It was a fond memory.

"Mr Don, brest customa," declared Chan proudly.

"I'm gonna be lynched," I groaned, putting my hands over my face.

"Mr Simmons, may I call you Don?" came Marion's voice now with an air of eerie serenity. I drew a deep breath.

"Yes, I would prefer 'Don'."

"Don, not 15 minutes ago you told this meeting how you'd overcome two of your biggest temptations, alcohol and fast food. My members and I are confused. Are there two Mr Don Simmons present this evening, or is this mountain of cholesterol all yours?" she barked.

If I tried to laugh this one off, she'd have my 'nads on a plate. I had to think on my feet. "If you would just bear with me for a moment," I said. I got up and walked purposely up the centre aisle towards Chan. The subscription fee, collected by Marion's hefty assistant Alison, accompanied each weekly visit to Weight Watchers. On payment, Alison handed you a raffle ticket in return. These 'subs' went towards the Christmas party, a night out at the theatre, and a meal thereafter ... great! The raffle was drawn each week and a table was set out beneath the stage, laden with donated prizes: baskets of fruit, flowers, paperbacks, pictures, handmade pottery, soups, perfumes, tins of biscuits and bottles of wine. This could be my get-out-of-jail-free card!

Everyone in the hall expected me just to keep on walking when I got to the back of the hall, even Chan, who had by now twigged the situation. No-one saw the quick wink and raised finger to my lips, asking Chan to keep schtum. Taking the yellow bags, I retraced my long walk back to the front of the hall, each step making the aged floorboards creak with the burden. Silence prevailed, yet, stony-faced I was smug inside, feeling a trump card coming on. After carefully placing the contents of the off-licence bags onto the table, I looked up at Marion and said, "Not ideal prizes I know, but I didn't have much time tonight."

She was fuming; I swear a small whiff of smoke seeped from her ears, invisible to all but me. Keen not to lose grace, she thanked me ever so quickly. Time to go, I thought.

The third round of applause from my audience was cut short by a raised hand from the Gestapo. "Mr Simmons, I'm sorry, I mean Don," her voice remained calm, "You have not explained to whom the food belongs."

So far this evening, the throng had been well entertained. I was not about to let them down. My eldest daughter, Trish the fanatical vegetarian, was obsessed with healthy eating. 'Freak' I called her. She always insisted that Chan provide her with a separate meal from the rest of the family. Chan hadn't mentioned Trish's food; in its own special little bag he considered it a separate order. I beckoned him to come up to the stage. Holding up the two big bags of now lukewarm Chinese, I said, "These bags, ladies and gents, are for my wife and three kids. This little gem… is for me." Struggling with the small carrier, I pulled out one container at a time. "Chinese salad, plain noodles and mixed seasoned vegetables," I proudly announced. There was a standing ovation. Game, set and match to Don Simmons!

Driving back home I dropped Chan off at his shop. He had tried to apologise for the whole debacle, but I assured him that he'd done nothing wrong. In fact we both ended up laughing like a couple of demented hyenas. Replacing the sweets and drink on the way was a small price to pay for the potential loss of face that had been at stake. And even though the journey was less than two miles long, I managed to finish off one bag of prawn crackers and start greedily tucking into the next.

•• ▼ ••

The new day broke with an intense yellow sunrise that had me as spellbound as a two-year old at Christmas. Its heat soon warmed the temperature in the car and forced the ground moisture in the vineyard valleys to rise to tree height, shrouding all around in mystical haze. I had to stop to dry my glassy eyes, so I pulled into an *aire* just below the Pyrenees and got out to restore circulation to my legs and take in this awe-inspiring spectacle. I took the last orange with me, peeled it and stood transfixed by the glory before me. "Thanks Belington," I said after a mouthful. "If it weren't for you, I would never in a million years be standing here at the foot of a mountain at six o'clock in the morning in me shorts and enjoying a fabulous orange. God bless you." I sucked in a lungful of French air. I still had an enormous craving nagging at my nerve endings, but this was better than any burnt tobacco fumes and more invigorating than a full Monty by anyone's standards. I guzzled back some water, smacked my lips and smiled at the glory. I then returned to the Range Rover for the final leg of my journey.

Driving through the night had given me time to get my head around abandoning my family. I consoled myself with the end result justifying the pain and cushioned it further by the reassurance of visitation rights. They would be out in a few months' time, I thought. I had also been planning my initial steps for the coming year and decided that the first priority was to employ a dietician-cum-trainer or both.

'*España 2 kilómetros*' — the sky-blue road sign bearing a little Spanish flag made me think of Marion again. "I expect to see half of you next year," echoed in my bonce.

"People won't even recognise me," I said out loud. An air of intrigue and adventure ran through my veins and made me want to pee again. I was getting bored with motorway driving, so once inside Spain I decided to take the N11, one of the 'truck roads'. I estimated that Pineda lay about a hundred kilometres from the border, so I had around an hour and a half's worth of driving time left. Roughly two kilometres from the crossing I came to the exit for Ola Jonquera and my final tollbooth. As I pulled alongside I could see that there were fixed prices for travelling that short distance from France. Two hundred and ninety-five pesetas for a family saloon! Fucking dear country, I'd thought, not having quite worked out the exchange rate.

"*Buenos días*," said a happy tanned face from inside the booth. The Spaniard was in his mid-fifties, bald and about as tall as he was wide. He had broken off a conversation with a colleague long enough to wish me a good morning and to point out the toll prices, before going straight back into what sounded like verbal diarrhoea with his mate.

I had brought a couple of grand in pesetas with me folded up in my jacket pocket, which was hanging from a hook in the rear. Reaching for it wasn't a simple task by anyone's standards, but I made it look like the desperate struggling of an escapologist, almost dislocating my shoulder in the process. I finally retrieved the wad and peeled off a 1,000-peseta note. I then began the now ritual farce of prostrating my enormity across the interior of the car towards the passenger-side window. The *Cajero*, seeing my plight, sprung up like a Meerkat and with his knees on his chair, leant most of his body out of the window to receive the cash. All this time he never paused for breath or deviated from the exchange of banter with his pal, but when I indicated that he should keep the change, he postponed his chat long enough to smile a toothy grin and say "Thank you *señor*" then lunged once more into Spanish with gusto.

The temperature was rising rapidly as the morning blossomed into a beautiful day. Just being here, driving in the sunshine made my spirits soar and I wound down all the windows to be cooled by the airstream. For the first time I was glad of the shorts that I had on because my legs were starting to perspire. I needed to fill up with fuel again but the first two garages that I came to in Ola Jonquera were crammed with commercial traffic, European haulage firms and container wagons to-ing and fro-ing with all manner of saleable goods. I gave these a swerve and settled for a smaller petrol station with a café bar beside it, on the outskirts of town. This was just perfect because the dull drawing ache of an imminent crap was building in my bowels and I doubted if I could hold out until Pineda. Since Monday my ablutionary habits had radically altered due, without doubt, to the dramatic change in my diet and my now minimal intake of poisons. My lack of 'wanting to go' every five minutes of the day would normally be cause for concern, but given the circumstances it felt justified. My liver and arsehole however, felt deprived.

After filling the tank, cleaning the windscreen and paying for the fuel amid more curious looks from fellow travellers and a baffled *Cajero*, I parked up and entered the café. It was for the most part typically Spanish, but also had an American diner feel to it, enhanced by a long stainless steel bar that ran the entire length of the eatery and supported by 20 or so chrome-plated red leather cushioned stools, two of which were occupied. The two hombres who rested there were enjoying a breakfast of thickly cut bread smothered in olive oil, topped with tomatoes and *jamón*. A dozen huge legs of Spanish ham were hanging from hooks on the wall behind the bar. I couldn't help thinking how unhygienic the meat looked. As I entered, the patron glanced up from pouring his two customers a glass of cold lager from a tap in the middle of the bar. He must have seen all sorts pass this way, so I'm sure my appearance didn't faze him in the slightest. After resting the beers down for his fellow countrymen, he made his way up to me, wiping his hands on his apron. A *mélange* of edible delights and liquid paradise assaulted my nostrils, beckoning me like absent friends. I was suddenly salivating and I breathed deeply in the rich aroma, before steadying my weakened self against a stool. I'd better not stay in here too long, I thought, remembering my purpose in Spain. I had wanted a cup of tea but the smell of freshly brewed coffee made me change my tune, a wise decision seeing as Spaniards in my opinion make lousy tea.

"¿Café señor?"

"*Si*," I replied.

The patron walked to the large espresso machine with non-stop commentary in his native tongue, presuming that I was a home-grown. He pointed in turn to a small glass and then a ceramic cup. I nodded at the cup and then at a bottle of milk, which was being offered. All the time the Spaniard gabbled away unaware of my ignorance. He must have expected some interjection, but as none was forthcoming, he simply wandered off.

I must learn this lingo, even if it's just to tell them to shut up, I thought.

Having survived the last 24 hours without a hot drink, I was now in dire need of some caffeine. I found that the coffee was excellent and finished the cup in no time. I indicated to the patron that I'd like another one, interrupting a wild conversation about last night's football match. Upon receipt of the second cup I thought that I'd try a bit of Spanish.

"*Graçias señor*," I declared proudly.

Apart from these two words and 'Si', my command of Spanish had been extracted from my addiction to Western movies. This meant that I also knew the words 'Alamo' and 'Rio Grande', but that was about it.

"*De nada*," he replied. I just smiled.

I had gotten half way through the second cup when I felt the urge to leave pretty sharpish. The warm liquid had caused a chain reaction in my lower intestine and now I was most definitely turtle necking. I trundled past the three amigos at an astonishing speed. To my delight the toilets were fashioned in a design that I was used to, not the holes-in-the-ground affair back in France, and were relatively clean to boot. I dropped my shorts just in time, because three days' worth of jobbies had been kept in storage and were desperado for a swim. I sat there for a while in quiet contemplation before standing up and retrieving my pants. To my astonishment my belt buckle receded back past its usual notch. For the first time in my life my waist size had reduced. I double-checked it just to be sure; it was true, I was losing weight. I was ecstatic. I raced to the wall mirror and gripped the porcelain sink. My unshaven pink chubby face was grinning like a clown on payday. I hadn't felt this good in years. If just three days of dieting could do this, what's a year gonna do? I thought.

I hadn't learnt about water retention yet. The endless urinating on the trip down had definitely contributed to a smaller waistline. My return to my coffee cup was met with knowing looks from the fellow customers and I winked at them in acknowledgement. I certainly felt a lot more comfortable and just wanted to taste that divine caffeine once more before I left. While I sat there, the *Cajero* from the tollbooth came into the bar for his lunch break and immediately fell into conversation with the other three. Their subject of course was soccer, a passion that was as essential to the Spanish as oxygen is to lungs. Gesticulating overtly, showing the others how the free kick should have been taken and how the defence should have dealt with the opposition's goal, his actions were obvious. I didn't need the language to ascertain the game's outcome. Barcelona had lost. The only thing that the men could agree on was to disagree and that was good enough for them.

I enjoyed the rest of the sideshow while savouring the last swig of divine coffee, and held up a 1,000 peseta bill to depart. As the owner walked back down the bar to retrieve payment, the toll guy also turned in his seat. He recognised me and came rushing down to thank me for the earlier tip. He said a few words while continuously patting me on the back, and then pointed to my coffee cup to ask if I wanted a refill. I got the gist, but refused saying that I'd had enough already. The 1,000 peseta note lay on the bar so the *Cajero* picked it up and placed it back into my hand indicating that he would pick up the tab for the coffee. I smiled again and said *"Graçias"* then made my way to the exit. As I reached the door the *Cajero* called out *"Buen viaje."* It meant have a good trip but it flew over my head.

Driving off in the midday heat I felt glad that I'd come off the motorway. Not only because I'd had a chance to see the glorious countryside, but I'd also had the opportunity to meet real Spanish people on their home territory, doing what they do, day in, day out. It was just a taster of things to come, but I liked what I saw. I felt that these were warm, welcoming people, not like the reserved guarded sods I'd left back in Blighty. I was going to enjoy it here. Forty-eight hours had gone by since an alcoholic drink had passed my lips. I felt good about that as well. I had come to realise that it wasn't necessary to douse your entire cellular structure in flammable liquid in order to make it through the day. I could reach my RDA of vitamins and nutrients through other healthier forms of intake. And Spain had a lot of those to offer.

CHAPTER EIGHT
The meeting

THE DIRECTIONS TO THE APPARTMENT and its accompanying map had started their travels to Spain as important pristine documents regally designated as the sole occupants of the front passenger seat, but had since endured the sufferance of multiple leaning-on by an unreasonably heavy elbow, and now resembled the discarded wrappings of a fish and chip supper. Even so I sought reference from them in a dirt layby on the outskirts of Pineda. It seemed straightforward enough: 'From the main road take a left turn past the petrol station next to the fruit stall (apartments in view). Follow the road down towards the beach, the complex is on your right.' Easy, I thought.

I found the junction within a minute; the garage was a bog-standard modern affair, large forecourt and canopied pumps. But the barrow that the fruit seller employed must have been at least 200 years old and looked barely able to support the mountains of fresh produce that had been superbly stacked upon its flatbed. There were all sorts of locally grown fruit and vegetables and some exotic-looking types as well, all of it perfectly mouth-watering. I made a mental note to visit this place once I had settled in. The quarter-mile stretch of road down to the beach was bordered on its left-hand side with a thick conifer hedge, reaching seven or eight feet towards the sky. I thought at first it was just the edge of woodland, but later that day, when taking in the view from my terrace, I could see that it was in fact the frontier of a large campsite. To the right of the road were agricultural fields in full production of a vegetable that I couldn't quite recognize. Its fragrance was tantalisingly familiar, crisp and fresh, a kind of curry smell raking up memories of my younger days. Mingled with the scent of sun-leached conifer trees, though, its identity was elusively shrouded. I halted at the security gate of my new home when it hit me. Celery! My granddad used to grow it in his garden. I remembered my Nan standing by the kitchen sink in her piny when I was about six-years-old, washing great wads of it. I would often nick a few sticks and seat myself at the big wooden table, so that I could dip them into a bowl of salad cream.

Happy days, I thought.

I checked the paperwork for the security gate number. "Star 668, hmm, the neighbour of the Beast," I said and leaned out of the window to press the keypad. The click of the gate opening startled a couple of basking lizards who suddenly became visible and shot off at breakneck speed over the boundary wall. I drove onto the forecourt; the sound of the opening gates also animated a man who was positioning some water jets on the grass verges. I noticed at once the immaculately manicured landscaping and the gorgeous array of Mediterranean plants; it pleased me no end. I loved a tidy abode and appreciated the enhanced value it brought to the property.

A pair of ink-black resourceful eyes followed the Range Rover as it traversed the driveway and came to a stop outside the first of a row of three apartment blocks arranged in a horseshoe-shape, all of which had an equal view of the gardens and the coast. I switched off the weary engine, opened the car door and put one boot forward to greet the heat-baked block paving, a historic first step into uncharted territory, my '*Nueva Vida*'.

As I stood up and stretched my fervently moaning carcass, the Spanish gardener appeared in front of me. I loved a character and this chap had all the trademarks of a top performer.

A worn-out straw Panama hat, tipped at a precarious angle, clung to his head by sweat alone. A dirty toothpick in his mouth was accompanied by a well-chewed cigar, both managing to keep their position despite the imbalance. He was dressed in grubby, blue work trousers, a whitish cotton vest that had seen a few birthdays and a pair of dusty slip-on canvas sandals. His skin, of course, was the colour of dark oak, but had remarkably few lines. I thought him to be 55-years-old but later discovered he was in fact 62, living proof of the healthy, life-extending eating to be found here. He looked very calm, knowledgeable and content with his lot. I liked him immediately. He smiled on approach, yet neither occupant of his mouth fell out even when he spoke. "*Señor* Simmons, *Buenos días*," he said, holding out a rough hand for me to shake. "José," he added, introducing himself.

"Don," I said, pointing at my chest. To my surprise, José's smile dropped and concern made a furrow across his brow. A cold moment passed between us and I felt troubled.

"*¿Tiene Usted la llave?*" asked José. I made a gesture to show that I didn't know what he was saying, so he pulled out a set of keys from his pocket.

"Ah, keys," I said and quickly showed him that I had my own.

"*Bueno, bueno,*" said José. "*Hasta luego,*" and with that he plodded off to resume his irrigation.

I couldn't understand the cause of José's sudden change of countenance and had no idea what his passing comment had meant, but I would realise its relevance in a short while. As for now I had the daunting task of hauling a consignment of luggage to the top floor of this three-storey building, and the very thought of it made me giddy. I entered the lobby through smoked-glass double doors carrying the first of my many suitcases. I was immediately affronted by the refreshing ambush of air conditioning, a commonplace luxury of modern times, especially in warmer climates, but sadly still an expensive toy to most British households. Its cool breath drenched me like a Cornish wave. I instantly felt clean and refreshed as I took in my surroundings with excitable vigour.

White marble dominated the floor and walls, while a crystal chandelier commanded the ceiling. A little gaudy for my liking but I could see that a great deal of money had been put into this place. To my immediate left and right were the ground-floor apartment entrances. Directly ahead a curved stairway extended to the upper levels, and to its left and right were the doors to the underground car park and the lift. I inhaled a chest full of climatically enhanced air and nearly passed out in the process. My body had yet to adjust to the radical change in temperature. My brain was still in self-coolant mode and had obviously overloaded on the cold stuff. I dropped woefully to one knee, ramming the cases to the floor with a clack. While I steadied myself, the pain of nicotine withdrawal raised its ugly head again, gnawing at my trachea, itching inside my lungs. Whispers in my head offered me quick relief in the shape of a small white stick, with warm vapours to cure all ills, but my determination took hold and I willed the temptation away. "Come on, Don. Get a grip," I said.

My arms took the strain as I raised the wobbling Titan to its feet. Just as I gained my dignity, the door to my left swung into life revealing the rear view of a man leaving his apartment apparently still engaged in conversation with an out-of-sight contemporary. A toy Yorkshire terrier burst out of the shadows and performed half-a-dozen circles in the lobby, chasing his own tail before returning to the door and sitting by his master's side. I thought it was oblivious to the foreign body making the hall look untidy, but a split second later the dog caught a whiff of a malodorous Englishman and began to yap. The resident cut short his dialogue and turned round to be confronted by a picture that would stay in his mind's scrapbook for eternity. Something unique, something unshaven, tired, bedraggled, sweaty, grossly overweight and ridiculously dressed: Don Simmons, in pain, bewildered and intent on using the stairs.

"*Silencio*," ordered the man, and the Yorkie obeyed immediately.

"Morning," I said, forgetting the time.

With an outstretched hand and a smiling face, the local strode over towards me, not once revealing the shock from his first impression. "You must be the new owner of the *ático*?" he said in perfect English.

I recognised the word for the penthouse. "Yes, that's right. Don Simmons, pleased to meet you." My new neighbour offered a firm and honest handshake, but much like the gardener earlier, his face lost its happy expression and became serious.

"Pleased to meet you too, sir" he replied.

"Oh no, please call me Don. Everybody calls me Don."

"That might prove to be a bit tricky, Mister Simmons. You see in *España* the word Don means 'sir' or 'lord'. You may cause bad feeling among people if you proclaim to be their master. Is that how you wish to be known?"

"Oh I see, no, of course not!" I said, suddenly understanding the caretaker's kneejerk reaction. "My name's Donald so, in England, everyone calls me Don."

"Well if it's all the same I would prefer to call you Donald. Please allow me to introduce myself," said my new neighbour, the smile returning to his face.

"My name is Fernando Rodriguez Monolito Pepe DeNegro. But you can call me Fernando. I live in the apartment just there, with my wife and little Circola here. We enjoy the beach and the sea air. Tell me, do you like to swim?"

"I do," I lied, "But I've never really found the time at home. I'll use the pool here though," I said timidly.

"Good. I'll probably see you around the pool then. I must take Circola out for her walk now. Err, you are going to use the elevator aren't you?" said Fernando, showing some concern.

"I was going to take the stairs actually, Fernando. I could do with the exercise," I said patting my stomach.

"Well, if you must!" he replied, cocking his head to one side in amazement. "If you need any help, I'd be happy to oblige later, *Buenos tardes*." Fernando turned and marched out of the lobby, closely shadowed by an overexcited little ball of fluff.

Call that a dog? I thought as I watched them go. I wondered how old Fernando was. It was hard to tell. He was definitely a fit bloke, straight as an arrow with a Nordic appearance, a short-cropped silver-grey flat top of a haircut and modern expensive clothes. He didn't look Spanish one bit and if it wasn't for the fact that I didn't bet anymore, I'd have put money on my neighbour having Swedish roots.

I lifted the cases. They suddenly felt heavier than before and my heart sank, but having made a public commitment to use the stairs, my pride took over. "Onwards and upwards," I said resolutely. With each gruelling step that I made every riser seemed to grow taller than its predecessor. Only halfway up the first flight I felt like I'd reached base camp of Mount Everest. I secured the cases on the treads and leant against the wall, wheezing like an asthma patient. "Fuck this for a game of cribbage," I hissed and closed my eyes for a second, but felt so dizzy I had to open them again and refocus. You idiot, I thought, why didn't you take the lift? I stayed there for about five minutes, like an inanimate blob of silly putty, hoping that no-one would find me in such an embarrassing state. Nobody did, so I took up my struggle once more and vowed there and then never to use the bastard stairs ever again. When I reached the first-floor landing, I was almost on my knees, dripping like a squeezed sponge despite the air conditioning. I plonked the cases down and resigned myself to pushing them along the marble floor bent double until I reached the cool stainless steel of the elevator doors. Once inside the lift I reached the penthouse floor in seconds. Still labouring with my breathing I again raised the cases and headed for my front door.

There were two *ático* apartments; mine was on the left-hand side of the landing. I fumbled in my wet Hawaiians for the keys, and after some fraught wrestling with the lining I removed the tangled bunch and put a key in the lock. With a faint shush, like the sound of an airtight seal being broken, the lock released and opened for me to pierce the darkened boundaries of the ultimate stage of my journey. The shutters were all closed against the ardour of a relentless sun, giving the place a subdued stillness that repelled disturbance. It felt as though I was somewhere that I shouldn't be, a burglar in my own home. Even in the poor light I could make out that the place was furnished with the bare essentials. Flicking on a light would reveal that it was all of the highest quality, but before I explored my luxurious sanctuary, I had to quell a thirst that Angel Falls would have had trouble extinguishing. I headed for the kitchen and almost ripped off the fridge door. It was one of those big American bow-fronted jobs with all the gadgets; its interior light illuminated the surroundings like a blinding beam from an alien mother ship in a Spielberg movie. Cold air licked around my moist torso enticing me inside like the ice queen, but to my bitter disappointment its only contents were a welcome bottle of Krug Champagne. "Bollocks," I said, irony's only manifestation. I sank a few inches into the tiled floor and then spotted the ice-cold water dispenser in an alcove on the front. Searching the cupboards for a glass, I found a tea mug and thrust it under the water outlet and pushed back the release arm. Nothing! I pushed it again, still nothing. The fridge needed a fresh 20 litre container of purified water. It had been emptied deliberately for hygiene purposes. I was dehydrating fast and turning rabid in the proceeds. Twenty-odd years of foreign travel had taught me one thing; never, ever drink the tap water. That pearl of wisdom went straight out of the window, as I flopped about the sink, let the water run for ten seconds and then dived in. Cup after cup after cup of tepid agua was poured down my throat and pyjama top. My mind said that I was still thirsty, but my belly said otherwise, so I ceased poisoning myself, leant back against the sink and took a few deep breaths. The water didn't taste too bad. They must have sorted out the drinking water, I thought. They hadn't - as I'd learn later!

    Like most of my acquisitions, the ultimate purpose of property was for me to make money; hence I always resisted falling in love with a house. This property in Spain was no exception, but its investment was three-fold. I could sell the apartment in a year's time for a profit, transform my lifestyle into one that actually sustained my life and win a quarter of a million quid at the end of it. I just had a couple of hurdles to get over. "Now let's have a squint at what I've bought," I said out loud.

    The kitchen was situated at the end of the hall to the rear of the apartment, and led open-plan into the dining room at the front. I flicked a switch. Ingenious halogen lighting revealed canary yellow walls, with light oak wooden surrounds, skirting and frames, and light grey stone floor tiles. An eight-seat dining table also in light oak occupied acres of space, but hardly cramped the room. A traditional Spanish dresser and a huge gilt-framed mirror completed the furnishings. To its left stretched an enormous sunken lounge, painted in dusty shades of orange and cream, the light oak theme carrying on throughout. There were a scattering of tables, cupboards and wooden chairs, but by far the dominant feature was a massive C-shaped settee covered in cream linen, which could easily seat ten people. In front of this was an equally massive low-slung iron and glass coffee table, finished in sage green. Its floor was beautifully laid with large polished terracotta quarry tiles laid in ever-expanding circles.

These two rooms and one bedroom faced the sea and all of them had access to the terrace via oak French doors, the lounge having two pairs. I couldn't wait to stand on the balcony and soak up my new surroundings; I wanted to be king of all I surveyed, at least in my head anyway. I sped over to the centre doors and pulled apart the heavy drape curtains to reveal firmly closed oak louvre shutters, light-restrictive with just a tantalizing hint of the world outside slicing through the leaves. "This place is like Fort Knox," I muttered. Finding my keys again I unlocked the doors and released the shutters from their manacles, drenching myself in sunlight. This area of the penthouse was stunning. Although the brochure had done it proud, in reality it took your breath away. I knew right then that I would be spending a lot of time on this terrace.

Although the building was an archetypical white Mediterranean apartment block on the outside, inside it was a veritable paradise. A white balcony wall encased the whole affair, with three cutaway sections fitted with horizontal metal grilles painted aquamarine. To my far left were raised terraced planters lush with dark green tropical foliage and fully blossomed pink and red geraniums. Amid this was a tiny sandstone watercourse where a bubbling stream of water cascaded its way down to a collecting pool, where it was drawn up to the top by a silent pump to begin its merry meandering once again. In smatterings of bottle green, diamond-shaped patterned ceramic motifs provided relief from the bland walls and gave the end wall some depth. Along from this a pantiled roof pagoda projected from the dining room wall and provided a refreshing alfresco dining area, complimented by two gnarled and twisted grape vines, potted in glazed terracotta and woven beneath the rafters by time. This section was furnished with an Indian wicker dining suite that could take up to eight people.

On either side of the living room doors were additional raised planters, this time backed by burnished terracotta ceramics, again in a diamond theme, but the foliage here was in red and brown hues and the flowers were scarlet and burgundy. The entire floor area was made of soft stone tiles in shades of peach, pink and umber. In the middle of which stood a tranquil pool, raised about six inches from the ground. It was made from a single deep-dish diamond-shaped vessel in cast iron and was the colour of aged copper. It had three small gentle jets of water that plumed from its centre at different heights, and made a soft bubbling noise that soothed the soul. The far right-hand side had been designed for sun worshippers and had furniture to suit. The planters this side were backed by aquamarine tiles and abundant in garlands of blue-and-yellow flowering trailing plants, while bougainvillea adorned the wall from a huge pot in the corner and stretched away over the roof where it tickled the sky. To the front against the balcony wall and in between the cutaways, long planters contained sweet-scented jasmine, gardenia and honeysuckle that fell towards the beach and carried perfume inland on a sea breeze. All of the plants were on an automated watering system, the brochure's blurb informed me, and needed tending only once a week by José who, I was further advised, was discreet and would fit in with whatever agenda the owners set for him.

Regardless of any pledges I had made in the past, I instantly fell in love with the apartment. This was a magical place, and already felt like home. I trod gently around the ático not wishing to disrupt the ambience. Making my way to the far left I saw something that until now had been hidden. Tucked away in the very corner was a white turret with half a dozen small steps that seemed to be carved out of the fabric of the house. Excited and intrigued, I climbed the quarter-circle steps with anticipation. Once at the top, I was rewarded with a commanding view of the coastline which meandered as far as the eye could see. A mile off to my right, snuggled into a peninsular, languished the popular town of Calella; to my left and only a quarter of a mile away laid the pretty village of Pineda De Mar. Directly ahead, beyond the enclosed gardens, was a tarmac beach road, then a single railway line, followed by another road made from hard-packed sand and then the beach rolling some way out to the sea. I was going to become as familiar with this dirt track road as I was with the history of malt whisky. The road in turn would get to know a great deal about me too, seeing that a large proportion of my body fluids would fall to its dusty surface and meld into its make up. For it would be here that most of my training would take place. The beach itself, though not overcrowded, was busy with horizontal brown bodies, some taking advantage of the shade provided by bright yellow parasols with the insignia 'Lipton's' written in red on their sides. "Bugger me, they have it here too!" I said, reactivating my unquenchable thirst. "I must get me some of that."

I stayed up in the turret for a good ten minutes, perusing my newfound paradise like Christopher Columbus in the crow's nest of the Santa Maria catching his first glimpse of San Salvador, my blue pyjama shirt flapping in the breeze. It was nearly three o'clock in the afternoon. I badly needed to shower and to get my head down before my brain exploded, but before all that I had to unload the rest of my baggage from the car and haul it skyward. Back inside the apartment I quickly checked out the bedrooms on my way out. All four had ensuite bathrooms, tiled floors and fitted wardrobes, and were painted in individual colour schemes of barley, pear, cherry and hickory blue, plain and simple and each with a king-size bed. It was an easy choice of which bedroom to make my own. I chose the hickory one, as it led onto the terrace. I couldn't wait to get in it.

Standing outside the elevator doors on my third and final journey, I was staring at my gross disfigurement in the polished steel. The ping of the lift doors opening coincided with the lobby doors being swung inwards. The noise jarred my exhausted nervous system and broke me from my daydream. In bounced the Man with Five Names followed by Circola the pretend dog.

"Those stairs are a little steep aren't they?" commented my neighbour.

I had been caught red-handed as a bottler. I went scarlet with embarrassment.

"I must admit, Fernando, that I was a little over-ambitious trying to scale them so many times," I said, trying to big up my feeble attempt.

"Do you like your garden? It's the envy of the whole complex. Van Grockle spent a lot of *dinero* up there. Is it to your taste?"

"I think it's just beautiful," I said, returning to my natural shade of pink. "Aren't all the penthouses landscaped then?"

"Alas not, my friend, some are quite bland. You should feel very proud."

"Thank you," I said, reactivating the lift doors. "Maybe I'll see you later on this evening?"

"I'm always around, Donald, *hasta luego*."

"Has-to loui glow," I replied. Fernando just smiled, turned tail and strode off, mimicked by the fluff ball. I got into the elevator still wondering about Fernando's age and nationality. These questions were going to keep on itching until I found out.

It was fast approaching four o'clock in the afternoon and it felt like a hundred sleep fairies were dangling from my eyelids. I made up my bed with the linen that Ann had thoughtfully packed for me, and then placed a family photograph on the bedside table. This was the first time in my entire life that I had ever made a bed up and the finished article looked like I'd done it with boxing gloves on, but to my tired limbs it would be the most inviting flop in the world. Before that I had to shower and get rid of this ridiculous attire, so I sat on the edge of the bed to remove my Trader boots. I hoisted one leg up to cross the other and heaved at the dusty hoof, but the bastard was stuck firm with moisture content. I pulled the leg up tighter to my belly, twisted my foot a little and put more force into a heftier heave. The boot inched off with a sucking sound akin to a cow giving birth, frustratingly slow until it cleared my heel and then whack! I smacked myself right on the nose. Blood rushed to my head and a constellation of stars danced before my eyes. I could taste iron on my tongue and ozone filled my nostrils. Blackness descended upon me like a heavy blanket; the boot had found my off-switch.

A pale obelisk sectioned the ceiling from the part-opened bedroom door to the opposite wall. When I finally focused I thought that I had died and ascended to some kind of waiting room, my only entertainment a giant TV screen with just the test signal to watch. I tried to move but paralysis had set in from being so motionless and it took several attempts to raise myself to my elbows and even longer to realise where I was. I checked my watch against the pale streetlight. It was almost 11:00 in the evening and I'd been out for nearly 7 hours. My back and legs were killing me; one foot was freezing cold and the other was on fire, but the thing that had mostly forced me into consciousness was the immediate need to urinate. My bladder felt like it would rupture at the slightest probe and my privates had shrivelled to nothing from the tension of holding it all in.

I willed myself to stand up and with one stocking foot and speedwalked to the bathroom. Lifting the seat just in time, I gushed sprinkler-style with piss that went in four different directions at once. On the floor, the rim of the toilet, my feet and over my Hawaiian shorts which had fallen to my ankles. I couldn't have cared less. It was one of those euphoric pisses that is so good it makes your teeth itch and provokes a deep intake of breath that burns in your chest like a feeling of post-orgasmic elation. I was in heaven and lounging on a cloud. Only a minute had passed but it seemed like ten. No sooner had I finished peeing, than the urge for a Winnie-the-Pooh gripped me, but a swift glance showed there to be just two forlorn-looking sheets of toilet paper clinging to the roll. A quick recce of the other bogs was called for. Slipping off my splashed shorts, I paraded around the apartment in my pyjama top and one boot checking cupboards and bathrooms for a fresh supply of Andrex. Only one-eighth of a roll could be scrounged, but it was enough to save me from having to perform the most difficult of manoeuvres, the British Bidet: in times of *escasez de papel higiénico*, the afflicted person is required to perform a handstand in the shower cubicle. This is a difficult undertaking for the average human being and in my case likely to prove fatal.

As I sat there contemplating the day's events, nursing my bruised nose and suffering my own internal gases, the obvious hit home. I would have to make a shopping trip my first priority — after a shower and something to eat, of course. I couldn't wait to explore the town and now that I'd finished my ablutions, a familiar emptiness was registering in the pit of my stomach. Perched on the throne, I found that the second boot was incredibly easier to remove and at last my rancid blue top could be discarded. All of my clothing had to stay where it landed. I was in no mood to play housemaid tonight.

As with the rest of the house, my ensuite was decorated with impeccable taste, tiled throughout in shades of the sea, stainless steel fittings and aquamarine frosted glass. My shower cubicle was a deep, open alcove lined with ocean-blue mosaics and boasted the most enormous stainless-steel showerhead I had ever seen. It must have measured 18 inches across. I fixed a cool temperature on the mixer dial and stepped into what felt like a tropical rainstorm, gently massaging my neck, back and shoulders. I sighed with relief and my stresses flowed away down the plughole.

Refreshed and now fully awake, I had no time for a wet shave so I used my electric shaver to mow down two days' growth. I slapped on some Polo aftershave, gave my armpits a squirt and dressed in a loose-fitting cream cotton shirt, beige linen trousers and a pair of brown leather sandals. I strolled out to the terrace to take in the night time vista and noted that it was not only still very warm, but it had become quite humid as well. The garden thermometer read 87° F and I knew that a walk into Pineda would be even more strenuous than my epic trek to the workshop last Monday. Even so, I was determined not to take the car, so I stocked up on handkerchiefs to mop up the by-products of a walk and filled up a bottle of water to replenish what I would lose.

The beacons along the coastline twinkled like streams of brilliant fairy lights complimenting the stars in the inky black sky. Taking full advantage of the temperate night air people were still sitting at the pavement tables of Pineda's restaurants. Within minutes the vanilla yeti was down in the lobby and heading for town. As I left the controlled environment of the apartment block the ground temperature hit me like a blast from a hair dryer. It was even hotter down here, which was going to make the journey all the more harrowing, but the need for sustenance had become pressing, so endeavour I must.

Cricket song laid down the perfect background noise for a Mediterranean night like this and inside the secure compound it was the only interruption to utter stillness. Once outside and on the beach road, the chaos of humanity drowned them out. Along this quarter-mile stretch of road, the pavement was lined with mulberry trees encased behind a low brick wall. At regular intervals, paving slabs had been placed atop the brick wall, providing the perfect resting place for weary travellers or a retreat for needy lovers. Some of the seats were already taken, but remembering my previous mistake, I made a point of stopping at every other one for a rest. Halfway there and my shirt was showing telltale signs of exertion, two hankies were sodden and the bottle of water all but gone. My chest was tight and I felt a little queasy, but nowhere near as bad as last Monday. I wasn't about to collapse and I wasn't sucking in air like a punctured bellow. I had the usual looks of disbelief from people passing by and heard their suppressed laughter, but I was used to this and thick-skinned enough not to let it bother me. Besides, I was on a mission, and a plate of Spanish cuisine had my name written all over it.

It was almost midnight when I reached a restaurant that could accommodate me and to my delight I found that they would still be busy until two o'clock in the morning.

I plonked my exhausted self at a table in the nearest corner on the street. A waiter was straight over, probably expecting a massive order, but all that I wanted right now was an ice-cold bottle of water.

"*¿Con gaz o natural?*" asked the waiter. I figured this one out and asked for natural. Between breaths I also asked for a menu. "*Si señor*," he said and vanished.

I pulled out my last remaining dry hankie and wiped my neck and forehead to the amusement of a couple of street urchins on pushbikes that were up far too late. I ignored them and looked around to study my fellow diners. The waiter was taking a hell of a long time and I questioned my order when I saw a tray full of frothy lagers heading for a crowd of Germans. Only Squareheads would want froth like that on top of their beer, I thought. Cold lager in frosted glasses on a hot summer's night — I was almost in tears. My throat was so dry that my oesophagus felt like it had been coated with a layer of glue; it stuck together every time I swallowed, then peeled away slowly as it recovered. By the time my water arrived I was fidgeting uncontrollably in my seat. It tasted divine spruced up with a slice of lemon; half a litre disappeared before I rested the glass back on the table. The typified Spanish tourists menu had a picture next to the description of each dish. The one that most appealed to me was the roasted half chicken, served with chips and a Catalan salad. I decided that I'd leave the chips and remove the skin from the chicken, even though the gorgeous crispy brown stuff was my favourite bit. This was going to be agony.

I hadn't quite quenched my thirst and especially because I was surrounded by it, the pull of alcohol grew intense. I allowed myself my one and only luxury, a G&T, but I couldn't have a Tom's Special, so when the drink arrived I ordered another tonic water. I tipped half of the generous measure of gin and half the ice into my water glass and filled it to the brim with tonic. I brought it up to my lips where its aroma tantalised my nostrils and effervescent bubbles burst open on my skin, then 'gulp', it was gone in one swift movement of the wrist. "Aahh," I sighed with delight, and my eyes glazed over.

It had been 63 hours since my last dance with the devil and I'd missed it so much. My hankie was employed again just in time for the arrival of my dinner.

I had never seen such a monstrous salad in all my life. It had several kinds of meat and fish, boiled eggs, cheese and even some salad items in there as well. The mound of curly chips on an oval platter looked mouth-wateringly delicious and the basket of fresh bread made me drool. My strength and resolve kicked in and I got strict all of a sudden. The chips were relegated to the rear of the table, just tomatoes were selected from the salad bowl and the middle of three slices of bread was extracted from their crusts. I ordered another G&T and devoured my meal with relish, feeling very proud that I hadn't gorged myself to bursting point, not least because I had the trek back to the *ático* to achieve. The urge for an after-dinner fag was immense and again I had to steel myself away. I patted the lifeboats stowed in my trouser pocket and thought of my aching chest when I sat on the garage wall. Gradually the urge quelled.

"Would you care for dessert, *señor*?" asked the waiter, bursting my bubble.

"No thank you, young man, I'm quite full," I said, this time surprising myself, "just the bill please. I've an early start."

"Very well," said the waiter disappointed. He wound his way through the tables once more and was back in seconds. I paid in cash, leaving a hefty tip, believing that if you look after the waiters then they'll remember to look after you, although this waiter would be hard pushed to forget *El Gordo*.

Because I hadn't behaved like the front-runner of an eating contest and had actually taken my time, the usual feeling of having swallowed a spacehopper was absent. This also meant that my ambling stroll back to the apartment was less of a strain. The temperature had cooled a little, which helped too. I reached the confines of the walled garden at around one o'clock and was pleased to hear that the crickets were still in fine voice. Standing on my terrace and looking out to sea, I contemplated the year ahead. There could be no doubt that it wasn't going to be easy, but with everything that I expected to be thrown at me, loneliness wasn't one of them. As I listened to laughter coming from groups of people on the road and the voices of holidaymakers returning to the campsite next door, for the first of many times to come, I thought about throwing the towel in. I missed Ann terribly. We had never spent more than a day apart before and I felt more than just a little lost. Like a chubby kid's first day at scout camp with a ten-man tent all to himself. It was the picture of Ann's face telling me that "she knew that I could do it" that snapped me out of self-pity. It was my family's life I was improving, not just my own. I headed for the bathroom, cleaned my teeth, had a slash and made my way to bed.

Passing the pile of luggage, I suddenly remembered the case of gin and was drawn to the bottle like a pin to a magnet. Before I knew it, I was unscrewing the cap and heading back to the bathroom. But tonight restraint ruled the roost, so I merely filled the cap with the gun-cleaning fluid, swilled it around my mouth and spat it out down the sink. Psycho-suggestion would give me the peace of mind that I needed at this stage.

At 4:30 a.m. A full bladder and a fart that would register on the Richter scale woke me from an impossible dream. I had been running up the sides of a pyramid with a baby elephant on my shoulders. No matter how many steps I climbed, I could never reach the top. The elephant exploded on my back and I found myself in my bed sweating beneath the duvet. I lay there for a second remembering who I was and then I felt the roll of thunder in my intestines. "Oh my God," I whispered. Leaping out of bed I hobbled to the bathroom and dropped my cacks just in time before a deluge of rusty water engulfed the toilet pan. It felt as if my entire insides had fallen through my arsehole in the form of battery acid as a smell of gangrene poisoned the air. I sat there for a while feeling totally deflated; the tap water had wreaked its revenge. After ten minutes I had regained enough strength to haul myself to the shower. After another record-breaking pee under the warm rain, I felt revitalised and surprisingly energetic. I brushed my teeth and decided that a drive around town was in order to find a convenient store and get some supplies, toilet roll being a priority. I was eagerly looking forward to the first sunrise in my adopted hometown and wanted to get to know my new surroundings as soon as possible. I slid onto the leather of my Range Rover and headed for Pineda.

Five o'clock in the morning is an eerie time of day. The whole world is asleep and the sounds that you make are exaggerated. Ghosts and vampires are thinking about turning it in for the night and early morning workers will soon be rising, but not just yet. I felt out of synch with the streets; I was wide awake in sleep time, an observer in a dreamscape. The air was warm, the lamplight milky and all around looked neat and tidy, but then again the night softens many a jagged edge.

I drove through Pineda and then on to Calella. The only thing open was the service station, so I nipped in and bought a four-pack of loo roll, some chewing gum and a five litre bottle of mineral water. As I drove back to Pineda, I noticed that there were a few people waiting at the railway station and that the small bar on the platform was open. It didn't seem out of place to see a man sitting there drinking a cold lager and eating a massive ham roll at 5:30 in the morning. If it weren't for my circumstances, I would have sidled up to him and had the same, but I was wearing my sensible head for the next 12 months, so I settled for a coffee.

The two glass doors of the bar were both open: one led in from the platform, the other led out to a little terrace that supported half-a-dozen tables and chairs, all vacant.

I nodded to the man enjoying his breakfast as I came through the door, and then in turn to the two blokes who were propping up the bar, drinking black coffee from glasses and puffing away on very strong cigarettes.

"*Buenos dias señor, ¿qué toma?*" said the bleary eyed barman. He was about 50, overweight, with slicked-back black hair tied in a ponytail and a long Mexican-style moustache. His white apron had seen a washing machine at some stage in the past, but not for a while. I figured that I had been asked what I wanted, so I just replied "*Un cappuccino por favor.*" The smell from the cigarettes was making me anxious, so when my coffee arrived I took it outside and sat at a table away from the door. I sipped through froth and watched the two fellows inhaling their lives away. I suddenly felt quite uplifted for having left that world behind and held myself slightly aloof of these lesser people who still indulged. I thought of Les sucking on a roll-up, Ray stuffing his pipe with Drum tobacco and the smoke haze that clouded above the heads of my drinking school. I desperately wanted a fag! Instead, I popped a stick of gum in my mouth. I tried to analyse why I hadn't been able to resist the temptation of smoking in the past, when now even the smell of tobacco smoke was offensive. I saw how ignorant and selfish I'd been when sparking up in company. Why had I given it up so easily? Because I had wanted to, I had decided to quit long before Belington's bet; that opportunity had only given me the pushstart that I needed.

A train pulled into the station at 5:45 a.m.; the two men at the bar dropped their cigarettes to the floor and extinguished them with a twist of a foot. Some bars in Spain prefer this; it saves having to supply ashtrays. They boarded along with the other commuters that seemed to have miraculously multiplied in the last few seconds and the modern little coast train slipped out of sight, heading for Barcelona no doubt.

I could have sat there all day witnessing my new world going about its business. I'd never indulged in watching people before, but I found it quite endearing.

The sky to the east had turned crimson pink and a splinter of tangerine had lanced the very top of the mulberry trees that shaded the little terrace. Soon the sun's unforgiving rays would be roasting the pavement once again, burning naïve tourists for a laugh.

I made a mental list of things to buy for the apartment, such as kitchen utensils, toiletries, iced tea and food. I needed to check the Weight Watchers literature first, but I had a general idea. Beyond beans on toast, jacket potatoes and opening takeaway food containers, my culinary skills ran dry. Two alternatives had been considered: a restaurant to cater for my needs, or a live-in chief to prepare meals and wash the dishes afterwards. No, there was only one way forward; I had to learn how to cook! When I arrived back at the penthouse, I decided to call Richard and ask him to get in touch with our Barcelona agent. I was hoping he would be able to assist in finding a gym and a personal trainer. It would cut through the language barrier and speed things up.

Language, another obstacle to conquer, I was going to add this to my list of 'must achieves', as if I didn't have enough on my plate. The only phrase of foreign tongue that I'd mastered was *'Frère Jacques, Frère Jacques, dormez-vous, dormez-vous?'* a line from the French nursery rhyme, but as my old dad used to say, "What fucking use is *Frère*

Jacques when you're broken down in a 45ft-artic on the Paris Périphérique?"

●●▼●●

They say something you never forget is how to ride a bike, but it had been more than 30 years since I had sat on one. The prospect never frightened me; I'd just rather have done it without an audience. It was eleven o'clock on Sunday morning. There wasn't a soul about and as I pushed my bike along the pavement in my largest tracksuit and squeaky trainers, I couldn't help feeling like a circus elephant rolling a ball around the big top arena. This first attempt at straddling the beast was rife with danger and I felt certain that I'd make a complete prick out of myself, so a vacant street was ideal. I positioned the Peugeot alongside the kerb to allow me an easy mount, although even with the dropped crossbar it would still prove difficult to get my leg over. I enveloped the saddle and was just about to push off when I heard "Good morning Donald". My foot slipped off the pedal, causing me almost to swallow a bollock. To my complete horror, grouped together behind me like the intro sequence from the Brady Bunch, was my neighbour Five-Names with his two sons and a daughter-in-law each in their mid-thirties, plus his two teenage grandsons. They were all kitted out in sportswear, evidently out for some exercise and all raring to go.

"Oh, morning Fernando," I said turning extremely red, "just breaking the old girl in, you off for a run?" I said trying to sound casual but stating the obvious.

"When my family comes over at the weekend we often take a jog along the beach path. Today is so pleasant; we felt that we had to get out. Oh forgive me; this is my son Pablo and his wife Sofia." They both nodded politely. "My eldest son Francisco and my grandsons Gerardo and Tico." They all nodded in turn, albeit somewhat nonchalantly.

"Alright?" I said, somewhat lost for words. After Fernando had introduced his new fat friend to his family, they said goodbye and set off at a leisurely pace, leaving me to negotiate my steed on my lonesome. Fortunately I hadn't forgotten how to ride a bike. Although a bit wobbly at first, I soon got into the stride and was pedalling for Britain, with the sun on my back, the ocean breeze in my face and a shoelace dangling dangerously close to the gear cogs. I passed the happy joggers on the sand bar and they gave me a resounding round of applause as I left them in my wake. It made me glow on the inside, urging me to go faster. Life was good and I gave them a little wave of appreciation. Small children stood in awe at the sight of a blue blobby bloke on a bike, hurtling along the beach on suffering tyres. While ice cream dripped from their cones, rippled down fingers and splashed in the sand at their feet. Oncoming runners sidestepped and looked back at the weighty wonder, forgetting for a moment that they were against the clock. I didn't see any of them, I was 13 again and racing along a dirt path in the woods with my mates, mouth open and taking in the local gnats.

Ten minutes into my joyride, I reached a beach bar selling ice-cold soft drinks and *el helado*. Its green-and-white striped canvas roof flapped in the wind, while its vendor, blissfully unaware of two pasty British kids queuing for a drink, was deeply engrossed in sweet-talking a Danish beauty in a thong. I thought that I had travelled far enough on my first outward journey, and feeling over-confident with the machine tried to perform a rear brake turn. Only I wasn't 13 any more, I was 26 stone and the tyres decided it was time to make it clear that they were beaten. The rear one popped off of its rim causing the bike to leave the hard-packed sand road and smack its wheel heavily against a boulder. The saddle jarred the bones of my backside with such force that I left the seat and found myself standing upright, astride the bike with my courting tackle just millimetres from the handlebar. "Fuck it," I snarled, totally pissed off and disillusioned by my antics. The British kids found it highly amusing and continued to laugh even after I had shot them my best grown-up's disgruntled look. The ice-cream man barely registered the incident and never once broke away from his cheesy chat-up lines, even though he was hopelessly outclassed. Most of the sun worshippers were unmoved or uninterested in a giant coming off his bike and soon beach life settled back into its normal rhythm and I melded into its pace.

I had no choice but to walk back to the apartment. Not wanting the embarrassment of being accosted by Fernando again, I pushed my crippled machine across the railway tracks and took to the pavement on the other side of the coast road. Here I would be shielded by the mulberry trees and could rest periodically on the wall.

It took me an hour to crawl back to the penthouse, made doubly torturous by the midday heat. Once through the side gate I made my way along the path, propped up pathetically by the one good wheel and dragging the sick puppy behind making a sound like a Wellington boot slapping against a bare leg. I passed Jose who was dutifully pruning a rose patch. He looked up as I approached. "Morning," I said with a weak smile. He gave me an upward nod and watched in bewilderment as the Englishman limped into the apartment block. I arrived dripping wet and medically in need of fluids, but luckily I remembered my wartime desert movies and knew not to drink too much too soon. Within 20 minutes I had polished off a litre bottle of water and discarded most of my togs.

The Peugeot stood in the hall looking very sorry for itself, "I'll deal with you later," I promised, "but right now what I need is a dip." I had been dying to grace the pool with my presence ever since I had arrived, but wanted to pick a time when it was free from lithe bodies — well, any bodies really — and right now the coast was clear.

The swimming pool was plumb in the centre of the complex to the rear of the apartments and occupying a very secluded position, where it was overlooked by only a handful of balconies. This was ideal because I was far from comfortable with the idea of exposing my grotesque exterior in a public domain. Admittedly, unless I took to swimming fully clothed, I was going to have to get used to being 'flesh out' in front of people; there was just no avoiding it. I had planned to use the pool in the early mornings or late afternoons to avoid other tenants, but today I couldn't resist taking a chance on it. Besides there were only 18 apartments and just one-quarter of them were in use all year round, so it felt pretty exclusive. Throwing my dressing gown over a mighty pair of Bermuda shorts and taking the largest bath towel, I sauntered down to the poolside. Still alone, I slipped out of my dressing gown and left it on the floor by the shallow-end steps. This again was a safety measure; in case I had to vacate the water in a hurry should someone approach. Gingerly holding both rails I reversed into the liquid expecting it to be ice-cold, UK-style. To my relief my pinkies were met with luxurious cool but not icy velvet that enticed my aching feet to delve deeper. The hot afternoon sun was recreating the work of a welder's torch on my unprotected flabby white back, so once the water was up to my knees, I let go of the rails to sink down for some cooling relief. I sunk like a stone and caused a small tsunami around the pool, emptying gallons of chlorinated water over the side.

Bobbing to the surface like a champagne cork, I trod water while wiping my blurred eyes with my big paws. The sound of a door opening close by sent me scuttling to the side. I clung to the rails for protection against an unseen adversary, someone who might find me offensive. My fears were allayed when I caught sight of Fernando coming down from his ground-floor terrace steps and heading for the pool, clad in nothing but Speedos, some sandals and a towel draped over his shoulder. In his hand he gripped a pair of swimming goggles and with his extremely toned bronzed body, I could tell that at one time he must have been an athlete of some kind and continued to observe a regime of regular exercise. Fernando reached the edge of the pool before he noticed me trying to hold myself statuesque in one corner.

"How's the water, Donald?"

I refrained from saying 'wet' but replied "Beautiful," instead.

"The best pool in Pineda by far," said Fernando as he walked to the far end. "Excuse me for a moment, Donald." He rinsed his goggles and then strapped them to his head. Diving in, he surfaced halfway along the pool and front-crawled the rest of the way with the inertia of a knife through thin air. "You've found time to take a swim then Donald?"

"To be honest, Fernando, I haven't really been in a swimming pool much since I was ten years old. I'm more of a casual floater." I thought that the truth was the best way forward, but I did miss out the bit about being shit-scared of water.

"I swim every day. You should make a habit of it too. Maybe you should join me, I could do with the competition!" He grinned and swam off. I laughed and watched with admiration as Fernando sped up and down the length of the pool, performing those flash turns at the ends where you don't seem to actually touch the wall. In no time at all he had completed 30 lengths, cutting through the water and twisting his head in perfect time to catch a breath. I didn't know much about swimming, only that if you didn't move about in water then you drowned, but I knew enough to detect that this man had been a professional at one time. Fernando eased himself effortlessly out of the pool and slid under the open air shower to rinse off the chlorine. He walked over to me while drying his hair and slipped on his sandals to rescue his feet from being griddled by the scorching tiles. All this time I hadn't left the sanctity of the steps and was just enjoying the weightlessness of being submerged.

"You'll have to join my wife and I for an aperitif or two some time soon," said the human fish.

"Yes, that would be nice," I replied. I couldn't think of an excuse at that moment. The last thing that I needed was another drinking partner; I had dozens of them back at home. Not wishing to seem rude I made arrangements for the following evening, secretly dreading being in the presence of alcohol. I hoped I could resist, as the big weigh-in was near and I couldn't bear to have come this far only to falter at such an early temptation. Fernando left, and once I was certain that I was totally alone, I pushed off with my first attempt at breaststroke for decades. I surprised myself by managing a quarter of a width before water found its way into my lungs. Wheezing and spluttering I scrambled back to the side for resuscitation. Three more attempts and half an hour later, I had still only managed to do half a width. Tuckered out, I retired to one of the sun loungers and caught my breath. "Next time old son, you're gonna manage a whole one," I promised myself.

CHAPTER NINE
The alliance

THE SATSUMA SUN SLIPPED SILENTLY FROM THE SKY in the remains of the day, making a little fizz as it dipped into the cold sea somewhere in the distant west. I watched the spectacle from my terrace in the comfort of a wicker chair, my feet propped up on another. Wrapped in my dressing gown and resting a glass of percolated coffee on my lap.

I smiled as the golden horizon gave one last resilient burst before retiring for the night. Dusk draped the apartment block in purple light and the air became heavy and full of scent. I reflected upon the day's events with wry amusement. No earth-shattering goals were scored but I had managed to conquer half a pool's width and for this I awarded myself a pat on the thigh. I knew that it would be some time before I felt comfortable going down to the pool twice a day and distressing the locals. I could see the newspaper headlines now: 'Elephant man causes hysteria among residents', but there wasn't a lot that I could do about this. Forty-six years' worth of built-up fat wasn't going to disappear overnight, unless I set about myself with an electric carving knife, but that would just ruin a good knife. I thought about Five-Names and wondered what he did for a living. I had a talent for matching people to an occupation by the type of car they drove. In Fernando's parking bays stood a high-end Mercedes, an American WWII Jeep and a 1960 Vespa motor scooter. I could tell from these that my neighbour was serious about motorcars, a romantic at heart and like most men, a lover of toys. None of this information helped to put a label on his profession, but I was working on it.

•• ▼ ••

The scientific fraternity generally frowns upon lying in the sun these days, but it is agreed that sunlight can provide vital vitamin D, which is essential for skin regeneration. A new word had entered into my vocabulary, moderation. I was about to apply this powerful new instruction to a spot of sunbathing. Given that someone with a tan is considered to look healthier, my plan was to spend an hour a day on my terrace bollock naked, in the vain hope of becoming a bronzed beauty —

well, slightly less objectionable to look at, at least! I hadn't got around to buying cushions for my sun lounger yet, so I pulled a mattress from one of the spare beds and dragged it outside. The garden thermometer read 92° F and it had only just turned nine o'clock in the morning when I lay down. My intention was to spend half an hour on each side, lightly basted in suntan lotion. Being new to solar roasting and also being out of reach to most of my body parts, I only managed to apply a tiny smear on just a few select areas, so the protection factor achieved was about as much use as a flip flop on a laver flow.

A trait of mine, which had always been a bonus in the past, was that whenever my head hit a pillow I was out like a light — very handy in the stressful world of business, not so useful when you are prostrate under a grill.

It was two hours later when I awoke to the sound of a sparrow flapping about in the waters of the fountain. I had curled into the foetal position and the mattress was absolutely sodden with sweat. I attempted to straighten out but my skin was so taut that it felt like it would crack at the slightest move. "Oh my God," I whispered. I was boiling hot and shivering at the same time and when I dared to reposition my limbs, they felt as if they were in slow-shutter time, like the animated images of a cartoon flicker book.

My only thought was to head for the shower and douse my sizzling skin in cold water. When I finally managed to limp to the bathroom, I chickened out of having a full-on freeze job and set the temperature to lukewarm, gradually lowering it as my body adjusted. It was the weirdest sensation: half of me bathing in North Sea conditions, the other half warming the water in a heat exchange upon contact with my skin. I withstood the torture for about 15 minutes and then shuddered back out to the bedroom to dry off. My Cheval mirror told a sorry story. The side of me that had sunk into the mattress remained ghostly white, while the other side glowed a sickly radioactive red. I looked like a monstrous rhubarb and custard sweet that had fallen out of a child's mouth. Even my testicles were two-tone with a perfect line down the length of my old fella. This spectacle reminded me of an occasion many years ago, when my dad had fallen asleep on a deckchair on Brighton beach, wearing his string vest. The inevitable happened, and he sported a rather fetching beetroot diamond motif across his front for the remainder of that summer. My condition was far more ridiculous and definitely harder to conceal.

Mooching about the apartment all day in just my underpants, suffering mild sunstroke and trying to avoid anything remotely abrasive near my sore bits, I must have drunk two litres of water and a litre of iced tea trying to keep my temperature down. I also tried wrapping ice in a flannel and laying it on my burning skin, but it melted so quickly that it just drenched the furniture. By the time seven o'clock came around I had to get out of the *ático* and chance a solitary dip in the swimming pool. Delicately wrapping my lobster bits under my dressing gown, I gingerly made my way down to the poolside. Checking that no-one was about, I stood by the edge and slowly unpeeled my shroud, letting it fall to the floor. No sooner had my hands grasped the rails to the steps than the sound of a patio door being opened broke the silence. "I don't fucking believe it" I groaned in astonishment. "That guy must have fucking radar in his room."

Bouncing along in his usual sporting attire came Five-Names to the poolside. "Donald, what have you done to yourself?" he said, clocking my misfortune.

"Fell asleep on the terrace," I said sheepishly, "for two hours!"

Although he showed concern, Fernando was also a little self-righteous and a tad amused that another newcomer had fallen prey to the sun's favourite trick. He examined the burns close up and announced that his wife would find me something to ease the pain after our swim, for we must have a swim together. "My wife keeps more potions in her medicine cabinet than a Chinese apothecary," he joked. I smiled at the emergence of my neighbour's sense of humour. "Also, I will give you one of my Viagra tablets!"

"Viagra?" I said, perplexed.

"Yes, it won't help the sunburn, but it will keep the sheets off of your skin," he laughed. I liked the cut of this man's cloth.

Once again the water felt fantastic and drastically reduced the heat in my skin. I bobbed about near the shallow end while Fernando completed his 30 lengths, finishing with a flourish and his usual seal-like exit from the water. This allowed me to attempt another width in true beginner's style. Half a width's success again, followed by more spluttering from the big'n, while Five-Names took a shower. When I finally ventured out of the pool, I did so without any self-consciousness. It took a while for it to register, and it surprised me. Had my new friend installed some extra confidence in me, or was Fernando so even-handed and forthright that I could relax in his company? Anyway I was at ease and felt good about it.

"I'll be up to the *ático* in five minutes, Donald. Listen out for me," instructed Fernando as he sprinted off to his home.

"Ok," I replied, not sure what to expect. Once upstairs I put on my baggiest shorts and a light running vest that would allow me to be comfortable while retaining some dignity. The doorbell rang and in stepped Fernando carrying a bottle.

"Good news," he declared. "My wife says this stuff is the best on the market; it contains aloe vera, excellent for heat reduction. Shall we go out on the terrace?"

I nodded and led the way, still uncertain of my friend's intentions.

"You do have the most beautiful garden up here, Donald. I'm very jealous you know."

"I fell in love with it from the off, Fernando, it's a very special place."

"It's what we call *tranquilo* in Spain, meaning peaceful, relaxing."

"You're spot-on there, old mate," I agreed. I later learnt that *tranquilo* also means to slow down or take things easy.

"Now take your vest off, Donald, and let me rub some off this cream into your wounds." He squirted a big, cold dollop into his palm.

Now I had always been a man's man: cars, football, farting. I would never have dreamt that another bloke would want to rub cream into my back, the two of us alone on a roof garden! What would the lads at the drinking school think of this? Reluctantly, I turned away and unveiled my stripe.

"A good make of sports clothing," commented Fernando. "I have some Ron Hill myself."

I held on to the vest like some kind of comfort blanket, a connection to the world I knew before. Yet my preconceptions soon melted away as the aftersun lotion sank into my skin and soothed the scorched flesh. I realised that it wasn't an unmanly thing to be aided by a fellow, especially a guy who didn't judge you but took you at face value. And there was strength to this man's character that went beyond kindness; he was compelled to do the right thing, the just thing, in the correct manner. He seemed to have the righteousness of a knight.

After creaming all the parts that even Heineken couldn't reach, Fernando handed the lotion to me so that I could finish the job. Aloe vera done, I asked my champion if he would like a drink, "tea or coffee?" I purposely avoided G&T to stem my own temptation.

"Black coffee will be fine, Donald, no sugar thank you, and do you have any ice?"

I came out of the kitchen some minutes later with a steaming pot of percolated coffee, two glass cups and a bowl of ice. I found Fernando in the lounge studying the whiteboard that I had erected the day before. "May I ask what this is for?" he said curiously.

I was compromised and had no choice. Besides I felt so comfortable with this man, I decided to tell him the whole shooting match. As the story unfolded I was surprised that I didn't receive the usual looks of astonishment. Fernando seemed completely absorbed by it and clearly excited, finding the part about Chris and Toni highly amusing. At the end of the epic tale he pierced me with his sincerity. "I think that you need some help here, Donald." The line of conversation stopped abruptly and we just stared at each other for a moment, waiting for the other to make the first move. I passed the ice while Enio Moriconi played eerily in the background. Five-Names dropped two lumps of ice into his coffee. Intrigued I did the same. Fernando sipped his refreshment like a connoisseur of the bean. I took a swig and winced as the coffee's cold bitterness assaulted the insides of my mouth before putting the glass down.

"Would you mind if I came along to your first weigh-in Donald?'

It was obvious that his interest went beyond mere spectatorship and I felt compelled to ask him why, but for now I would just let the ball roll and see where it landed.

Before leaving, Fernando asked if he could borrow the Weight Watchers paraphernalia overnight, to see what it contained. I agreed, of course — by now, I had a good idea what was brewing.

Beams of sunlight came in through the louvre slats, cutting the air with laser-sharp precision. Minute dust particles danced erratic patterns between the thermal differences, enjoying the freedom of their miniscule world. It was eight o'clock on Tuesday morning; dawn was two hours past and I lay comatose, lost in oblivion. I had thrown the sheets off during my sleep and was lying on my front butt naked, perfectly aligned rhubarb and custard crossed with sunlight zebra stripes from left to right. I looked like an exhibit from a recent Damien Hirst show. A loose pillow feather had found its way to my nose and had formed a trap door that opened and closed with each breath. Its tickle started to register with my conscious mind and slowly provoked me into an irritated mode. I finally brushed the thing away with a swipe by which time I was aware of the daylight and slouched into action.

Manoeuvring into a sitting position I rummaged in one of my suitcases for a fresh pair of swimming shorts. Finding a choice pair of fluorescent green Baggies, I struggled into them and hobbled off to the bathroom. "I must put those clothes away some time," I muttered. Splashing cold water on my puffy face, cleaning my teeth and drinking a glass of bottled water was all the preparation I needed for a swim. I slid into my dressing gown and sandals and swaggered down to the pool. Fernando was doing his usual impression of a Sea World inmate and didn't notice me approach until he had completed his exercise, then he swam over. The deep-fried whale was just descending into the water, which I found pretty chilly this morning even though the temperature was 80° F.

"Morning Donald, did you sleep well?"

"Like a log mate, woke up in the fireplace!" Fernando didn't get the old joke, so I kept to straight talking. "I slept rather too well actually, hence my late arrival, sorry!"

"Not a problem, Donald. Tell me, can you do the front crawl?"

"I'd crawl anywhere if there were money involved," I joked, sinking up to my chin. "No Fernando, I've only ever managed to do the breast stroke, badly."

"Then let me teach you my friend. You'll find it more suitable as an exercise," said Five-Names very enthusiastically.

"Er, ok then," I replied with a wince. We started in the shallow end with Fernando holding me under my belly, while I prostrated myself on the water's surface. He taught me how to kick my legs in slow time and showed me how my arms should windmill, alternately pulling me through the water. I managed this even though my burnt arm stung painfully with every stretch of the skin. Then after letting go and bringing me upright, he showed me how to breathe on every fourth stroke by turning my head sideways to the right and sucking in air quickly before returning to the forward position. "This is gonna take a while, old mate, my coordination isn't that good," I said.

"You'll be fine, just relax a little and do as I say," advised my neighbour. Holding me again under my middle, Fernando walked slowly as I kicked and crawled and swallowed pool water, with him giving me instruction all the way. "Bring your head up more Donald, that's it. One, two, three, breathe, good, good."

We carried on like this for 20 minutes until I was quite exhausted, then we took a break. Red on both sides of my face, I burped and hiccoughed and gasped at air for quite some time, while Fernando calmed me with words of appraisement. By now, the day's temperature was rising and Fernando was worried for my skin, so he decided I should try to swim one full width before we retired. He stood at one side of the pool and told me to push off from the other. Putting into practice everything that I had just been taught I kicked away from the ceramics in good style, like a hunting Orca in pursuit of a doomed penguin, but I soon descended into churning up the pool like a Mississippi paddle steamer taking on water. By some miracle and sheer determination I made it to the opposite bank half-drowned and exhausted, but receiving copious praise from my tutor. "Well done, Donald, well done. You're on the right track. Tell me do you think that you could ever give up alcohol?" The question came out of the blue and it took some time to compose myself.

"As I said last night, Fernando," I spluttered. "It's my one grip on my past and it's only a tiny reflection of what I used to consume. Psychologically, I can never cut it out. Besides a couple of gin and tonics won't do me any harm."

"That's true, but they will hinder your weight-loss objective."

"I understand that, mate," I responded, getting agitated. "But I've just gotta 'ave 'em," I said, out of breath.

"Fair enough," said a resigned Fernando, diffusing the situation. "Tell me more about your knee problem."

I gave him the official version from Dr Amstone, but told him that I'd never accepted the doctor's prognosis, even though I knew it to be true that 80 per cent of my problems could be cured by drastically reducing my weight. Back then a lifestyle change was inconceivable. I knew what was going through Fernando's mind. I had come up trumps with a personal trainer, but I just wanted to play it out a little longer, to be 100 per cent certain. The time was fast approaching ten o'clock and the evil disc in the sky had been stealthily turning up the gas one notch at a time, so Fernando brought the session to an end.

"Remember that it's drinks tonight at my apartment, Donald. I suggest that we go to my place after your weigh-in. We don't want to increase your true weight any more than we have to."

"Good idea, mate, I'll see you just before seven." A couple of G&Ts would quell my nervous stomach, but I could wait another ten minutes for a drink.

"Ok, *buenos dias* Donald."

"Bwen us dee us," I replied, searching for my towel.

José had witnessed the morning's events from over the top of a yew hedge that he was clipping and had found the scene compulsive viewing. Now I was looking for a towel that I hadn't even brought down with me. It made José shake his head slowly with disbelief. I shook myself like a drenched dog, sending saggy skin and flab flying in all directions. I stamped about on the paving slabs, rubbed my hands together several times and then rewrapped my soggy body in my dressing gown before heading upstairs.

"*Otro hombre loco en esta casa,*" said the gardener to himself, then carried on clipping.

••▼••

My stomach felt like a bubble factory, all I had eaten today was a bowl of cornflakes with skimmed milk, two bananas, a gallon of water and three cups of coffee. And just like last week, I was still pissing for England. The zero:zero reading from my digital scales stared up at me like two worried eyes, dreading the impending crush that they were about to receive. I'd placed the scales next to the French doors in the lounge, where the floor had an even surface. They would remain there throughout my stay, so as to give consistent results. I couldn't believe that I was feeling so nervous about having my first weigh-in and was glad to have someone like Fernando on hand. I was aching to see if I had lost any weight at all; from the inching-up on my belt strap to the way that I felt in general, I thought that I must have shed something. My worst fear was that I had actually gained a few pounds, or maybe remained the same. Anyhow, zero hour was nigh and the truth would out. It was obvious that Tuesday nights were going to be pivotal in my race against time, and prone to the unexpected from time to time.

The sound of the doorbell told me that a ten-minute countdown had begun. Five-Names was as punctual as a Swiss clock and really eager to get things going. "You look worried Don. You shouldn't be, even if it is bad news this time, we'll get over it," he said, beaming confidently.

He called me 'Don', I thought. 'Sir' would have been better. I puffed out my cheeks and nodded. I was wearing the vest and tracksuit bottoms that I intended to parade in for every weigh-in. I positioned myself in front of the scales and mentally prepared for touchdown.

Fernando crept up beside me, "*Buena suerte.*"

"What does that mean?" I asked.

"Good luck, old boy!"

"Thanks, Fern. Here I go then." As if to make myself lighter, I inhaled a huge amount of air then climbed aboard. "Two and a half pounds, I thought I'd done better than that!" I boomed. We both stared down at the readout.

"What was your starting weight again?" asked Fernando.

"Twenty-six stone," I replied.

"Then look again, my friend," said Five-Names, doing a quick calculation. The disappointment soon lifted as I realised my error. The reading said twenty-four stone, eleven and a half pounds. In my panic I had overlooked a stone!

"Fuck me," I said "It's falling off." I shook Fernando by both hands.

Five-Names switched the scales from pounds to kilos and said "You've lost 7.5 kilos, well done!" He was as delighted as me, and couldn't wait to tell his wife. I changed into a cotton shirt and some slacks, slapped on some Polo and we both headed for the landing. On reaching the lift door I said, "I'm feeling quite fit tonight, I think we'll take the stairs!"

"Are you sure you're up to it, Don?"

"Yeah, no prob, it's downhill, innit?"

"Oh well," said Fernando, resigning himself to the inevitable. By the time we had reached the second floor I was panting like a gun dog. "Let's take the lift," insisted Five-Names. The stainless-steel doors closed in unison with my heavy eyes, then in a second opened again in the lobby. My breathing hadn't calmed yet, so I asked for a moment in the hall. Once the wheezing had stopped we continued to Five-Names' apartment. The door was ajar, where a whirling, gurgling, black-and-tan ball of fluff with a little red bow in its head greeted us in the hallway. "*Hola* Circola, *hola!*" Fernando blew kisses at her; she sniffed at my feet and then flew off to the lounge. 'Mummy' was waiting for us in there and she rose to her feet when we entered.

"Donald, may I present to you my wife, Anna?" She held out a tiny, gracious hand. It felt extremely soft and light and I engulfed it with my massive mitt. She looked straight at me, clearly curious to the bone about the half-burnt creature before her.

"You have the same name as my wife, Ann. I'm delighted to meet you."

Not understanding a word that I had said, she just smiled sweetly and put her hands behind her back. She was smart, elegant, with a pleasant face, had flawless skin and a petite hourglass figure. Smaller than I had imagined, she seemed younger than her 60 years.

"Alas, my wife only speaks Castilian and Catalan, Don, so I will have to interpret. Your wife is called Anna as well? What a coincidence."

I remembered there were two languages in this part of Spain, so I assumed that she must be a local.

"G&T for you Donald?"

"Absolutely, cocker," I replied. Fernando rushed off to the drinks cabinet to fix us all an aperitif, while *Señora* DeNegro remained glued to the spot, slightly twisting her hips. I smiled back at her and quietly pom pommed to myself, awkwardly lost for words. "I'm afraid that it's not as special as Tom's, but it is very weak I promise you, Donald."

Five-Names then handed his wife a small glass of Oloroso. They exchanged a few lines of Catalan and then he went back to the drinks cabinet, returning with a glass of Rioja for himself.

"Donald, I have something to discuss with you, a proposition. Would you care to join me in my study?"

"A proposition? I'm always ready for a bit of business, Fernando."

"Oh, it's not a business venture, but it is to your advantage. Shall we?" Fernando gestured with his head that we leave the room. He asked Anna to excuse us as he led me down to his study. On the way I checked out his apartment. It was smaller than my own, but smart, cordial and beautifully designed, in fact rather like his wife. The walls of Fernando's office were lined with two glass-fronted trophy cabinets that faced each other, above which were two matching bookshelves crammed with photographs of a young swimmer in action. At the rear in front of the balcony windows stood a huge mahogany desk.

Likes a big desk does he? Just like me, I silently noted with approval.

The floor was made of slate grey tiles; the furniture was of a rich dark wood and the walls were eggshell blue. It was a very cool room and smelt of coconut cream. I was gobsmacked at how many trophies Fernando had won and stood mesmerised by his Olympic achievements. Two bronze medals and two silver medals for the 200 metres front crawl, and a gold medal for the 4 x 200 metres freestyle relay.

"You kept this lot quiet, you old bugger."

"All in my youth," said Fernando modestly from behind his desk. "Come and sit down, Don. I need to speak with you."

I sat down, knowing what was coming.

"I've given a lot of thought to what we talked about last night, and before you stepped on the scales this evening I considered that the task you had set for yourself was impossible. How did your friend Terry describe it, a 1,000 to 1? I'd have given you worse odds, but your weight loss in just one week has impressed me and revealed your determination." I didn't know whether to smile or to keep a serious face, so I just raised my eyebrows. Fernando paused for a moment and then said, "Would you let me be your personal advisor throughout the next year?"

I finally let my emotions loose and with a big smile replied, "I thought you'd never ask, old boy! Of course I would, you're more than qualified."

"Well not entirely, Don,' he said earnestly. 'I can train you physically but I'm no dietician and I am definitely not a physiotherapist, although I know someone who is. They could advise us if things went that way."

"Look, I've read through the Weight Watchers material and it seems like a workable diet, but I'm not used to a points system. I've always relied on calorie-controlled methods. Let me explain to you the way I know and then we'll align it to the Weight Watchers plan. Would that be ok?"

I nodded in agreement.

"For example, your daily routine without any exercise at all: shopping, dressing, washing, driving, etc, even watching the TV will burn up about 3,000 calories for a man of your size. You need to put those calories back just to retain your existing weight. The trouble is that you, my friend, have been putting away about 5,000 calories a day and not burning off any excess at all."

"Tell me about it," I said.

"I will. Have you heard of the term 'the Thermic effect of food'?"

"Er, no," I replied, dumbfounded.

"Well, it's used to describe the energy expended by our bodies in order to process the food that we eat. We expend energy by burning calories. Processing protein, for instance, requires the greatest amount of energy, about 30 per cent. Dietary fat, on the other hand, is so easily turned into body fat that there is little thermic effect, perhaps two or three per cent of the total effort.

"Ok," I said, becoming ever-so Homer Simpson.

"It's this body fat that we have to attack my friend, but we can't go at it hammer and tong. The worst diets are the ones that lose weight too quickly. You'll only put it all back on, and they can be very harmful to your body. The best way is to lose around a pound a week; 52 pounds in a year can't be a bad thing!"

"Blimey, no!"

"But we have to achieve more than that if you are to reach your racing weight or half your starting weight that is. We have to lose three pounds a week!"

"I've made a good start, Fern."

"So you have Don, but a lot of that as you know is down to water retention. Fortunately you have been drinking lots of water to compensate for this. Burning calories requires plenty of water in order for the process to function properly. Also, burning calories creates toxins in your body, almost like a car produces exhaust fumes, and water is vital to flush them through. So we'll keep up the water intake especially because of the hot climate you've chosen to train in — dehydration is an ugly thing my friend.'

"Does iced tea count as water?"

"Certainly, you can drink as much of that as you like. Now, getting down to the nitty gritty. We have to get you to burn up more calories in a day than you are consuming. For instance, a pound of body fat is equivalent to about 500 calories, so in theory all you have to do is only eat 2,785 calories a day and you'll lose three pounds a week. Simple!"

My mind boggled with the logistics.

"But I intend to train you to be fit enough to run a half-marathon and that means exercise, lots of it. Of course, working out will not only eat up more calories, but it will build up your metabolism, making food easier to digest, and thus increase the thermal effect and build up your muscle content too, which will carry on burning up calories long after you've stopped exercising. Am I boring you?"

"No, no. It's just a lot of information to take in at one time," I said, breaking out of my glazed-over state.

"Good, now where was I? Oh yes, so because you'll be burning up a greater number of calories through exercise, you'll have to eat more to compensate. I've done a rough calculation of what to expect. Look at these figures." He showed me a detailed calculation. "After tonight's success you now only have to lose 11 stone and 8 pounds in 12 months. That's less than four pounds a week. With all the added exercise, it will mean that you'll burn up 42,000 calories per week. If we only put back 39,404, you'll lose those pounds, no problem and get fit in the process" he said, as proud as a sated lion.

"Wow," I said. "You certainly know your stuff, but it all sounds very complicated. Can't we just go with the points system?"

"We can work with them as far as the diet is concerned, but Weight Watchers does not bear in mind an exercise plan, so we have to include our calorie calculations as well. But don't worry about that, my friend, I'll take care of the mathematics, you just concentrate on the hard work." Fernando went to his computer and printed off several sheets of paper. He'd put in some hours during the day and had compiled a seven-day diet based on Weight Watchers' recommendations and allowing me 36 points a day to start off with, building up to 54 when full training began. I could see that alcohol had been included, but alas beer, lager and whisky were absent from the list, only red wine and the occasional gin. The evening meals were made up of five courses, and my dread of attempting all things culinary resurrected itself as I tried to picture myself in the kitchen torturing innocent food. Fernando had anticipated my fear of fending for myself and so had arranged for all the evening meals to be cooked at his friend's restaurant. The Weight Watchers brand could be shipped in at a later date from Marion.

Several more sheets of paper were produced; they included a mapped-out 13 and a quarter mile running course around the beach, the hillside and the outskirts of Pineda and Calella, and an exercise programme, which comprised a progressive chart for running, swimming, water aerobics, cycling and weight-lifting. I was suitably impressed if a little daunted by the array of activities and thanked my new coach for all his hard work so far. Although I felt that he had been a little presumptuous, nevertheless a massive burden had been lifted from my shoulders and I felt that fortune had smiled on me once again.

"You'll notice that I've stepped the training in bi-weekly increments. We'll work for three days, have two days' rest, and then work for two days again. We'll swim every day though. You'll need the rest days to begin with, Don, but we'll increase the programme as your weight comes down. *Tranquilo*, remember Don? I agree with every word that your friend Terry said. No running or jogging until the weight comes down. Would tomorrow suit you to begin?"

My mind was racing. "Yeah, I suppose so. What time do we kick off?"

"Seven o'clock by the pool?"

"Superb. I can't wait to tell Ann. If only I had a phone."

"Here, you can use mine. Use it any time you want to. I'll just go and fix us another drink. Tom's Special?"

I gave him the thumbs up and began dialling England, rehearsing an opening speech in my head.

"Up, up and away in my beautiful, my beautiful balloon." I began to sing the opening line to an old TV advert, where the woman eating the wonder slimming bread had become light enough to sail away on a hot-air balloon. Ann laughed on the other end of the phone. "Airship more like! How you doing, love?" she asked.

"I've lost more than a stone actually, you Doubting Thomas."

"You've not. I wish I could lose it that easily!" she moaned.

"As if you need to pet."

"You seen my bum lately?"

"Alas not my sweet, only in my dreams." I sighed and went on to tell her all about my new good fortune and of course the bad. She thought that I had done brilliantly but begged me to stay out of the sun. I assured her that I'd try hard but it was easier said than done during summertime in Spain. I tried not to take the piss and only stayed on the phone for 15 minutes but in that time I found out that Mathew had been reprimanded at school for selling Playstation games in class —Good old boy, I thought — and that Trish had split up with her latest 'Swampy' lookalike. All in all, everyone was fine, apart from Les who was walking around with an expression on his face like Droopy the cartoon dog. I felt for the old fella, but he'd get over it. We said our goodbye's and more than enough 'love you's' before I finally put the phone down.

When Fernando returned he brought Anna along with him and we sat chatting for a good hour, mostly about each other's families. I found out that they had three children: the eldest son, Francisco, ran the family textile business in Barcelona; Pablo was a doctor married to Sophia, a nurse; and their youngest, Gina, was married to a physiotherapist.

"You're a handy bloke to know, Fernando."

Five-Names just smiled. There were many strings to his bow, but he revealed them on a need-to-know basis only. Anna asked me if I wanted to stay for dinner but I declined her invitation saying that I was extremely tired and wanted a good night's sleep before the big push in the morning. Fernando said that there would be plenty more opportunities for evening get-togethers and at their front door wished me *Buenos noches* from both of them. Besides I had been fantasising about a jacket potato that I had slung into the oven two hours ago. I planned to microwave some baked beans to go with it and wolf it down on the terrace to the sound of cricket song and the smell of evening primrose!

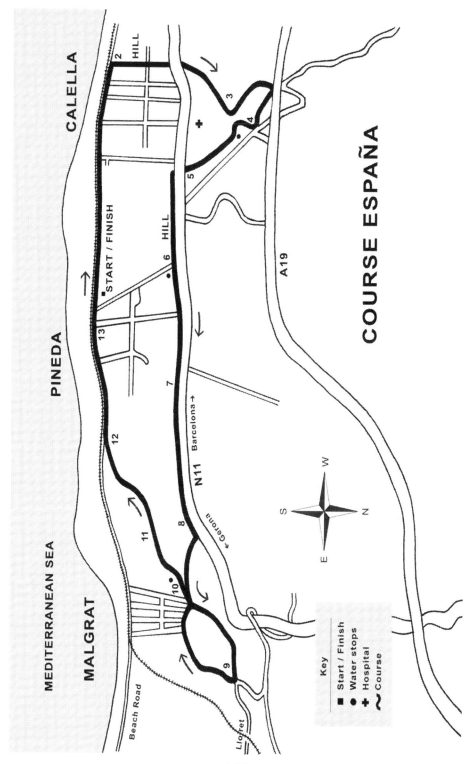

CHAPTER TEN
Reality bites

THE TINY FISHING BOAT CUT THROUGH THE SEA like a smudge across a spoilt watercolour; a distant phut, phut was the only sound to disturb an otherwise perfectly still morning.

I focused on the little green vessel for a while before switching off from the present and contemplating how the rest of today would pan out. It was 6:00a.m. The sunrise over the Mediterranean was breathtaking, and I watched it from my beautiful terrace garden barefoot, with the sea breeze kissing my toes and angels caressing my tear-streaked face.

Fernando didn't intend on wasting any time. Not only did the training programme start today, but I would also be taking my first glimpse of the course and the hill — oh yes, there was a hill.

Meeting Manolo, my newly appointed cook, visiting his restaurant and sampling his cuisine was also of prime interest today. Fernando hadn't spoken much about his friend, but Manolo was aware of the importance of my diet plan and was more than happy to cater for me. As I sipped my percolated Java, the bitterness made my lips purse. What I wouldn't give for a sweet frothy cappuccino. I wondered whether Fernando would allow me one a day.

My sanctuary on the roof was the ideal place for contemplation, to plan ahead and think clearly; it was also a perfect spot for being char grilled under the morning sun. My burnt offerings were starting to itch like buggery. Flakes of skin were decorating my shorts like giant's dandruff, while my shedding flesh resembled the landscape of a dying red planet.

As I peeled away and inspected the transparent sheets of gossamer dead cells, I thought about calling Marion and informing her of my triumph. She'd be flabbergasted but genuinely pleased; I could order my first shipment of Weight Watchers products while I was at it.

I had mixed feelings about seeing the course for the first time today. We would be driving the route and stopping at various key points, such as mile markers and first-aid stations. I wondered whether the tour would jam-pack me with inspiration or have the opposite effect and send me on a downward spiral of depression. Fernando had told me the previous evening that everything that we did this year would be for a reason, and that once I had seen for myself the course that Pablo had so kindly mapped out for me, it would put this outrageous sabbatical precisely into perspective.

I picked up the training programme once again and felt my chest tighten. It all seemed too much for a man of my size, but as Fernando had said, if you only cover a quarter of the course on a pushbike in an hour and a half at this stage, it would be fantastic. *Tranquilo*, that was the key, taking it easy because the race hadn't started yet. Common sense must prevail in these early stages, because a heart attack was hovering at the front door and it had its own key. An orange diamond-shaped spark on the horizon kick started my lardship into gear. "Shower time," I said to myself and stomped off to the ocean room. Once rinsed, I decided to eradicate my whiskers with a wet shave, but halfway through I wished that I hadn't. The razor was taking off slivers of peeling skin from around my lips, which stung like crazy and clogged up the pathetic blades of my Wilkinson fucking Sword. It took me all of half an hour to scrape off the stubble, which left half of my face looking like a baboon's arse and had me running late for my first training session.

Fernando stood by the pool in his Speedos, hands on hips impatiently waiting for me to arrive. When I finally turned up, puffing like a steam train and full of apologies, my coach ticked me off. "You will have to improve on your timekeeping, *señor*. I'm a stickler for punctuality!"

I wasn't used to taking orders from anybody, but in this situation I knew that I was definitely the underling. Besides, Fernando's command was something that I could stomach comfortably. The champion swimmer slid into the water with his usual grace, while Mr Late-on-Parade took to the stainless-steel steps, giving them a little more stress than they were made for. The instructor took over.

"Right Donald, what we need to do is improve on your swimming style. What you achieved yesterday was excellent, but your technique is appalling." I liked his version of good cop/bad cop.

"I want you to warm up first, so while I do a few lengths you grip the side of the pool, stretch out flat and practise the leg movements that I showed you, ok?"

"Right you are," I said. The porpoise swam off. As I lathered up the pool with my legs, my animated mind imagined that I was actually pushing the whole pool sideways and that when I finally let up, we would find ourselves relocated by the boundary wall.

"*Tranquilo* Donald, you're acting as if you're lashing out at an approaching crocodile" ordered Fernando on completion of his lengths.

"That's it, like the ticking of a clock, remember? Good." He let this carry on for a couple of minutes before giving me a rest.

"So how steep is the hill then?" I asked, concerned.

"You'll see later. Let's just concentrate on the swimming for now shall we?"

I gave the 'Oh, alright then' look of a dim-wit and we set to it. "This time I'm going to hold your ankles while you crawl. No kicking, just concentrate on the arms." I threw myself forward with gusto and it was only by sheer chance that my trainer got hold of my feet. What followed was a period of thrashing about, the likes of which I'm sure Fernando had never seen and it took him a good 20 seconds to realise that I hadn't taken a breath yet. He released his pupil's legs and pulled a purple-faced monster upright.

"What are you doing? Trying to drown? You're supposed to take breaths on every fourth stroke, not hold it till you reach solid ground!"

I couldn't speak. My eyes stung from a chlorine overdose and I was desperate for air. "Look, I will show you in slow time." The coach mimicked the front crawl in thin air, cocking his head to the right on the fourth stroke and exaggerating a breath.

"Ok, I got it," I gasped. "Can we stop for a bit? I've taken on a few litres."

"Of course my friend, take as long as you want."

We began again after some time, resuming yesterday's position with Fernando holding me by the waist while I went through the motions, until it was time to put it into practice. "Right Don, lead with your right arm and push." I set off with all the elegance of a startled hippopotamus, churning up the water and creating a mini-tidal wave that lapped the pool at least a dozen times. Even so, and in my own inimitable style, I once again managed to complete a width. "Bravo, bravo Donald. An awful approach, but well done," said the schizophrenic instructor. "We better have some breakfast. The drive around the course will begin at 9:00. I'll meet you in the car park — don't be late."

Fernando skipped off leaving his spluttering apprentice to recover on my lonesome. I took five minutes to revive myself and then hauled my drenched hulk onto terra firma. I flopped onto a sun lounger and drip-dried under the morning sun, creating a large puddle on the paving slabs beneath me. "Not too bad this swimming lark, after all" I told myself. The early rains that flooded an ants' nest under my feet were the talk of the colony and had caused much distress, especially in the nursery, where the fire department had to rescue dozens of egg cases.

After ten minutes of solace, I pulled on my dressing gown and headed back to the penthouse. Breakfast consisted of orange juice, black coffee (no sugar), two boiled eggs and brown toast lightly spread with margarine. The boiled egg had become a recent addition to my list of achievements, although I'd found that three minutes to boil an egg was a total load of bollocks — far too runny for anyone's taste. I wolfed it down practically in one spoonful. My appetite was enormous after all that splashing about, but the meal proved to be more than enough to quell my rumblings.

After dressing in shorts and polo shirt, I set off to meet Fernando in the car park, where he was waiting in his genuine 1944 GPW Willys Jeep in totally original condition. She hadn't had the slightest bit of refurbishment; the only addition was a couple of cushions on the front seats which was a necessary improvisation because the suspension was so hard you were likely to get bounced out at the nearest opportunity or incur spinal injuries without them. It didn't seem possible that this old girl had been to war, but out of the 360,000 Jeeps made for WWII she was one of the survivors. I loved military vehicles; I'd sold plenty of them in my early years, ex-MOD stock, with a huge profit margin. Right now I was back in the 70's, flared burgundy suit and a kipper tie, contemplating whether or not to have a tight curly perm.

"Jump in, Don," said Fernando, looking like a movie star in his white vest, tanned body, gelled-back hair and Police sunglasses. I couldn't jump anywhere, not even if my life depended on it, so I had to be content with sliding on to the passenger seat and pulling my legs in one at a time. The jeep took on a lop-sided tilt rather like the Flintstone car collecting its portion of spare ribs. We drove out of the complex waving to a rather disgruntled José. He was a bit miffed at having his 9:30 a.m. game of *boules* with Fernando cancelled due to Five-Names' newfound hobby of 'Reduce-the-Englishman'.

"I bought this little gem for my grandsons to enjoy, when they're old enough of course."

"Of course," I chuckled. I knew that it was really Fernando's toy.

Turning left in the direction of Pineda we quickly came to an underpass beneath the railway line that led onto the beach road. Here, Fernando stopped the jeep.

"That little quarter-of-a-mile stretch will be the only part of the course that you will cover twice. It's the start and the finish line, so you'll love and hate it both in the same day. It is here that you will question your sanity. You will wonder why the fuck you came to *España*. You will want to lie down and die, just to escape the pain."

Cheery words indeed and they served to make me very pensive. It was the first time that Fernando had sworn in front of me and it sounded very strange, but it underlined the commitment needed to complete this year successfully. We turned right and continued along the beach road. As we passed the apartment block I locked onto my terrace garden, billowing out green splendour against the bland whiteness of the block. My head followed its line as we left it behind.

"You love your terrace, don't you Don?"

"It's wonderful," I said. "I can really focus up there."

"I can relate to that," said Fernando. "Getting mentally prepared is equally as important as physical training, and up there is an ideal location."

Following the hardpacked sandy road, the sun beat down upon the open-topped jeep making all the exposed metal parts scolding to touch and slowly roasting its two occupants. My sweat glands were in overdrive and the old trusted handkerchief came out to play. "This is the hottest part of the course, my friend. There is no shade here at all, but fortunately it's not too long a stretch." He wasn't kidding — it was only ten o'clock and the temperature had risen down here to 100° F. As we turned the corner by the go-kart track Fernando informed me that this was the first-mile marker and from now on would be known as 'No-Cart Corner', because there will be no carts to carry me the rest of the way.

"Very fucking funny," I replied. We skirted the old cemetery walls that announced the start of Calella. Fernando remarked that I would see some big changes in the face of Pineda over the next 12 months. "Why's that Fern?" The driver flicked a finger towards the densely packed beach; there were literally thousands of people enjoying the fruits of the coastline. "Bloody busy, innit?"

"It's peak season, Don. Keep that picture in your head my friend; I'll remind you again in four months' time. There are two faces to a tourist town, you know!"

This course was one of contrasts: the first mile being the most unprotected from the sun; the second being the total opposite, in full shade. Although we were unable to drive this part, Fernando pointed to the walkway that ran to the far end of Calella; it was almost three-quarters of a mile.

"*Un paseo por la sombra*," said Fernando.

"What does that mean?" I asked.

"A walk in the shade," replied Fernando. We sat there staring at the lush, cool avenue of trees gently swaying their healing fronds in the summer breeze. Fernando went on to explain that these were banana trees, although a completely different type of plant to the fruit-bearing palm of the tropics. These beauties only produced little yellow berries, but could live up to 2,000 years unlike the other banana trees, which only live for a year and are widely becoming fruitless through some kind of genetic mutation.

That was too much information for Mr Simmons, but I could see why the Spanish used them for shade. It was like looking down an emerald tunnel; the walkway's surface was tightly packed sand as well, but smoother and on a better level than the beach road.

"If only the entire course was like this, Don, then my position would be redundant; you would sail round it. But unfortunately for you it isn't. Come, I will show you." Where the beach ended, the road went into an underpass. The avenue of trees also ended here. "We'll cycle down here later, Don, then you'll be able to see just how effective those trees really are."

"Are there any other shady spots along the course?" I asked hopefully.

"Five, in fact they're all underpasses. When you enter one of those covered in sweat, after being in the burning sun, it's like running into a cold storage room. The shock can be quite dangerous to the heart so we'll have to make sure that the runs are made in the cooler parts of the day."

Three of the underpasses went under the railway line, while the other two traversed the N11 motorway. I welcomed them with open arms as they would be ideal and much-needed respites. We emerged from the subterranean murkiness into a dazzling white-hot sunlight on the other side; at this point I wished that I had brought my sunglasses because I was temporarily blinded by the brightness.

"This is the two-mile marker my friend, and the start of the hill," said Fernando.

What lay in front of us was a gradual incline of about 1:20, nowhere near the monster that greets you after a mile on the High Wycombe course. Even the two smaller hills in Wycombe were bigger than this! Fernando had based this course on the description that I had given him of the one back home, but he obviously hadn't understood the severity of the Wycombe beast. On the other side of the next underpass I felt that I had to say something.

"Fern, I think you might have misinterpreted my description of the hill back home. This one here just isn't big enough by comparison." Fernando pulled into a side road between two apartment blocks and slowed to a crawl.

"Is that steep enough for you?" he boomed, gesturing up ahead.

"Fuck me!" I said aghast. I looked at Fernando, whose grin said it all. "That's not a hill, that's the north face of the fucking Eiger," I declared.

"Then that's what we'll call it, the fucking Eiger," he resounded, double declutching and putting the jeep into first gear.

The apartment blocks here had obscured the presence of the hill, but now it rose up before us like some kind of awakened leviathan. It was so severe that I was pushed back hard into my seat. It reminded me of the ascent to the top of the roller coaster at Blackpool's pleasure beach, its incline was 2:5.

"This is the worst part by far, my friend. Once we make that bend ahead, it's not half as bad as this" reassured Fernando. The hill was made up of three parts: the gradual quarter-mile incline once out of the underpass; the quarter-mile Eiger; and about half a mile of twisting section affectionately known as 'The Snake'. Once at the top of this meat grinder, the road meandered gently up through ancient olive grove plantations, their grey-green leaves looking sucked dry of any nourishment and desperate for a drink. The undergrowth here too was brown and listless, very arid and choked with dust. I sensed its thirst immediately and felt a strong urge to murder a pint of ice cold lager at The George.

All of a sudden we left the lazy heat-soaked kingdom of traditional farming and entered the modern world, where row upon row of heavenly scented ripe strawberries saturated the steep banked hills on either side of the road. It was like being awoken from a bad dream by a vivacious Penthouse Pet.

A gang of four, no doubt poorly paid, African migrant labourers had the arduous task of harvesting this crop. They were bent double, engrossed in their mundane work, dressed in dark blue overalls and Wellington boots, singing traditional songs from home to keep up their spirits. They straightened and waved at the passing jeep regardless of whether or not they knew us; it was simply a welcome break from the monotony of their task. The concrete road led up to a few farms and a fruit-packing plant that dominated the area. It looked out of place up here and slightly sinister, the sort of place where people entered at their own risk, never to be heard of again.

"Do you like strawberries and Muscatel, Don?"

"I love strawberries, me old mate, but can't say that I've heard of Muscatel? Is it a cream of some sort?" My usual method of devouring strawberries was to drench them in double cream and then cover the whole dish in a thick layer of sugar — glutton's delight.

"It's a very sweet wine. The combination with strawberries is not to be missed — they complement each other exquisitely," replied Fernando. I remembered that I had seen both items on the diet sheet and all of a sudden warmed to the idea. Five-Names instantly read my mind and cut me a raised eyebrow.

"Well, if it's alcohol I'd certainly consider sampling it," I said with relish.

Fernando laughed. "I've already instructed Manolo to keep a steady hand on the alcohol!" I appreciated the joke. I wasn't a wine drinker at all and would have preferred cream and sugar any day, but Fernando had worked hard to formulate a beneficial stratagem for this project, so I wasn't about to question his motives. We passed a red ribbon tied to an olive tree that indicated the third mile; the road had now completely levelled out. "That's the hill finished with, my friend." I was pleased to hear that.

"*La Granja* down there belongs to a man called Taboada," said Fernando, nodding towards a lengthy drive that led to a substantial white-rendered house. It had a pristine terracotta pantiled roof, an enormous porch, a huge balcony and a white post-and-rail paddock that fenced in several Andalusian horses. From the stone-pillared gateposts down to the magnificent house, the cobblestone drive was lined with orange trees in full fruit. The scene awakened my business instincts briefly as I surveyed the cash-drenched fruit orchards.

"Did you say Ganja?" I asked.

"No," laughed Fernando. "*Granja*, it means farmhouse. Taboada's a very wealthy man; he owns most of the land around here. Fruit's not just good for your health, it's good for your wallet too," he said. We hadn't discussed each other's wealth, although we had spoke about my business interests and Fernando obviously knew that I had bought an apartment in Spain for just one year's occupation. This must have said volumes about my standing. Fernando had simply taken it for granted that I was loaded, but even if I had been the poorest creature on the planet, he was sufficiently interested to want a share in my challenge that his offer of help would have remained the same.

A few hundred yards on, Fernando stopped the car again. "When you reach here my friend, you'll have completed one-quarter of the course," he said, gesticulating towards a blue ribbon hanging from a tree.

If I ever get here, I thought. The stop was double edged: a reminder that I still had three-quarters of the course to complete but a standpoint from that bore witness to spectacular views of the coastline. A perfect uninterrupted 180-degree vista of breathtaking scenery that stretched as far as my eyes could focus. I could see to the other side of Malgrat de Mar some four miles away to my left and way down to Sant Andreu de Llavaneres on my right. In between, golden beaches mellowed by the heat haze dominated the coast, interrupted politely at intervals by tiny stone fishing harbours and the red and white prominence of Calella and Pineda. The railway line was quite distinct, hugging the contours of the beach like an endless brown snake. A perfect cloudless sky melded into the beautiful azure Mediterranean, only discernible by a slight darkening on the horizon. Pockets of vegetation rambled upwards over the rocky terrain, rolling inland on an emerald crusade intent on claiming the land, only to end up being harvested by the very people that had given them life.

"It'll be worth the struggle getting up here just to look at this every morning, won't it?" said Fernando.

"Mm," I agreed. I was lost in thought.

"You seem worried, *amigo*. What's troubling you?" asked Five-Names. I blurted out my fears about the Eiger. I couldn't imagine anybody running up that monstrosity, especially a blimp like me. "Fear not, my friend, that hill is not intended to be run up," he said calmly. I was confused. "Let me explain. Until we can complete the whole course, we shall cycle small sections of it at a time, say two or three miles. You can't run anywhere yet anyway!" I felt and looked slightly hurt by this comment. "Once you are down to jogging weight, we'll do the same thing on foot, all except the Eiger that is. We'll tackle that bugger last! When we're out cycling, we'll dismount and walk the thing. When we're out jogging, we'll walk the thing. It'll be a pointless exercise to try and run up there; it'll use up too much energy and burn you out for the rest of the course. When and only when you are fit enough we'll attempt to jog the hill, very slowly. I've allowed for this in our time schedule."

Fernando reached into the jeep and pulled out a folder that had been occupying the back seat. He showed me a breakdown of the times needed for each section of the course to achieve our objective. The Eiger should be jogged in no less than three minutes. I felt faint; it took me three minutes to put my shoes on. Fernando broke the silence. "Shall we?" he said, nodding at the jeep.

"Go for it," I replied, following his style and thinking more positively.

The concrete slab was now taking a most definite decline. Five-Names doubled the clutch again and once more selected first gear. "This is probably the most dangerous part of the course," he said, quickly making a sharp left turn onto a very unmade road.

All of a sudden we were rally driving on something akin to a Kenyan bush track and getting bounced out of our skins by the screaming, bucking GPW. The gradient was as bad as the Eiger in reverse, and I felt sick as more than once my soul left my body courtesy of the G-force, before returning back with a snap. Thankfully this portion of the course only lasted for 200 yards; it then regained sobriety by acquiring a tarmac surface and developing into a more sensible gradual slope.

"Wanna do it again?" joked Fernando with a great toothy smile.

"Fuck off!" replied an agitated jelly.

We were back among the strawberry plantations, their heavenly scent soothing my rattled nerves. The green fields sprawled across the open landscape and accompanied the road to the bottom of the hill. Soon we passed the four-mile marker pinned to a fence post and left behind the rural splendour, emerging abruptly into urban tourism.

Surrounded by scores of hotels, bars, restaurants, shops and plenty of people, I suddenly felt very exposed and insecure, wedged in this ancient tin box. I was definitely not blending in with the crowd. It was the same paranoia I had felt about exposing my gluttony at the swimming pool. It was fear of ridicule, only on a grand scale, because right now this place was swamped with holidaymakers and a fat git in a tracksuit fighting a seemingly losing battle would certainly make me a target. Fernando could see that his big novice had tensed up. "Don't worry, Don. By the time that we're jogging the course, all of these places will be closed for the winter. It's like a ghost town from November to April."

His words quelled a building tide of apprehension and I relaxed back into my cushion. Not everybody had the same enviable attitude as Fernando. I was my own worst critic these days. I had only become conscious of my size as a result of this bet with Lord Belington, and although it had turned out to be a good thing, I still needed to get my head round the reason why I was here and totally focus on that. I told

Fernando of my fears and had expected the sort of words of reassurance and encouragement that my mentor offered. What I hadn't expected was Fernando's fierce defence of large people. "Not everybody who is overweight can help their size. We live in a world of temptation without education." Strong stuff indeed, and the sentence reverberated around my head for some time, making me think of my two youngest children June and Mathew.

On any marathon course, you will always find the following: first aid stations (FA); toilets (T); feeding stations (FS); and mileage markers (1m–13m). Our first feeding station was situated at the start of the hill at a small bar that spit-roasted dozens of chickens on the wall in the street. Our second station along with a toilet stop was smack in the middle of tourist town, in a bar called Papa's. We pulled over at the kerb and Five-Names pointed across the street to a red flashing neon cross situated high on the fascia of a row of shops. "That's the first-aid station; it's open seven months of the year. Hopefully you won't be needing it my friend. Most towns in *España* have them. They are very resourceful."

I wouldn't have noticed the place on my own. It was snuggled between two garish souvenir shops, their frontage jam-packed with airbeds, plastic sandals and cheap tack. Everything on sale was of questionable quality. "There's someone I'd like you to meet," said Fernando, "He's very resourceful as well, come on."

We both got out of the jeep and climbed the steps to Papa's. From the outside it looked typically Spanish, with a cool veranda, tiled floor and wooden furniture, white walls, Andalusian ironwork, eight-foot high terracotta pots and grape vines that strangled anything that stood still for long enough. It felt like this bar had been overlooked by commercialism, but I was brought back down to Earth again when I saw that the A-boards were advertising full English breakfasts, home-made curry and steak and kidney pie and chips. Just when I had taken in the menu, a man in his early fifties with copper-tinged grey hair spotted us. He rushed through serving a table of drinks, and then sashayed over, completing a slalom course around empty tables en route.

"*Buenos dias Fernando, mi buen amigo. ¿Que tal?*" said the patron. I naturally presumed the jolly round-faced man to be Spanish, his accent and mannerisms being perfectly in tune with this part of the world. However I was wrong.

"*La vida es dulce en este memento, gracias,*" replied Fernando. "Don, I'd like you to meet a fellow countryman of yours. This is John and he owns Papa's bar along with his wife Anita."

John held out his hand, "Pleased to meet you, over here on holiday?"

"Don Simmons pleased to meet you too. Actually, I've bought a place over in Pineda, in the same apartment block as Fernando. I'm, err, staying for a year."

John looked perplexed. "I wondered where you had met this old bugger. Did you fall asleep in the sun?" he asked pointedly.

I sadly had to own up.

"How about a drink? He asked. It was like inviting a vampire to a neck-kissing contest in daylight; the pain was intense.

"There's nothing I'd like more down me neck than a tall glass of ice-cold lager with a whisky chaser, but that's a complete no-no these days. I wouldn't mind an iced tea if you have it, John?"

"Peach or lemon?"

"Um, peach sounds great. What about you Fern?"

"Coffee for me please, John, with ice."

"I know," said John, disappearing behind the bar. The trainer and his *protégé* sidled up to the bar and sat on large wooden raffia-seated stools. If Spanish tradition was the intended impression outside, then inside was a complete contrast. The huge elongated bar played host to an impressive array of British beers, lagers and ciders, while the glass shelves behind the bar bristled with every kind of spirit imaginable. They even boasted a selection of malts. I started to drool.

I learnt that John hailed from Watford in Hertfordshire. He had studied as a carpenter's apprentice before coming to Spain in the 1970s. His only recollection of High Wycombe was in fact the big hill; whether you entered the town from the north or the south, the hill was a dominant feature. In fact if you came in from Amersham, the town centre looked like the low point in a massive big dipper that loomed up into the clouds on the other side. He had met and married his wife after a couple of years of working in bars; her father then owned the bar that we were now sitting in. Papa only put in a few cursory hours in the early mornings these days, for old times' sake. John's son and Fernando's granddaughter were in the school orchestra together and that's how the two men had met. On many occasions both sets of parents would share a car to go and watch their children's performances in Barcelona or further afield; consequently, they had become extremely good friends.

Because the establishment held a corner spot on the street, two of its sides were open to the wide terrace via several dark oak double doors that allowed a cool wispy breeze to glide through the shady room. Ceiling fans purred above our heads and the whitewashed walls peered out from behind a bizarre melange of faded '70s football team posters, football scarves, bullfight promotions, pictures of the meals on offer and the obligatory collection of foreign currency. A dozen or so large wine casks were festooned around the walls and on every table were placed pub beer mats and bottles of Daddies sauce. I felt strangely at home abroad and although getting anxious at being immersed in all the evils that I adored — barred from touching a drop, a fag-paper's width from heaven — I felt quite at one with my surroundings. Then I was delivered a killer blow.

One of John's waiters brushed passed me with two massive oval plates, brimming over with the full Monty. I breathed in and closed my eyes, following the aroma like a Bisto kid and nearly fell off my chair. "Two eggs, two sausages, two rashers of bacon, mushrooms, beans, plum tomatoes, toast and a pot of tea. That's our full English breakfast, Don," said John, returning with the drinks. The words rolled off his tongue as if joined together; a streamed sentence that he had wrapped around the tastebuds of his customers 10,000 times before. I was failing fast, suddenly ravenous. All I could think about was tucking into a big, greasy plateful of Monty. The bar faded around me and I was transported back home into my kitchen being spoilt quite literally to death by my loving wife.

"Don, Don, I think we had better explain to John the reason why we are here, don't you?" said Fernando, wrenching me from nirvana.

"What? Oh yes," I said coming round.

"It is some gauntlet we are running here, John, by coming into your bar, but Don has to face his enemies in order to conquer them."

John immediately grasped the plot and listened intently as Fernando and I unleashed the whole kit and caboodle on him. By the time we had finished it was approaching eleven o'clock. The bar had swelled with customers and John needed to help out his staff, but we had impressed on him our commitment and need for a strict regime in order to complete my training. Being the compassionate man that he was, John agreed to let his bar be one of our food stations. He would even have a key cut for us to use when the bar was closed at the end of the season, or for early mornings. I could settle up the bill later.

I finished my peach tea. Although it was not as rewarding as a cold lager, it quenched my thirst like perfumed rain on a desert plantation. "Where's the toilet old bean? I need a piss like there's no tomorrow," I confessed.

"In the far corner, down the corridor, second on your right," nodded John. He watched my wide load waddle past tables of punters till it was out of sight. He puffed out his cheeks and told Fernando, "Got your work cut out for you there, mate!" Fernando just smiled.

In the toilet I was relaxing into another monster slash and rebuilding my resolve. I was feeling good about my efforts so far; including the smell of cigarettes becoming offensive, although it was a shame that whisky and fried food weren't having the same effect. Back in the bar I ordered two bottles of still water before my companion and I headed for the street, waving our goodbyes to a much occupied John across the bar.

Passing more shops we made our way towards the N11. Crossing it would take us back towards Pineda. Stopping at the junction, Fernando noted that the road was busier than usual and this was definitely not the way for me to cross. "The course takes you under yet another subway a hundred yards to our right," he said. Once over the N11, Fernando pointed out the five-mile marker, a lamp post, but this time unadorned by a ribbon. The next mile would become my second-least favourite. It had a slight incline and was enclosed by buildings on either side; although they offered some shade they made me feel very claustrophobic, bearing down on me like hyper-critical tutting monoliths. This was the only part of the course that was totally enclosed and we were soon out of it. We passed a small restaurant called The Elbay, the six-mile marker. "I have some good news, my friend," announced Fernando, pulling into the petrol station with the fruit stall. "This is the halfway point; there are toilets here too." Five-Names filled up with petrol while I got out and strolled over to inspect the fruit. It was the finest quality available and while I ogled its succulence and freshness, picking up various pieces to sniff their fragrance, I was conscious of the ancient salesman watching this two-tone giant with his curious ink-black eyes. I hadn't been true to the promise that I had made to myself, because up until now I had bought my fruit and veg from the supermarket, but seeing the wonderful selection on offer made me decide that this was the gear for me. I would cycle up from the apartment at least twice a week and give the old boy some business.

"*Hola Josep*" said Fernando from behind me.

"*Hola*" replied the salesman in very croaky tones.

"This is Josep," Fernando by way of introduction. "He's been selling fruit here for a million years. Josep is Catalan for Joe. See the petrol pump attendant?"

I nodded.

"His name is Joe. What with Jose our gardener, who is Castilian, you now know three guys named Joe."

"Oh," I said nonplussed.

After buying a couple of bags of oranges and having Fernando explain to Josep who this man-mountain was, the two of us sat in the shade of a mulberry tree and devoured the sweetest oranges I'm sure I will ever taste in my life. They tasted exactly the way orange blossom smells and left you wanting more.

"This guy is the best," said Fernando, pointing a sticky finger at Josep.

"You're not wrong there, mate," I replied, feeling that now was as good a time as any to ask my mentor the two questions that had been burning holes in my head for the past week. "If you don't mind me asking, Fern, how old are you?"

Fernando laughed. "I'm sorry Don, people are always questioning my age. I'm 68- years-old."

"Fuck off, you're not," I retorted in disbelief.

"I am," he affirmed, still laughing. "I've a young man's haircut — it makes all the difference you know."

"I'd have put you down for at least ten years younger, I'm impressed."

"I shall tell you my secret and you will learn its ways. It'll be the most prized possession that you'll have, but it will take me a year to tell you," said the mystic as he popped another orange segment into his mouth. I thought about my own appearance and my immature descent towards the grave. I was suddenly desperate to turn back the clock and start over again with the knowledge I knew now.

"I have another question for you."

"Oh yes?" said Fernando.

"What nationality are you?"

Five-Names laughed again. "What do you think I am?"

"I think you're answering a question with a question, that's what I think. No, everything about you says that you are Spanish apart from your appearance. To me you look Scandinavian."

Fernando pouted and slowly nodded. "Well, let me tell you my heritage, my friend." And so he began the potted history of Five-Names. "My great, great grandfather, Frederick Olefson, was from Norway. He was a merchant sailor who fell in love with and married a girl from Madeira. The couple ran away from her family because she was only 16 and they settled in South Africa, where my grandfather Tommas and his brothers were born. After little success as a diamond prospector, Frederick quit Africa and returned to mainland Europe; first to Portugal where he tried fishing for sardines and then to Spain working on an orange grove near Valencia. Tommas and his brothers did well at school and most of them went to college. Tommas met my grandmother Isabella at the University of Madrid where they studied medicine and after passing out as doctors they married and moved to her family home town of Barcelona, where they both practised medicine until the children came along."

I was totally absorbed — this was better than any Mills & Boon yarn.

"My mother Angelina was born second. She showed great promise as a swimmer and went on to swim for *España* in the world championships; that's where she met my father, Rodrigo Montoya DeNegro, a diving coach for the youth team. They fell in love, married, and then along came me. I guess that I still carry Frederick's genes."

"That's some story Fernando. Are your parents still with us?"

"Unfortunately not, my friend, my father died just after I was born, fighting against Franco in the civil war and my mother passed away just last year. She was 89-years-old; she had a good 'innings', as you would say."

"You may have mixed parentage, mate, but you definitely have an English sense of humour," I replied.

"I had a mate from the British national team; he came from Cambridge. He had a wicked sense of humour and we spent some hilarious times together, but that was long ago. Do you want a piece of this?" asked Fernando, offering me some of his orange.

"Have you had enough?" I said.

"Yes, I've had plenty."

For a person who up until a week ago thought that fruit was only for the seriously ill, I had radically changed my views and was stuffing oranges into my gob like a captive monkey. I had always prided myself on having a poker face whenever necessary, but Five-Names had seen right though me. "You have another question for me."

I looked down at my sandals and then up again at Fernando. "I should have asked you this earlier, Fern. Why are you helping me?"

"Ha, ha, I knew that this one would come up. I'm a sportsman Don, I enjoy a challenge and, like all competitors, I thrive on scoring goals. Life around here has become mundane just lately, you can imagine. My only successes these days are getting Circola out of the apartment in time before she craps in the hall. Getting too comfortable makes me irritable, you coming along like this is like a godsend to me, you've given me a purpose, and besides you have had the same red flag waved at you that I received many moons ago. I too was given the same odds of 1,000 to 1 of winning a gold medal at the Olympics; the challenge inspired me."

"You won!"

"I did Don, and so will you my friend."

If encouragement and confidence was all I needed to carry me around that course in an hour and a half, I could do it tomorrow, but I was going to need a lot more than just incentive to bring me home. While we were sitting there deeply engrossed in oranges and Q and A's, I had been oblivious to a train of tiny red ants that had made their way up my leg and were now taking an interest in my nether regions. It seemed like a good place to start a picnic so the lead ant got stuck in. Josep cocked his head at the sight of two grown men dancing under a mulberry tree, both of them patting the inside leg of the larger one.

Nursing my stinging groin wedged into a red hot metal box sometimes known as a jeep wasn't the most pleasant of experiences, but suffer I had to because the rest of the course had yet to be inspected. The next two-and-three-quarter miles of dusty N11 was flat country, and the road was lined with tall fir trees heavily laden with cones that had started to scatter, carpeting the road and bike lanes like a minefield left by a retreating army. We turned off and headed in the direction of Lloret De Mar on a downward slope towards the coast. Of course what goes down doesn't always stay down and neither did the road. I was just arguing the toss in my head between what was worse: a long, gradual incline or a short, steep climb and thinking that I'd already seen both, when we reached a crossroads at the nine-mile mark and turned right, in front of us stood another meat grinder.

"Oh shit" I muttered.

"It's not as steep as the Eiger, Don, and only a hundred yards long. I would expect you to be able to jog or cycle this one." We pulled over to the side of the road with a sharp halt, causing hot dust to shoot past us, clouding our view for a moment as it reacted with the afternoon sunlight. "Once we're over this one, it's downhill or on the flat all the way home. Do you have a name for him yet?" asked Fernando.

"It's your turn. I've already named a bloody hill today," I replied distinctly disgruntled.

There was a short pause and then Fernando said, "I name this hill 'possible'!" "Why's that?" I asked.

"Because this hill is possible to overcome."

"That's terrible," I barked. "I'm gonna call it 'The Knackerer'."

"Uh?" said Fernando.

"Because it'll knacker me every time I run up it."

Both of us roared with laughter.

"At least when you cycle up it you'll have a good run up, that decline must be 400 yards long. You could virtually roll to the top!" said Fernando.

"Halle-fucking-lujha" I said.

Once over the brow of the hill the coastline was on view again, but at a lower altitude, so we couldn't see as far as before. The scenery along this stretch of road was quite beautiful; densely forested hills with the odd villa visible now and then.

"How come you didn't buy a property up here? You could have had your own swimming pool and a gymnasium," enquired Five-Names.

"Fate brought me to your doorstep, Fern. I honestly believe we were meant to meet."

Fernando smiled. I know he felt it too.

The ten-mile marker was a few hundred yards from a garage forecourt. It was the last toilet stop and food station, and was owned by a man called César, a good friend of Francisco and a dead ringer for a young Cliff Richard. We drove in and I was formally introduced.

"*Buenos dias, Don Quixote*" said César.

"Donkey who?" I asked.

"*Don Quixote*. Haven't you seen the film 'Man of La Mancha' with Peter O'Toole?" asked Fernando.

"No," I replied.

"One of the best songs ever recorded!" said Fernando. "To dream the impossible dream, to fight the un-fightable foe …" sang Five-Names. César joined in.

"Is he taking the piss?" I enquired tentatively.

"No," laughed Fernando. "It's all about conquering adversity. We have faith in you Don, come on sing! "This is my quest to follow that star, no matter how hopeless, no matter how far …"

I just stared at them both with a bemused Eeyore expression.

"Fucking nuts, the pair of you," I said, chuckling to myself.

The next two miles led us through well-cultivated farmland. An overabundance of super-irrigated fruit and vegetable plantations were in full swing: tomato tunnels, lettuce fields, melon patches, orange groves — in fact every kind of produce that you would expect from market gardens.

Of course, celery was very apparent, its aroma invading my nostrils and being out here in this Eden-like environment made me appreciate why my granddad had loved his old allotment so much. Even I found myself making a mental promise to grow a bit for the family in the back garden when I got home next year. The shade along this stretch was quite limited, the trees being few and far between, but two of them acted as marker posts, blue to indicate that three-quarters of the course had been completed and a red one to show the 11th mile. Fernando stopped the jeep once more. "Well Don, you have a choice. This last section of the course can be run on two different surfaces, the tarmac or the beach road. They're of about equal distance and both offer only minimal shade from the sun. Which would you like?"

The beach road seemed the more welcoming so I opted for that. We drove under the last cool underpass and after passing a mile and a quarter of head-to-toe eye candy, we were back at the apartment gates. "Well, what do you think of our little course?" demanded Five-Names.

It was one o'clock in the afternoon and I was more than a little road weary. I couldn't find anything constructive to say. In my mind I was suffering the effects of gross malnutrition and I had seen enough scenery to scramble anyone's perspective. Today I was particularly struck by tongue-tiedness, managing only to utter 'err' and 'um' before Fernando intervened and suggested we go around once more, this time without stopping.

Half an hour later we were back at the same spot and although I had nothing to compare it with, the course still looked phenomenally hard. "Time for lunch," said Fernando at long last. I was beginning to think that feeding the apprentice had been scrapped for today, and so was monstrously elated at the sound of the dinner bell.

We ate on Fernando's terrace which was a neat and tidy affair with pastel green slabs and just a few pots and planters filled with geraniums, impatiens and lobelia. We sat on extremely comfortable rattan chairs, ate a mixture of fruit slices delicately prepared by Anna and drank mango and lychee tea. I just kept on surprising myself. A week ago I would have poured such a brew over Les's head if he had brought it up to the office. I wondered how the old fella was coping without his sparring partner.

By 2:30 p.m. the pair of us was up to our chests in pool water. Anna stood on the side giving instruction in the art of aerobics. Fernando was ever the enthusiast; I felt like a twat. Not only had I stripped down to my trunks all grotesque and two-tone in front of a lady, I was now turning, twisting, walking in water and waving my hands about like a right ponce. Fernando assured me that water aerobics would be the perfect way to exercise without putting too much pressure on my joints at this early stage of the training. I still felt like a twat! On top of this we had a heckler.

"*Voy a bailar contigo mañana,*" shouted José from a rockery.

"What did he say?" I asked.

"He said that he'll be joining us tomorrow. That old codger has never once used this pool, not even on the hottest days of the year. I have a running bet for a bottle of Cognac against him taking a splash," said Fernando.

"He'd better take that cigar out of his mouth first," I replied, "they're so hard to relight when they've been in the pool!"

CHAPTER ELEVEN
Nuevo cuisine

"TWENTY-FOUR STONE ELEVEN AND A HALF POUNDS?" There was a slight pause. "That's a loss of sixteen and a half pounds. Are you sure, Don?"

"Yep."

"That's quite a lot in one week!" said Marion in a disbelieving tone.

"On the level, Marion. Fernando is my witness."

"Well, well done you" she said in her best patronizing effort to date. "Of course you realize that most of that is water retention, don't you? It gets harder from now on you know. You may even suffer a couple of weeks without weight loss …"

I stopped her in mid-rant by placing an order for her products and giving her Manolo's address to send them to. I knew the reasons for my dramatic reduction and didn't need a lecture. Even taking into account my abandonment of jewellery and the lack of heavy clothes, it was still well over a stone that I had lost and I was made up. The all-important seven o'clock Wednesday night weigh-in report and chats were destined to become rituals, and I needed Marion as a friend and confidante. I had decided to suck up a little, and the order that I had just placed with her was a hefty one, bursting with profit for the coordinator. "My offer to fly you and your husband out here for a holiday still stands, you know? You can catch your star pupil in action, live at the beach if you like."

"I'll pass on your kind offer for the moment, Don. We have two weeks in Dorset booked already; lovely little place on the coast, nice and quiet, good cream teas and there's a bingo hall."

"Sounds great" I said, mimicking Marion's condescending tones. I finished the conversation by thanking her for her support and promised to check in again next week, same time.

"Barrier up, bridge open," I confirmed after putting down the phone. I sat in Fernando's office and swivelled in the big leather recliner, with my sandals kicked off and my feet cooling on the cold stone floor. This would be the last time I'd have to borrow my coach's phone because I had gone back on my earlier resolution and ordered a line to be installed. On reflection I had realised that it was a necessary evil.

I contemplated the evening ahead and tried picturing Manolo's restaurant in my mind. Fernando had described its whereabouts, in a side street off the beach road from Pineda, not far from where I had sat on my own on that first night, drinking G&Ts and feeling sorry for myself. How dramatically different I was feeling now. In just six days I felt like a changed man. I definitely had a spring in my step; admittedly, it was only one of those flimsy wire things that you get inside a ballpoint pen, but a positive spring all the same.

Fernando and I took to the streets. The thunderstorm on Tuesday night had cleared the air of the oppressive humidity that the town had been suffering, and there was even the luxury of a sea breeze, most unusual for this time of year I was told. It rippled through our clothing like cool silk ribbons unfurled by invisible gymnasts as they flitted between the mulberry trees. It definitely eased the walk; I only had to stop once to catch my breath.

We came at length to the first of many bars that lined this stretch of the coast. Fernando stopped. "This bar is the only one that stays open all year round down here, apart from three weeks at Christmas, but then of course the whole of Spain hibernates for Santa Claus. It'll be an ideal location for a coffee stop on your way back to the *ático*. Hugo the owner makes excellent coffee; I take one here most mornings."

"Sounds wicked," I said, suddenly sounding very immature.

Fernando raised an eyebrow.

Three hundred yards on, we turned left into Manolo's street. As with most roads that meander down to the sea, this one had a gradient – nothing to an average Joe, but perplexing for a lardy like me. I needed time to gather enough oxygen in my blood supply to make the ascent without passing out, so I leant on the corner of the block for five minutes. The buildings in this part of town had a more traditional Spanish style and were tucked away from the hustle of a holiday resort. The three-storied houses sported coats of white or cream and most were in need of a lick of paint. They all had coloured shutters of various hues, the dominant being sky blue. The ruddy pantiled roofs, some with broken and slipped canals, jutted out over the walls with angular prominence, but hardly offered an easy passage for descending raindrops as they lacked guttering. In fact, when it rained, anyone leaving the building had to brave a waterfall at the outset. A few shops mingled among the houses: a butcher, a greengrocer and a hardware store that abutted an alcove in the wall that housed a faded and chipped painted Madonna. This was obviously a parade for local denizens and I loved its charm immediately.

"Come on, let's get me to me trough. Me stomach thinks me throat's been cut," I said, adopting a Yorkshire accent.

The image of Manolo's bar was completely different in my mind to the drab facade that presented itself. If it weren't for the two glass-fronted menu boxes that languished on either side of the doorway, you wouldn't have recognised it as a restaurant at all. Any unsuspecting passer-by would presume it to be a working man's bar, and that's partially just what it was. A bar crammed to the gills with local artisans, fishermen and farmers, chancing their luck at the fruit machines, slapping down dominoes or supping San Miguel through their moustaches. The noise that spilled onto the street was approaching illegal levels, and the mixed aroma of cigar smoke, lager and roasted garlic that wafted up my nostrils left me hopelessly smitten. Surely Jason was sailing perilously close to the Sirens tonight, with such temptation just a mermaid's breath away? Why on Earth would Fernando choose a haunt like this for his charge to moderately dine in? I still had total trust in my coach, but this was unnecessarily testing. A television entertained itself high in one corner, but in an instant it became the only source of sound when we entered the room. Lee Van Cleef and Clint Eastwood stood just inside the doorway while the greasy Mexican outlaw horde surveyed us with guilty, twitching eyes. Somewhere in my mind a pocket watch played a familiar old tune.

The whole bar suddenly cheered and shouts of '*Buenos tardes*' and '*Bienvenido Quixote*' could be deciphered between wolf whistles. I had made no secret of my mission here in Spain and neither had Fernando. Anna knew and so did her friends; Manolo had told his wife, the cook and the waiters, and pretty much the rest of Catalonia as well. It seemed the whole of Calella was anticipating the start of my challenge and, in this bar at least, the atmosphere was fervently in my favour. Bets had even been placed. We made our way through the smoky room at a snail's pace. I was being properly introduced to each and every one, amid plenty of back patting and handshaking. Five-Names knew everybody here and appeared to be held in high esteem.

The décor inside the room was very plain and traditional, with white walls, quarry-tile stone floors and dark wood furniture. The L-shaped bar was wood-framed and roofed by a fishing net that had somehow managed to catch two plastic lobsters, numerous bunches of black grapes and a lonesome traffic cone. Behind its marble top, the bar housed stainless-steel chiller cabinets, an impressive ceramic coffee machine, three huge wine barrels laid on their sides, several beer taps and a mountain of liquor stacked on mirrored shelves. The restaurant itself was in the backroom down some wide open steps and had a warm, welcoming look to it. Gingham tablecloths covered heavy oak dining tables that had matching chairs with barley-twist legs. In the centre of each table was a small glass vase, which cradled a single cornflower blue, Anemone. The walls in this room were painted apricot and played host to mounted iron candelabras whose light gave off a magical luminescence.

Before I managed to reach the restaurant, I was introduced to four more colourful characters: Andrés, a Dutchman with a slight Scottish accent picked up from his Aberdeen-born wife; his business partner Pedro; and Juan and Carlos Ferreira, better known as the *Mañana* Brothers. If you wanted some building work done, the brothers were your men, but be prepared for them to start the job at least a month after the commencement date that they had set. Or the day after that!

"I'm so glad to have met you at last," said the enthusiastic Dutchman.

"My reputation seems to have preceded me tonight," I replied.

"Some of us wanted to see you in the flesh before committing to our bets," piped up Pedro.

I suddenly felt very vulnerable, less than human and more like an exotic acquisition that'd just been paraded around the ring. The hurt was etched across my face.

"Don't encourage them, Don. These are honourable men but they have a wicked twist; they only back complete outsiders, it brings them greater rewards," interjected Fernando with a smile.

I relaxed. This lot reminded me of my drinking school, and I made a note to get my own back on them one day. Besides, who was I to criticise the betting on human flesh? I'd been doing it for years with boxing, football and motor sports; I wasn't about to be a hypocrite.

"That's alright, mate, we'll all be reaping greater rewards when I fly over that finish line, you mark my words," I proclaimed.

"Ten out of ten," said Andrés. They all burst out laughing. He and Pedro were well defined in expensive tailoring, lightweight summer suits and thin cotton shirts. Their shoes were positively handmade and they both adorned themselves with heavy gold chains and bracelets. They were obviously in my league and I acknowledged it in one sentence. "If you want to buy something tasteful with your winnings boys, I could cut you a great deal on a couple of Bentleys. I'd even fly you over to Ruislip for a test drive."

"We'll hold you to it," said Andrés. When the Dutchman first heard of my trial, he was more than just interested in making a few pesetas. This game was right up his street because he, too, pounded the beach road a couple of times a week and also found time to put in the odd game of tennis or squash at his club. He certainly looked fit for a man in his early 50's.

All four men were drinking ice-cold tap lager and adoring every drop. I massaged my parched throat; I was fast becoming maddeningly arid. In front of the men on the bar stood four empty little tapas plates, each sporting varying degrees of olive oil residue. I was so hungry that I could have eaten the plates. The men were talking to me, but all I could hear was my own voice in my head wondering what odds they'd given me. Andrés was more than qualified to give an impartial opinion of my chances. "You are looking to run a mile in under seven minutes then? I struggle to do that kind of time over four miles, Don. How are you going to keep it up for thirteen and a half? Mind you, you do have Fernando on your side," he said, casting a confident glance at Five-Names. All of the men turned down their mouths and nodded in agreement.

Suddenly I was back among them. "I have total faith in my coach, gentlemen," I reassured the crowd. I wondered whether the odds had moved up from 1,000 to 1.

"I'll tell you what Don, if you pull this off..." — thankfully he wasn't pointing at his groin. "...I'll pay for every man in here tonight to eat and drink as much as they like, for one evening in the restaurant."

"And if I don't?"

"Well, that's easy my friend, then you pay," said Andrés with a smile.

"A tempting challenge mate, but my bet with Belington was the last bet ever, so I cannot take you up on that."

Seeing his charge on the verge of a confidence slip, Fernando quickly stepped in.

"This is so my friend, but there is nothing stopping me from taking up the wager seeing that we are affiliated, Don. So because my honour is at stake too, I'll pay for the evening if my champion fails."

"Deal!" said Andrés and the two men slapped hands.

Pedro called for silence as he stood on a chair and translated the wager to all and sundry. The whole bar erupted and much beer was spilt.

"Right, to the restaurant my friend," said Fernando and ushered me forward.

"*Hasta luego*," he said to the group.
"*Buen provecho*," they replied in unison.
"What did they say?" I enquired.
"Enjoy your meal," replied Fernando.
"Not arf," I said. By now I was positively ravenous. Reflecting on the group's parting remark, something that all continentals say to one another, I felt it to be a very affectionate expression and one that was sadly missing from British custom. I couldn't remember being wished happy eating by friends or family at any time in England and there had been plenty of opportunity.

The kitchen was on the right-hand side as we descended the small steps. It had no discernible door, which perturbed me a little, but at least you could see that you weren't being served up local alley cat or an ex-Crufts champion. It seemed a little overcrowded but looked spotlessly clean. Although the kitchen had a standard commercial layout, hanging from its ceiling was an impressive oblong pot rack and below a massive wooden table laden with ingredients. The enchanting aroma that had beckoned me from the street was more intense in here and obviously came from a huge earthenware cooking pot that was being intently fussed over by Manolo, his wife Christina, and their chef Philippe. They had not noticed their customers' arrival, so Fernando shouted something equivalent to 'service' and they all turned around at once. Big smiles were produced and the husband and wife trotted over to greet their guests, hastily wiping their hands on the tea towels that hung from their aprons. I was surprised to find such a well-presented couple running a restaurant; they looked more akin to members of the jet-set league, but then I figured, why not if this is what they enjoy doing? Manolo's features were 100 per cent Spanish; swarthy and handsome with an enduring sparkle in his eye, he was definitely a ladies' man and his confidence was infectious. Christina could have graced any catwalk in the world; she was so mystifyingly beautiful that I could hardly make eye contact through fear of her knowing what I was thinking.

"*Buenas tardes mi amigo. Bienvenido, bienvenido,*" said Manolo, shaking Five-Names by the hand.

"*Buenos tardes,*" said Christina, kissing Fernando on each cheek.

"*Encantado Señor* Simmons *mucho gusto.*"

Fernando did the business with the necessary translation, as the couple declared that it would be an honour to serve me for the coming year and that they were delighted to be taking part in such a momentous challenge. I was floored by their honesty and warmed to them immediately. They were my kind of people, both grafters and happy to be right in the thick of it. They showed us to our table, which had a triangular 'Reserved' sign on it, and was set for four people — very handy given that I would be occupying the space of two. Christina said something that made Fernando and Manolo both laugh aloud.

"She said that this was the best table in the house if you like noise," said my coach.

"Gonna get rowdy is it?" I enquired.

"This is a very popular restaurant; it can get quite hectic in here."

"If the food's as good as it smells, I'll be too absorbed to notice." I plonked myself down onto one of the chairs and took in the ambience. The patio doors were drawn back, giving me a full view of a small cobbled courtyard at the rear of the house. It was brimming with glazed pots of all sizes containing sweet-scented blooms of every colour. Planted in the centre were two trees, a lemon and an orange, both in fruit and almost ready for harvest. The brilliant yellow and orange orbs contrasted vividly against the glossy green leaves. I had never before wondered where oranges and lemons came from, they were just there in the supermarket, but here was horticulture staring me in the face. You could grow these fruits in your back yard and pick them fresh whenever you wished. They looked so majestic that I wanted to touch them just to check that they were real.

A soft breeze danced through the open doors and pirouetted across my table refreshing my chubby chops. Twenty or so other tables had been set and Fernando explained that between 12:30 and 2:30 in the morning, every table would be taken. Manolo's was renowned for its menu of the day, a typically Spanish affair that most of the restaurants offered, comprising three or four courses, plus bread and wine; and the price was always low. Apart from Friday and Saturday nights, the general evening trade wasn't especially busy for Manolo, which was great news for me. I didn't relish the idea of sitting at a packed restaurant every night; it would be too much like dining at Burger King. Besides because the Spanish don't usually eat until after eight o'clock in the evening, I would probably be the first to arrive and first to leave, that's if my fan club managed to rein in its attentions.

The main focal point inside the restaurant was a large, open brick fireplace situated on the opposite wall to the kitchen. Two columns of random-sized limestone blocks supported a 15-foot oak beam mantelpiece which was decorated in the centre with a huge hand painted vase, tenderly stuffed with more anemones. A pile of logs on either side of the columns suggested that this fire saw some use in the winter, although the thought of it cracking away in its hearth right now made me feel hotter than a cod fillet on a Friday night. I tugged away at my shirt collar. While I had been glancing around, Christina had gone back to the kitchen and brought back two bottles of water. "*Sin gas, Señor?*" she asked, and gave me the prettiest of smiles. She really was quite beautiful.

"*Gracias Christina.*"

"*De nada.*"

Manolo was explaining tonight's menu to Fernando. It would be a week before the Weight Watchers products arrived, so he and Miguel had improvised with the information that he'd already received. My first meal at Manolo's read as follows:

Artichokes, anchovies and olives in sauce
Don's salad (Medium)
Spinach omelette
Vegetarian pasta tubes
Strawberries and Muscatel
Two pieces of bread
Don's sangria or two glasses of red wine

Two glasses of water were soon dispatched into my parched black hole and a third glass was being prepared for take-off when I realised that I was making a hog of myself. Fernando had only sipped through a quarter of his but hadn't cast any disapproving glares in my direction; so I sat there contemplating the liquid in my glass like Jabba the Hut presiding over the fate of Han Solo.

"That's good Donald; I was just about to suggest that you have one or two glasses of water before your meal. It'll help with the digestion, and will also make the wine last longer!"

"Sorry Fern, I'm so dry I could drink a small stream."

"Sangria or wine, old boy?" asked Fernando.

I had spotted a jug of the good stuff earlier being handed over at the bar. Masses of ice and chunks of fruit bobbed about on the surface and made the whole deal seem so tempting. "I'll go for the sangria, I think. I never cared for wine much anyway, bit of a girl's drink."

"It's made with wine!" exclaimed the indignant connoisseur.

"Yeah, but it has other stuff in it, like fruit 'n' that d'nit?" I argued in my defence.

"Yes," laughed Five-Names "and yours is a special brew, much healthier for you than girlie wine, so a wise choice my friend."

"Special Brew, now you're talking."

I had always been resistant to change, especially in the food and drink department. I liked what I knew and rarely wandered. But my old attitudes towards experimenting were going to have to take a u-turn this year, along with the rest of my antiquated habits. To me olives and anchovies were items to be left off when ordering a pizza, and I'd never even seen artichokes before. Now, all of a sudden, I was having all three for a starter. Mind you, I was so hungry at this point that iced monkey brains would have gone down a treat. I was about to find out that circumstance was full of delightful surprises.

Fernando had already eaten his first cocktail stick tapas and the look of appreciation on his face persuaded me into suck-it-and-see mode. I picked up a stick and pulled off the lot in one go. Bitter, sweet, salty, oily, nutty, intense fish, the almost medical taste of the olives, and a hot pepper sauce assaulted my tastebuds all at once. My eyes almost left their sockets as a pleasure–pain *mélange* erupted on my tongue; endorphins rushed to the alarmed nerve endings and brought sweet relief. My saliva glands went berserk and flooded my mouth, causing an involuntary smacking of the lips.

"Bloody hell!" I managed to spurt out.

"Manolo is renowned for his tapas; people flock from all over Catalonia to this restaurant, and you my friend, I'll have you running here too before long."

"Run here? I'm thinking of moving in!" I said, wiping my face on a napkin. Fernando chuckled and poured me a glass of sangria. "Here, another first for you I believe." He handed the glass to me, and I held it up to the light.

"To your very good health *señor*, God bless you," I declared and dived in.

"Of course it's only a shadow of the traditional sangria. Yours has no sugar or spirits and it has less wine than usual, but there's more fruit to bolster its body, it should be quite refreshing," said Five-Names, as I polished off the nectar and emptied the fruit pieces down my neck.

"Fuck me," I said, resting the glass on my belly.

"Can it wait 'til after dinner?" asked Fernando dryly.

I laughed. "Fix me another one of those, barman please."

"You'd better take it easy, my friend. You don't want to bloat yourself out."

"Quite right, old son, I'll pace myself." I took a piece of bread and mopped up the juices on my plate. "Fantastic grub," I announced, "Shame there are only three little sticks apiece though."

In contrast the salad platters arrived and nearly took over the table. This was only the medium-sized plate but its contents must have laid bare an allotment. A splendid rainbow of orange, yellow, red, purple and green sparkled in the candlelight and dazzled its beholder. "There're even flowers in there," I said amazed, spotting the Nasturtiums.

"It's all good for you," reassured the coach.

A chef had once told me that you should always eat with your eyes. I thought that he was just spouting clichés, but now I understood the very essence of his words. Tucking into my vegetable mountain with guarded optimism was a bloke who once referred to salad as 'rabbit food'. Yet as I munched and crunched my way through delightful new flavours and textures, complemented with an excellent salad dressing that Manolo had prepared, I became quite fond of my long furry ears, buckteeth and pink twitching nose.

The next piece of unexplored territory to present itself came in the form of a spinach omelette. Watching Popeye cartoons as a kid had really put me off the idea of eating greens from a tin, and not being a regular at the greengrocer's, I didn't know that the leaves came fresh on the stalk and cooked up like strong cabbage. The dish arrived in a flurry immediately after the salad, hot and steamy like a flat yellow moon, its heart a deep river of green. Enhanced by garlic and some seasoning, it smelled divine.

"Well, Popeye wasn't a fat fucker," I told myself, "and he always beat the shit out of Brutus, so what the heck?" It tasted delicious and I berated myself once again for not being more experimental in the past.

"It's normally served to you like a slice of cake, as the wedges are cut from an enormous omelette, but tonight Miguel has prepared us individual versions of his speciality," informed Fernando.

"Good old boy," I replied through a mouthful. I took a swig of water and looked back at the bar. The four amigos that had been watching every course raised their glasses to acknowledge approval of their investment. I winked at them. The main course arrived as swiftly as the last and consisted of tricolour penne in a chilli and tomato salsa, tossed with herbs. This too was out of this world, but I was glad for the small portion because somehow I was already nearing cut-off point and wanted to save some room for the strawberries and muscatel, plus another glass of sangria.

"They're a bit stingy with the wine aren't they?" I said, staring at my shallow glass of Muscatel that arrived with the dessert.

"It's supposed to be an accompaniment to the strawberries, not a thirst quencher, my friend," explained the highly amused Fernando.

"Oh well, down the hatch," I said and sank the lot in one go.

Five-Names just shook his head.

"You're right, it is bloody sweet." I winced.

"Like I've said before, *tranquilo*, *tranquilo*, strawberry, sip, strawberry, sip, it's much nicer that way."

"Can I have another one and start again then?"

"No you cannot!" said Teacher. "Just eat your strawberries and be grateful."

I chuckled again and popped the biggest one into my mouth. Just then an old lady entered the room and placed an armful of neatly folded tablecloths into the drawer of a large dresser. Recognising Fernando, she shuffled over for a chat. Fernando introduced me and her face lit up as though a switch had been thrown. She clasped my hand between hers and squeezed it so tightly that my blood supply was in danger of being cut off. Her endless stream of Catalan flowed straight over my head, and I could only nod and smile sweetly in return. At last she finished and bid us both '*Buenos noches*' before tottering off.

"What was all that about?" I quizzed in bewilderment.

"I don't know, never met her before in my life," said Five-Names.

I obviously looked pained.

"Only kidding, that was Christina's grandmother. She's 89-years-old and still working. She wanted to welcome you to Spain and wished you all the success in the world. She has a hundred pesetas riding on you."

Now the pain was really kicking in. I ate my strawberries brooding over my predicament and then said at length that I needed to learn Spanish. I asked Fernando if he could help me.

"I don't think I could have you fluent in a year, Don. Old dogs like us can't be taught so easily you know, but I think that I could maybe have you conversational by the time you go home."

"That'll do, mate, I feel so excluded when people are talking here, it puts me on edge, if you know what I mean?"

"I know exactly what you mean. I was in your position during my early tours in Europe, but being young and inquisitive I picked up your language quite quickly. English is the international language of sport anyway and very necessary."

"I suppose it is, but I feel so ignorant."

"What we can do is learn some basic phrases, greetings, how to ask for things and so on, and then I'll teach you some vowels and nouns, everyday stuff that you'll use. Try to learn perhaps three words a day and then use them in place of the English equivalent, we can worry about the grammar later."

"Vows and nows, what are they when they're at home?" I asked, sounding like a student.

"Don't worry about it tonight, we'll get to them later," reassured Sir, before sinking the last of his Rioja.

I picked up the tab while Fernando thanked Manolo and Christina for the heavenly meal. I would mostly be eating alone from now on and I promised a punctual return tomorrow night. We exchanged goodnights with them and then we two cowboys headed back to the ranch amid more cheering and backslapping. We stopped off on the way at Bar Hugo's for a nightcap cappuccino and reflected on the day, which we both agreed had been constructive if knackering. It had been a day of enlightenment for me, and even though my head was awash with brand new ideas and experiences, this was the first time in years that I'd felt so content without the aid of a bottle of Scotch and 40 fags!

CHAPTER TWELVE
Hot head

HOW CAN A 100 PER CENT routine over a 12-week period be so distinctly different every time? Not only each day, but every hour and every minute.

That's how the past three months have played out, yet when Fernando had laid down his initial plans for my training schedule; it looked about as riveting a prospect as standing guard over a dripping tap. His regimental roster gave me the absolute minimum of time off between each activity; admittedly it had left me totally drained, but I found that it eliminated the three main enemies of a slimmer; depression, apathy and boredom.

"Crazy golf — the amazing new workout video with Mr. Motivator". Nope I couldn't remember seeing a national multimedia campaign to support that one. Yet there it was on my exercise programme. I couldn't for the life of me see what benefits crazy golf could bring to the table. Maybe it was just one of Fernando's favourite things to do and he had slipped it onto that day's roster for personal reasons. Anyhow there we were on our bicycles three months ago heading along the beach road for the course.

Banana Avenue lived up to its reputation. It was as cool as a refrigerated cucumber and had an ideal running surface, as flat as a billiard table and somewhere between soft and firm underfoot. "You have a saying in England, Don. 'You have to take the rough with the smooth.' This is as smooth as it gets my friend."

"I can't wait for the rough," I said sarcastically.

The crazy golf course was along the front, close to the go-kart track and was the usual gaudy sterile affair. Like the ones in England, it looked hardly used and I wondered how on Earth the owners ever prospered from the thing. I reluctantly followed Fernando up to the kiosk and queued behind two ginger Liverpudlian kids who had escaped their parents but failed to protect themselves from the sun, resulting in extremely pink freckled shoulders. Five-Names bought the tickets and collected the clubs but instead of using the usual entrance, we were led like two distinguished guests through a side gate, because the turnstiles were only made for the more nimble among us.

First obstacle up was a poor replica of the Tower of London. It took me eight goes to breach the portcullis, much to the amusement of my coach who was definitely a shark; his hole-in-ones were too much of a coincidence. By the end of the round I felt quite exhausted, but without having overexerted myself or incurring much pain. "You see, you will use muscles that you have forgotten about. Trust an old master," said Fernando.

"Yes master," I said, impersonating David Carradine in Kung Fu.

We visited the pool three times a day now and the improvements I had made from my first aquatic debacle were nothing less than astounding. I could easily complete 30 lengths of front crawl and had become an expert in the ancient art of underwater handstands, yet I was still having problems with the old diving in. Fernando presumed that I was attempting an entry in the Guinness Book of Records for the most-performed belly flops in a summer season. The energy that I used climbing in and out of the pool must have burnt up a million calories, but at least now I could dive in without most of the water diving out! Not only was I getting used to the fact that water was actually good for your insides, but I also looked forward with eager anticipation to being immersed in the stuff.

Yet another challenge I had set myself was to be able to swim one mile (or 134 lengths of the pool to be precise) by the time I left Spain. I had cracked 30 lengths, so it was all downhill from then on. Water aerobics had now become a major feature of my exercise programme and as much as Anna wanted to assist in my progress, she felt it best that a professional should coach me. I was promptly enrolled for a class held three times a week in the public pool at Malgrat, where I was to be instructed in the very fine arts of aqua-combat, aqua-jogging, aqua-fitness and dance. My teacher was a rather buoyant 50-something woman from Orpington called Susan, who liked to be decked out in flower-spangled swimming caps and water-resistant war paint. My initial reluctance to attend these classes manifested itself in a typical macho stance, "I'm not gonna prance about in the pool with a bunch of tarts!" It masked a deep underlying fear of exposing my hideousness to the rest of humanity and the embarrassment of a fully-grown man bobbing up and down like a cork in the shallow end. Fernando recognised my severe lack in confidence but insisted that I went, so I duly obeyed my boss. The first week of sessions were excruciating and I retreated further into my shell with every visit.

Fortune delivered me from this 'fate worse than the death' during my second week of attendance, by sending two new gentlemen into the fold. Suddenly, the classes took on a new life. Although these new recruits hardly suffered from the same weight problem as yours truly, they had their own agenda for keeping in shape. Through the translation services of her husband, Anna had informed me beforehand of their imminent arrival, and although Fernando usually recited every conversation word for word, I had the impression I was being kept suspiciously out of a loop. The grins on their faces suggested there was a secret they weren't sharing with me. "You'll see," said Anna, with her tongue firmly in her cheek.

It was at the start of our third lesson that week when a shrill echo shattered the humid stillness of the pool and reverberated off the tiled walls.

"Cooeee."

All eyes shifted from our instructor and focused on two of the most camp men that you are ever likely to meet. Ronnie and Robert fluttered in like paper butterflies on a wire, outrageously attired in costumes that spoke volumes about their lifestyle. Catalonia's most flamboyant and brazen drag queens had entered stage left and stolen the show, as ever, to immediate acknowledgment. Their reason for joining the class was straightforward: their dresses were becoming a bit too tight — a sound enough reason for any man.

Ronnie and Robert proceeded to offer extensive but obviously shallow apologies for their lateness, but Susan looked unimpressed. With dramatic flair, Robert tested the water with one toe, letting out a girly scream as if it were freezing cold, which it wasn't of course. It quickly became evident that these two characters rarely left the stage. Everybody in the pool found their antics hilarious, but what tickled me more than anything was their bathing gear. Robert, the elder of the pair, was kitted out in a Victorian one-piece swimsuit of lime green and purple hoops that greatly emphasized his undercarriage and spare tyres. If he had walked out of a bathing machine on Brighton beach a hundred years ago, he would have instantly been given a right slap! Ronnie had other ideas. Known locally as the Shirley Bassey of the Costa Brava and blessed with a pair of legs that would have been the envy of glamour models, he had opted for a fluorescent pink Lycra thong with a matching rubber swim hat that sprouted blue and yellow daisies, and blatantly took the piss out of Susan's.

If I was the epitome of shyness in this class then these two boys reigned supreme at the opposite end of the scale. There wasn't a single lesson when their antics and colourful ways didn't have me curling up with laughter, but more importantly, I no longer felt embarrassed at performing aerobics. When you've got the likes of Shirley Bassey and Dame Edna Everage to entertain the crowd, no-one is going to take a blind bit of notice of the fat git struggling in the corner! In time, I found that the classes taught me how to perform exercises that I couldn't have possibly attempted on dry land without rupturing something. More than that, water aerobics showed me that being graceful was nothing to do with being effeminate; in fact, it can build strength and character, two forces that I would later depend on. Ironically last summer I had stubbornly rejected my children's pleas for a swimming pool to be built in the garden because I had considered it a waste of money. Now, I earnestly adopted a politician's resolve to deliver a complete u-turn on that mandate and arrange for a pool to be constructed as soon as possible.

•• ▼ ••

In time, Fernando and I wholly conquered the crazy golf course and were able to complete a full round of hole-in-ones, which meant we were ready to try our hand at the proper game. Fernando had booked us in to an exclusive course in the hills behind Calella for Saturday morning and I was keen to get up there. We were going to start cautiously with just nine holes for the time being, as it was going to be a stark contrast to putting balls through castle gates and clown's mouths and we wanted to find out if it suited our needs. I had never pounded the greens before while Fernando had not played in years, so he had the slight advantage; both of us would undoubtedly become the annoying beginners that jam up traffic on the fairway, but we all have to wear L-plates at some point in our lives. Only one tradition was going to be broken at this golf club — we wouldn't be visiting the 19th hole!

•• ▼ ••

Cycling had become my favourite form of exercise. For me it represented a kind of escapism and let me view the course from a different perspective and level. As planned, Fernando and I had started off with just two-mile stretches at a time, one day in the direction of

Calella and the next towards Pineda. We then increased the distance by half a mile each day until we had covered half of the course from each direction. For the following two weeks the routine was changed and we cycled the whole 13-and-a-quarter miles each day, excluding the Eiger. Then we went back to riding half the course, this time including the Eiger but only as pedestrians.

Our first ascent of the hill took its toll. It was 75° F in the shade and I had to stop 15 times on the way up. Eventually I stood at its peak triumphant, like Sir Edmund Hillary looking down on his world, but as I was standing there, feeling glorious a deep depression suddenly engulfed me. I felt drowned, as if someone had lifted the lid of my skull and poured molten graphite into my empty head. "How long did it take me to climb this fucker?" I moaned out loud. "I'm never gonna do this!" Fernando was quick to stamp out my negative downturn with the power of positive thinking and some logic. The Earth's tectonic plates weren't about to shift and rearrange the Spanish landscape into a flat plane, so we would approach the situation with methodical reason and discipline; it was simply going to take time.

During week 12, Fernando had taken me to a private hospital in Gerona for a medical and stress test. Roberto, his son-in-law, had recommended the visit and arranged the appointment. It involved me being wired up to various monitors while I walked on a treadmill; the treadmill wished I hadn't! Surprisingly, I passed the test with flying colours, much to the disbelief of the doctor after learning about my former lifestyle and having seen the anti-svelte on the scales. "¡*Asombroso!*" was all that he could say: I was lucky to be alive.

My sixth and seventh weigh-ins yielded duplicate results, a loss of four pounds in each case. Marion and Fernando were both pleased with these readings, but Mr Impatient wasn't and my disappointment showed. "Is that all?" I groaned, looming over the digital readout between my toes. "I must have shat out a four-pounder this morning!"

"It's excellent for one week my friend. You must learn a little serenity," said Five-Names.

"Time's shifting at a pace, old mate, and I'm still a fat bastard!"

"Well I wouldn't put it like that. You're ahead of target with your weight loss, look at how much you have lost already and think of how much healthier you are without all that strain on your heart!"

"Yeah, but I don't feel any lighter."

"You will my friend, you will." Unbeknown to me, Fernando had a little plan up his sleeve and quietly left the *ático* to put things into action. Instead of going home, he slipped out of the apartment block and headed up to Josep's fruit stall where he arranged for three and a half stone of fruit and vegetables to be collected in a large box the following afternoon.

The following day, Anna politely asked me to collect some groceries from Josep for her and I was happy to oblige. Never again would I whinge about not losing enough weight; from now on I would celebrate every ounce discarded. That quarter of a mile walk back from the fruit stall was the perfect shock tactic to strike home just how far I had come. Confronting my enemy face to face by having to carry the equivalent of my own lost bodyweight in fresh fruit and veg was like having a bullet up the backside. By the end of the twelfth week I had a total weight loss of four stone and eight pounds and was feeling great.

WEIGHT CHART

Starting weight: 26 st. 0lb

Week
- 1. - 24 st. 11lb 8oz
- 2. - 24 st. 5lb
- 3. - 24 st. 1lb 8oz
- 4. - 23 st. 10lb 8oz
- 5. - 23 st. 6lb
- 6. - 23 st. 2lb
- 7. - 22 st. 12lb
- 8. - 22 st. 7lb
- 9. - 22 st. 2lb 8oz
- 10. - 21 st. 13lb
- 11. - 21 st. 9lb
- 12. - 21 st. 6lb

Total loss 4 st. 8lb

A rousing dawn chorus awoke me from another blissful sleep. I slid into consciousness, still snug under the duvet and guarded against the first autumn chill that came creeping through the open French doors.

Sunlight bounced off the terrace floor like polished gold and beckoned me outside to witness yet another beautiful sunrise.

Slipping into my dressing gown I shuffled out on to the terrace where I was bedazzled by an awesome spectacle. It had rained in the early hours of morning, just a light sprinkling from the edge of a rather low weather system that dominated the south western sky. An immense blue-grey storm cloud occupied 50 per cent of the firmament, all ominous and foreboding while, in the other half, bright sunlight reigned supreme. The sun's long arms reached out and pierced water droplets falling towards the sea, creating a magnificent double rainbow in full arc. It caught my breath and I was held enthralled while the wind did a shrivel job on my landing gear. "What a beautiful sight," I murmured, "two pots of gold!"

After five minutes of contemplation, my thoughts turned to the road conditions. It was Wednesday 29th of September and I would be attempting to cycle the course in less than an hour and a half today. I had long since worked out the firmest least-bumpiest route along the sandy beach road, but when rain mixes with that stuff it clogs up your tyres and slows you down to a near standstill — all very strength-sapping. Luckily the rain had only been a light misting and wouldn't have penetrated much below the sand's surface. This was the first day of my 13th week; last week, I had managed to drop a further three pounds, which now made me an almost ballerina-like 21 stone and 6 pounds. Fernando and Anna had gone to Barcelona to complete a business deal and would be staying with Francisco overnight. The mere mention of a business deal got my juices flowing about the thrill of chasing a few quid. My mind got to wondering about my own business back home, but I firmly shook those ideas off and reminded myself that today, I was in charge. I felt like a kid who'd been let off the reins for the first time. Even though Fernando's pearls of wisdom still repeated in my head, accompanied by the eternal '*tranquilo*', they were faint words for the obsessive. We both understood the psychological significance of breaking the hour-and-a-half barrier on the pushbike today; the inspiration would give me more motivation to achieve the same time on foot. Yesterday's attempt was just over the marker (1:33:28 to be precise), so an extra push today would see me through. The weather was on my side, cool with no wind; the morning drizzle was nothing more than a superficial encumbrance. The only downside was that my support and encouragement had gone south and I would have to attempt this one alone. The pangs of solitude had been all too evident in the swimming pool at 8:15 a.m. where I felt like a whale calf that had been separated from its mother and was wallowing alone in the mid-Atlantic — just a tad insecure.

On the bike and 30 seconds into the course, I was racing along the beach road, where my tyres were picking up some sand, but not enough to worry me. My frame of mind was good and I was flying along at warp-factor five. At No-Cart Corner my stopwatch read 0:05:10 I had completed the first mile in record time. The second was not as spectacular, but still a record at 0:05:32. At this rate I could possibly knock off 15 minutes from my previous best. Not surprisingly *'tranquilo'* had fallen *silencioso* in my ears, crowded out by excitement and enthusiasm. I was so intent on achieving the hour and a half, that all logic had been abandoned. Managing to ride for 200 yards uphill from out of the underpass before stopping to walk the Eiger, I made a snap decision to take only four rest stops instead of the usual five. This irrational decision was a foolhardy choice and one that I would surely regret later, but one less stop gained me more time and at the three-mile marker the clock read just 0:20:40.

"Brilliant!" I said to myself proudly. "Now let's really hammer it downhill to Papa's then take another rest". Judging by the amount of sand on the road up here, it must have rained a lot harder than it had in Pineda. The smell of damp earth blended beautifully with olive wood and the last of the summer strawberries, and together they invigorated my senses. Speeding past La Granja like a jet-propelled bison, I considered my options down through the Kenyan bush trail. I knew this course so well now that I had three choices: the left-hand side, which was the most frequently washed, was smoother but took you dangerously close to a savage thorn bush that took great pleasure in maiming you for life; the centre path was good but you had to negotiate several deep-rutted crossovers that could easily jar you off the bike; or the right-hand side, which was the driest but had huge rocks jutting out, such that it couldn't be taken at speed. I plumped to go left — bad move!

As soon as my tyres left the concrete surface and hit dirt I knew that I was in trouble. The rain had made deep gullies in the soft soil. Both sets of wheels locked into one gully such that I couldn't escape. The ground took me where it wanted to and the bike began to shake violently. I panicked and tried in vain to slow the thing down by applying the brakes as well as scraping one foot on the ground, but it was hopeless because the sand was too wet. This capricious canyon, viciously carved overnight, was suddenly brought to an abrupt end by way of a hefty boulder that was only partly visible in the mud. The Peugeot came to an unexpected stop; I didn't and in an instant found myself flat on my back, having somehow performed a full somersault without a single recollection of its execution. It was a baffling event, as though a fragment of my life had been edited out and thrown to the cutting-room floor; there was no conscious memory of time between coming off the bike and hitting the deck.

With the wind knocked out of my sails and nothing but bewilderment in my mind, I took time to right myself. I checked for damage — nothing broken, just a sore back, grazed shins and cut hands. It's funny what goes through your mind immediately after a life-threatening accident. All I could think about was that I was wasting precious time on the ground and should be back on the road in order to make the hour-and-a-half deadline. Rolling onto all fours with the blood pounding in my temples, I shakily stood up only to find that my chariot had come out of the crash in a worst state than me. Its front wheel now boasted a classy V-shape and both forks were sporting new elbows, a classic entry for a modern art exhibition but not very useful as a form of transport. "Bollocks" I spluttered vehemently, and picked the old girl up from her sorry resting place.

Attempting to push the bike along using its back wheel proved to be impossible, so I resigned myself to abandoning my no-longer-so trusty steed on the side of the road for retrieval later on and made my way to Papa's, keeping my balance on wobbly legs and feeling a complete plonker. A little way along I felt what I imagined to be a fly landing on my head and instinctively reached up to brush it away. It was then that I discovered my injuries to be more serious than I had first thought. My hand came down covered in blood and a further cautious inspection revealed two large gashes, each about an inch long, on the top of my bonce where I must have hit a rock. Right on cue, a gnawing, stinging pain suddenly made it self apparent, a violent headache started to brew and I began to panic. A thick stream of blood trickled down over my forehead and broke across the bridge of my nose; secondary rivulets were snaking their way past my ears and down my clammy neck towards my shoulders. I had nothing to hand to stem the flow, so I resorted to pulling off my t-shirt and converting it into a dressing. Placing this on my wounds helped a little and I quickened my pace, conscious that there was now a degree of urgency for getting medical help. I hoped that the medical centre would be open and could quickly patch me up, but when I finally arrived there, I was devastated to find that it was closed for the day.

Heads were turning my way in the street, as the sight of me started to arouse some rubbernecking. My own fear for my injuries deepened. I crossed the road to Papa's and tried the door, only to find that it too was locked. I hadn't actually spoken to John since my first introduction to him some time ago, just the occasional nod or wave as I trundled past on the bike. As yet I hadn't taken advantage of his offer of hospitality, but right now it was to be sorely tested. My heart waned at the thought of my pathetic helplessness, as I tapped on his door. I was spiralling into oblivion fast, but suddenly perked up at the sound of keys being turned in the lock. It was John himself who opened the door to a wretched desperado, an unforgettable sight that he would frequently recount to his friends in the following weeks. It felt as though I'd lost about a pint of blood by now; it had coated itself over my upper body and made me look like a battle-crazed berserker. The expression on John's face conveyed a thousand exclamations, but he was stunned into silence. "Sorry mate, I've come off me bike," I whined feebly.

"You look like you've come second in a bullfight. Come inside quick."

He took my arm and ushered me to a table, shouting something in Spanish to the two lads behind the bar. They both looked shocked at the sight of me but in seconds one of them had brought over a couple of tea towels and some water. John removed my makeshift bandage and immediately reactivated a fresh stream of blood. "A bit nasty this," he said, leaning over the wounds and then hastily putting a clean tea towel over them. Shouting something else in Spanish, he wet a towel and cleared the caked-on blood from around my eyes, while the second man brought over a set of car keys.

"Come on mate, we're off".

"Where're we going?"

"To the hospital, old son, it's not far."

The trip to the hospital did indeed take just two minutes and blew a few cobwebs out of the cook's old Citroen; it hadn't touched 50 miles an hour for a long time. Hobbling into the casualty department, I felt quite faint, probably from so much blood loss, but I was still mindful enough to be impressed by the pristine condition of the A&E department and how quickly I received medical attention. In England I could have taken a numbered ticket, gone home, had a bath, eaten my dinner, watched Emmerdale, gone back to the hospital and still had a four-hour wait!

The young doctor spoke reasonable English and asked me about the accident, while examining my wounds. In particular, he wanted to know if I had lost consciousness at any point. There was a tap at the door and in walked John, who had realised that I might have needed some help with the language. He spoke extensively to the doctor in Spanish who once again tried to ascertain whether his patient had passed out during the fall. To be honest, I was feeling that I might pass out right then and there, and that a large whisky would be the only thing to pull me round. The doctor then explained to John the procedure that he was going to take. It would involve an x-ray followed by three or four stitches on each of the cuts. Providing that the x-rays were ok and that I was feeling fine, he would then let me go home. John translated for me and I in turn confirmed to the doctor that everything was clear. The doctor put a hand on my shoulder and said something in Spanish. The nurse and John both laughed.

"What was all that about?" I asked.

"He said that next time you want go headbutting rocks you'd better wear a safety helmet".

"'E's right there!" I said, thinking of Harold's last words back in the cycle shop.

After the X-rays, my big lump was wheeled back into the examining room and placed next to a table carrying all manner of horrific-looking implements. The nurse came up behind me and pulled my head back into her stomach; she smelt of fresh linen and rose water, which made me think of my aunt Sheila back home and it soothed me. The next thing I heard was the sound of an electric razor, and then watched in dismay as thick chunks of black hair tumbled to the floor. "I was growing that," I joked.

There was no reply. She cleaned the wounds with an ice-cold liquid that stung like a motherfucker, and then proceeded to stitch me up. Each needle thrust through raw nerve endings and severed flesh; it sent jets of pain hurtling all over my face, making me feel nauseous and giddy once again. I must have turned as white as her tunic as she stopped halfway through to give me a glass of water. She could see that pain was not my forte.

Three hours after arriving at hospital I got the all-clear from the doctor. John had offered to wait, but I assured him that I would be fine and could get a taxi back to the apartment. I told him where I had left the bike and he kindly insisted on retrieving the wreck before someone else did. He also offered to call Fernando, but I said that I wanted to explain and apologise to my mentor in person. I had not taken his advice to take things easy and as a result, I had ended up in Casualty; my defiance could have jeopardized everything!

All the way home from the hospital, the taxi driver kept sneaking a look at his oddball passenger. It was comic enough to have a 20 odd stone bloke testing your suspension, but to have him shirtless, splattered with blood, with an erratically shaven head complete with fresh stitches sewn into his scalp like cranium zippers, was not an everyday occurrence. Gingerly touching my bald patch became something of an obsession for me; it was such a dramatic contrast to my remaining hair. I had caught glimpses of my reflection in the side window of the taxi, but nothing prepared me for the sight I was about to see in the bathroom mirror. My bonce resembled a number-eight pool ball, with the white circles in closer proximity to one another. I looked ridiculous and suddenly felt acutely embarrassed; so many people must have pissed themselves at the sight of me between here and the hospital. There was only one solution: to shave the whole lot off! I had already invested in a pair of scissors to cut out those bloody annoying itchy labels that populate every new garment, now they were going to see some proper action. I was glad that the nurse had shaved off so much hair around the cuts; the last thing I wanted was to pull the stitches out with a cackhanded slip of the scissors.

Cutting through matted dried blooded hair was interesting, something akin to chomping through corrugated cardboard with curling tongs. I gradually managed to bring it down to a shaveable length, albeit hacked and chopped, and found that I resembled an unfortunate vagabond about to be tarred and feathered. Taking a hot, wet flannel to my scalp, I dampened the skin, then applied shaving foam, selected a fresh Gillette disposable and got stuck in. When I had finished shaving I took the flannel and wiped off the excess foam, revealing a few stubborn whiskers that I had missed on the first sweep. I attacked the survivors with a second wave and voila there I was, a bonehead. I gazed inquisitively at the person staring back at me in the mirror. My first thoughts were of a novelty Humpty Dumpty eggcup holding a white hardboiled egg. My face had become relatively tanned, but my scalp had been protected until now by thick black hair. It hadn't been exposed to the evils of the ultraviolet and remained a ghostly English white. I could only laugh at the comical state I was in. The person staring back at me definitely wasn't the person looking out of these eyes. "Who are you?" I asked my reflection. Then I saw something else, my old self, my younger self emerging from the years of abuse. I stared intently: four and a half stone had come off the old fellow and now for the first time since the programme had begun, I could see a difference. It started to spook me, a glimpse of what I was aiming for, of what I was to become after I had shed 12 stone — the man that Ann had fallen in love with.

The schedule for today was in tatters; I really didn't fancy a swim, but felt that I needed to justify the time that had been wasted in hospital. I sat down to ponder while drinking half a litre of isotonic drink. Fernando had been planning to introduce some short walks along the beach road into the programme. It was only 6:30 in the evening and the temperature was a pleasant 65° F, perfect for a walk, so I wandered into the bedroom to put on my knee supports and a fresh tracksuit. My old knee supports were quite loose now, which either indicated a reduction in leg mass, or a stretch in the supports fabric, either way I pulled a new pair from out of a drawer. These felt much more secure.

Apart from a few joggers there was nobody about. It really was a fine evening for taking a stroll. The day's earlier events seemed almost dreamlike and I was lulled into a very mellow mood. At No-Cart Corner I was on the point of turning around to head home again, when not 20 yards further on a runner in his early twenties overtook me. I estimated him to be around 6 foot tall, 14 stone and in excellent shape. He sped past me at about nine miles per hour and in no time had put some distance between us. It made me reflect about all that I still had to achieve and I felt another depression looming. At that moment a sudden wild surge whipped through my veins and to my surprise I took off. For the first time since Don Simmons was 12-years-old, he was running! The blood throbbed painfully in the cuts in my head, my knee cartilage crunched like hazelnuts under a sledgehammer and the sand beneath my feet grumbled at the giant's approach. Alright, so it was only 30 yards that I ran, just to the next telegraph pole, but it was worth it. What a magnificent feeling, even though I was gasping for breath and my heartbeat thundered in my ears. I could run, I could sprint for 30 yards, and still live to talk about it.

I didn't recall passing out, but the small crowd that had gathered around my crumpled torso on the sand assured me that I must have. A couple of lads helped me to my feet while I regained some semblance of balance. I brushed myself down without a word and gathered as much dignity as I could muster. Taking a deep breath and without a word, I pointed towards the empty sky. The crowd followed my finger in wonderment. With their attention diverted I turned and walked away, leaving a rather puzzled group of individuals staring into space.

The next day after breakfast, I drove the Range Rover up to Papa's to retrieve my mangled machine. John was out but his two employees were there. They looked surprised to see their crash victim, perhaps because they had recovered the Peugeot and felt that I was lucky to be standing, or maybe they were shocked at the sight of my chrome dome. Some pidgin Spanglish was exchanged and I thanked them for their assistance the day before. One of them helped to load the bike into the car and I drove home again. The bike and I stood in the coolness of the dimly lit underground carport, two companions both bashed up and forlorn. I was wondering what to do next and the bike was pleading miserably to be taken back to Stan and Harold's shop, when suddenly a Mercedes swung into view and pulled up beside us. The car window lowered, and on seeing the state of us, Anna put her hand to her mouth and gasped. "My God, what has he done?"

"Looks like you have visited the barber shop and got the wrong side of his razor," replied Fernando wryly, shaking his disappointed head.

I didn't know quite how to reply so I just shrugged with a stupid look on my face. Once upstairs and sat around the swimming pool sipping Anna's homemade iced tea I unreeled the disapointing story, apologising profusely for messing up Five-Names' strategy.

"Do not beat yourself up any more, my friend. Accidents will happen. The main thing is that you are not too badly hurt," said Fernando generously. "Tell me, how do you feel about getting back on the bike?" he asked.

"As long as she's had no other bloke in-between, I'm up for it."

"What?"

"Yes, I'm fine with that. No fear whatsoever."

"Oh good," he said, still trying to work out the meaning of my one-liner. "Then we must see about getting her repaired, I know just the place. This afternoon I think we should see about making that part of the course safer. We'll go over to the dirt track and take a look at the spot, and then I'll call someone who can help."

"Ok" I said, leaning back into my sun lounger. Fernando was not about to let me dwell on my misfortune.

"I want to change your training programme for the next two weeks, but it's nothing to do with your accident," he quickly added. "I just want to introduce something new. In four or five weeks' time you should have beaten the 20 stone barrier and will be able in my opinion to take up some light jogging."

"Is that the same as regular jogging only with fewer calories?" I joked.

Fernando cleared his throat and said "Just so," before carrying on. "I think it best that we warm you up a little by starting the two-mile walks that we've talked about." I cringed inside, not wanting to let on that I had already started that strategy and had disobeyed yet another order in the process — let alone revealing that I had even run a little. I kept schtum and added a few more grey hairs to my chest.

"A couple of miles twice a day, I'll draw up a schedule tonight."

It sounded like a prescription and a bitter pill at that, twice a day! "Sounds good to me," I lied.

The Kenyan dirt track looked different in the bright sunshine of another day, its lethal aspect now eroded by the wind. There was no evidence of subterfuge or conspiracy from the spiteful rocks that had so expertly ambushed me the day before, just a bumpy road. Fernando surveyed the scene and then reached for his mobile phone. After a lengthy discussion with an invisible peer, he turned to me and smiled.

"I have spoken to a friend at the *Consejo Municipal* and he is going to send a machine over to level the ground here. We shouldn't have any more problems. We were lucky, because the *Consejo* would not normally consider spending any amount of money on a road such as this, but a favour for a favour goes a long way." I wondered what sort of favour Fernando was doing for his amigo, but shelved it. Once again, I was just grateful to benefit from another of Five-Names handy 'friends'.

On our way home we called in at John's place to thank him personally for all he had done. He assured us that it was a small thing and to think nothing of it. While seated at the bar I cast my eyes lovingly along the glittering shelves of siren-like spirits that were urging me to release them. Worse still, at the beer taps was a medley of British and European brand names all polished and welcoming. Right now I could rip the arse out of a barrel of beer and throw the lot down my neck in one swallow. My fingers gripped a bar towel, wringing it tightly with frustration.

"Like a drink while you're here?" asked the owner of the bar.

"I'd wrestle Big Daddy for one!" I blurted out.

"I thought you were Big Daddy," retorted John. "Hold tight, I'll be back in a mo." Five minutes later he was back with two steaming hot cups of PG Tips. It wasn't what I'd been salivating over and I had mixed feelings — gutted and pleased — about accepting it. Fernando had been more than generous with my daily intake of alcohol and I really shouldn't take the piss.

One o'clock and the long lunch break was still in progress. We had an hour to kill before the cycle shop opened, so Fernando suggested a stroll along the beach.

"According to a news report I saw in Barcelona this has been one of the hottest Septembers on record."

"I can believe that, I'm melting over 'ere!" I replied. The beaches that were once teeming with sun-worshippers at various stages of radiation sickness were now almost vacant apart from some latecomers at the bargain end of the bucket. We had only been walking along for a few minutes when I reacted violently to the heat and clasped both hands over my polished skull. "Corr, me 'ead's on fire!" I yelped.

"I'm not surprised, my friend. Haven't you put any protection at all on it?"

"How's a condom gonna fit over this?" I quipped.

"Spanish condoms are larger by necessity my friend, but you have a point. Here I have something, how do you say, right up your alley?"

"Keep away from my alley, mate, and just stick something on me 'ead."

With that Fernando produced a white cotton handkerchief from his pocket, tied a knot in each corner and perched it expertly on top of my burning dome. "Comfy?" he inquired.

"Perfect." I replied.

"Typically English," he said.

"What do you mean?" I said, somewhat disingenuously.

"Your *sombrero*, it's an English *sombrero*," said Fernando brimming with pride at his improvisation.

CHAPTER THIRTEEN
Walk before I can walk

EVERYBODY FORBADE ME AND I KNEW THE RISKS, but I couldn't wait any longer. A milestone on my treacherous journey was threatening and I wanted to pass it sooner than I should. It was Wednesday 27th of October; the summer hordes had shuffled back into mundane drudgery, the temperature had become more accommodating and I had stepped triumphantly into a smaller size of track suit — extra large.

I bubbled with excitement and anticipation, irrepressibly animated because last night I had got my own way and had persuaded Fernando to bring forward the date of my first walk around the entire course. My Tuesday night weigh-in had shown me to be down to 20 st. 2 lbs, only 2 pounds away from the benchmark that Fernando, Terry and his pals Phil and Steve had insisted on. Surely the equivalent of a bag of sugar wouldn't make that much difference? Reluctantly and partly because of the hunger pangs gnawing at his insides, Fernando had agreed to let me walk the course today. Although deep down he knew it wasn't the right move and that a disappointment was heading my way, he also knew that Calella's adopted son was losing weight too rapidly. We were quite a few pounds over target, which could prove to be dangerous for my health and disastrous for the game plan. This Englishman was getting over ambitious, increasing his exercise programme and eating less than he should. Fernando knew that he had to put me back on track or it would all end in tears, but first, some Catalonian shock treatment was in order.

All that I could think about was time, the time it would take me to crawl around the thirteen and a half miles. Fernando had chastised me saying that there was no need for heroics; how long it took was not an objective right now, just a precedent for improvement. Completing the thing would be our kudos, then every following two weeks we would hope to do better. I accepted that Fernando would set the pace and I respected my mentor's reasons for holding back the reins. As with the swimming and cycling, he had disciplined methods and I had mostly adhered to them. Every attempt at the course would begin at 9:30 in the morning for two reasons. First, it mirrored the Wycombe start time and secondly, most of the morning traffic along the N11 would have found its destination by then. A good thing because after 30 years of filling my lungs with cancer, the last thing that I wanted to do was to top them up with carbon monoxide.

Breakfast had been a simple affair; a bowl of cornflakes boosted with a banana and three cups of black coffee, which only served to heighten my jumpiness. I had been up since six o'clock and had had two turnouts already; a third one was imminent and it was only half-past seven. Patience had never been my virtue and if this was a prelude to pre-race nerves, what was I going to be like on race day? I would be in need of my own septic tank! My anxiety seemed to come from a fixation about the importance of having a worst-time scenario on which to build. A trait from my gambling days was that you needed to know the odds in order to realise your chances. I put more importance on this than Fernando did, who simply regarded the walk as part of the training programme.

As it was course day I was exempt from all other exercise, which was a relief because I didn't relish the fact that I might leave a bobber in my wake in the pool.

The heavy arm on the kitchen clock sank to the bottom of the dial, I clenched my buttocks and minced off to the bathroom — I was going to have a brontosaurus by the end of the day.

After showering, I unpacked a brand new set of Ron Hill's, laid them out on the bed and smiled. There's something quite magical about new clothes; the way they smell, the way they feel, they're a real confidence booster. You almost feel like a catalogue model parading down the street, imagining that passers-by are thinking, "Wow, look at him! There goes a trendy chap." Only in my case the word 'handicap' was a more apt description. I reached the front gate about 9:10; after that first reprimand, I had learnt the importance of timeliness when dealing with Fernando and was typically way too early. There was nobody in sight. It was a beautiful autumn day, bright, fresh and still warm enough for a pair of shorts. A heady smell of wet conifer scented the air, a gift from the previous evening's downpour. Not wishing to linger for a minute, I trundled over and crouched down at the poolside to run my hand through the water and was met with a welcome surprise. It was warm for the first time this season; the heating system had been switched on for the winter. I looked forward to testing it out later as some of the morning dips had been quite cold recently. I had really had to motivate myself to take the first plunge, but was always vindicated later by the feel-good factor of achievement. I wondered if I would feel the same way after today's proceedings.

Returning to the front gate, I was greeted by Fernando who was coming in from the street, followed at a short distance by Anna and Circola who was tension-testing her lead to new standards. Anna's other hand gripped a small rucksack.

"Morning Don, how are you feeling?" Five-Names enquired.

"Fine thank you Fernando."

"I'll just put this in the bin then I'll be with you." I watched with some disdain as Fernando dispatched a fresh warm dog egg into the waste bin.

"*Buenos dias*, Don," said Anna, finally reaching the gate slightly out of breath.

"*Buenos dias*, Anna," I replied, smiling to compensate for my poor Spanish vocabulary.

"*¿Este día es importante?*"

"Yes, I mean *Si, si*," I said, half guessing what she had meant.

Well aware of my pitiful command of Spanish she always made the effort to keep it simple. "*Tranquilo, tranquilo*," she implored, with exaggerated concern.

"*Si, si*," I said again.

She knew the madness of this morning's meander and had come to realise that I always tried to run before I could walk. Today, though, I was surpassing myself, trying to walk before I could walk! Somebody was shouting abuse from the right. We turned to see José and his wife Maria coming towards us. Fernando translated for the ignorant.

"He said that he'd love to come with us, but he's already done 13 miles around the garden this morning!"

"Fuck off" I whispered, with a broad grin in his direction.

Maria made a gesture to say ignore him and then asked if I was ok.

"*Si. delgado y contento*," I said somewhat disjointedly.

"*¡Bravo! Su español está mejorando*," she said, putting her hands together in approval.

"*Si, si*," I replied, finding myself stumped once again.

She patted me on the shoulder and melted me with sincerity. "*Tranquilo*," she advised.

"We have ten minutes to go, Don. I think that we should do some warm-up exercises to get the blood flowing," said Fernando.

"I'm warm enough, Fernando!"

"You're a hothead alright!" he replied, with some truth in his quip.

"Now stretch out those arms to the side and do tiny windmills, Quixote, and increase them slowly. I don't want you taking off!"

"Likely!" I barked back.

The supporters on the sideline watched and chatted with fascination as the two amigos bent, stretched and limbered up until it was time to go. Although I felt more relaxed now, my pre-walk nerves were still inflicting intestinal mayhem. I wondered again how it was, after so many years of being on the frontline of so many big deals involving thousands of pounds, that a simple thing like walking a few miles could get me so wound up. The raw facts were in front of me: I was facing an opponent that I might not be able to overcome, or even contend with, and coming second place just wasn't part of my vocabulary. I had built from scratch one of the largest and most highly respected second hand motor vehicle businesses in Europe, by overcoming adversity, but this time I may have bitten off more than I could chew. It was universally agreed that this challenge was bordering on the impossible; today's walk was going to put achievability into perspective and the truth would most definitely out.

A sudden northerly gust produced a tiny little dust devil that twisted and squirmed in the gateway for a while until it lost momentum and faded to nothing. "Time to go!" said Fernando, looking at his watch once more. We synchronised our timepieces and set off at a slug's pace. As the well-wishers cheered and offered words of encouragement, us boys were soon down at the beach road and turning right. My nerves had all but vanished now and in true Simmons style I was raring to go. Fernando had different plans. As agreed the coach would set the pace and we walked the first mile as if we were out for a Sunday stroll. We even stopped a couple of times to chat to people in the street, which niggled me something rotten. Not wanting to undermine my trainer, I curbed my frustration.

We rounded No-Cart Corner and waved to Bernardo the mechanic at the track, who was wiping his hands on an oily cloth and chewing on a cheroot at the garage door. Through *en paseo por la sombra*, I got my first glimpse of autumn as a golden mulberry leaf swayed gently to Earth in front of my face and landed silently at my feet. It sent a sharp chill down my spine and reminded me of home.

"We'll be knee-deep in these boys before long," I said.

"Fortunately for us the street sweepers do an admirable task around here, but occasionally a few leaves make their way to the shore. The crabs use them as surfboards until they get too waterlogged," replied Fernando, with a straight face.

I did a double-take before I realised the leg-pull and both of us chuckled. At the foot of the hill a wave of dread washed over me and my heart sank a little into my stomach. I had walked the Eiger before but had always cycled up to it, got off my bike and leant on the handlebars all the way to the top before turning around and freewheeling back down at breakneck speed, dashing through the underpass like a bullet through a barrel, the wind revitalizing my soul.

So far I had managed two miles quite comfortably, but these next two were going to test me. Just before the Snake we had to stop. I was suffering from double vision, and venting water like the rose of a watering can — even my tongue was sweating — and I panted like a big cat on the plains of the Serengeti under the midday sun.

"We'll take five, my friend. Here, have some water," offered Fernando, pulling a bottle from his rucksack. I grabbed the bottle and gorged myself. "*Tranquilo*, Don, you'll only give yourself stomach cramps."

Severely reprimanded, I obeyed at once and took on the appearance of a wild hamster taking morning dew from a ripened raspberry. The first shadow of doubt grazed my troubled mind and I began to question my ability to complete the rest of the course. "I've got to own up to it, Fernando; I don't think that I am quite ready for this yet. You were right; we should only have attempted half the course."

Fernando hadn't finished with the treatment yet so he pumped me with enthusiasm. "Did you know that Zulu warriors would think nothing of running 50 miles before fighting a battle?"

"Yeah, but I'm not enhanced by hallucinogenic mushrooms and the promise of a blissful afterlife am I," I wheezed.

"No, just the promise of 250 grand," replied the enforcer.

"You're right ole son, let's go!" I said. Fired up once more, I set off like a greyhound shooting out of its trap.

"Maybe them warriors in the top field will have a punnet of strawberries waiting for us," I mused, stomping off with renewed vigour. Fernando caught up with me and slowed the pace right back down again. By the time we had reached the olive groves I had come to the conclusion that for me cycling and walking were about as far apart as malt whisky and Gaviscon and that I much preferred the first. Yes, I much, much preferred the first.

At the four-mile ribbon I checked my stopwatch; it said 0:52:32. Reality bit hard: it was going to take us four hours to complete the course at this rate. It seemed like another lead bar had been strapped on my legs as we trudged on. Up ahead, a hare emerged from a melon patch and stopped in the middle of the road. Unfazed by our approach, it stayed in place and soaked up the morning sun, scratching his right ear with a rear paw. I was so engrossed in the pastoral scene that I didn't hear the telltale signs of a sprinkler system coming to life. This, my first introduction to automated irrigation, delivered the liveliest left hook that I had ever received. It caught me straight in the ear with a deafening blow that made me react so violently that I caught Fernando in the ribs with a raised elbow. Both of us let out a comic-book 'argh' in succession, but as I had taken the full force of the water jet, Fernando remained bone dry while I was thoroughly drenched and took on the appearance of a river-deluged St Bernard shaking his cocked head in an effort to dispel the flood. It tickled Fernando pink and although his ribs hurt, he was more crippled by the hilarity of the scene. The hare sniffed and loped off into the next field.

"Very fucking funny," I said, soaked to the skin in a deadpan Oliver Hardy stance.

"Didn't you hear it starting up?" teased Five-Names through his tears.

"I was too busy watching that rabbit," I protested.

"Hare," he corrected.

"What?" I said, touching my head.

"It was a hare not a rabbit," replied Fernando.

"Whatever" retorted Grumpy.

"Come on; let's go down to Papa's. We can have a drink and a short rest, you'll feel better then." We pressed on. "I don't know what you're so miserable for anyway, I always feel refreshed after a nice cold shower," he said, sniggering again.

"Bollocks!" I said.

We made three more stops on the way round; one at the fruit stall to buy some much-needed bananas and oranges, one at César's garage to use the toilet, and one last stop at the peak of the Knackerer to avoid a possible collapsed lung. When we finally tramped through the front gates, some 3 hours and 49 minutes after we had begun, I was gaunt and ashen, hobbling, wheezing, rinsed with sweat and clinging to my coach like a sackful of soiled laundry. Fernando, on the other hand, swanned into the grounds looking as though he had just emerged from a salon.

He helped his wounded soldier up to the *ático*, sat me in the air-conditioned sanctuary of the living room, fixed me a long glass of iced tea and cut up two whole oranges to replenish lost vitamin C. Before leaving, Fernando asked me to give him a knock on my way to Manolo's that evening, because he would like to join me. I could only manage a nod in assent.

After what seemed like a week of just sitting there staring at the window, I summoned the effort to lean over to the table and claim my sustenance. The drink went down in one action, then I devoured the fruit in slow motion, peeling away each segment from its pith with my teeth and savouring the nectar. I continued to stare out to sea for some time until I formulated the idea of having a hot soak in the tub to revive my lost limbs. The cherry bedroom had a jacuzzi-fitted sunken bath in its ensuite and it seemed to me that this would be the ideal solution for putting the fizz back into my life. I leant forward again and pushed off from the settee, straightening up with the suppleness of a dried cabbage leaf. Fortunately nothing snapped off, so I painfully hauled my mass to the bathroom. I poured in some herbal-scented foam bath that Anna had kindly given me and turned on the taps. While the bath filled, I discarded my crumpled running gear and piled it into a heap on the floor. Leaning on the sink I gazed into the shaving mirror for inspiration, but found none, only a deflated ego and a flatulent hunk of flesh. Thoroughly pissed off I slipped into the tub. The warm waters gripped me immediately. I relaxed a little and began to think about the walk. What a joke! Fernando hadn't set the pace today, I had, and it was pitifully slow. I tried to apportion the blame for the pathetic time it had taken us on the half-a-dozen stops that we had made, but it was a lame excuse. The fact was that if I hadn't had all of those breaks, I would never have finished the course at all. Despite my former confidence in conquering all odds, let alone my eagerness to jump in and wrestle with the sharks, the plain truth was that I had walked into a bolted door today and willingness alone wouldn't serve as a master key.

Three hours and forty-nine minutes — Fernando had dismissed the time as a mere formality, but the fact that he had asked to join me for dinner tonight raised my suspicions that my coach was more than just a little concerned, as much about the state of his apprentice on the finish line as the time it had taken us. The long and short of it was that we had just eight months in which to knock off 2 hours and 19 minutes from my best time to date. Those starting odds that Terry had given me seemed all the more glaringly realistic now, but I did have one consolation: I had achieved what I had set out to do today. Now I had a number on which to improve, only there were league upon league of improvements to be made. I switched on the jacuzzi, laid back and closed my eyes. The streams of liquid turbulence felt like a dozen tiny hands therapeutically soothing my aching limbs and it wasn't long before I drifted off into a deep sleep.

The airbed drifted on docile gentle currents, being swayed only occasionally by the faintest of ripples from an otherwise millpond Indian Ocean. My legs dangled in the sea, drawing the attention of schools of tropical fish that were frolicking beneath me in the coral reef that encircled the island. They tried in vain to extricate a tasty meal from the apparent free lunch but their tiny mouths couldn't penetrate living tissue, so they tried tickling me to death first. Occasionally a cold rivulet would make its way up a valley in the bed and shock the boiling skin of the bathing beauty, causing me almost to spill my vodka and tonic. It was a minor irritation to an altogether perfect life and I was enjoying it wholeheartedly. A feather-light tradewind carrying the fragrance of citrus and cinnamon wafted in from the west and nudged the airbed over the reef. Its sharp formations sliced through the fabric like a razor blade across stretched silk. Air vented the bed in great unstoppable billows and it collapsed like a retractable flick-knife. Sea spray and bubbles were the only evidence of a once-happy customer, for I was sinking to the bottom of crystalline waters like a jettisoned stowaway wearing concrete shorts. I had lost the power to swim and my oxygen supply had used up, but still I managed to keep a hold of my tall glass of sea and tonic. The world was turning black as I began to pass out; my brain told me not to breathe in — don't breathe in, you cannot breathe in water, water will kill you — but an unseen force made me, made me open my mouth and suck in that liquid death. I woke with a gasp and a physical jerk that forced waves over the side of the Jacuzzi. For a few seconds I thought that I had in fact actually died this time and was now in Heaven, because all around me was white and deathly quiet. White spheres surrounded me, little white orbs with a hint of rainbow and the smell of lavender ...

"Oh fucking hell," I said from the grave, realising that I was in fact engulfed by bubbles.

The Jacuzzi had whipped the liquid soap into a massive frenzy and the ensuing froth had almost reached the ceiling. A large inhalation of breath had pulled in a fair amount of chemicals and I was now coughing up the nasty stuff like a tuberculosis patient. I climbed out of the stew and leant on the sink again to regain my composure. "How many times must a man die in one day?" I asked myself. I was now way too hot and bothered to be relaxed, so I stepped into the shower and set the temperature low. It took the sting from my pain and awakened me fully. At last I could think clearly and construct some kind of Plan B, should things go badly tonight over dinner. I grabbed a towel and headed for the balcony, making a detour via the kitchen to pull a bottle of water from the fridge.

At the poolside, I sat for hours in a rattan chair, with my tired legs resting on a second chair, until the sun went down. I floated many ideas but nothing solid had emerged by the time I needed to get dressed and phone my favourite dietary consultant. When I attempted to get up I found that rusted gate hinges had secretly replaced all of my joints. Most of them creaked into life, but my knee joints were locked solid and I had no trusty WD-40 on hand to lubricate them. Lowering my legs one at a time, I hobbled the length of the terrace several times over to get the blood supply flowing and liven them up. While speaking to Marion, I still had to massage my calves to ward off cramp. Her response to this week's phone-in report was to state the soberingly obvious: I was losing too much weight too soon and I should try to moderate it in some way. I promised to do so, recounting that Fernando was openly concerned as well, but I neglected to tell her of today's walkabout through fear of another roasting. I had had enough bad vibes for one day.

I called for Fernando and the two of us promenaded along to Manolo's bar. My physical discomfort in walking was all too obvious to my coach. We spoke of the weather and Barcelona's coming football match and we wished '*Buenas noches*' to a few acquaintances along the way, but of today's trial we said nothing. I had the feeling that it was all being saved up for an after-dinner meltdown. In the three months that we had been coming to Manolo's, we hadn't once stopped for a drink at the bar on the way through to the restaurant, so today's order of two G&Ts came as something of a surprise. The members of the gambling fraternity were all there as were a party of the Simmons Supporters Club, all six of them eager to hear the results of the big test. The first great gulp of a Tom's Special was like having a cuddle from my mum, comforting and familiar, and helped me to settle into conversation. Fernando delivered his version of the story, which was far kinder than the one I had envisaged having to recite. I told them about the sprinkler incident, which had them falling about with laughter; even I found it funny now. Thankfully none of them seemed concerned about the hideous length of time it had taken to walk the course. Instead, they all thought it fantastic that I had completed the course at all and gave me a pat on the back for my effort. Suddenly I felt a hundred times better than I had before. Andrés, who was there with the manager from his clothing business, was wildly excited and I could almost see the *peseta* signs in his eyes. "Good lad," he kept saying in his Dutch-Scottish accent.

The *Mañana* brothers had found their way into the bar just before Fernando and me, and were arguing about the integrity of swimming pool liners and their cost effectiveness compared with ceramic-tiled walls. Carlos was a short, overweight, well-tanned man with a large but neatly trimmed moustache. By all accounts, he was very traditional in his approach to work and incredibly meticulous. Juan, on the other hand, liked to think he was thinner than his brother and wore trousers that were far too tight, accentuated at the waist with a huge belt, which gave him an almost wasp-like appearance. Juan was hyperactive and always on the lookout for a shortcut to finish a job more quickly. Some said that he liked to turn up to a new contract, sweep the floor and then hold his hand out for the money. If asked to spell the name of his god, his reply would be 'P.E.S.E.T.A'. This meant that if a job worth one peseta more came in after yours had been booked, yours would go to the back of the queue! Juan was bearded, lighter skinned than his brother and considered himself as a bit of a ladies' man. Quite a claim for a 5' 2" relic from the 80's! Unfortunately for him the only ladies he could interest usually worked in the middle of the night and charged him for their services.

I liked the brothers immensely. They were eternally cheerful and never had a bad word to say about anyone. They had an endearing smell about them of wood chippings, linseed oil and fresh rain, and their gold-toothed smiles were highly infectious. According to rumour, the truth about the *Mañana* Brothers was that they did excellent work, eventually.

The last of the group were a couple of individuals who seemed to be permanently playing dominos, ancient fellows with skin the colour of weathered mahogany, who, if they hadn't have moved occasionally, you'd have presumed to be part of the furniture. They lived in the same clothes day in and day out; one donned a black beret and the other a flat cap, and couldn't have had more than six teeth between them. Occupying the same table every night under the television by the entrance to the restaurant, they would interrupt our conversation every now and then with gems of Spanish wisdom such as *"esa es mi butifarra gordo"* (that's my fat sausage), or *"enséñarles la talla de tu zapato"* (show them your shoe size), which provoked giggles from the locals but only left me baffled.

I took another dive into my gin and tonic, and was flooded with nostalgia; briefly, I was back in The George and its aura reassured me. Promising our friends that we would return later for a chat, Fernando and I bundled into the restaurant. As was normal for this time of the evening, we were the only diners, and the room had its usual ambience of 'out of season and should be closed, if it weren't for these two bloody nuisances who booked late'. I jumped when Manolo grabbed me by the shoulder from behind, like a station sergeant nicking a wanted criminal down a dark alley. "*Enhorabuena por hoy mi amigo.*"

Thinking I'd understood the patron, I replied, "*Muchas gracias*, Manolo."

"We have a long way to go yet," said Fernando in Spanish to his friend.

"Yes, yes but big olive trees start from little stones as you know, eh?"

"As I know. Now how about some service, huh? Honestly things are getting scrappy around here lately!" said Five-Names with a smile. Manolo tugged his forelock and backed off into the kitchen in mock subservience.

I was curious about the exchange the boys had just had. I also wanted the cards laid firmly on the table making clear the state of play and my future prospects, so in between mouthfuls of anchovies and artichokes, I questioned Fernando in my inimitable, subtlety-free style. "Am I for the scrap heap then, old mate?" We had been working together day after day now for more than three months in such close proximity, that we had gotten to know one another's mannerisms quite well. Fernando had a tendency to bite his bottom lip when something was troubling him. He had started doing it when we were halfway around the course today, and was still nibbling away at it tonight. I sensed that it was crunch time. Even though my coach had always maintained that times were not an issue, I knew that he was deeply concerned by my performance. Maybe the unexpected gin and tonic was a cushion for telling me that it would be pointless to continue!

"Almost my friend, what do the Americans say, 'You can't polish a turd'? Well, we're going to have to try!"

"Oh," I said slightly hurt. The whole project pivoted on the pinhead of Fernando's integrity and I was bracing myself for a direct blow to the chin.

"These are the facts. Your time was 3:49:56 for completing the course today. In slightly less than 36 weeks' time, you will be asked to run an almost identical course within an hour and a half. Somehow you've got to eradicate 2 hours, 19 minutes and 56 seconds. It's a hideous task that's probably impossible to achieve. I have given a lot of thought to our predicament this afternoon and at one point I nearly called you up to offer my resignation but, after taking advice, I reassessed the situation and have decided to change our entire training programme starting from tomorrow."

I sat back in my seat conjuring up all manner of extreme procedures that might be adopted, and all of which were likely to be painful. "Who did you talk to?" I asked.

"We'll get to that," replied Fernando, mysteriously.

"Do you think that we achieved anything today?" I asked in desperation.

"We did what we set out to do — complete the course!"

Fernando's sternness unnerved me. It felt as though our relationship was being pushed to an uncomfortable outer edge and although my completion time was pathetic, my main concern was the state that I was in on the finish line. "Yes but I'd used up every piece of energy that I had to get round!"

"You got *round* from years of unabashed self-abuse!" The old Fernando was back in the driving seat armed with quick-firing, shameless sharp wit. He had the gift of healing heavy hearts in an instance with his positive attitude. "Listen," he said. "Here's what we've got to do." He pulled out two sheets of paper that were neatly folded in his back pocket and flattened them on the tablecloth. "It's shit or bust time, is that what you say in England?"

I laughed. "One does indeed!" I replied, and leant over to examine the new training programme. The figures were depressing. There were more reps in the gym; more lengths in the swimming pool, and the schedules had been totally rearranged. Fernando went through it with me while Manolo cleared away the plates and brought out a course of chicken in white wine and mushroom sauce. "Every other Wednesday you'll walk, then jog, and eventually run the course. Every second Sunday you'll do a 100 mile cycle ride, taking you through breathtaking Catalonian countryside."

The thought of '100 miles' made me grimace.

"Every Thursday, you'll have golf instead of your bike and sauna routine.

I smiled, weakly.

"Each day you will walk a different third of the course, starting from tomorrow. I will take you to your start point in the jeep and pick you up from your finish. This will continue until Wednesday 17th of November, exactly three weeks from today, when we attempt the whole course again." I turned pale at the prospect.

"After that my friend, we're going to attack the thing every two weeks and we're going to shave off an average of eight minutes every time we do it."

I attempted to speak, but was cut short.

"Your knee predicament and the possibility of heart problems are greatly enhanced now. I am not sure whether they can take the punishment of an increased programme, so I have contacted an old friend of mine who has retired from the athletics circuit, but is now a physiotherapist at Barcelona FC. I have explained the situation and he has agreed to give you a thorough examination this Friday."

I tried to speak again.

"I've also spoken to my son and son-in-law on the question of your heart; on their recommendation, you are to have a medical every week until you reach a target weight of 14 stone. The work will be intense but at a steady tempo."

"Hurry up and take your time!" I said getting a word in at last.

"What?"

"It's something I used to say to my people at work to get them motivated."

"And it will work for us too, Donald. Now do you agree to all these new proposals, because without them my friend we are fighting a lost cause?"

I stared at my chicken; it was a piece of breast meat that had long since lost its heartbeat. I imagined the beast lying on a mortuary slab, a cold dead bird with my head in place of his and I shuddered at my own mortality.

"Devil if I do, and devil if I don't!" I said at length. "I've no choice, so where do I sign?"

•• ▼ ••

Three weeks of gruelling hardship passed without me finding a fluid rhythm or pace. The swimming pool I swore had been elongated; the Peugeot complained about the extra mileage; and my first pair of Asics finally lost the will to live with a blowout while up on the Snake. I now knew the course better than I knew the contents of Chan's takeaway menu, but I still found something new to admire at every turn: the autumn harvests, the ever-changing hues, the sadness of the sea for losing its appeal. I held on to my wanderlust but kept my mind and body totally focused on the job in hand, every minute of the day I ate, slept and breathed that course.

One shining moment happened within those three weeks that had the pair of us jumping around the room like a couple of lottery winners. It happened on the first Tuesday night, when digital revelation confirmed that my weight had gone from the twenties to the teens. Fernando had anticipated the fall and had brought along his camcorder to preserve the moment. It was definitely one for the archives.

Two of the 100 mile cycle rides were now behind me, the first one being accompanied by Fernando and Pablo, who was just out for a Sunday jaunt. The three of us set out at a rather hazy and chilly 5:30 a.m. but within a couple of hours the sun was smiling on us sweetly and made Fernando's 'good idea' seem much more acceptable. Some of the picturesque places that we passed through did wonders for keeping up my morale; ancient villages in the hillsides and coastline untouched by greedy modern-day settlements and still drenched in a sleepy charm. The rocky streams, bridged by wooden platforms, meandered down to the sea, frivolously innocent of the turmoil and confusion awaiting them in the open jaws of the resorts below. I adored the cool pine forest above Lorret de Mar with its musty smell of damp woodland and the way in which the sunbeams broke through the dark canopy to form iron grilles holding back the mystical gloom. Although I was exhausted, I couldn't wait to do the course all over again and it made the return into quasi-concrete Pineda, at 7:30 that evening, something of an anticlimax.

Later, at Manolo's I relived the experience while savouring another five courses of exquisite culinary delight. At times I hardly even noticed what was on my plate I was so engrossed in recall. The idea of spending the whole Sunday riding a bicycle out in the country four months ago would have been my idea of an idiot's outing, much preferring instead the confines of a pub sofa on which to get severely drunk. The day's exercise had given me an extremely large appetite, but instead of sneaking up to the kitchen to ask for more, this Oliver Twist was content to stroll home feeling totally privileged for today's gifts. On my terrace I climbed up to the crow's nest with a mug full of diet hot chocolate and nestled there pondering the starlight in the endless black firmament.

Thirty minutes later I was softly snoring under a light duvet in my monster bed, blissfully unaware that moths were being driven insane by a white-hot moon that had come down from the sky and perched itself on my balcony wall.

Walking just one-third of a half-marathon bears little relation to walking the whole course. So adding up the three best times on each individual third of the course, which happened to be the last three attempts, did not provide a true perspective of my overall performance. I wished it were so, because totting them up came to a time of 2:49:52, a fantastic improvement on three weeks ago. Fernando had told me that if I could reproduce anything like that time in the next three weeks, then he wouldn't hesitate to place 100 per cent confidence in his student. Although I felt comfortable with each segment of the route, I was under no illusion that once I tackled the full course my troubles would begin as soon as I had completed that first third. Why Fernando had chosen this method of training was a mystery that I hadn't questioned, but all was about to be revealed.

It was Wednesday 17th of November, point-critical in determining the achievability of my quest. The pre-race nerves had started early; it wasn't even 7:00 a.m. and some warm pipe had been laid in the bottom of the toilet bowl already, and I was turtle-necking again. I wondered whether I would ever conquer this anxiety-related poser and shuddered at the thought of suffering the ultimate embarrassment of coming under siege from 'jogger's trots' halfway around the course, even though it might make me the centre of attention with the local fly population. For the time being, the dilemma wasn't an issue as I had at least five toilet stations scattered around my practice course plus the distinct advantage of starting out from home, but what about on race day? I had no idea about the facilities at High Wycombe. What if there was only one Portaloo for the entire competitive collective? I would fill the thing on my lonesome! What I needed for peace of mind was staring me right in the face, my own piece of porcelain. I owned dozens of motorhomes at my showroom in Reading, so I could just take along a Winnebago and park it on site. I could shit myself empty before the race began without the fear of a desperate mob outside the door. Bingo! I would call up Ray in the morning and get one organised.

Ice-cold milk fell over the crisp cornflakes causing some of it to spill over on to the work top. It was soon accompanied in the bowl by a crudely chopped banana and a dusting of grated cinnamon. Two pieces of toasted Weight Watchers bread liberally coated with local honey and a pot of percolated coffee made up the pre-course breakfast. The honey complemented the coffee to perfection. It was two hours before the walk began, giving me plenty of time to digest the meal, but given the way my intestines were reacting this morning, it might just pass straight through me whole. My nerves were getting the best of me, so I tried to distract myself with unrelated subjects to take my mind off the walk, but all roads led to Pineda. It was no use. My whole body was captured in a force field of doubt, an unreachable itch that only being out on the course could scratch, and I paced the room impatiently in nothing but my socks and underpants.

Several more trips to the bathroom, gallons of black coffee and a tremendous amount of psyching up brought me to a quarter-to-nine — time to bring it on!

Fernando and his son-law, Roberto, met me down at the front gate; the doctor was there as promised to give me the once-over before I started off. He would also accompany Five-Names in the jeep as a precaution and carry out regular check-ups along the way. Although glad to know that the doctor was on hand, I hoped that I wouldn't have need of him. We went through a ten-minute limbering up routine, then I made sure that my knee supports were firmly in place and Roberto checked my blood pressure and pulse — the Titan was ready to go! I felt like a Grand National jockey anxious for flight yet held back at the start by a thin wire; I probably looked more like Red Rum than the lightweight jockey. Birdsong from a nearby palm stirred the morning air and a passing lizard froze solid to avoid being detected by any lurking predator. Roberto broke off from conversation with Fernando and came over to read the riot act to me, the basic do's and don'ts of exercise over distance. In a nutshell, it read 'Do not kill yourself.'

It was decided that the doctor and coach would head off in the jeep and wait for me at every mile-point to offer water, encouragement and medical assistance if needed, in equal amounts, while the large one would endeavour to smash his previous time to pieces. Nine twenty-nine: Five-Names and Chubby stepped up to the gate and synchronized our watches. Whispers and murmurs from behind us revealed that my loyal trio of well-wishers had come to see me off again. Don Quixote gave them a smile and a wink.

"*Buena suerte*" they shouted, wishing me luck.

Fernando, steady as a rock, held one hand in the air while all the time looking at his watch. He counted the seconds down: "Five, four, three, two, one — Go!" A cheer went up and I stepped out into the street. At No-Cart Corner an offer of water was refused. I was a little dry but could easily plod on for another mile before taking on fluids. The temperature on my balcony this morning had read 62° F, so with the breeze coming in from the sea I figured it to be around 58° F down here, a thankfully perfect temperature for a half-marathon.

The banana trees stood rather barren now and they offered little in the way of shade. Their branches had been hacked back by the council's tree surgeons making them look like immature pineapple heads. Waiting at the end of the avenue was a cold bottle of water just desperate to be drunk. I obliged this time but was only allowed one cupful before being directed towards the underpass. Once at the foot of the Eiger I stopped for 30 seconds to take on oxygen and wipe my face with a handkerchief, and then made two more stops at the start of the Snake and by the olive groves at the top of the hill. The sweat was now rolling from my shaven head and threatening to blind me; I was making good use of a towelling wristband that was so drenched that it could have accommodated live fish. I passed Albert, a lone African worker tending to the dieback in the strawberry fields. He mimicked my actions as a man on his last legs delirious for a drink. I laughed and showed him the finger; Albert laughed too and then we both returned to our respective tasks.

By the time I had reached mile three I had regained my composure and was back into my stride. I was truly thankful for the second cup of water that the boys had let me have; they knew that it would be essential after the hill. They decided to skip mile four and instead rendezvous at Papa's bar which marked the end of the first third of the course. The bar was closed for the season but they had let themselves in and were waiting for me at the bar. As I climbed the steps up to the front door I checked the stopwatch: 0:58:22. I had shaved off another minute from my personal best for this part of the course. Recharged, I felt confident, focused and brimming with enough vitality to break the three-hour mark. Even so Roberto insisted on giving me a once over, which I passed with flying colours.

Pressing on to traverse the N11, I once again refused water at the five-mile point. At the Elbay restaurant I checked my stopwatch for the second time and found that I was even further ahead than before. My excitement was starting to get the better of me and I was prematurely speeding up. Water was readily accepted here, but I took it a bit too dramatically for Fernando's liking, drinking it on the move as if I were competing and had no time to stop.

"I'm gonna do it!" I shouted back enthusiastically. By the time I had reached the crossroads at the nine-mile marker, and the end of the second third of the course, my mistake of cracking on too soon was taking its toll and the dream of completing in less than three hours was slipping away. Limbs of lead and a torso full of mercury were pulling me earthwards and my earlier feeling of sustainable vigour was swiftly draining away. I recognised the red warning light and I signalled to Fernando that I was in trouble.

"Sit down on the grass now!" ordered my coach. I complied and shakily withered to the floor, flattening a patch of once-carefree daisies into the subsoil. Both men began massaging my weary legs, and then Roberto continued the treatment while Fernando sponged my head and neck with cold water. It brought sweet relief to my boiling skull, as if a layer of sizzling flesh was being peeled away to reveal a fresh face on a beautiful spring day. Next the boss worked on my shoulders while his son-in-law checked for vital signs. My blood pressure was up and my heart was racing, but not to dangerous levels. My pupils weren't dilated and I could remember the name of my favourite malt whisky, so I was allowed to continue. After repeating the sponge-down, Five-Names made me change into a clean running vest and instructed me to sit there for five minutes to take on board a half-litre of glucose water.

"Now retie your shoelaces, take ten deep breaths and set off again slowly."

I nodded, did precisely as I was told and set off at a relaxed pace. The Knackerer was looming in front of me, the last ball-breaker before the long downhill home, and I intended to ascend it at the softest of paces.

"*Tranquilo*" shouted out Five-Names. I raised a thumb in recognition. The time-out had taken ten precious minutes off the clock, but without the rest this marathon man would have had to call it a day. It put the quest for a sub-three hour walk firmly beyond reach especially at the more moderate pace I was now forced to take. As I trudged up the hill, breathing laboriously, a murky depression set in. "This has been a complete waste of fucking time," I said to myself. "Who am I kidding, thinking that I can run a half-marathon? I can't even pissing well walk the fucking thing." I was falling deeper into despair. "I'm gonna jack it all in tomorrow. Fly home and pay Belington his winnings. Bollocks to it!" Just then a topless cabriolet flashed past, featuring César standing upright in the back singing The Impossible Dream' at the top of his lungs over the sound of a furiously honking car horn. It cheered my spirit no end, and as I saddled the brow of the hill, a refreshing wind caught me full in the face, whipped around my waist and pulled me down the inverse slope with the power of a recoiling bungee cord. My dark mood completely evaporated and my reserve tanks span into action. I had just 45 minutes to finish the course in time and I launched myself into the challenge like a hell-bent critter.

César's garage forecourt went by unnoticed, as did the two observers in the jeep. Fernando could see that once again the Chubster had increased his speed, and shouted out *"Tranquilo,* tran-fucking-quilo!" but it fell on deaf ears. I was now perspiring from every pore, giving the illusion that I had recently been basted in hot oil. I was panting like a pit bull on a choke chain and oblivious to the world around me. I had one vision: passing through the gates of the apartment with my arms stretched high to the triumphant sound of the Rocky theme tune — beyond that, nothing else mattered.

Towards the 11th mile I slowed down slightly to give the illusion that I had listened to my coach and disguised my shortness of breath so that the doctor would not interfere. "I feel fine, really," I said as I welcomed a cup of water followed by a second. Having managed to escape suspicion, I broke free again and once my team were out of sight, sped up to almost jogging speed. Fernando wasn't fooled at all, but gave me the benefit of the doubt just to see if I could push myself that extra bit further and find the special flair that winners need. Roberto, on the other hand, wasn't happy about it at all, but dutifully respected his father-in-law's opinion.

The fruit season had long since finished, but salad produce was still being grown under polytunnels. The acidic smell of vine tomatoes and cool leafy lettuce conjured up a mouthwatering vision of a fat juicy BLT with a generous helping of mayonnaise, the grilled bacon all tender but with a crispy rind and slightly salty. God, how I missed grilled bacon!

I stopped to tie a flapping shoelace and noticed a small yellow and green spider, legs akimbo in the middle of his web, just inches from my face, its delicate silken thread strung brilliantly between the branches of a Potentilla. "No fast food for you, eh old chap?" I said to the arachnid. "You have to work hard for every meal!"

"Piss off ya big bastard!" said the eight-eyed monster wishing he were six feet taller.

At mile 12 I assured my service crew that all was well despite my crimson face advertising the fact for all to see that my blood pressure was sky high. As soon as the jeep had passed me, I glanced at my watch. I had only 15 minutes to complete a mile and a quarter. I wasn't ready for it, but I had no choice; I started to jog, albeit in a pathetic style. I looked more like a spacehopper in clown shoes than a fleet-of-foot marathon runner, but it gave me the extra speed that I needed. Deciding that it suited the pace better, I took the tarmac road instead of the beach, but before long my knees were crunching up cartilage and the pain became unbearable. I had to stop jogging and return to the snail's pace, which was just as well because I had come to the road leading to my apartment block. I walked the last stretch like a Teletubby on LSD and fell through the gates, deprived of the basic elements that keep human beings standing. My jelly legs supported nothing and I fell onto all fours gasping like a goldfish out of its bowl, only vaguely aware that two pairs of feet were about me. With my last ounce of strength I managed to push the button on my stopwatch before my head filled with black ink and I passed out.

Stringent ammonia poison hurtled up my nostrils and assaulted the back of my eyeballs. I woke with an aggressive start, lunging at an invisible foe before realising that I hadn't the strength to hold my body upright and fell back to the ground with a bump. I lay there for a few seconds trying to remember who I was and who were these two blurry figures standing over me.

"You're still alive then?" said my coach ruefully.

"I ..."

"I've been a stupid idiot? Is that what you're trying to say?"

"I'm sorry Fern I got carried away!"

"You'll be carried away alright, in a mahogany box!" said my coach as he lifted me upright with the aid of the young doctor. "What possessed you to break all our rules?"

"I ... I just had to go for it," I said in a confused state.

"Well, you did it my friend; you broke the three-hour mark!"

"Bugger me!" I puffed.

"You almost buggered yourself," said Five-Names, "but your time was 2:59:58! Well done."

I feebly lifted my arm and checked my stopwatch. I couldn't believe it! I sat there like a crumpled sweat-stained Buddha, grinning from ear to ear. "What kind of language is "tran-fucking-quilo" anyway?" I wheezed at my mentor.

"That, my friend, is a special language that I made up especially for you!"

CHAPTER FOURTEEN
Unexpected presents

THE SINGLE TRACK RAILWAY LINE that hugs the contours of the coastline on the Costa Brava was a key feature in the view from my terrace garden. I had often watched the early morning train amble by, speckled with the first of the day's commuters heading for Barcelona and beyond. The service boasted smart new trains, which stopped at ancient stations along the line; it was a curious mix of modern technology with old-fashioned nostalgia. At night the last train home would be peppered with late-night stragglers, shift workers, party revellers or face-locked lovers oblivious to the worn and troubled world. I promised myself that one day I would take a ride on that line; it would be my first-ever train journey abroad. So when the opportunity arose during a long weekend in December when Anne, June and Mathew came to stay, I seized it!

As I boarded the ultra-quiet train through sliding doors, it struck me that the train was much like the latest rolling stock on the London Underground, but inside the carriage one dramatic difference impressed me immediately: the spotlessly clean interiors. The two-hour journey took me along the shoreline through some of the pretty villages that I often cycled through and many more that were new to me. Digital information streamed across long display screens in every carriage and an intercom announced each station in advance of the train stopping there. The stationmasters clearly took pride in their platforms, which were quaint and adorned with planters and brightly coloured furniture — just how they used to be in Britain, once upon a time. Seduced by the charm of this particular train line, I pledged to ride on it more often.

My journey terminated within the bowels of Barcelona airport and ten minutes later I was waiting in the arrivals lounge as nervous as a divorcee on a blind date. The flight had been delayed by 20 minutes so I walked to the gents to kill some time. Washing my hands after an awkward urination between a Japanese tourist on tiptoes and an adolescent crater-faced airport worker who spent more than enough time shaking off the drips, I became engrossed by my reflection in the mirror. It's funny how different you look when you catch sight of yourself in unfamiliar surroundings. Although I had witnessed my gradual transformation when glancing in my own mirror countless times over

196

the past five months, the person standing in front of me now was a complete stranger. It wasn't only my appearance that had changed; my whole attitude to life had transformed into one of enlightenment. I was almost out there on the fringe with the yogist's and Buddhists. Well, I had once looked like a Buddha, now I just fraternised with some of their ways. "You are what you eat!" I reminded myself, like the ancient sage of dietary health.

My transition was both physical and philosophical although the mental changes were probably only visibly apparent to me. The old adage came to mind, 'If you feel good, then you'll look good too'. I just hoped that my family wouldn't be too alarmed by the impostor in my shoes. An announcement that their plane had arrived prompted me to head for the arrivals entrance, where an eternity passed until they appeared. Yet it was while waiting for my family that I realised for the first time in my life that I no longer stood out in a crowd. There were no sideways glances, sniggers or wide berths; I was just part of the collective. Suddenly I spotted June and Mathew who, using their luggage trolley as a sleigh, came hurtling out of baggage reclaim like a two-man toboggan team getting up to speed on the Cresta run. I almost shouted out, but my reserve got the better of me. Then I saw my beautiful wife emerge from Spanish officialdom, like a bird-of-paradise flower erupting from a tight bud. She looked more lovely than I had remembered and as radiant as the sun. Ann caught up with the kids as they entered the lounge and they parked themselves by a post while they scoured the crowds for Daddy. I hesitated at coming forward because I wanted to enjoy their reaction on seeing me for the first time. At the same time, I was struck by the amount of weight my two youngest had gained, especially since Ann had ruled that there would be no more fast food after I had left for the Continent. I could stand it no longer and slipped between a rowdy bunch of ex-pats and a Spanish family waiting for their returning exchange-student son, to make myself known. Yet still I remained invisible to them and it scared me. There was nothing for it, I had to approach them. Lunging forwards with arms open and smiling like a loon, I kissed Ann on the cheek and almost squeezed the life out of her. She stepped back wide-eyed and in apparent shock. The children were mortified by the affront of this hairy foreigner slobbering over their mum. If I hadn't spoken there and then, they might have laid into me.

Six months ago I wouldn't have been seen dead in anything other than a designer suit of some quality, accompanied by fine shoes, a clean-shaven face and a whiff of fashionable cologne. Today's attire would have been regarded as something verging on criminal in the eyes of Simmons the car salesman. Dressed in a khaki shirt and shorts (even though it was too cold for shorts I had simply got used to them), complemented by Caterpillar boots with socks rolled over the tops, and sporting four days' growth on my face and a number-two buzz cut on my bonce, I looked as though I had just stepped off the set of Born Free. To top it all I smelt of oranges! Having lost seven and a half stone and being bronzed to local standards added another layer to my disguise and it dumbfounded my troop. No wonder the kids thought Ann was being mauled by a maniac. I had taken them all by surprise.

"It's me, really love! Can you believe it?" I said patting my stomach with both hands.

"Prove it!" said Ann, tightening up her eyes and pouting. The kids just stared open-mouthed and fell the quietest they'd ever been in their entire lives. "Alright, we have another daughter called Trish at home in England, who is looking after our two dogs; we have a thriving car business, its head office is in Ruislip and me best mate is called Les!"

"You could have squeezed that information out of him during interrogation!" she quipped.

"What's your favourite thing to have for breakfast?"

"Cornflakes with banana slices and black coffee no sugar!" I said with pride.

"Kids, call the police. Your father's been abducted. What have you done with him you monster?" she laughed, and walked over to embrace the man that she'd loved for a thousand years. "I'm so proud of you, Don," she whispered. "You look fantastic!"

"Only halfway there yet my darling, God, how I've missed you!" I kissed her forehead. Mathew and June still stood there agog. I realised that I was ignoring them and turned my attentions their way. Letting Ann go, I said "Have you missed your old Dad then?"

"Our 'old Dad' yes!" said Mathew sullenly.

"He's still inside 'ere son. He's just been to the body shop and had a refit!"

"Well, I like my new daddy!" said June defending her father, and she rushed over to grapple my diminished waistline.

"That's better," I said, pulling Mathew under my armpit to give them a double cuddle. A minute later we were heading for a taxi, with me in command of the trolley, a happy wife on one arm, a skipping daughter on the other and a sulky son lagging behind.

"I hope that not everything has shrunk, Mr Simmons?" purred my wife.

There's nothing worse than a reformed fast-food junkie, and I was ready to recite the party line to my family. My mind boiled with draconian means to end all means.

I was going to sit the children down and instruct them on the errors of my ways. I intended to make them fully comprehend in the space of five minutes that theirs was a course to obesity, a miserable, self-loathing road to ridicule and an early grave — all this from the instigator of gluttony, the promoter of individual choice at meal times, the lard-arse who led by example. I was racked with emotional turmoil; it was my fault, yet I felt angry with them. I had dragged them around the easy-option, fast food places, filling them with carbohydrates, sugar, E-numbers and monosodium glutamate until it was coming out of their ears, and now suddenly they were in the wrong? I felt ashamed, but I had to act, I had to instruct them on healthy eating; in short, I had to take responsibility and be a parent for once in my life. That side of business had always been left to Ann while I ran around breaking all the rules, acting like one of the kids, playing with cars and an endless supply of money. How reckless had I been? More important, how was I going to correct all of my wrongdoing in just four days? I had to try.

"Ooh McDonald's, Dad can we stop at McDonald's please?" squealed June.

Mathew sat upright for the first time. Obstinate and self-righteous to the point of insensitivity and in a position of command from the front seat of the taxicab, I launched my campaign. "No, no, your Dad's gonna cook us something to eat when we get back to the apartment. It's not that far now!" I replied.

"Oh, Mum said we could go to McDonald's when we got here!" said June with a protruding bottom lip. Both kids followed the golden arch with their eyes, turning their heads as it went sailing past.

"You're going to cook for us, Don? Cook?" asked my wife.

"Well, prepare. I've got loads of fruit in the refrigerator. I'm gonna segment it and serve it on the terrace with tall glasses of iced tea!"

"Umm, delicious!" said Ann.

"Don't like bloody fruit!" muttered a voice in the back.

"Language Mathew!" I snapped.

"Cold cups of tea?" queried June.

The rest of the journey was spent in silence, with me experiencing a mini-anxiety attack, Ann thinking about a night ahead of passion, and the kids suffering from a processed protein withdrawal. The cab driver longed for a fag.

Suddenly we were at the apartment gates. I gave the driver a decent tip and we unloaded onto the pavement. "One suitcase each!" I said, desperately trying the jolly-hockeysticks approach. A strong wind blew up the street from the beach, rattling leathery fronds against the palm trees' rugged trunks. It was a grey day and the sea looked devastated.

"I thought Daddy lived in a sunny place?" enquired June.

"It's mostly sunny, my darling. Just today it's a bit miserable," I reassured her.

I punched in the number and accessed the security sidegate. June was struggling with her little wheeled suitcase, so I took charge of it. Already bearing the burden of Ann's case, I was reminded of the last time that I had crossed the forecourt laden with luggage. This time the passage was markedly easier and I entered the lobby without so much as an exaggerated breath. As if by magic or because he had his radar switched on again, Fernando appeared from his apartment with the whirling hound by his side.

"Ah Donald," he said.

Turning to my wife, I said "Ann, I'd like you meet the most important man in Spain, my trainer and best buddy Fernando Rodriguez Monolito Pepe DeNegro, or Fern for short." Ann's smile lit up the lobby; she had heard so much about Fernando and was delighted to have met him at last. She held out her hand as he approached.

"I am enchanted to meet you Ann. Please do not listen to your husband's outlandish claims of my importance, I'm simply offering him the benefit of my experience" he said graciously. "How was your journey? Not too arduous I hope?"

"We had a short delay in taking off and then some hairy safari guide picked us up from the airport, but apart from that it all ran smoothly," she replied. Fernando looked at me faking concern. I just chuckled.

"These are my two youngest," I said, waving a hand towards a visibly bored Mathew and content little June who was now engrossed in tickling the belly of a very appreciative Yorkshire terrier.

"Mathew and June, I'm very pleased to meet you. I bet you missed your father terribly?"

"I have" said June, continuing to seduce Circola.

Mathew managed to conjure up a half smile and looked nonchalantly around the room.

"Puberty?" Fernando asked me.

"McDonald's deprivation!" I replied.

"Oh I see. Listen, I must take my little girl here out for a stroll right now, but before you go out tonight why don't you all come round for an aperitif? I'll introduce you to my wife Anna; you both share the same name!"

"That'll be lovely. We'll see you later then, have a good walk!" said my wife.

"We will. *Buenos dias*," he replied, as man and dog skipped out into the garden.

I turned to my son. "There's no need to be rude, Matt. You should answer when people speak to you, especially Fernando. He's done a tremendous amount for me!"

"Oh come on you two; let's not have any bad feelings. You haven't seen each other for five months. We're on holiday, remember!" said Ann.

"Too right," I said, recognising the threat of barriers being put up. I slackened my hard line a little for the sake of harmony. "I'll tell you what; we'll dump the cases upstairs and go out to a pizzeria that I know. I've not eaten there myself but I've heard the food's pretty good. Sod the fruit, eh!"

Ann elbowed me in the ribs. "I mean we'll forget the fruit, but listen up kids. Your dad doesn't eat junk food anymore and I know it'll be hard for you, but you're gonna have to give it up too. You can have it as a treat now and again but not everyday, got it? You're both getting far too chunky." They nodded sullenly, but the prospect of pizza was burning at the front of their brains.

The restaurant was no more Italian than a Devon tearoom but the food was superb. Ann and I both had salads — dutifully I discarded the bacon and cheese from mine — while the kids devoured two 12-inch meat feasts with alarming ferocity, each washing them down with a pail of Coke. I watched with mounting disgust. I was supposed to love and protect my kids, not encourage them to metamorphose into two maggot-bodied waste disposal units. I had failed miserably and would have felt no better if I had let them starve. Anxiety got the better of me and I had to leave, throwing a 50-peseta note down to cover the bill.

"Come on," I said and frogmarched them out of the building.

Back in the Land Rover, I was raging with guilt, biting my bottom lip while mentally punishing myself. Ann got in beside me and the two chubsters clambered into the back. They were quite happy now they'd been fed, but were totally unaware of the turmoil going through their dad's head. Back at the apartment I showed them the swimming pool and gave them some towels. I was off to walk a third of the course and didn't want to keep my coach waiting, plus the road was the best place to vent some steam. I could contemplate on the hoof and hopefully come up with a plan that would suit all parties.

Fernando had suggested that I take a few days off to be with my family, but I knew that any lapse in my routine was potential suicide. Besides my wife had absolute commitment to this crusade and totally forbade any time off on her account.

The course blurred by without my noticing as I churned over the problem that was weighing me down. Finally, I came to the conclusion that the only direction was to steer my children down the same dramatic path that I had taken. June and Mathew would have to follow a diet plan overseen by Marion and enforced by Ann. She was going to have to go through hell with it and I was shot through with guilt even now, for I couldn't be around to offer my support or stamp my authority on the programme. I would tell her gently, but not until tomorrow, as I wasn't going to spoil tonight. Making good time again, I was picked up by Fernando who congratulated his *protégé*, however I said little in return. My coach could see that I was in a pensive mood so he left me to it, simply adding, "See you at 7:00, my friend," when we parted company.

Drinks at Fernando's were pleasant enough and Ann was relieved to have met Anna and find that Mrs Five-Names wasn't as attractive as I had led her to believe. Apart from a few uncomfortable silences, they got on fine, with Fernando providing his customary translation services and me offering a few phrases of my newfound second language. The children just sat on the couch mystified by the whole episode.

Having been informed of the arrival of Mrs Simmons and *los niños*, Manolo had prepared a table for four. I asked for the menu for my family but was keen to avoid a repeat of the day's earlier mealtime trauma, Ann jumped in immediately with a helping hand. Much to the children's disgust, she declined the menus and asked that they all be given the same food to eat as her husband. "All for one and one for all" she announced.

I was quite moved by the gesture. As tears welled up in my eyes I gently held her hand across the table. "You don't have to do that," I said.

"No, but I'm going to. We work together in this family!" she replied with resolve.

After an enjoyable meal that the children just pushed around the plates with their forks, my entourage was eagerly introduced to each and every one of the barflies. It must have taken us a good hour to wade through the sea of welcomes and good wishes, before heading out into the night and taking a slow stroll back to the *ático*. We stopped at Bar Hugo for a coffee. The kids were given orange juice despite their pleas for Coke and together we sat around a table as one, Ann with her arm through mine and her head on my shoulder, June smiling at us lovingly with her chin resting on her downturned hands and Mathew eyeing up the sugar bowl, hoping to sneak in a lump at the first opportunity.

Later that night when the kids were soundly asleep, Ann and I made love under a blanket sky, the temperate wind perfect on burning skin. I spread out the mattresses from the sun loungers onto the terrace floor, while Ann slid out of her fine cotton dress into nakedness. Her silky limbs were still as slender as the day we had met. I was giddy with anticipation and rushed to embrace her, kissing her intently while fumbling with my clothes. Ann helped me disrobe and we fell together like two entwined clematis ravaged in a storm. She took control and straddled me like a bareback rider on an unbroken stallion. Scorching hot inside her was a brilliance that she had longed for and it burnt with every thrust. It was like making love for the first time and her mind splintered into a thousand fragments upon every climax, the incredible force taking her breath away.

When I finally came, a hundred million neurons illuminated at once in my frontal lobe, a billion starburst fireworks exploding into infinity on a Bastille night to remember.

It was much needed relief. On many an occasion, I had commented to Fernando that I was no farmer, but I was carrying around a couple of ache-rs.

I breathed in the longest, slowest breath ever inhaled. I held it in my lungs for an eternity where it felt like paradise had arrived, the sweetest burning ache in my chest since my last cigarette. Finally I let the air out through my nostrils and made a satisfied humming noise. I kissed Ann on her forehead, her nose and her eyelids, then her mouth, before counting one, two, three in preparation to disconnect, but she clung on to me like an engaged octopus intent on keeping hold of its prey.

"Oh no you don't!" she said defiantly. She held me for a couple more minutes before she finally floated back down from her cloud and let me go. For Ann it was like having a new man who was totally familiar with every sensual line, crevice and curve; a new man with a map to her heart.

We peeled away from each other with the adhesion of sticky tape from a roll and stayed still, enjoying the moment. I lay quietly on my back with Ann snuggled up beside me on her side, one leg over my thigh and her hand on my chest. Soon the night air was raising a few goosebumps so we decided to retreat indoors and snuggle under the enormous duvet. Suddenly I had a craving for something that I hadn't longed for in ages. The pull of nicotine had raised its ugly head again, but I forced it down with my sledgehammer will.

"I love you so much Ann, I'd do anything for you, you know …"

"Oh I don't love you at all," she interrupted. "I'm in love with some wild jungle-loving bearded git who kidnapped me at the airport this morning!"

I was bludgeoned for a second and then I laughed. "You should see him performing water aerobics, that'll really turn you on!" I replied.

"Ooh kinky!" she retorted.

"No, seriously love, I'd like to talk to you about the kids, I'm really in pain here!"

"Yes I know," she said, "I've seen it! And it's my fault entirely. I know that I said I'd keep them off junk food, but it's such an easy option when you're out with them and they're whingeing on and on and on. God, it sounds so pathetic, I feel really feeble!"

"Nonsense," I insisted, taking the reins. "How's it possibly your fault? I'm the one who got them addicted to the crap in the first place. If it weren't for my hideous eating habits, they'd have grown up being used to a normal healthy diet with the odd burger featuring now and again."

"Rissoles!"

"I beg your pardon?"

"Rissoles, that's what we had when we were kids. Mum used to make them out of the leftover roast lamb from Sunday, so we usually had them on a Monday night. Mmm, big thick greasy patties mixed with chopped onions and seasoning, served with loads of onion gravy, marrowfat peas and mashed potato."

"Stop it Ann, I'm salivating, I'll be forced to take a bite out of you if you keep on."

"The café's open!" she said.

I needed no other invitation and soon we were making love for a second time. It was just as provocative as the first, but this time more intense and lasted twice as long. When we finally released each other we were both covered in beads of sweat that soon became chilled from the night air that had seeped into the bedroom. We lay there exhausted but with just enough strength left to pull over the goosedown quilt and banish the cold. We fell into a deep sleep and dreamt of nothing that either of us could particularly remember.

The morning awoke us with the whispering fragrance of sea grass shaken by the wind; it felt like a mermaid was gently blowing on our faces. An absolute feeling of well-being washed over me and I smiled to myself before I could remember quite why I was smiling. Of course — Ann was with me. My lovely wife stirred and stretched out all four limbs in thorough contentment. I reached across and stroked her spine with my big fingertips. She purred with appreciation.

"Sleep well love?" I enquired.

"Umm, blissfully" she replied. "What's for breakfast?"

"Whatever you're making my sweet."

"Rat bag, I'm on holiday, remember?"

"Yeah, just kidding, I'll rustle up something exotic from a cornflake box!" I quipped.

"I'm going to talk to the kids this morning and lay down a few ground rules so that they know where they stand. I don't want any confusion over their new diet regime."

"Diet regime, at their age? I don't like the sound of that. You hear horror stories of children on diets!" she said sitting up.

"Not a fad diet or a fashion thing, a healthy diet, a controlled diet. And I think that we should enlist the aid of Marion as soon as you get back home."

"This all sounds a bit too drastic. Can't we just sort it out ourselves?"

"Marion's the way forward, love, trust me. Look what she's done for me, Ann. We've got to save our kids from obesity; it's the plague of the modern world!" I proclaimed from my soapbox.

"Ok love, but let's do it gently, eh? Mathew's very sensitive right now and June's so impressionable."

"You know me love, Mr Tactful!"

Something stirred in the corridor outside and then all hell let loose. In came June with guns blazing, scrambling up on the bed shouting, "Wake up Mummy, wake up Daddy." She then started to bounce up and down like a cartoon kangaroo, threatening to turn me into a eunuch with every bound.

"Alright, calm down, calm down, we're getting up," said Ann.

"What's for breakfast? What's for breakfast? What's for breakfast …" continued the marsupial.

"You'll see," I answered. "Now skiddadle while we put some clothes on."

She bounced off the bed and hurtled down the corridor to wake up her brother.

In the kitchen Ann perched on a bar stool in one of my running vests that fitted her more like a mini dress and watched approvingly as I worked my magic with a percolating machine. Junie was still bouncing in her nighty, this time disintegrating the sofa by pretending to leap from one cloud to another. Mathew came skulking into the room like a disinterested automaton and plonked himself on another stool.

"Morning son, you look refreshed!" I said sardonically.

"What's for breakfast?" asked the living dead.

"Cornflakes and bananas," I replied.

"What?" barked Mathew with a grimace. "I wanna bacon sandwich!"

"Don't you swear at me, young man, that kind of fare is banished from this kingdom so put all thoughts of it far from your mind. It's cornflakes or fruit — take you pick!"

"Mum!" he wailed.

"Don't look at me, Matt, I didn't do the shopping. Anyway some fruit will do you good; it's great for your complexion," she said swinging around on the barstool.

Mathew huffed and looked down at his feet. I fixed cornflakes and peach slices for everyone except Mathew, and all three of us sat around the breakfast bar. "I'll tell you what, son," I said between mouthfuls. "If you come walking with me this morning, I'll treat you to a sandwich at a bar I know, whaddyasay?"

Mathew raised his head. "Walking? How far do we have to walk?"

"I'll be honest with you, son, it's a long way — four and a half miles."

"That's nothing," said Mathew, thinking he was on to an easy treat. "I walk that to school."

"So you do," I said remembering, but there ain't a mountain on your way back home, I thought to myself. "Right, go and get dressed then, wear some trainers, we set off at 9:30!" I shouted at Mathew's back as he scuttled down the corridor to his room.

"Are you sure this is a good idea, Don?" asked a concerned Ann.

"I'm gonna show him how unfit he is, make him see for himself. He'll be more inclined to listen to reason then!"

"He's 13, Don, he doesn't do reason!"

"We'll see," said the master.

"Daddy, are you going to have your Full Monty now?" asked June.

"No sweetheart. I'm full up as it is. Did you like your peaches darling?"

"Yes thank you," she replied, "but can I have some more breakfast, please?"

"How about a banana or an orange, they're the best oranges in the whole of Spain!"

"Have you got any crisps?" came the response.

We reached the top of the Eiger and rested on a street bench to take on some fluids. I wasn't worried about the time today; we would rest as long as we wanted.

I could walk up this hill now with ease, but looking at Mathew was like looking at a reflection of my former self: crimson-faced, puffing and wheezing, sweat-stained and unable to talk. I took a bottle from out of my backpack and offered it to him. He lunged at the water and guzzled it way too fast, which made him bloated in no time and initiated a huge burp.

"A boy of your age should be able to run up that hill no problem. You're out of shape son, big time. You've been eating too much crap and it's gonna have to stop. Come on." The reprimand over, I set off again before the boy had time to recover. I marched along the Snake at a quick pace, occasionally checking over my shoulder to see if Mathew was still there. He lagged weakly, at least 20 yards behind; eventually alongside the strawberry fields I stopped and waited for him to catch up.

"Nice up here innit" I said.

"Yeah," puffed Mathew, with his hands on his knees.

"They're a part of the rose family!" Mathew looked about, wondering what I was on about. "Did you know that in Finland there's a town called Mansikkala?" I continued, "It means the 'place of the strawberry'. There are huge strawberry farms there and with the aid of the midnight sun, the fruit ripens almost 24 hours a day."

"No," wheezed Mathew nonplussed.

"Just thought I'd mention it," I said, smug with my gem of useless information. "Let me take you down, 'cause I'm going to, Strawberry Fields ..." I sang as I strode off.

Mathew waited for 30 seconds, mouth open, before setting off again, dragging his Nikes behind him. The road being level now allowed him to catch up with me and soon we were negotiating the Kenyan rally track and heading down into Calella.

Outside Papa's, we met Fernando who was surprised to see the nipper with me but wisely made no comment. I asked my coach if we could all go to the station bar because Mathew hadn't had any breakfast yet and I had promised him a sandwich.

"Never miss breakfast my friend, you'll always regret it later!" said the wise one, "Besides I could do with a coffee," he added as a sweetener.

"You only had cornflakes in the cupboard!" sulked Mathew.

"Just the job!" said Mr Enthusiastic. "Come on, get inside. We've a lot to do today."

Mathew found Fernando to be just a little too buoyant for his current mood, but he really fancied a trip in an American military jeep, so he clambered into the back post- haste.

We entered the station bar just as a train was departing south. Mathew and I occupied a table while Fernando got a round in. He brought back two espressos, an orange juice and a huge *jamón* sandwich that was more like half a loaf, but I figured that my son could handle it. "It's not bacon I'm afraid, it's local ham, but it's better for you," I said authoritatively. Mathew's eyes were bulging from their sockets as he launched into the bread like a starving hyena sinking into a zebra carcass.

Fernando sat with legs crossed, observing the boy with deep concern.

"I'm not going to lecture you to death, son," I said at length, "but your mum and me are so worried about the amount of weight that you and June are carrying that we're putting you both on a diet."

Mathew stopped chomping and looked at me in disbelief.

"When you get back to England you're gonna go to a class that I went to called Weight Watchers, and you're only gonna eat what the lady there says you can eat."

Mathew swallowed a big cheekful.

"That's no more burgers, fried chicken, Chinese, Indian or pizzas, in fact no more takeaway food at all. No sweets and no fizzy drinks, only healthy food from now on son."

Mathew's heart sank, visibly.

"I'll put my hands up to having encouraged you to eat all that junk in the past and I'm sorry, but it all ends here. You saw how knackered you were walking up that little hill today? Well, it will only get worse. Soon you won't be able to climb the stairs. And no bird likes a fat bloke, believe me son, I get no second glances."

Mathew's world fell out of his backside; his every waking moment had revolved around food. His parents might have well have put their hands around his throat and extinguished his air supply. He was gutted and declined to make conversation again for the rest of the weekend. June was just about as miserable, for she had had a similar dressing-down from her mother, but it hadn't sunk in quite as deeply as it had with Mathew. And so it continued. I maintained my programme with a stiff upper lip. We ate at Manolo's every night; Ann and I made wild, passionate love between the sheets; and the kids moped around the apartment, longing for a Playstation and proper food.

The taxi ride to the airport on Monday afternoon was a sullen affair. I tried to joke my way through it, but no-one was having it. I was torn between feeling guilty about ruining the kids' vacation and feeling justified that I had saved their lives. My unbreakable iron will was forcing me to see this year through in Spain and I had put no higher priority than winning the bet with Belington, but if Ann had asked me to I would have knocked out the pilot and flown the plane home myself just to be with them and share their pain.

We arrived at the terminal and piled out of the car. I tipped the driver heavily for having to put up with such a 'load of sourpusses' and we slipped into the airport. After checking in, the girls wanted to parade the shopping area for some gifts to take home so we arranged to meet up by the departure gates in time for the flight. They trotted off, leaving Glum and Glummer in an electrical goods store. I seized my chance; I had just half an hour to patch it up with my son, send him off to England with a smile and make amends for being such a despicable role model in the past.

"Fancy a beer son?" I said suddenly.

"Huh?" replied Mathew, snapping out of a dream.

"Do you fancy a nice ice-cold lager with your old dad?"

"Er, alright then," said the boy, shrugging his shoulders and not quite believing what he had just heard.

I knew that he wouldn't turn down a beer, as I had plied him with enough of it over the years with sips from my own glass. Mathew's red chubby face showed signs of a smile emerging, but he kept it hidden for the time being. I gestured to an open-plan bar across the mall.

If a product or new gadget ever impressed me, my first thoughts are always the same: 'I wish I had shares in the company'. Spanish-bottled *cerveza sin alcool* was one of those things. Not only did it present itself as a premium lager, but it had the taste of one as well. My first guzzle of cold lager in five months was like experiencing rebirth and I savoured the refreshment as it rinsed away 1,000 miles of road dust. I watched Mathew take his first swig from his own glass and then took delight in telling him that it contained no alcohol; he wouldn't have been allowed it in here anyway. Then I made a joke of saying that they should ship a load of it over to Uncle Ray. This did the trick and made Mathew laugh. I took the opportunity to apologise for all the lectures that I had bestowed on him and his sister during their short stay. Mathew shrugged his shoulders and said that it didn't matter, but he was just masking his hurt. I had to approach the weight-loss question again so I decided to offer him a deal. It was the only way that I knew how.

I told Mathew that if he could lose three stone over the next year and that if he keeps it off, only gaining weight in correlation to his height, then I would treat him to a 50cc scooter on his 16th birthday. His friends were all promised a moped for their birthdays, so it was an ideal carrot to dangle. Accepting my terms and beaming from ear to ear, Mathew shook on it. Getting one's child to do something through bribery might be frowned on in some circles, but my main concern was getting my children healthy. If a little bit of the old Simmons-style cunning tactics had to be used, then so be it. June's titbit had been a promise of a trip to Disneyland next year with three of her pals if she could also lose a stone in that time period. This also worked, so I was a happy man. It looked like Trish would no longer need a separate cupboard for her food, since everyone would be eating from the same bowl from now on!

The kissing, the cuddling and the 'I love you's' at passport control went on for an eternity and kept the airport officials quite entertained. The four of us were in tears. If any father was trying to make amends for his shortfalls at that precise moment, it was me. The kids begged me to come home with them, which didn't help to ease my conscience of how rotten I had been. I told them that I couldn't, but when the race was over, things would change at home big time; I would more than make it up to them.

I kissed my wife once more and asked her what it was like sleeping with a stranger.

She patted my belly and said "Lovely dear, I can't wait to meet his mate in six months' time!"

"I hope your husband doesn't find out about you sleeping with all these strange men!" I teased.

"My husband and I don't keep secrets from one another!" she said coyly. Ann turned and walked away, followed by the children who kept looking back while their passports were being checked. There was one last look back from the other side of the barrier and a final wave before they slipped out of sight. I tugged out my handkerchief and mopped my streaming eyes before heading for the train terminus. I had been totally humbled and needed the solace of a quiet railway carriage seat to comfort me.

WEIGHT CHART

Week
13. - 21st 8oz
14. - 20st 10lb
15. - 20st 5lb
16. - 20st 2lb
17. - 19st 11lb
18. - 19st 7lb 8oz
19. - 19st 4lb
20. - 19st 2lb
21. - 19st
22. - 18st 10lb
23. - 18st 7lb
24. - 18st 2lb 8oz
25. - 18st

Christmas in a foreign land just never seems right, especially without the warmth of your family and familiar things such as crackers, Paxo, the pre-lunch visit to the pub that has you inexplicably drunk on so little alcohol and, of course, The Great Escape on the telly. I had received various invitations to Christmas dinner, all heart-felt and with the best of intentions, but I had turned them all down. If I couldn't be with my family this year, then I would spend it alone.

Fernando had suggested that I go home for the holiday period, but I rejected the idea. The temptation to visit the drinking club and get involved in an almighty piss-up was far too dangerous to consider, let alone subsequently finding myself incapacitated with drink and gorging myself to bursting point. I had always been a major player in that game, but now, having six months without a single relapse, I was buggered if the festive season was going to upset my routine. Christmas for me would be a very different affair this year; aside from the over-indulging, I was also used to the dubious delights of an over-occupied house full of friends, distant relatives and people I'd never met before such as Trish's boyfriends or loners kidnapped from the pub. This year I would be on my Jack Jones and entertaining for one.

Manolo was closed for a week so I had bought in a hefty supply of frozen readymade meals and was prepared to stress the oven to the max. Having meals made for you is a relatively easy way to control your diet, so cooking, albeit just bunging a container in the oven, threatened to be something of a trial. Manolo had given me four bottles of house wine on my last visit. I had topped up on fruit and veg at Josep's stall, and was all set for the festive season. I had even bought a little plastic Christmas tree, complete with coloured lights and a fairy; all I needed now was a paper crown.

Fernando's apartment and mine were the only ones occupied now. Even José and María were away for two days; they had gone to stay with her brother in Tordera, which was about six miles away. I had been invited to join them for a game of bowls, but had declined graciously. All the same I felt extremely honoured to be welcomed into people's homes after such a relatively short time of knowing them; it made me feel like I belonged. "It's just another day," I kept telling myself. "Lots of people spend it on their own, it's nothing special." Even so, I longed to be home with my family and the bitterness of being away was ripping my throat out. I resolved to survive the festive season by shelving my emotions and religiously bulldozing through my routine. The goal of many more Christmases to come was high on the agenda, so this misplaced lonely yuletide was just a glitch on the calendar, a necessary evil that I had to endure.

The day dawned slowly. Five seconds ago I had been gently swaying at the end of a parachute transfixed on an up-and-coming patchwork quilt — England. The sky was a still and tranquil place to be, disturbed only by the occasional whine from my straining guidelines. I touched down perfectly, like a feather on a marshmallow and my chute slipped away to become a goosedown duvet. I opened my eyes and smiled warmly; it was Christmas Day. I decided that I would open my presents after breakfast, so I took my usual early morning swim and trawled calmly through the tepid water, feeling the chilled air with every raised arm. This was the first Christmas morning of my adult life that I hadn't woken up feeling like a dehydrated furry turd, needing six Mars Bars and a litre of Coke to put me back on track. It was like living someone else's life and I loved it.

Back in my kitchen I munched my way through a couple of slices of toast liberally spread with local honey and sipped at my black coffee, all the time staring at my little pile of presents. This has to be another first, I thought. No bottle-shaped gifts! People must be taking me seriously," I murmured. After eating, I gathered my pressies and headed for the terrace. The first three were from the kids and were all books. Trish had bought me Vegetarian cooking; Mathew's was The Complete Guide to Marathon Running; and June had misunderstood the plot altogether with A Clubber's Guide to Spain.

A fourth package contained a box of 38 Christmas cards from associates and my friends, ranging in tone from the sweet to the downright filthy. By the time I had finished reading them, tears were rolling down my cheeks. The one that got me the most was from Les, it was misspelt and said, 'I miss your moning'.

José and María had kindly bought me a set of *boules*, something that José might live to regret now that I could get some practice in. Manolo and Christina had given me two Dunlop tennis rackets, after overhearing that tennis would be introduced into my programme. Anna and Fernando had also opted for a sporting present, although much to my amusement rather than use wrapping paper they had simply tied a large red ribbon around an expensive set of golf clubs. "See me on the crazy-golf course with these boys!" I said, delighted. The last present that I opened was from my wife, a little box that had kept me guessing. Ann had always bought me clothes for Christmas and, of course, the obligatory bottle of malt whisky would sneak its way into my stocking, so this tiny gem had me foxed. I was surprised to find inside an eternity ring, an ideal gift given the recently bolstered realisation that true love never dies. Apart from my wedding ring, I'd stripped myself of jewellery months ago and now that my porky fingers were steadily turning into chipolatas, even this ring was also going to be shelved. I tried on the new ring but it was just too tight for any of my digits — another challenge for me, I noted. "I'll be seeing you in a couple of months," I vowed, putting the ring back into its box for safekeeping.

It was time to 'phone home', and spent the next two hours talking to Ann and the kids. I had them queuing up for a chat and nagging at the person in front to 'hurry up' because it was their turn to talk to Dad. I got the lowdown on everything, from the latest antics of the dogs to the position Arsenal held in the premiership; from the 'wickedness' of the latest mobile phone to how busy it was in John Lewis. Of course I also got a progress report on Mathew and June's diet and learned that 'some arsehole' had opened a door onto Trish's Beamer in a car park, causing an indent on her otherwise peerless paintwork. When I came off the phone after a multitude of 'I love you's' I was totally forlorn and deflated. Suddenly I had a sense of being contained, as though I were living in a lead-lined box and nauseous from the smell and taste of plumb.

I looked out of the window; it had started to rain and my books were getting wet on the terrace. Normally by now I would have been back in The George for a few pre-Christmas dinner sherbets and boasting about how much money I had spent on the kids' presents. There would be the odd game of spoof and the most outrageous exaggerated stories that you'd have ever heard. I would have taken centre stage, as always, with cigar smoke, beer and malt whisky choking up my arteries like fur balls in a cat's throat. I had to get out. I decided on a 50-mile bike ride to cure the doldrums, and promised myself a plate of pasta Nicosia, a Spanish salad and a couple of glasses of Manolo's red wine on my return before delving into one of the kids' books. This Christmas I was a far cry from the bloated incoherent gasbag who could never ever satisfy his insatiable appetite for voluminous amounts of yuletide fare.

••▼••

Mile 40: Head down, squinted eyes guarded against the constant drizzle, pains in the thorax but the pedals keep going round and around.

Mile 41: Arms on the handlebars, lost in thought; the features blur by unnoticed.

Mile 42: Drop down into low gears to negotiate a hill climb, bike dripping wet and unresponsive; pissed off with the continuous cold jet-spray fired up from the rear wheel on to my back and down into my shorts.

Mile 43: Few cars on the road today but every one of them intolerant to cyclists and fly by far too close, drenching me with icy puddle water. The road rolls by underneath me with an uncaring slushy hum that is grating upon my nerves.

Mile 44: Thighs burning and shin bones feeling like they might splinter under the strain; my fight for breath becoming an intense effort and steam is rising off my back like the wisps from a hot-water spring, impressive for 12 inches but then overawed and diminishing into the ether. Pedal, tarmac, pedal, pedal.

Mile 45: Thinking of home and a long, hot shower to rid this skin-numbing cold; a plate of pasta and some red wine knock-out drops savoured in the comfort of my sofa. Keep pedalling …

A ten-foot smear of fresh blood dispersed by the rain snapped me from my reverie and had me clutching hard on the brakes. Obviously something had been knocked down and had dragged itself into the tall grass beside the road, but what? I screeched to a halt and dismounted in one action. My immediate thoughts were to help the poor wretched thing, then I stalled wondering whether it might not be an injured animal at all but a slain human being, another cyclist wrestled from his ride and slaughtered by a maniacal half-man, half-beast with a penchant for murder on Christmas Day. This may be a lure into the killing field. "Silly bastard," I told myself, wiping a dewdrop from my nose. I then heard a hauntingly pitiful cry that pulled my heart through my chest. It was a plea more human than animal that alerted every nerve in my body and sent adrenalin flooding through my system. Emboldened, I rushed towards its source and lumbered through the undergrowth where I came across seven newborn sand coloured shivering pups trying unsuccessfully to suckle from their almost lifeless mongrel mother. Her entrails were exposed and woven into a mess of umbilical cord and womb sac and her legs were clearly broken from the impact of the force that had hit her. By instinct she had gone through labour to bring her puppies into the world even though they faced certain death, and now she was clinging onto life so she could try to protect them. A miracle was what she needed, and that miracle came in the shape of me!

Eye contact in humans is something primeval. It lances through the barriers of modern society and contacts forgotten senses that need neither words nor actions; it expresses divine intent. The look from that dying animal was one that I could not begin to explain, but it brought out a pity in me that has generally become lost to mankind. Between us it was understood that she could let go of her frail hold on life, leaving her weary head in my hands and her pups to my love, in the cold, wet grass on the side of the N11 on a rainy December the 25th. I stroked the little dog's motionless soaking face and promised to care for her babies as if they were my own. Taking off my jacket and T-shirt, I lined my saddlebag with the shirt and placed the frozen squirming things inside. The icy cold drizzle would have normally made me shudder, but right now I was in a bubble and didn't feel a thing. I wanted to bury the mother there and then, but having no tools available pledged to come back the following day and do the job properly. As I replaced my jacket, I had just one thing on my mind now, milk. If I didn't get some sustenance into these little mites within the hour they would surely all perish. Unstrapping the saddlebag from its pannier, I tucked it inside my jacket in a hope that my body heat would protect the pups from hypothermia and rode with all my might back towards the *ático*.

"Baby milk, powdered baby milk," I muttered to myself, "and a dolly's bottle, that's what I need." I suspected I'd have more chance of finding a dinosaur turd. What I needed to track down was a chemist that was open today, of all days. There had to be one, surely people got sick on Christmas Day as well. A thought occurred to me: Ask at the police station, they would know of the emergency chemists.

Screeching to a halt outside the cop shop, I laid the Peugeot down and raced up the steps carefully clutching at my saddlebag. The door was locked! "Fucking hell," I shouted, before noticing an intercom button on the doorframe, patiently waiting to be pressed.

"¿*Si?*" came the response.

"I'm looking for a chemist that is open," I said.

"¿*Que?*" said the voice.

"Oh, what's the word for it? Far ... farm ... farmer, *farmacia*," I blurted out at last.

"Ah *si*," said the desk sergeant again, and gave me the address of one in Pineda.

I fled from the station like a wanted man running scared from a vengeful posse, and arrived pink-faced and steaming, beneath the chemist's traditional green-flashing cross. Outside normal opening hours the emergency chemists in Spain are manned by only one member of staff, so they close the doors and operate on a hatch system rather like a garage forecourt. The doors in this case were shuttered, through which I could glimpse an extremely beautiful girl in her early twenties, swaying her body in the most provocative fashion that I had ever seen. What the hell was a gorgeous young thing like her doing selling plasters on *La Navidad*? Didn't she have someone who adored her, worshipped her and would die if she ever left his sight?

"*Felices pascuas*," she greeted me in a voice that could melt diamonds.

I felt myself turn a bright shade of red and lost all power of speech. Luckily, a sudden movement from under my jacket jerked me back to life and I attempted to ask for seven tins of baby milk and seven feeding bottles. She just about understood my request and set off to retrieve my goods, no doubt asking herself how a man of my stature could produce seven children, or even want to. Returning to the kiosk with just the milk, she indicated that they were out of bottles. Bollocks, I thought. This was the only place open for miles; I would have to improvise. First I thought about using a rubber kitchen glove with a hole in the finger, but didn't know the word for glove and 'Marigold' alone clearly wasn't going to do the trick either. Looking around for inspiration, I found the answer to my problem staring me in the face. There on a cardboard display case by the window was Durex!

"Why is there always a pretty girl serving you when you need to buy Johnnies?" I complained inwardly. Taking a deep breath and pointing to the display I said "Durex" and turned positively purple.

She smiled, understanding totally that seven babies were enough for a man at my age. "*¿Cuantos?*" she asked.

It had been a while since I had bought a condom and I couldn't recall how many you got in a pack so I plumped for seven again.

"*¿Por esta noche?*" she said impressed.

I tried to explain that they weren't for me but for my dogs, but all I got was a knowing 'of course' look from her; clearly she had heard every excuse in the book. Determined to prove my innocence, there was nothing for it but to open my jacket and peel back the lid of my saddlebag to reveal the magnificent seven. The look on her face said it all. Her heart was deluged by a tidal wave of love, pity and guilt — for thinking such wicked things about this rotund saint standing before her in the rain. Breaking every house rule, she unlocked the door and let a stranger into the shop. Instinct told her that I was to be trusted and it was the only way she was going to get a proper look at the puppies. She proceeded to give me some useful advice on feeding them and recommended that I give each one as much as it would take every two hours, night and day until they were two weeks old. After that, I should feed them less often but with larger quantities. I was also going to have the task of forcing them to defecate by wiping their bottoms with a damp cloth. Mum, of course, would have used her tongue, but I didn't think I could quite manage that.

Realizing that the pups were newborn, the assistant asked me how I'd come by them, so I carefully re-enacted the road accident and my chance find. She praised me for my kindness and asked if I would like anything else. To be 20 years younger and a bachelor came to mind, but I swiftly whitewashed those thoughts. In truth, I wished that the mother of these seven little orphans were still alive and longed for the gratification that only a large glass of whisky could provide. Both of these were spirits and neither of them was about to appear, so I shook my head and started to pull a wad of notes from my bumbag. The assistant refused to accept any payment, saying it was the least that she could do. So, the season of goodwill still had meaning after all!

Once inside my apartment I reached for the central heating dial and turned it up to full blast. I could hear the system charge into life way down in the boiler room for everywhere else was silent in the building. Pulling the saddlebag from out of my soaking jacket, I gently placed it onto a work surface in the kitchen and set about making the pups a bed. A grocery cardboard box was ideal and I lined it with one of my car blankets, the softest one I could find. Placing the almost lifeless forms into their new home and covering them with my T-shirt, I retrieved a bedside reading lamp from my room and set it up over them to raise their body temperature. Now it was time to make up some milk. I figured that one condom would equal one feeding bottle and that it should be enough for the first feed. It had been 20 years since I last made up baby milk and had to resort to reading the label for instructions. It said to use boiling water but I couldn't pour that straight into a condom so I made up the milk in a glass jug and waited for it to cool down.

Ripping open the packet of Durex and fumbling with the slippery teat reminded me of one adolescent night I'd spent trying to roll back the unfamiliar product inside out, getting it half on and then having it fall off during the act. It made me chuckle and eased the tension a little. I towelled off as much of the lubricant as I could and stretched it out. "Surely no one could fill that!" I gasped, both impressed and amazed by its length. The next job, actually getting the milk inside, was a tricky operation that took many attempts to perfect. In the end I found that placing the condom into a tall glass and rolling the ridge over the rim of the glass, gave me the right support so that I could pour in the liquid without needing a third hand. I tied a knot in the end, pinpricked the teat and set about nursing my seven unexpected Christmas presents. The puppies had warmed up a little by now and were squirming in their nest. I picked up the first one, turned it onto its back in the palm of my hand and tried to push the wet bendy teat into its mouth. The pup wouldn't respond so I resorted to force, slipping my little finger into its mouth and then placing the teat inside and giving it a squeeze. To my relief it did the trick and the little fellow sucked greedily for 15 minutes until it was bloated and fell asleep. "Bloody hell, this is gonna take all night" I groaned, as I contemplated the remaining six. I could already see that was going to need to mix up more powder because this lot wasn't going to last.

After the pups had been fed, it was time to get them to defecate and I set about the grim task with a bad taste in my mouth, or there would have been had I done it au naturel! Wetting a hankie with warm water I stroked each one's bottom in turn. I couldn't believe the response as pure liquid came trickling out. For the most part, it was odourless but I had no doubt that would change very shortly. Three hours later after I had showered and cooked my evening meal, I sat on a stool shovelling mounds of pasta into my mouth and sipping on Manolo's delectable wine. I couldn't take my eyes away from my new family. They lay fast asleep, snuggled together under their sun lamp, twitching occasionally or stretching out a paw. I felt brilliant, proud, homely and content. Of all the lovely Christmas presents this year I had been kindly given, none could surpass the gift of life I had received seven times over.

There followed a long sleepless night but I got through it and still with a smile on my face. In the morning I managed to find a veterinary surgery that supplied me with the correct nursing milk for puppies and a large syringe with teats that made life so much easier. I contemplated keeping the condoms for future use, but quickly shook my head to that thought. Word of mouth meant that many people soon found out about my 'Immaculate Conception', bringing scores of well-wishers and interested parties to my door. Finding good homes for my pups was not going to be a problem. I had found my own favourite almost from the word go, a strong little mite with an independent nature who strangely enough disappeared whenever I had company. When the day came for the puppies to be re-homed, this one still hadn't been claimed but he had no need to worry — he already had a home with me. I named him *Siete* and sensed that we were going to be mates for a long time.

CHAPTER FIFTEEN
The calling

WEDNESDAY 9TH OF FEBRUARY WAS A DAY LIKE NO OTHER; a day that would forever flicker in the archives of my mind like the dusty reels from a nickelodeon. It was the day that I first laid eyes on *mi casa*. I had shaved off another thin veneer from my best time to date. Coming in at 2:22:03 this morning and collapsing into a gasping jittery heap had been a major achievement. The fact that I could by now jog the course helped enormously to improve the times that I was making and with a weight of just 16 stone 8 pounds, my body needed less energy to propel it through the streets. I still felt nauseous, asthmatic, and giddy, and had the impression that a Challenger tank had parked on my chest, but at least my legs remembered their purpose. Even Fernando was impressed.

"Did you get anything for me at the supermarket?" he asked.

"What?" I puffed.

"Well, you must have done your week's shopping while you were out, looking at the time it has taken you."

"What?" I spluttered, breathless.

"Only kidding, old chap. You have broken your record again. *Enhora buena mi amigo*. Take the rest of the day off."

"I always have the rest of course-day off," I managed to wheeze.

"Yes, but today you actually deserve it!"

"Oh, thank you boss!" I said, cap in hand.

"*De nada.*" Fernando pocketed his stopwatch and strode off, leaving me to water the grass with perspiration. Course-day afternoons usually consisted of a two-hour soak in the bath, a sleep out on the terrace in my favourite wicker chair and maybe a swim before heading off to Manolo's for dinner. Today, however, I was listless and woke up after only an hour into my slumber, itching for something to do. It had just turned 3:30; the sky was a perfect blue with a scattering of cottonwool clouds, criss-crossed with aircraft contrails. I was reminded of the dogfight scenes in the 1960s' classic film The Battle of Britain.

"Good afternoon my arse! Put ya hands up ya Bosh bastard," I said to myself in a Cockney accent, mimicking my favourite line. I was as stiff as a board; perhaps a stroll down on the sand might loosen me up and get rid of this unwanted dose of the fidgets. The air had a distinct nip in it now due to a light northerly wind that had sprung out of nowhere, so I crept into the barley room to fetch a sweatshirt. As I walked into the room, a through draft from the open balcony door brought to life a flimsy net curtain that danced up and down before ensnaring itself on the rough edges of a louvre shutter. I was drawn out on to the balcony where I focussed an area that I had seldom paid much attention to. The rambling hills that billowed to the back of Pineda were a patchwork of thick forest and farmland that was dotted with a scattering of white houses. Magnetized by the view, I suddenly felt it: that was where I needed to be this afternoon. Loathe to admitting it to myself but I actually wanted to climb another bloody hill.

I could, of course, have taken the car, but I hadn't used it more than three times in seven months and I didn't want to drive it today either. Fernando would have been more than happy to come up there with me if asked, but I wanted to explore this one on my own, to soak up the spiritual experience more than anything, and for that I needed to be alone. A sudden burst of noise from a 'fart and hop-it' in the street interrupted my train of thought and gave me an idea. I hadn't ridden a moped in 20 years; to be honest I would have absorbed any machine that I sat on and would have had to have it surgically removed from my posterior. Even though I owned a motorbike shop, my love of two-wheeled transport had always been from one perspective — they made me money. Today, though, a moped was exactly what I needed.

Anna opened the door just wide enough to peer round it cautiously, but when she saw who it was she threw it open and welcomed me warmly in, making a fuss of Siete who was happily perched on my arm. Circola frantically tried to get a better look, shredding my kneecap raw in the process (much to my annoyance) before sniffing, growling and running off down the corridor to hide.

"Can I leave him with you for the afternoon, I need to go out?" I said in pidgin Spanish.

"Of course you can, I'd be delighted," she said.

"Circola?" I enquired.

"Oh, she'll be alright," she insisted.

I smiled and handed over the soft bundle which clearly intended to lick to death the sweet-smelling lady.

"Have you been using the bath oils that I bought for you, Don?"

Still haunted by my near-death experience in the bath, I ducked from answering with a hasty, "*Si*. Is Fernando here?"

"In his study, go on through."

"*Gracias Señora.*"

Five-Names looked up from his computer where he'd been pretending to do some research while playing FIFA international soccer. Seeing him behind his large desk reminded me how I used to spend an unjustified amount of time in my office. It felt good to be liberated from all that.

"Not sleeping old boy?" he asked, closing down the game.

"Couldn't Fern, I need to ask you a favour actually!" I replied.

"Of course, what can I do?"

"Could you lend me your scooter? I'd like to go exploring." I went on to tell him about the hills behind the apartments that had caught my eye and of a calling to venture up there alone to accept my destiny. Bemused by my sudden use of hippie terminology, Fernando looked secretly relieved not to be invited along, probably because the Spanish team was beating Brazil three–one and it was still only half time.

"You'll have to wear, how do you say it in English, a crash hat?"

"Crash helmet."

"*Si, si*, a crash helmet. It's law now!"

"No problem, where are the keys?"

"In the kitchen, but it needs petrol!" he shouted to my back as I left the room. This was one of the rare occasions when Fernando didn't have the correct vocabulary for an item, but looking at the helmet he was probably right the first time. A hat was more like it, being about 30-years-old and having no visor, still it would do for the purpose. I squeezed my fat head into it, folding my ears down in the process and making me look as though my face was about to burst. A more apt description might have been that a baboon had curled up in the helmet for a snooze and left his rear end exposed for all to see. Still on the plus side, a few months ago the prospect of me riding a moped would not even have been entertained, let alone physically possible.

Within minutes I was bombing along at a breakneck 22 miles per hour and heading for the hills. After filling the tank at Joe's garage I took the N11 towards Gerona, a part of the course that I usually covered by human power. It felt mighty peculiar to be propelled along a route that looked wonderfully unfamiliar. Half a mile on I turned left and started an upward climb. Fernando had warned me that the roads up here were not the best in Spain and he was right. Before long, the tarmac gave way to a dirt track pitted with potholes that I negotiated with all the flair of a circus chimp on a unicycle. I stopped a little further on to look back at the view.

From here I could see most of Calella and Pineda and a fair part of the course, but I was still a long way from the top. I rode on with strawberry fields to the left and strawberry fields to the right. Up ahead lay a pine forest whose cedar-scented hand beckoned me forward. Seduced by the aroma, I had no choice but to enter its cool, damp stillness. The canopy of dark green sweet-smelling boughs was pierced by the glares from a hundred thousand pairs of eyes of woodland critters who had been disturbed by the din of my machine. I soaked up the essence and bathed in the laser beams of dappled sunlight that fell on me as I ambled up the track. Once through the forest I entered an olive grove where up ahead the road forked. To the right the pavement diminished into a grass track barely discernible apart from some wheel ruts. Again, led by my compulsion I veered right, ankle deep in rain-quenched meadowland and carried on until I was halted abruptly by a rusty chain that stretched across the width of the drive. Hanging from its middle was a faded sign, illegible from where I sat on my idling bike, so I killed the engine, steadied the thing and got off for a closer inspection. The sign had obviously been there a very long time; it read '*Se vende*', for sale.

Years of corrosion meant that the agent's phone number was no longer visible much to my frustration. What was or what had been for sale? "Act first and ask questions later," I told myself, as I cocked a leg over the chain. I froze in mid-straddle, alarmed by the sound of a barking dog coming up fast and the distinctive jingle of bells and bleating from an approaching flock. Stepping back and almost losing my balance I peered to my right and caught sight of 50 or so goats being herded my way, stopping to nibble on tufts at any opportunity before being forced ahead. I watched for a while before the dog and its master came into view; the spirited collie had let his owner know of an intruder long before I appeared. The ancient farmer looked the best part of a hundred years old; his brown leathery face was wizened and deeply lined from a century of sunshine while his short frame was hunched from a lifetime of graft. He wore a grubby and torn blue work jacket teamed up with a worn-out black beret and carried a rather mature boater bag, slung over one shoulder. The dog stopped barking and jerked his head to one side. The pair of them stood motionless, contemplating the big git at the end of their drive. The old man's weary eyes seemed to be reading my body language like an open book. Both of us waited for the other to speak but neither of us did. I was stunned by the awesome picture-perfect scene before me; a real-life oil on canvas of breathtaking Catalonian beauty, depicting traditional rural life against a backdrop of olive trees and pine forest falling away towards golden beaches and an aquamarine sea. Only now was I aware that from up here I could see at least five miles in either direction of coastline; to me it was Nirvana.

The old man had seen enough; he leant on his stick and resumed walking. As he went by, I nodded and he returned the gesture; as he did so, something passed between us, something indescribable, a primitive knowing. Following the herd's progress through the olive trees, I noticed a group of buildings that I had missed earlier, nestled in among the plantation of trees. As I studied the landscape more closely, other buildings became apparent: an elegant farmhouse, a barn, some smaller houses and various outbuildings. There was an entire complex up here, a hidden hamlet — and a perfect retreat just crying out for restoration. The hairs rose on the back of my neck and my cheeks flushed with excitement. The house had been calling me and I, at last, had heard its cry.

It had just turned seven o'clock when Anna answered the frantic knocking at her front door. She opened it and raised a finger to her lips, whispering "Shush, you'll wake the puppy!"

I hastily apologised and pointed towards the study. She nodded in acknowledgement and I hurried down the hall like an excited bull on insemination day. Fernando was still at his computer, only now Spain was thrashing Italy and it was five minutes from time.

"You're right about those roads," I said, tossing the keys to Five-Names.

"How did the bike handle them?"

"I came off twice but I don't think she's too badly scratched!"

Fernando looked worried.

"Only kidding, she's a handy little tool!" I went on to tell him of my find and its whereabouts, spilling over with such enthusiasm and joyous detail that I hadn't noticed my coach's frown.

"¡Finca López!" said Five-Names, rolling his eyes. At that moment, Anna came in to arrange the blinds and stopped what she was doing on hearing her husband mention the López farm. Fernando explained to her where I had been.

"¡Bonita!" she said.

"Yes it is," agreed Five-Names.

"*¿Se vende?*" I said. The couple looked at each other and both laughed. "Is it for sale?" I asked.

"Yes and no, Don. The property has been up for sale for more than 20 years, but it will never sell my friend, not in a 1,000 years!"

I had sold hundreds of houses in my time, but the sale was usually a lot quicker than that.

"What do you need a farmhouse for anyway?" continued Fernando.

"I didn't know that I did until today, but I have been wondering lately whether I really want to go back to my old routine when this race is over. I might just want to retire here, but a wife, three kids, two ponies and three dogs would be a bit of a squeeze in the *ático*."

"Very true, Don," agreed Five-Names. "I am pleased that you would want to retire in España, but there are plenty of other farmhouses you know!"

"No, I want this one!" I insisted.

Fernando sighed. He translated our conversation to Anna and then turned to me. "I'd better explain to you about the Lopez saga. Sit down my friend, as this might take a while!"

I obliged, eager to learn some local history.

"About 25 years ago, Juan López and his wife died within a few months of each other. Some say she died of a broken heart, I personally think that she just missed having someone to nag and wanted to be on his back again. Anyway, he had always been a hardworking traditional Catalonian farmer, born into the cultivation of olives, grapes for the wine market, almonds, goats' cheese and pork. The old fellow was honest, well- respected and dedicated to his family, of which there were four boys and two girls. One son happened to be homosexual; he was ostracised by the community and ran off to live with a man in Ibiza. I understand that he's now returned to the mainland and lives in Barcelona. Another son, the youngest, trained to be a veterinary surgeon and had a practice down in Villanueva y Geltru until he retired. The two eldest brothers took control of the farm when their father became too old, even though they had very different ideas for its future and were constantly at each other's throats. Meanwhile the daughters took turns in looking after their parents, in between caring for their own families.

When Juan died he left specific instructions in his will for the farm to be run in the traditional manner and forbade the family to split up the land under any circumstances. He also instructed Antonio, the eldest son, to be sole executor of the will.

This caused a bitter row between the brothers; Pepe moved out of the farm and they haven't spoken to each other since. Five of the six children wanted to sell immediately, but the girls and Pepe wanted a bigger share because they had put far more into the business than the others. Sadly, none of them could agree upon a figure. Nobody considered Eduardo in the Baleares and Gerardo was happy to receive anything he could get, but he refused to get involved with the dispute. In the meantime Antonio placed his two sons and their families in the two smaller farmhouses and vowed never to destroy the dreams of his father, 'whatever the cost'.

Anna who was standing with her arms crossed on the back of Fernando's chair, nodded intermittently in agreement. She knew the story off by heart and didn't need a transcript.

"Right then," I said, feeling that these were only minor details and unable to see where the problem lay.

"That's not all my friend, by a long shot," continued Fernando.

I sunk back into my chair.

"The López children are all in their 70's or 80's now. The goat herder that you saw yesterday is almost definitely Antonio; he is 82. They live a long time, the López people, and personally I feel the only way that a sale will ever take place is when all six of them are dead!"

"*Todos muertos*," repeated Anna dramatically.

"But then there are the dependants. 23 of them, I believe, and they have children as well, most of them adults. You have met one of them, Anna's friend Lolee. Every one of them is in contention for a share in the place, but nobody will settle for an equal share. The larger families want a higher payout, but nobody will foot the bill for an arbitrator. It's never going to happen, Don, because there are far too many people to please."

"It'll happen!" I said as I stood up and looked at my watch. It read 7:45 p.m. and my stomach was rumbling like a moonshine distillery.

"Listen amigo, if you won't take it from me then let me take you to the agent who has dealt with the López estate for all these years. He's a friend of mine, and he'll still be at his office!"

I knew the estate agency very well. It was close to the church in the old part of Pineda, and I had stopped there many a time to browse the properties in the window, a pastime that had become semi-obsessive for wont of something better to do. Weighing up the true value of the properties for sale against the asking price was something akin to entertainment for me and a link to my old life — I just couldn't turn the habit off. Very few of the people I knew in Spain were aware of how much I was worth. No doubt, there had been speculation and I imagined most of them would have drawn their own conclusions from the extravagance I had displayed, such as buying a penthouse suite just to flop in while I trained for a year, or like leaving a 60 grand motor in the car park to gather dust. To win this new trophy though, within half an hour, I really needed drive home that I not only wanted *Finca López* but had the necessary credentials to it.

My associates back home had always attributed my fortune to me being an excellent salesman, be it cars or property. Not so, I would tell them, my road to success lay in being a good buyer; I always bought with a healthy profit margin ahead of me. Daylight robbery some people called it, while others labelled me ruthless. However, making a killing on a property wasn't on the agenda this evening, I was hunting for myself. I had been drawn up a hillside and enchanted by a dilapidated farmhouse that had captivated my heart, only the second property ever to have that effect on me, and fire was running through my veins. I had come up against some pretty awkward and almost bizarre real estate deals in the past, but this little beauty was unreservedly the most complex. It was going to take more than an open chequebook and a gobful of spiel to pull it off.

Miguel rose to greet Fernando as we walked into his office. They knew each other well, and two of Fern's children had bought houses through the agent. The opening conversation was in Catalan, and included Miguel's secretary, Mila, who seemed to be able to converse and type a letter at the same time. Linguistically silenced, I stood there feeling like the invisible man, impatiently rolling my thumbs with my arms behind my back. "The runner?" queried Miguel, finally turning his attention towards Mr See-Through. Although my grasp of the local language was extremely poor, I knew this word all too well.

"The runner," I confirmed, taking up the agent's offer of a handshake.

"You speak Catalan then?" He said in English.

"Very little, I regret."

The conversation continued in a mixture of Catalan and English with Fernando as translator.

"I hope that you didn't mind me calling you 'the runner' Mr Simmons?"

"Not at all," I laughed. "I take it as a compliment."

"Tell me, how are you finding the *ático*? I dealt with the exchange you know!"

"You did? Well there's synchronicity for you," I said contently.

Miguel looked puzzled. Mila came round from her desk and introduced herself. She was tall, slender and gave off an air of cool sophistication that caged a vixen underneath. She appeared to be about 25-years-old, with long dark hair neatly pinned into a bun and thick black eyelashes encircling the bluest eyes I had ever seen. She smelt of Calvin Klein's Eternity.

"Enchanted," I said rather demurely. The next ten minutes hinged around me: questions about diet and weight loss and the times that I was now achieving — all the usual stuff — heaping so much praise on me that I thought my inflated ego would rupture. Nevertheless, their charm was seductive and almost lured me into the open jaws of master salesmanship. Deciding it was time to 'talk business', I announced that I wanted to buy a local farmhouse in a secluded spot with plenty of land. Miguel expertly wound a tether around his potential victim and slowly pulled me closer, turning to the question of a price range. I casually flaunted the million-pound marker and the shark's eyes ignited. Letting go of his catch for a second, the estate agent rushed over to a filing cabinet and hauled out several folders. "We have a number of properties that would suit your requirements *Señor* Simmons, one in particular ..."

Fernando interrupted abruptly, "He wants the López farm!"

All the ropes recoiled with whiplash speed and the agent's savage jaws snapped firmly shut. Agitated eyes flashed about the room between the *immobilaria* and his secretary in abject disappointment. Their forlorn faces appealed to Fernando for help, but he just gave a nonchalant shrug. I on the other hand was quite enjoying the scene that I had caused; the electric disharmony was just what I needed to gain the upper hand. Even the hardest of estate agents would be panicking now, having sniffed the aroma from the profit of a killer sale, only to have it blown away a second later with no chance of a reprisal.

Miguel turned to Five-Names in despair; "You must know the López saga!" he pleaded.

"I do, but I wondered if there had been reconciliation?"

"No, and there won't be, not in our lifetime." Mila resigned herself to a no-sale and returned to her seat to resume typing. I could tell that they both thought that this one had got away, but I wasn't going to let it lie.

"Are you the López' sole agent?" I asked, trying to penetrate their apathy.

"I'm afraid so," said Miguel dejectedly.

"Good because I've got a proposition for you!" I hadn't, I was just thinking on my feet. "Do you have the details on this property?"

Miguel rolled his eyes and gestured to Mila for her to retrieve the much-travelled folder. "This is the fifth brochure that we have prepared for the family!" he said wearily.

I understood the anguish that must come from more than 20 years of fruitless advertising, but I hoped to put an end to all that. I was handed the papers.

"But it's all in Catalan!" I exclaimed.

"It's a Catalonian property!" concluded Fernando.

Miguel went back to his desk and slumped into his seat. The brochure had four pictures of various buildings, one of which I recognised as the main house, but I couldn't read a word so I handed it to my coach to translate. The sulky shark was muttering in Catalan to Fernando, apparently telling him that I wasting my time, but Five-Names persevered on my behalf. While I listened, Miguel said nonchalantly that he would make tentative enquiries to see whether the farm was still up for sale, but his hint of sarcasm made it clear that he thought this was simply pouring yet more money down the drain. The more that I heard, the more eager I became. A breakdown of the property listed two grand farmhouses with outbuildings, a large barn and two worker's cottages also with outbuildings, all approximately 300 years old. The two main houses were intriguingly identical, although the one that I had seen hadn't been lived in for a quarter of a century. Fifty per cent of the land was made up of woodland dominated by pine forest and almond trees. There were also vineyards and an olive grove covering approximately 21 hectares, together with pasture, pig sties and a small dairy as well as adjacent land rented out to neighbouring farms. The total area must have enclosed the majority of the hill and the revenue that it brought in was equally distributed to all six children after Antonio's profit and running costs.

Antonio López lived in the main house with his wife, while his two boys and their families occupied the two smaller cottages that were situated somewhere in the forest.

"How old is this brochure?" I asked.

"Oh, six maybe seven years," replied Miguel, who was now sat next to Mila searching for a suitable alternative to the *Finca López*.

I asked for a pen and piece of paper, which Mila duly supplied, wiggling her hips and showering me in her scent once again. Nice bottom, I thought as she catwalked away. The asking price on paper, working on 200 pesetas to the pound, would have been roughly a million pounds, but adding to this general inflation and the recent surge in foreign house prices, the current price was more realistically likely to be two million. It was an absolute steal at the asking price and I would have normally shed blood trying to acquire this place to make an easy profit, but making a profit wasn't an issue for once. I simply had to have the house.

What I needed now was to get Miguel on board the Simmons bus. I offered a sweetener to see where it would go. "Miguel, how much commission do you usually charge on a property deal?"

The shark looked up from his paperwork and replied "Around six per cent of the selling price."

I paused for a few seconds. "Tell you what I'll do then."

The trio waited with baited breath.

"If we can secure a deal with the López family, I'll pay you commission at ten per cent on the current market value of the farm, which I estimate to be two million pounds sterling!"

Miguel dipped his head and shook it slowly. "You don't understand do you?" he said softly. "Your offer is superbly generous. I normally wouldn't let you know that — I'd just whip the contract out and snap your hand off — but the problem remains the same as it did 25 years ago. All six family members have to sign, and the best that we have managed to achieve so far is having three of them in a solicitor's office at one time. That was then; we now have the complication of a further 23 liggers trying to steer the play of events and all pulling in different directions." He looked at me expecting a reaction, but got nothing save a stony face. "Look, even if we did achieve the impossible and gathered everybody in agreement, are you willing to pay that much money for a property that has sitting tenants?"

Fernando had to translate most of this and from it I could see that the promise of green had sparked a tiny flame of enthusiasm in the greedy boy's eye. I needed to dig further. "Can't I just buy the derelict house, a few acres and the right of way?"

"We've tried to go down that road before Donald, but the López family have made it quite clear that the farm cannot be carved up into smaller lots under any circumstances. That is set in stone!"

"Hmm," I said. "What's all this about sitting tenants?"

Miguel continued, "Well, under current Spanish law, if you buy a property that has tenants in any of the buildings, you are legally required to evict them via court action. This can be very expensive, take a long time and cause a lot of heartache. Antonio has lived on that farm his whole life, so even if he was given a substantial amount of cash, he still wouldn't want to leave the only home he has ever known. Plus, he also retains the right to work the land for six years after a sale, if he so wishes."

"I see," I said, twiddling the pen through my big fingers and staring down at my notes. My mind raced. I had to come up with a super plan and come up with it before Manolo shut-shop for the night. My destiny lay up in 'dem der hills' and the only way to make this dream a reality was going to be through respect, diplomacy and understanding — and a mountain of cash, of course.

Time was distorted to an insect's perspective, neuron fast for me but at half speed for the rest of the world. In those 60 or so seconds I devised a preposterous proposal that no right-minded individual would have normally considered. I knew that the land and property were protected from any major upheavals and that restoration work could only be carried out under the strictest of supervision. Development or any further construction was out of the question. These factors pleased me greatly because it had been the natural beauty of the old house that had attracted me to the property in the first place. I swivelled round to face my audience.

"Right, as I've said, the current value of the farm should be two million pounds, but with Antonio and his children occupying three of the four houses on the estate and him having farming rights and tenancy rights, it lowers the value considerably. Am I right?" I looked at Miguel, Fernando translated, and Miguel nodded in agreement.

"Good, so the actual value is probably about a million. So this is my offer ..."

All three of them leant forward a little. "I'm willing to pay two million pounds including your commission rate of ten per cent. I will also pay each of the 23 descendants a sum of £50,000. Plus, if the deal goes through within the next two weeks, I will pay you, Miguel, a further £25,000 as a bonus."

They all leant back again in astonishment, but I wasn't quite finished. "I'll also give you, Mila, a gift of £5,000!" She drew her hand to her mouth and blew me a kiss.

Fernando raised an eyebrow; he knew that I was loaded but had no idea that I could be so frivolous. Before anyone had time to speak I continued with my offer. "I'll honour the rights of the tenants and allow them to live in their respective houses until the day they die, or if they wish they can leave at any time. They can continue to farm the land indefinitely if they want, but I will take financial control. Antonio can expect a hefty wage as farm manager, his sons likewise." I could see in Miguel's face that after 25 years, the impossible just might begin to happen. "And finally," I said, "I want to sign over a deposit within two weeks from today!"

Miguel could contain himself no longer. He jumped up out of his seat and rushed over to shake hands with Father Christmas. He hadn't been this excited since his wedding night and was visibly shaking. "We'll make it happen, *señor*, you have my word on it!" he said in Catalan. Five-Names did the necessary and we all shook hands together. Miguel said that he would be in contact and bade us goodnight, while Mila twisted in her seat picturing a new wardrobe of clothes and a dedicated shopping trip to Madrid to buy them.

"Are you out of your fucking mind? Offering that old codger such a hideous amount of money for that rundown heap of stones on the hill!" said Fernando, once we were out of the shop.

"Watch out for that dog turd," I replied, pointing to the pavement.

Five-Names negotiated the fresh egg with nimble expertise and continued his rant; it was only the third time that I had ever heard him swear, so I knew the man was upset.

"I always knew that you were deranged by taking up this bet with Belington, but now I know that you have no brain. Your brain has been removed! Are those autumn leaves that I see blowing down the street? No, they're peseta notes falling out of Don Simmons' arse!" he raged sarcastically.

"Thank you for your concern my friend, I appreciate your intentions, but ..."

I stopped and faced Fernando in the street, hoping to appeal to his sensitive side. "... Money's no object mate. I'm in love and I've just gotta have it!"

The Spaniard held his tongue, slapped silent by the emergence of an emotion he knew too well. We walked on, both of us mulling over our controversy. Five-Names understood passion, knew its insatiable drive and compared my proposal with his own past crimes. "I'm sorry my friend," he said at some length. "I have no right to tell you what to do with your money. You've earned it, so you enjoy it!"

An emotional weight took its leave from my shoulders and I thankfully felt at one with my coach once more. I rallied the evening with some light talk.

"Thanks old boy, I'm just about to enjoy some of it right now!"

We had arrived at Manolo's, where Anna was being entertained at the bar by the outrageous antics of Andrés, Pedro and the *Mañana's*, and some highly flirtatious comments from Carlos. She looked pleased at the arrival of the rescue team, as the usual cheer went up when we entered the room and we grinned in response.

"Gentlemen, release my wife!" commanded Fernando in true regal fashion.

"With pleasure, your Grace, she's become quite unruly in your absence," replied Andrés. Anna smacked his shoulder in reprimand and courteously he waved us all through to the restaurant.

The talk at dinner was all about my offer. Although it seemed to be a certainty that the deal would go ahead, I wasn't counting my olives just yet. Anna's compassion shone through when she put the whole affair in perspective, saying "By this time tomorrow 6 elderly couples and 23 families would be a lot more comfortable and financially secure, plus 25 years of bitter rivalry would be over." The question that had been lingering on Anna and Fernando's lips was finally asked: Did I intend to live in Spain indefinitely? My answer was simply. I had been drawn to that idyllic spot in the woods by the hand of fate and had never felt so complete in all my life. It was where I belonged.

•• ▼ ••

My last *boule*, the lightest one that I owned, was readied for my final shot. I arched my back, came up on my tiptoes and swung my arm, flicking my wrist at the last moment for extra height in a desperate attempt to displace José's perfect shot covering the *cochonnet*. The gardener had been throwing *carreaux* all afternoon and I had come so close to beating him, but still no cigar. I had already christened my two opponents a couple of petanqueurs, but only I seemed to find this funny. The *boule* sailed through the air in slow-mo like a shot from the Matrix movie; its antagonists followed it unreservedly. Wallop, it hit Fernando's closest *boule* and scattered every other one apart from José's.

"Bollocks!" I said. "What a wanky shot!"

José stuck his cigar in his mouth and smiled contentedly.

"I'll have you one day, you fucker."

José sniggered. Just then Anna called from her balcony to tell us that Miguel was on the phone with urgent news. We dropped everything and ran indoors like tearaway schoolboys on pretend horses. The conversation was mostly one way, with Fernando uttering the occasional 'yes' in Catalan. Anna and I looked on anxiously to hear the outcome. Five-Names put down the receiver and gave me a quizzical look.

"Well?" I said.

"Were you standing by my scooter when you saw the old goat herder yesterday?"

"Yes why?"

"That was Antonio alright. He has agreed to speak with you. This is the furthest that Miguel has ever got with him. He has always been the main opposition to the sale. What on Earth did you say to him?"

"Nothing, I just gave him the nod!"

Five-Names looked puzzled. I re-enacted the gesture, but it clearly didn't have the same effect on him.

An urgent meeting had been arranged with all six dependants for seven o'clock that evening at the farm. Miguel had also informed Fernando that as from eight o'clock that morning all but one of the 23 children had received a letter and an invitation to lunch at a relaxed hotel in Pineda for one o'clock that day. They had all been informed of the 50-grand payout should the sale go ahead, so a full house was expected. One family member had been on holiday in southern Spain, but Miguel managed to fax the hotel and obtain a positive response from the López offspring. It looked like the two estate agents had moved like shit off a greased shovel to get this one in the bag. They had stayed at the office until one o'clock in the morning, returned there by six a.m. and used half-a-dozen motorcycle couriers to ensure that the invitations were in place before eight o'clock. Miguel had also personally delivered letters to each of the six López siblings. Miguel's incentive of a £225,000 commission had done the trick. All I needed now was the Simmons' charm and I would have a result.

Darkness leant on a rhubarb sunset; its icy shadows reminded me that winter was not done with yet and I promptly retrieved a chunky cardigan from my closet. I knocked for Fernando and we took off for the farm, picking up Miguel on the way. We three characters might have been selected from an exhibition on the variations of male attire. Miguel in an Armani suit, Fernando in an Adidas tracksuit and me in desert boots, flame-red baggy shorts and a Starsky and Hutch cardigan. My dress sense may have relaxed but my astuteness had not; I needed to know everything that had taken place earlier at the hotel lunch. Miguel told us that the meeting had generally gone in my favour. Everyone apart from Antonio's sons, who wished to speak with their father before making a decision, wanted to urge their parents to sell. What everyone really wanted to know was the identity of the prospective buyer. Miguel had informed them that his client, although wanting to live there, fully intended to run the farm in the traditional manner with its current personnel as management. It was more out of curiosity than concern, but for the people that I was about to meet, my character was point-critical for moving this project forward.

The Willey was an excellent touring vehicle for languid summer evenings, but in mid-February it was positively the wrong bit of kit to take up a mountain. Sitting in the back in his flimsy designer suit, Miguel shivered like a fragile newborn fawn. I still had the feeling that I was trying to buy something that wasn't for sale and that this meeting was just a formality, a part of the stalling process manufactured by Antonio. I hoped that I was wrong. At the point where I had taken the right-hand fork the previous day, Fernando veered left instead, taking us through more pine forest and a larger portion of the olive grove until we reached the main entrance to the farm. The two farmhouses were identical; they sat at right angles to each other, one facing south and the other facing the rising sun. Between them were an orchard and gardens. Apparently the houses had been built by twin brothers, the founding members of the López family business, who had matched everything the other did in life, including the day they died.

Sancho the Border collie scrambled to his feet the moment we entered the drive and announced the arrival of the jeep as it ground to a halt alongside the courtyard well. I cast my eyes over the array of vehicles that littered the yard, from which I judged their owners to be hardworking souls with little prestige about them: two old Japanese four-by-fours, a dirty Citroen CV van that had seen better days, and two brand new John Deere tractors. Drawing on my experience of sussing out showroom visitors before moving in to make a sale, I had gained their mark before entering the building. A thick-stemmed, gnarled and ancient grapevine dominated the doorway; although it was still winter-dormant, it seemed eerily conscious of a stranger's presence. I swore the thing tightened its grip on the building as we entered — even the plants up here were defiant in the defence of their heritage.

The previously buoyant and crowded kitchen fell deathly silent when we stepped in. The gaze of 20 or so people almost hurt. I felt guilty, exposed and vulnerable yet in the company of honest people whose knowledge spanned centuries and far exceeded my grasp on the ways of the world. They understood the weather, the earth and knew how to create life with their bare hands; these people were the backbone of a land in which I was subservient. Pine logs crackled in the hearth of a large stone fireplace and gave off warmth that not only removed the chilly night air, but filled the room with an ambience of well-being. I made a quick scan of the kitchen; it had heavily worn terracotta quarry tiles on the floor, its thoroughfares shaped concave and polished with time. Massive oak beams surrounded by whitewashed plaster dominated the walls, but above the work areas they were tiled with the most hideous brown and orange reliefs that I had ever seen. The surfaces were either terracotta tiles or black-veined marble and, in the centre, hanging from the ceiling was a traditional wooden pot rack. Either side of the fireplace were a couple of paisley-patterned, padded armchairs, which had gotten too close to the fire.

You don't have to take your boots off to come in here, I thought.

Most of the congregated family were dressed in plain and dowdy clothes, typical of a farming community, all except one who wore a bright yellow Ralph Lauren dress shirt. Eduardo stood out like a lone Barbie doll in a boxful of Action Men. They definitely had a clan look about them: rather short and stocky, almost square with a walnut complexion and jet hair; the elders were mostly bow-legged.

The introductions over with, we sat around an impressively large oak table that could comfortably seat 14 people. I had been warned that Antonio López was a very stubborn man and set in his ways. He spoke to his immediate family for about ten minutes before turning to Fernando and making a statement. I watched with a mixture of admiration and anticipation. Finally Five-Names turned to me. "It's yours. Antonio won't try to stop the sale."

I was shocked. I thought that more of a fight would be needed. All the same, I could tell that the story wasn't complete. "And?" I said, keen to establish what the catch was going to be.

"Antonio told me that he had always wanted one day to have the money to buy out his brothers and sisters, so that his sons could continue the 300-year-old tradition of López' working the land. While he appreciates that no-one lives forever, but if he were to pass away suddenly his empire would tumble like a house of cards. The hyenas would move in and a Catalonian tradition would crumble into dust. By selling to you, he can partly fulfil his father's legacy by keeping his name above the door and the business within the family. For that, he is very grateful to you."

Antonio's wife had her arms around her husband's shoulders. He leant back into her bosom, drained of all the zest that he had possessed yesterday; the sparkle was gone from his ebony eyes, but she held him upright, proud of all that he had achieved and 100 per cent behind his decision to sell. She'd had enough of the fighting and wanted them to enjoy the few remaining years they had left together.

"Yet, this is also the saddest day of his life," continued Fernando. "Antonio feels that he has failed his father, failed his children and has lost the family name by making this decision. He will never know happiness again."

For the first time, I began to regret ever having laid eyes on the house. Listening to the pained speech of the López patriarch, I felt like a heartless criminal. If I was going to live here with Ann and the children, I didn't want to be surrounded by eternal damnation nor did I want to be a despised landlord either, greeted with false camaraderie every time we crossed paths. A compromise was needed, and fast. Deciding to play for time, I got up to stretch my legs and walked over to the fireplace. Forty eyes followed my footsteps. Three hundred years of López history was in this kitchen, 300 years was now on the chopping block; could I just bring down the cleaver? No, there had to be a better way.

Turning my attention from the flames, I noticed that two of the youngest grandchildren had fallen sound asleep in one of the large armchairs. The ambient rosy light flickered across their angelic faces, highlighting their innocence and their blissful unawareness of what was going on. All at once, I knew what I had to do.

"Fern, what's Catalan for 'partner'?" I asked my coach.

Five-Names looked over and smiled, "*Soci.*"

The head of the tribe raised his head and jolted back into life; another coin had been put in his meter.

"Ask him this," I said. "Would Antonio consider me as a partner? I'd let him buy out his brothers and sisters, but carry on running the farm. He and his sons could live here forever and we'd split the farm's profits 50/50. All I'd ask, if he wouldn't mind, is permission to rename my house and plant a border of trees to give it some privacy!"

Fernando carefully translated my offer to the silent audience, whose hearts pounded against their ribcages. The fire's flames danced up the chimney. Antonio's wife Carmina broke ranks and waddled over to 'the office', a space under the sprawling oak staircase equipped with a wooden desk and two wooden filing cabinets. She opened a drawer and removed the largest key that I had ever seen in my life. Placing it on the kitchen table in front of her new partner, she spoke to me directly in Catalan.

I didn't understand a word, so I turned to my coach for subtitles.

"She said that yesterday her husband saw a man looking at his father's house on the edge of the olive grove. He was a big man with a nervous tic, but an honourable and respectable man. There was something about him that suggested they would meet again ..." Fernando stopped short.

"And?" I said.

Fernando looked embarrassed, for once. "Me being your friend confirmed his judgement of you." He was choked with pride at the warmth and respect that the community held for its Olympic gold medallist.

I swallowed hard to keep my composure. Addressing the family, I vowed that I would strive to learn their language, for I was powerless without it. Fernando translated accordingly as Antonio handed me the key while saying something to me in his native tongue.

"He said you'd better learn the lingo if we're going to be filling out tax forms together," laughed Five-Names.

Handshakes were exchanged around the room followed by kisses galore, some soft and perfumed, some crinkled and prickly, which were planted on every available cheek. The jollity woke up the babes in the armchair who quickly spotted the massive spread that had been produced from out of nowhere and displayed on the table: jugs of homemade wine, bottles of the farm's spring water, a mighty charger of home-reared ham, bowls of olives, plates of *pa amb tomqueat* and huge wedges of cheese. It was a lethal concoction for a weight watcher so I politely declined the invitation, but Fernando urged me to indulge the tradition otherwise the family would be insulted. Even though we had a table reserved for us back at Manolo's, there were times when even the strictest of rules have to be thrown out of the window. As we feasted, Five-Names told me a little about the farm. Apparently wild boar still ran through the woods and the odd wolf came to rummage through the dustbins. "I wonder what great door this fabulous old key unlocks?" I said, gripping the hefty piece of metal.

"Oh nothing," said Fernando. "It's just been in the drawer for years and Carmina just wanted to get rid of it!"

The spring water was the sweetest that had ever passed my lips, and I even found time for a little wine, but the ham was like bumping into a childhood sweetheart. I had forgotten how beautiful meat was. It fell apart in my mouth and sent my tastebuds berserk. If it weren't for the fact that I was in company, I could have easily downed half the hock. I contented myself with a bowl of olives instead, every now and then wishing that I were alone. Everybody in the room was delighted that the sale had gone ahead, although I suspect Antonio's sons thought the Englishman had more money than sense. I had surprised myself too: a lifelong sole trader, always being master of my own ship, and now I was going into a partnership, something that I'd sworn I'd never do. This time, though, for whatever reason, it felt right to share the post.

The three of us left the meeting with moods as individual as our dress sense: Miguel busily spending his pay cheque in his mind; Five-Names delighted to see a happy ending; and me with my mind on my new future. Tomorrow I was going to hit the routine hard and notch up a gear with the training. Although all the paperwork would be sorted out in a couple of weeks' time, I decided to put off viewing my new home until after race day; besides, I wanted Ann to be with me when I went through the front door for the first time.

"The only downside to you buying this property" said Five-Names as we headed down the hillside, "is the company you have chosen to restore it."

"Huh?" I said.

"It's taken 25 years to sell that house and it'll take another 25 for the *Mañana* brothers to complete the job!"

Miguel and I laughed, but Fernando remained unnervingly serious.

CHAPTER SIXTEEN
Helping hands

THE SMELL OF FRESHLY CUT GRASS was the only nice thing about being this close to the ground; it spiralled in front of me slowly, like the after-effects of a funfair ride, and threatened to bring up my breakfast. Dribble hung from my mouth like cold clear jelly on a slow descent to Earth. I had flashes of Ridley Scott's Alien about to take someone's spleen out and of a certain Oxford and Cambridge boat race where at the finish the camera closed in on a rower who had clearly spent every ounce of energy in competition and lacked even the strength to wipe away the bucketload of saliva that oozed from his cake hole. My heart felt like it might just punch its way through my ribcage and each breath had the capacity to inflate a blimp.

I was down on all fours with my fingers splayed out, arms rigid, a towel draped over my steaming head and panting like a woman in the final throes of labour. Once again I had pushed myself too far and, once again, I was paying for it. My body lacked the basic blood-sugar level necessary to remain conscious and I collapsed sideways with all the grace of a discarded sandbag. I woke up ten minutes later in the recovery position under a poolside parasol with Fernando fighting off a swarm of flies that were eyeing me up as an easy meal. Sitting up, I felt the blood drain from my head. I had a dull ache at the back of my eyes and without warning a stomach spasm brought forth a tide of cornflakes, coffee and bile with such gusto that it shot past my shoes.

"That'll help with the diet!" quipped Five-Names. "Stay there while I get a bucket."

"I don't need a bucket now," said sick boy.

"No, but I do!" said my coach. Finding one of José's watering cans instead, Fernando filled it with pool water, marched back to his charge and let me have the lot, full in the face.

"Jesus!" I cried.

"You're certainly moving closer to him," replied my coach. "Come on, we'll clean this lot up later." Five-Names helped me to my feet and hauled me up to my apartment via the lift.

"How did I do mate?" I asked, spent and leaning against the elevator wall in sweat-stained disarray.

"You made a mockery of the rules once again."

"Yeah, but what was my time?"

"Down by 6 minutes and 20 seconds."

"That's good, innit?"

"The time's good, but your health is suffering. This is not the way forward my friend."

I managed a wry smile but my mentor wasn't so jubilant. The lift door opened at the penthouse, Fernando hoisted me up again and dragged me to my door. Once inside I sprawled onto the sofa while he ran a bath for me. "We've reached a crossroads, my friend. While you are having a soak, I'm going to decide which path to go down. Come and call for me at seven," he said sternly and strode out of the door.

I hummed the theme tune to the old, popular TV soap, Crossroads, a few times before crawling to my bath, my mind boiling with scenarios. I had given my all today; there was nothing else to give. A crossroads? It felt more like a cul-de-sac. 17 weeks to go, and my ultimate goal still seemed to be light years away. I sank into another void. The last thing that I remembered before falling asleep was Fernando saying, "Call for me at seven ... seven ... seven ..."

Siete was licking his master's blistered toes protruding from under the duvet, in a feeble attempt to receive some nourishment from the delicious toe jam. I hadn't had the energy to feed him this afternoon and the poor hound was ravenous. Six and a half hours had been wiped away from my calendar as if they never existed. I felt, heard, smelled, dreamt nothing in those lost hours until the angel of death loomed over me and softly spoke my name. Fear shot through my veins like a blue jolt of 50,000 volts and my eyes flicked open in an instant. A murky grey shape hissed an unintelligible language right in front of my face; its rancid garlic breath, mocking and repugnant, threatened to anaesthetise me once again and claim me for the underworld. The smell of garlic, cigars and grass cuttings... Grass cuttings? I finally emerged from my semi-comatose state only to find myself staring at José's ugly mug.

"Aahh!" I screamed.

"He's still alive," said the gardener nonchalantly before heading for the terrace.

Fernando had been frantically trying to rouse me for the past 15 minutes and had finally resorted to enlisting the help of the caretaker and his spare set of keys.

"What the fuck's going on? Why is it dark? Why are you two in here?"

I sat up in confused panic.

"We're in here because I thought that you were in trouble! It's dark because it's 8:30 and what's going on is that we two are going out to eat the best steak that you've ever tasted in your life!" said Five-Names.

"What about Manolo's? What about my diet?"

"Don't worry; I've cancelled Manolo's tonight. As for your diet, it can suffer a little setback, besides you could do with the protein. Now come on. Jump in the shower and wake yourself up."

"You couldn't get us a pint of water first could you mate? I'm as dry as a Pot Noodle!"

"What's that?"

"Never mind."

"I'll get your water. You should have drunk more before you went to bed, it's not good for your system!" said Fern, wandering into the kitchen.

"The sound of that steak is though, me old mate," I replied as I put on my dressing gown. I had often talked to him about my favourite meal — grilled tomatoes, fried mushrooms, onion gravy, medium-rare steak and chips, but reckoned I had a one-in-hell's chance of getting it this year. I sat on the bed licking my lips.

"Where are we going then, Fern?" I demanded, as Five-Names reappeared with the water.

"La casa langosta."

"That's a fish restaurant!" I protested.

"Yes, but its steaks are renowned throughout the province. You'll not find a better steak between Barcelona and the French border, and that's a promise!"

"I'll be the judge of that one, old chap; I've had a few in my time."

"Yes, I can believe that!" said my coach, mocking me. "Come on we'll be late. I'll meet you down in the jeep in 15 minutes." And with that he left me to it. While I showered I wondered what Fernando was up to. He had obviously come up with a master plan and a good one at that, or we wouldn't be celebrating, but celebrating what? I dried myself and wandered down to the kitchen for another glass of water. As I opened the fridge door and grabbed a litre bottle, I realised that for the first time in 20 years, I could see my crown jewels without the aid of a mirror. There I stood with a bottle in one hand, illuminated by the fridge light and taking pleasure in the sight of my own private parts when José popped his head through the kitchen doorway.

"*Buenos noches Señor Desnudo,*" he said with a big tombstone smile.

I jumped a mile. "For fuck's sake José, I thought that you had gone long ago!" I spluttered, covering my manhood with a transparent bottle.

"I water your plants," said the gardener in broken English.

"Well, go water your own, you big shit. You're gonna do me in creeping round the house like that. I'll see you tomorrow for a game, yeah?" I said, motioning a *petanque* throw.

"*Si, si, señor. Buenas noches.*"

"Bugger me," I said, leaning against the worktop and swigging from the bottle. "Where's me dog?" I asked myself and yelled for Siete. The puppy came running in from the living room, wagging his tail faster than the human eye can track.

"What have you been up to you little bugger while you dad's been asleep?" I said, almost rubbing my dog's ears off.

Oh let me see, thought Siete. I ate a newspaper, then I sicked it up on the veranda, dug up some geraniums and pissed in the fountain. Oh and I've just demolished one of your trainers, so fucking feed me would you!

"I bet you want some dinner, eh boy?"

"Sunk in has it?"

"'Ere you are, some of your favourite," I poured out a large helping of dry dog food into Siete's bowl and topped up his water dish. Just then I heard frantic tooting coming from the car park, so I ran to the bedroom and threw on some clothes. Grabbing my keys on my way out of the door I shouted "See you later, boy!"

"Bring back some proper food this time!" barked Siete, through a mouthful of reconstituted pseudogrub for the younger dog.

La casa langosta resided in the centre of Pineda in a cobbled square between a florist's shop and a handmade furniture store. In theory if you wanted to you could buy your lady some flowers, get her drunk over lunch and then try out the beds next door. Fortunately for me the only thing open at this time of night was the restaurant. Fernando introduced me to Sergio, the owner, who showed us to our table. They spoke briefly in Catalan from which I managed to pick out the words 'runner' and 'wager'. I didn't need the conversation translated; I knew that the whole town was betting on me, and Sergio was probably no exception. I was unintentionally becoming a minor celebrity in town, but being a big fish in a small pond can have its drawbacks: it can inflate your ego, restrict any progress and, ultimately, you could find yourself letting people down.

Sergio offered us an aperitif on the house, but Fernando insisted that we would prefer a brandy after the meal. Now you're talking, I thought. What we needed first was plenty of water and Sergio made sure that we received preferential service. The salad arrived and I realised where Five-Names had nicked the idea for 'Don's salad'. It tasted as good as Manolo's, if not better, but I said nothing. The waiter poured Fernando a snifter of local red; Five-Names tasted it and gave his approval, then we both received a glass. "Not a bad drop of wine this!" I could feel my lips forming the words and heard my own voice making the sounds, but still my brain refused to admit it. As far as I was concerned, wine still failed to qualify as a man's drink.

"An excellent year, I feel. It has captured the wild flowers that grow in the meadows on the slopes of a vineyard near Santa Coloma."

"Mm, buttercup and daisy," I said without a clue.

Twenty minutes later the main course was placed in front of us: two huge oval plates brimming with mushrooms and tomatoes lightly brushed with olive oil and grilled to perfection, English-style chunky chips, thick onion gravy that could only have been Bisto, and medium-rare sirloin steak fit for a king. The waiter even placed a jar of Colman's Mustard on the table.

"You delicious old bastard, how did you know?" I declared jubilantly.

"You've told me enough times about your favourite meal, I could have cooked it myself."

I smiled, "Thought you'd give it a go then?"

"If it's good enough for the goose," said the wise one.

"Gawd bless ya," I said in Dickens-mode, with a mouthful of succulent meat, juice, mushroom, chips and gravy. My more-refined coach relaxed into his chair and waved his steak knife at his amigo's chest." You have buttoned your shirt up the wrong way my friend!"

"Worry ye not Fern. Just get that steak down you neck, it's fantastic."

"I told you so," laughed Fernando and the two of us proceeded to devour our meal in complete satisfaction. Between mouthfuls, the conversation centred around an analysis of our progress, the results being weighed up against the damage it was causing and the reality of achieving our objective. Fernando's optimism had not wavered in the least but he now realised that if we didn't change tack once again, we were never going to make it. He wanted to enlist some help and knew precisely the right man for the job.

"Do you think that you could persuade Terry to come out for a couple of weeks, starting from April?"

I was taken aback; I hadn't foreseen that question coming. "I can phone and ask him but I can't just expect him to drop everything and zoom out here. He's a busy old boy!"

"Yes I appreciate that, but couldn't you make it part of his employment or something? A paid holiday perhaps? Don, we really do need his help!" Fernando knew that Terry had a wealth of knowledge when it came to running, having run the Wycombe-Half eight times already and countless other marathons to boot. It was clear to him that without Terry we would be sunk in the water.

"Let me think of something. I'll give him a bell tomorrow," I said pensively. A dessert of strawberries arrived so I changed my brandy order to a Muscatel, of which I'd now developed a hankering for.

The phone call to Terry had started well. He was pleased to hear from me and enthused about everything that I had achieved, especially the weight loss. From there the conversation deteriorated briefly, when my reason for phoning him became apparent. Terry protested that he couldn't possibly make it at such short notice; it was his son's birthday party that week and his own training schedule couldn't be interrupted. I gently brought him round, saying that if he could make it the following week, I would pay him his hourly rate for every hour that he was here, plus he and his family could have a free two-week stay in the apartment this summer. It was an offer too good to refuse, but Terry being a man of principles said that he would talk it over with his wife first and let me know tomorrow. I knew that he had been hooked and sure enough the next day, I got the ok from England. Fernando breathed a sigh of relief, but another lost week meant that we were cutting it fine.

••▼••

Problems and rows were par for the course in my early days as a secondhand car dealer and I had come across my fair share of dodgy traders, lawless pikeys and ruthless gangsters; they all seemed to be part of the game. It was some time before I gained a modicum of respect as a no-nonsense honest dealer who wouldn't take shit from anyone. I wouldn't back down from a soul and if smacking a few heads together meant not getting shat on, then so be it. My reputation had preceded me, but the way I saw it was that you either ran, talked your way out of a situation, or fought — and sometimes talking just wasn't enough. Of course, being a fat bastard narrowed my options down a bit, so I had become pretty handy with my fists. All the same, I considered my rucking days to be long gone and never expected to be called into action again, especially not today.

It was Sunday 7th of March and I was on the last three-mile stretch of my fortnightly cycle ride, the 11th time I had been around the 100 mile course and, as expected by now, it had become a whole lot easier and more enjoyable. I had time to appreciate the early lilac blossom if I wanted to, but ever the competitive beast; I made each cycle ride an event to better my previous time. Even allowing for getting caught in a couple rainstorms and one time helping a farmer with some runaway cows, I had still managed to clock up progressively improved times. The weather that day had thrown at me at least three seasons. When I started out at six o'clock, it was bitterly cold with some icy patches on the road; by mid-morning a warm thunderstorm had blown in from the sea; and by the afternoon, it was bright and sunny with just a hint of a breeze, wonderful for a country jaunt.

There's many a splendid thing to be seen on a long stretch of road, and two miles outside of Pineda was the most pleasing of them all: a half-mile strip of coast road known affectionately as BJ Boulevard. On either side of the street, ladies of the day would display their best assets with the minimum of modesty. Strutting their stuff up and down their patch in outrageously skimpy outfits, whatever the weather, they luridly tempted anything with a cock. I was a familiar face to most of these girls who knew that I wasn't out for business. My proper English gentlemanly approach with a cheery 'Good morning' as I passed, often got me a blown kiss and a wave. I was fascinated and amused by the girls' antics. Admittedly I was sometimes aroused too because some of them were really quite gorgeous, but being a faithful old dog, I was never tempted. Besides, I couldn't cope with a crab comb!

As I neared the end of the line the bike began to shudder, then I heard the tell-tale flapping noise of a sure-fire puncture in the rear wheel.

"Oh bollocks!" I sighed, bumping to a stop. Considering the mileage that these tyres had covered, it was a wonder that this was only the second puncture I had sustained in all the time I had been in Spain. I pushed the bike onto a piece of waste ground and flipped the machine upside down. Palm trees offered some shade from the now blazing sun, but I didn't take up their offer due to the presence of a white plastic chair and stolen parasol advertising Orangina. This was someone's territory and the quicker I could repair my inner tube and be on my way, the better! Stan and Harold had provided me with all the necessary pieces of kit to perform roadside repairs and I soon got into the swing. Thinking back to my youth when things like scrumping for apples over neighbours' fences and building trolleys out of bits of old pram, planks of wood and string brought back glorious smells such as creosote and mossy tree bark. The smell of rubber reminded me of changing tyres on my doorstep using a pair of Mum's kitchen spoons, which I would ingeniously reshape for her, earning myself a thick ear as a reward. The sound of clip-clopping interrupted my reminiscences, as a pair of red stilettos came into view through the spokes of my prostrate machine and glittered before me like the footwear of a tainted Judy Garland. The sweat that had built up on my eyebrows now avalanched into my eyes, making me squint from the effects of salt water and sunshine. I lifted my head and followed an exquisite pair of long legs right up to Heaven. They halted at a pair of pink, lacy knickers that just about covered the Morris Minor bonnet, under a red mini skirt no bigger than a scarf.

"*Hola*" said their owner.

Raising my head higher, I was delighted to see that the top half was just as pleasing as the bottom. Wearing a rainbow-coloured knitted vest cut just below her nipples, revealing the firmest pair of breasts that I had seen since my school days, the 'lady' had long, dark wavy hair that cascaded over her shoulders and defined a face so pretty and not unlike that of a young Elizabeth Taylor. She could only have been about 18-years-old and her violet eyes reduced me to a puddle. She spoke Castilian but her accent was eastern European, making her words hard to understand. Six times she asked me if I wanted sex and six times I refused her, questioning my sanity every time. If ever there were a test for one's marital vows, this was it. When I struggled to my feet and stood face to face with her, I became almost powerless. She radiated sex appeal like a beacon and I had to back away some distance. Reaching into my shirt pocket I pulled out a hefty-peseta note and handed it over; in the nicest way possible I was telling her to piss off. She looked confused but took it anyway, then wiggled off chewing the inside of her cheek and glancing back to give me a look that asked 'But why?'

I breathed a sigh of relief and went back to repairing my bike. Every few minutes the two of us would lock eyes and she'd give me a little wave in appreciation of my benevolence. Every time a little tingle was detected in my loins, I'd dismiss it and carry on with the puncture. She sat under the parasol, cross-legged, waiting for her next customer; I knew that it wouldn't be long. The tyre popped back on with ease and I located the valve and attached it to the pump. Within seconds I had the right pressure in the wheel and was turning the Peugeot upright again. As I was placing the repair kit back into the saddlebag, I heard the crunch of car tyres stopping abruptly on a loose road surface. I looked up to see a German-registered black Mercedes emerging through the dust.

'Ere we go, I thought. Drop yer drawers and ten bob's yours! How wrong could I have been? Even from 20 yards away I could see that the girl was filled with pure fear; I could almost feel her trembling. I didn't like the look of this. Two men in black suits burst out of the car and flew at the girl. A big shaven-headed bastard was shouting something at her that sounded like Russian; the second, a five-foot nothing, pockmark faced weasel of a creature, was smirking beside them enjoying the abuse that the square-headed ape was raining down on the tearful girl. The weasel's eyes flicked around the immediate area, he must have caught sight of me but obviously didn't consider me a threat. Another man, older and more relaxed, had noticed me however. He sat in the front passenger seat, talking into a mobile phone and was watching me, watching them. The gorilla ripped the girl's handbag from her shoulder and emptied the contents onto the pavement. Among the lipstick, chewing gum and condoms he found the money I'd given her. Swearing like a demented lunatic, he reduced the girl to a helplessly shaking wreck. Holding the note to her face, he spouted more abuse, screwed the note up and then threw it at her. Not content with this, he half turned and delivered a harrowing backhander to the side of her face. I felt the pain as flesh made contact with bone. She let out a pitiful moan as a spurt of blood and saliva shot sideways from her mouth and splattered on the pavement. It made me feel physically sick and triggered an animal instinct in me to steam in.

Crimson rage flooded my senses. The girl had been floored and was now on her knees begging him to stop, but the big bastard just smirked and kicked her hard in the stomach. Although the guy on the phone hadn't shown any emotion towards what was going on, he was bound to get excited when the heat turned up, so I decided he would be the first to have it. Looking around for a weapon I picked up a huge limestone boulder, let my bike fall to the ground and launched my attack. Shouting "Leave her alone you fuck!" I hurried towards the passenger side of the car. The two on the sidewalk swung around, surprised that anyone had the balls to interfere. Before the guy inside had a chance to get out, I hurled the rock through the side window and into his face. It landed with a dull thud on his testicles and left pinned him to his seat. Moaning in agony, he didn't try to leave the car anymore.

Square-head reacted instinctively and ran to the boot of the car to get tooled up, leaving the weasel unprotected. "You're next you cunt!" I growled through gritted teeth. A boxer once told me that if you want to hit someone, aim for what is directly behind him. In this case it was a range of mountains about six miles distant and the little shithead's face just happened to be in the way. He was silenced with one curl and then kicked in the crotch for good measure. By now the gorilla was frantically grappling in the boot for his weapon. Seizing my chance, I ripped the tattered parasol from the ground and with the cold barbarity of a matador, went in for the kill. The ape located his Uzi 9mm from under a suitcase and flicked off the safety catch. Turning to empty a clip into his attacker he found himself on the receiving end of a rusty dirt-caked parasol pin which pierced through his cheek and exited the far side of his mouth. The lance stunned him motionless and he dropped to his knees, letting go of the gun in the process and clinging on to the rim of the boot for stability. Dodging the flailing Orangina advert, I swooped in and slammed shut the boot lid on the thug's fingers, shattering bones into fragments. Not wishing to leave him as the odd man out, I delivered half a dozen penalty shots in the gonads as a special treat. Releasing the boot catch caused the gangster to fall to the floor, revealing a gun that was just begging to be used. I picked up the Uzi and riddled all four tyres with short well-aimed bursts. The gunfire made the mobile phone user wet himself in expectation that he was next, but I had no intention of killing anybody today. Unbelievably, the gorilla tried to get up so I let him have a blast in the foot, which put paid to his tap-dancing days. The little shit had come around and was also trying to get to his feet. Charles Bronson gave him a Glasgow kiss and it was goodnight Vienna.

All along the strip, business had halted and although nobody came near, a long line of hookers and clients craned their necks to get a good look at the show. Still on her knees, the girl with a now tear-stained porcelain face couldn't believe what she had just witnessed. Surely her prayers had been answered? Her hero had come, not on a brilliant white charger, but on a silver Peugeot bush bike, to release her from her shackles. She was clearly in shock, wide-eyed and deathly cold. Thinking fast, I knew that we had best be gone to avoid a lot of untimely aggravation from the police. I absolutely could not be involved with this situation. I quickly wiped the gun clean of my fingerprints with my hankie then, hurrying towards the girl, I took her hands and gently raised her to her feet. I gathered her meagre belongings from the floor and rapidly shoved them into her handbag. Speaking in Spanish I said that we had to get out of here immediately and that I would take her somewhere safe. She nodded and followed my lead.

Now the big dilemma was whether to hoist her on to the handlebar, or to plonk her onto my saddlebag frame. I opted for the latter. I got onto the bike first, and then she straddled the machine giving the frame a treat of a lifetime. I thought the bike might be hard to handle with a passenger but quickly realised that she was as light as a meringue, and probably just as edible. We sped off towards town, turning into the beach road by Joe's garage just as three police cars and a riot van hurtled past, heading for the crime scene.

"We made it," I said, letting out a long whistle.

"You are English?" said the girl in surprise.

"Absolutely," replied her saviour. "And your English is better than your Spanish, where are you from?"

"Tirgu Mures, central Romania," she managed as we rattled over some stones on the grass verge. Idyllic images of wildflower meadows in a medieval-framed landscape entered my mind.

"What on earth made you get involved with that pile of shit back there?"

"Can we stop now, my bottom is hurting!"

"Of course, we're here now!" I braked outside the apartments and got off the bike, as Fernando and Anna rounded the corner with the two dogs. Looking like a boy that had just been caught peeing in the bushes, I froze not knowing where to start. Fernando shook his head. "What have you been up to this time?" then noticing blood on my clothes and the state of my passenger's face, concern set in.

"What's happened?" he said hurriedly.

I gave him a brief and rather frantic synopsis of the recent carnage. The girl started sobbing again and Siete, bored with the lack of attention, sat on the lawn and started licking his balls.

"Let's go inside" urged Five-Names, ushering us forward.

"I'm sorry, my dear, I didn't catch your name," he said in Castilian.

"Please use English *señor*. I'm better in English. My name is Anouska," she said proudly, "but most people call me 'Nush'."

Before I could intervene, my warped humour was conjuring up wisecracks about Nush giving nosh. I firmly trod down those images because they really weren't that apt under the circumstances.

Once inside the apartment, Fernando made me go through the whole episode in greater detail, while Anna cleaned up Anouska in the kitchen. After hearing the story again, Five-Names got up and hurried to the terrace where he made a quick call on his mobile phone. Within minutes more sirens and the blade-slap of helicopters could be heard heading for the boulevard. The girls came in to the living room, Anouska looking more like the girl that had first captivated me. Fernando handed us both a large G&T and sat down to listen to her story. It transpired that Nush and her sister had been brought to Spain under the pretence of working as lap dancers, but were instead imprisoned and forced to work as prostitutes. Her sister Natalia had refused to go out on the streets so the big bald bastard had beaten her up so badly that she had been confined to her bed for the past two weeks. She most definitely needed medical treatment but none had been given.

Anouska started shaking and tears rolled down her beautiful face once again. She rocked back and forth, wringing her hands and calling her sister's name. Her distress was heartbreaking to witness. I sat beside her and put my arm around her, holding her close to my chest.

"It's alright, it's alright," I whispered. "We're gonna take care of you and Natalia." I swivelled round and looked deep into her amazing eyes. "No harm is gonna come to you again, I swear, ok?"

She nodded.

"Come on, let's get your sister!"

"You had better get changed first mi amigo," said Fern. "This is the Russian mafia we are dealing with. They're well connected, and the word could be on the street already of who to look for."

"You're right mate. We'd better act quickly. I'll run up and stick on some slacks and a shirt. Can you call up Pablo and ask him if he'll come over to check the girls out this afternoon? If he's not too busy that is."

"Of course, I'll see if Roberto can come over as well."

"Right-oh," I said and was gone.

Ten minutes later the damsel, the knight and the Olympic hero piled into the Range Rover in its subterranean resting spot and slammed the doors. "I hope she starts," muttered Don Quixote, ramming keys into the ignition. The Discovery fired into life. "On the button" I said, relieved. We headed for a small, rundown hotel in the old part of Calella. Parking a block away so as not to arouse the suspicions of any minders, all three of us got out and gingerly approached the front of the building. The plan was for me and Anouska to enter together, me acting as a prospective client, while Fernando kept a lookout from the street. He knew some of the guys in a bar opposite and stood talking with them while watching the lobby door. Anouska had only ever met the three guys that I had seen to earlier and there was always one of them hanging about the hotel, guarding their wares. Surely they had associates who would step in if they knew their colleagues were in trouble. Nush used her passkey to gain access to the lobby. Inside, the ceramic-tiled walls and stone-paved floor kept the dark corridors positively fridge-like and we both shivered while waiting for the lift to come down. I assumed a boxer's stance and held my fists at the ready, in case a would-be gangster appeared on the other side of the steel doors. The lift went 'ping' and its doors opened to reveal nothing. I relaxed. We got inside, went up to the third floor, came out into the hall and walked along to the room without seeing a soul. The place was deathly silent. Anouska cracked open the room door, took a quick look inside and then rushed to her sister's side. I strolled in behind, checking my back as I went. Natalia froze at the appearance of a new man on the scene; she thought perhaps that he was another gangster coming to slap her about some more. While the girls spoke rapidly together in their own tongue, Natalia's eyes constantly darted between her sister and me. She stroked Nush's bruised face and they hugged each other weeping. Finally Anouska said "This is Don, he's going to get us out of here."

The sister was fluent in English as well and just as beautiful as Nush if not as sexual; more of an Audrey Hepburn and a little more reserved.

"Pleased to meet you, sweetheart," I said. "Can we get a wiggle on?"

"Uh?" said Nush.

"Can we get going? Time is of the essence I think!"

"Oh, of course" she replied. The girls set to work immediately, stuffing their belongings into a couple of large holdalls and within two minutes we were out of there.

"Normally I'd carry those bags for you girls, but I want to stay hands-free in case our friends turn up!" said the protector.

"That's ok, we can manage," said Natalia, clearly struggling.

"Give me a handle, come on!" I said heroically, and we bundled down to the street unchallenged. Five-Names gave the all-clear from across the street, then hurried to help with the luggage. All four of us rushed to the car. We threw the bags into the back and scrambled onto the leather seats.

"Bollocks!"

"What is it, Don?" said Fernando quickly.

"Fucking parking ticket!"

There was stunned silence for a second, until raucous laughter filled the car. We shot off back to the *ático* like a gang of thieves fleeing from a high-class jewellery heist. Inside Fernando's apartment, I was pleased to see that both of the doctors had turned up. After the introductions, Anna, Fernando and I made our way out on to the terrace, while the boys gave both sisters a thorough examination. The prognosis wasn't good. Anouska had received a cut lip and had a bruised cheekbone below her right eye, but nothing too serious. Natalia, on the other hand, had two cracked ribs, a suspected torn stomach lining, bruised kidneys, a fractured thumb, a broken tooth, a hole on the inside of her bottom lip, multiple bruising to her arms and legs, a bloodshot eye, dangerously high blood pressure and was suffering the effects of malnutrition.

Pablo administered a tranquiliser, gave her a course of antibiotic pills and an injection of multivitamins. He also strapped up her thumb and her ribcage and told her that she must rest for at least a week and eat well-balanced meals little and often. "That was a foolhardy thing you did, Donald. You could have got yourself killed!" said Fernando with ice-cold ferocity. For the first time, he was fearfully serious.

"I couldn't help it, old son; the poor little bugger was getting mullered!"

"Yes, but the Russian mafia! It's a good thing that you are just a passing cyclist and not known to them. Still, if people start asking questions there are plenty of girls down on the strip that are familiar with your face. Let us hope that nobody is bothered by their arrest!"

"I wonder what sorta shape my 'mates' are in?"

"Roberto is making enquiries right this minute. He'll uphold your anonymity of course!"

"Good old boy!" I said, grateful once more for Fernando's catalogue of useful contacts in high places.

The young physiotherapist came out onto the terrace puffing his cheeks. As he spoke to his father-in-law, he handed him a list which Fernando read in disbelief.

Turning to his charge, he said in stern tones, "They're quite a colourful bunch that you have tackled this afternoon my friend. It seems they rank high on Interpol's 'wanted' list in three countries, for a wide range of games: murder, money laundering, drug smuggling, human trafficking and slavery."

I couldn't find the right words to say, so I declined to comment.

"At present, all three are under armed guard at Barcelona general hospital," he informed me.

"Right ..." I said slowly.

"Do you want to know what damage you caused?"

"Go on then," I said sheepishly.

Fernando took a long breath and shook the paper in his hand rigid. "One man is in intensive care. He has, let me see, eight broken fingers, six missing teeth, perforated cheeks with an inch-wide puncture in both sides, a lacerated tongue, two fractured ribs, severe gunshot wounds to his left foot resulting in an amputation, a blood clot in his testicles and septicaemia."

I raised both eyebrows and started to chew the inside of my mouth.

Fernando continued, "Another man has a dislocated jaw, a broken nose, four missing teeth and a ruptured scrotum. He is also suffering amnesia."

My brow furrowed.

"The other man was not so badly injured but is in a state of severe shock. He has a cracked cheekbone, a broken jaw, a broken nose, multiple lacerations to his face and acute bruising to his groin area."

I let out a short, silent whistle.

Fernando paused. "How did you manage to cause all this carnage on your own?" he asked with dismay.

"I just lost me rag!" I protested.

"What?"

"Look, they were really laying into that poor little cow. If I 'adn't done something she'd 've been the one who ended up in hospital, not them!" I said, defending myself.

"Yes, I understand your compassion. But the Russian mafia? You couldn't have picked a more ruthless outfit to upset. They'll never let it lie, you know!" said Five-Names.

"I didn't know who they were. I just knew they had to be dealt with!"

"Well, let us just hope that they never find out who dealt with them!"

Roberto spoke to his father-in-law again.

"It seems that the Guardia Civil also picked up four other characters that had come to assist your punchbags and have arrested them too. They've made quite a catch today! Apparently the injured men were adamant that a maniac on a pushbike had attacked them, but luckily for us the police think that the *mêlée* was the product of gang rivalry and have dismissed the phantom biker story as pure fiction. So, you are unbelievably 'off the hook' as far as the law is concerned, my friend."

"That's handy," I said thanking my lucky stars.

I looked around at my Spanish friends who all appeared to be in a state of shock. Anna had been spared the gory details but had got the gist of what had happened. They had all seen a different side to the man they thought they knew, a side they would sooner forget as it left a bitter taste in their mouths, but it had earned me a shitload of respect.

"How could the simple act of repairing a puncture cause so much havoc?" queried Fernando after a few minutes of quiet contemplation.

"It used to piss my mum off as well," I joked.

••▼••

I stared at the tiny G-string airing on the back of a dining-room chair. "Crikey, she'll catch her death in that!" I said out loud. Bits of female kit were strewn around the house with gay abandon and the waft of expensive scent reminded me of the perfume departments in large stores. Still, it was refreshing to have female company about the place for a week and titillating in more ways than one. The sisters cooked the most superb-smelling cuisine that drove me crazy because I didn't dare to join in their meals. They would also think absolutely nothing of parading around the apartment topless, oiled up and sizzling from sunbathing on the terrace or fresh and fragrant after a long soak in the bathroom. This caused natural stirrings in the old underpants department and forced me to take more than my fair share of cold swims.

Being unquestionably honest in a relationship is nigh on impossible, especially over great distances, and suspicions are easily aroused. Although I wanted to tell Ann everything, I neglected to mention just how beautiful the girls actually were, or the fact that they treated me to a peep show every day. She wanted to come over immediately when she heard about my Rambo episode, but I persuaded her that I was in absolutely no danger and had remained anonymous in the event. A confirmation from Fernando helped to allay her fears, but she still phoned every day for a month just to make sure.

Natalia made excellent progress in her time at the *ático*; she ate plenty, rested fully and adhered to her medication. Before the girls left, Roberto came round one more time to check on her and pronounced her fit to travel and most definitely certainly fit to look at. The sisters had decided to stay with relatives in Rome who would take care of them for a while, so I bought them one-way tickets and gave them a thousand pounds each to get themselves started. I also did the wise-old-father routine and advised them to take up safer forms of employment. I was pretty confident that they had learnt a huge lesson in life and I felt especially proud of myself for playing a part in their salvation. The hugs at the departure lounge in Gerona airport went on for longer than they should have and I received an unexpected kiss full on the lips from Anouska. It was the softest, sweetest kiss that I'd ever had in my life.

"You'd better go now," I said, "or I'll be pogo-ing out of here!"

She smiled and said, "Thank you, angel." And with that the two of them skipped out of my life forever.

The Russian mafia was temporarily extinguished from Calella, its seven members being deported back to their homeland to receive hefty prison sentences. I heard through Fernando's contacts that my three sparring partners got several life sentences between them and wouldn't see the outside world again for as long as they lived. They still insisted on their story about a madman on a bicycle being the cause of their injuries, but the police considered the matter to be a closed case. The ladies on BJ Boulevard had closed ranks and protected my identity. They took to showing their appreciation for me helping one of their own by flashing their tits and blowing kisses my way whenever I cycled past. Not wishing to appear rude, I tended to ride this part of the course at a leisurely two miles per hour!

WEIGHT CHART

Week
26. - 17st. 10lb
27. - 17st. 8lb
28. - 17st. 3lb
29. - 17st.
30. - 16st. 11lb 8oz
31. - 16st. 8lb
32. - 16st. 4lb
33. - 16st.
34. - 15st. 12lb
35. - 15st. 9lb
36. - 15st. 4lb 8oz
37. - 15st. 3lb
38. - 14st. 13lb 8oz

With Terry's arrival imminent, I was pleased that Tuesday's weigh-in revealed that I had broken the 15-stone barrier. I was losing an average of around three pounds a week and bang on target. The last time I had seen Terry, I weighed a massive 26- stone and couldn't walk the length of my showroom without the fear of coronary arrest. I could now run up a one-in-five hill without feeling breathless.

Terry had caught an early flight into Gerona airport and was due to touch down at 8:30 a.m. Fernando and I went to meet him off the plane. I preferred Gerona, as it was closer to home and, being smaller, a lot more user friendly. The downside was that I was unable to play my little game of 'Hide the thin, Don' among the arrivals crowd. The panel beater came through from baggage reclaim and locked eyes with his boss immediately. As if he had been pulled in by some kind of magnetic device, Terry headed for me and then stopped a few feet in front of my face, gobsmacked.

"Is it really you, Don?" he said, transfixed on his governor's eyes.

"Certainly is mate, what do you think?"

"I think I'm at the wrong airport! Blimey, where did you go?"

I just laughed. It was fantastic to see my old friend again; he would give me the confidence boost that I needed for my final three months. I turned towards my coach to introduce him.

"Tel, I'd like you to meet Fernando … I couldn't have achieved any of this without him, he's a godsend!"

Terry put down his bag and shook the Spaniard's hand. "I've heard only good things about you *señor*," he said, earnestly, "I'm very pleased to meet you!"

"And I of you, my friend, it seems to me that we have a common admirer," he nodded towards the big boy in the baggy shorts.

"A common pain in the bum more like!" said Terry.

I laughed again.

"I can see that you know him well," replied Five-Names.

"C'mon, give us your bag!" said the pain. "We've a lot to talk about and I can't wait to show you the course."

Safely stored in the jeep, the intrepid trio headed back to Pineda. Even though Terry knew in advance how much weight I had actually lost, the shock of seeing it in the flesh (or lack of it) was blatantly apparent. Several times I caught him staring at me and although unaware of it, he seemed mesmerized by my metamorphosis. It was quite a bizarre feeling to be on the receiving end of such attention.

"What do you want me to do then?" Terry asked.

"Better let Fern fill you in on the gen, me old mate. He's the task master!" I replied.

"Yes well, what I thought that we might do over the next four days is, first, drive around the course so that you can get a feel for it. Then I thought that we could all cycle round it — of course, you can walk around if you like — and finally on Wednesday I would like you, Terry, to run the course on your own so that you have first-hand knowledge of our training circuit. I'd also like to go through our other training schedule with you to see if you spot any negatives or have some additions to make. Basically, my friend, we want a second opinion on the best way forward, because we are wide of the mark for coming in on time and I am running out of ideas!" said Fernando, negotiating a tight bend rather too fast for the jeep.

"I see," said Tel, hanging on to his seat cushion for grim life and trying to get to grips with the full schedule of activities that had been prepared for him. "Of course, I'm not a professional trainer you know, but I do have 20 years of running experience under my belt, so I'll do my best to help."

"That's my boy!" I enthused, looking something like a film producer in the Police sunglasses that I had nicked from Fernando.

The Willey hugged the contours of the coastline like a limpet on an oil slick, while the wind took the opportunity to refashion our hair, time and time again. Allocated to the uncomfortable rear seat, Terry hugged its contours, expecting to be jettisoned at any moment.

"Don sees this challenge as an individual one and from a personal point of view he is right, of course," said Five-Names. My coach clearly wasn't going to waste a second of Terry's valuable time over here, and wanted to get down to business straightaway. He continued, "To undertake such a life-transforming project and driven by the prospect of such a large wager, you couldn't have more personal reasons for the endeavour. But I've always favoured having partners in sport. I believe that they inspire you to greater heights. What do you think Terry?"

Terry nodded, thoughtfully biting his bottom lip.

"Is Wednesday your usual course day, Don?" he asked.

"Every other week, yeah."

"Then I think that we should both run it, but in our own time. I mean set off together and see what times we can achieve!"

"What race each other?" I gasped in horror.

"No," said Terry laughing. "Race ourselves!"

We entered Pineda around ten o'clock and Five-Names asked whether Terry would like to see the course straightaway or to freshen up first. Terry thought it best to lunge straight in and get to grips with the beast. Since we were in the car anyway, it made sense to whizz round and get another hair makeover before taking Terry back to the apartment.

"... and this is the Eiger," I said proudly as we turned into the steep climb. I looked at Terry, hoping for some kind of reaction, but he just checked out the pavement and road surface and stayed silent. All along the circuit I tried to impress him with various views and points of interest, but Terry was more interested in the running conditions, identifying the pit stops and mile-markers, the latter looking rather faded now. When we finally arrived back home I was like an excited kid. "Well what do you think?" I said to the deeply meditative one in the back.

"Well, it has two things in common with the Wycombe course," he replied, "in that it has a hill and it's 13-and-a-quarter miles long. Other than that, it's completely different."

I was taken aback by his abruptness and a little hurt that he wasn't as enthusiastic as I had hoped he might be.

Terry continued, "The Wycombe run is mostly on paved surfaces through suburban streets; it's a totally different animal. Your one advantage though is that you've been training in high temperatures, something that British runners aren't used to. July is a tough month to run races in, so you won't feel the heat like everyone else will!"

"Not all bad news then," I said feebly.

If not bowled over by the course, Terry was definitely impressed with the *ático* and looked forward to spending a couple of weeks here with his wife and children later on in the year.

"Who's this little fellow?" he asked between several hot stinky licks to his face.

"That's Siete, and he's just been licking his arse. I think he likes you!"

Terry gagged and pushed the beast off. "I'll shower now if it's alright?"

"Knock y'self out. Try the barley room," I suggested, "It's the second on the right."

After his shower, Terry changed into more fitting attire for the Mediterranean.

"Nice shorts, Tel," I said. "Shame about the lily whites though," I indicated to his legs.

"Some of us have been hard at it in the workshop, boss, not lounging around on deckchairs sipping iced tea," he pointed out.

"I know, it's tough at the top, innit?"

Terry huffed and said, "So what times have you been achieving then?"

"Well, I walked the course to begin with, as you know, until I got down to 16 stone. After that I started to jog it and then eventually to run it, 'ere I'll show you a breakdown of my last 11 times."

COURSE TIMES

Run - Hr:Min:Sec
1. - 3 : 44 : 30
2. - 2 : 59 : 58
3. - 2 : 47 : 11
4. - 2 : 39 : 48
5. - 2 : 35 : 10
6. - 2 : 29 : 58
7. - 2 : 27 : 01
8. - 2 : 22 : 03
9. - 2 : 18 : 30
10. - 2 : 12 : 10
11. - 2 : 07 : 58

My aim for Wednesday was to break the two-hour marker, but this meant knocking off a gruelling eight minutes, a tough task for any novice long-distance runner. In truth, I was hoping that Terry would give me the incentive and the means that I needed to achieve my goal. He aimed to run the course in 1 hour and 15 minutes, subject to good weather. He took a piece of paper and listed the times that he would expect an experienced runner to achieve per mile on the Wycombe half-marathon, if they were to complete it in an hour and a half:

WYCOMBE COURSE TIMMINGS

Individual miles (mins) and their Cumulative (mins)

1. - 07:30 (hill)
2. - 06:30 - 14:00
3. - 06:15 - 20:15
4. - 06:30 - 26:45
5. - 06:30 - 33:15
6. - 06:45 - 40:00
7. - 06:45 - 46:45
8. - 07:00 - 53:45
9. - 07:00 - 60:45
10. - 07:00 - 67:45
11. - 07:15 - 75:00
12. - 07:15 - 82:15
13.2. - 07:40 - 89:55

"There you go, that's what you've got to achieve boss. I think that we should gear our thinking to training for the individual mile rather than the whole race. Then we can put it all together later. I'll know more about that particular method after I've been around a few times."

"That's quite a different approach to what I've got used to," I said. "Do you think that'll do it?"

"It's a tried-and-tested method," Terry tried to assure me. "It does work, but it's just my initial thoughts. Let's give the beast a pounding first and see what she throws at us, eh?" he added enthusiastically. "Now what's for lunch?"

"I'm making you lunch, am I?" I said, with my tongue in my cheek.

"Well, I am the house guest!" he declared.

"Then I'd better snap to it your Lordship! We've got honeydew melon, Weight Watchers vegetable soup and a drop of local bread."

"Sounds delicious, what are you having?"

"Your share if you keep being cheeky."

We both chuckled and I went into the kitchen. This was going to be an enjoyable two weeks. It felt great to be in the company of an old friend again and brought a welcome *esprit de corps* into the *ático*.

That evening, all three of us ate at Manolo's and enjoyed each other's conversation, which continued over a long coffee at Bar Hugo followed by a tall glass of sangria back at my place on the terrace. Terry settled into the pace of life easily as if it were the only lifestyle he had ever known. While crickets and tree frogs serenaded each other in the garden below and the surf gently massaged the beach, he turned to me to impart some sound words of advice. "You know, whatever you go through and whatever you have achieved at the end of this year, always remember one thing…" he paused dramatically.

I looked across at him and nodded to show that I was eager to hear his giant words of enlightenment.

"You should never ever under any circumstances stand up in a canoe!"

The next morning Terry joined me on the terrace in his boxer shorts. He came through the French doors yawning and stretching his arms.

"Sleep well old son?" I enquired, with a knowing look.

"That's the first lie-in I've had since I can remember. If I'm not woken up by a blast from Capital Radio during the week, then it's one of the kids destroying my kip on a Sunday. The smell of your coffee brewing woke me up; I was having a lovely dream," he said ruefully.

"You get that round 'ere," I agreed.

"Been up long?" he yawned again.

"Up before the birds, old son, I like to watch the sunrise splinter over the mountains."

"Hmm, we get that in Ruislip too! What're we up to today?"

"First off, I'm gonna take Siete round the block for a Tom tit, then we're going for a swim, so have a cuppa and go get you trunks on."

"Trunks? I didn't bring any!" replied Terry, fending off my puppy's affections.

"I'd lend you some of mine, but they'd look like an inflatable raft on you. Just wear your boxers; no-one will be down there at this time of day."

"Ok."

The water felt fantastic and visibly woke Terry up more than I'd seen canteen coffee do at work. I did my usual 20 lengths, which left my friend goggle-eyed in astonishment, and before long we were meeting up with Five-Names at the front gate with the Peugeot, Fernando's Marin and Anna's 'ladies bike'.

"I bet I know which one I've got!" said Terry sarcastically.

"She's very comfortable, my friend — big soft saddle," said Five-Names, patting the seat. And off we went into the morning whistling the theme tune to The Famous Five. We stopped many times during the ride as time wasn't an issue and there were scores of sights to take in. Terry especially liked the view from above the Taboada farm, and had to be wrenched away so that we could continue with the course. Once we had completed our tour, we headed up the coast to Blanes and took lunch at a fine restaurant overlooking the sea. This gave us a chance to talk about the course and the training programme. Fernando liked the idea of the 'one mile at a time' approach so we decided to put it into practice the day after the big run.

"Seen much of Les, Tel?" I enquired tentatively.

"Oh, only every day. He's been acting like an abandoned greyhound since you've been over here, expecting you to arrive in every car that pulls up!"

"Is he still on the roll-ups?" I asked.

"Did he ever stop?" replied Terry.

"Oh yes, we both gave up for about a week before I came out."

"Well you wouldn't have known it," laughed Terry. I chuckled too and let my mind wander home for a moment.

"We had better get back now, gentlemen," Fernando advised us. "The gym is booked for 2:30 and it will take an hour to get there."

On the journey back we passed along BJ Boulevard, where the ladies paid their usual tributes to me; I just winked or blew kisses at each one in return, but Terry nearly crashed his bike into the kerb. When he finally caught up with us he asked if the girls always did that.

"Only to me," I said modestly.

"Really, why?"

"I've no idea mate, but it brightens my day."

"Blimey," said Terry, flabbergasted.

It was Wednesday morning, at 9:25. The weather had panned out beautifully, 65° F with a cool westerly breeze. The usual suspects lined the driveway along with Gina and Francisco, who had offered to help with the feeding stations. I had chosen to wear a vest for the first time this year, to be like my running buddy who was decked out in the skimpiest gear I have ever seen and a pair of Nikes that should have been binned months ago.

"But they're comfortable!" the Experienced One had protested.

As Fernando sent us packing, plenty of cheers and whoops could be heard rattling around the apartment block. "They like a good send-off around here," I explained.

"Mmm, so I see," replied Terry modestly.

We were pace for pace for about 200 yards and then Terry increased his speed, leaving me to follow in his footsteps. Further and further ahead he went until he was no more than a blur in the distance. Once I was in the first tunnel I lost sight of him completely and contented myself with running the course in my usual way, giving it all that I had, but secretly hoping to find that little bit extra. By mile ten I thought that I had this one in the bag, so I pushed a little harder, helped by the downward slopes. I levelled out and hit the beach road sweating like a squeezed sponge. I came in hobbling and did the customary dramatic collapse into a heap of sodden flesh on the lawn, while Terry looked on with his hands on his hips and a puzzled look on his face.

"You hurt, boss?"

"No, I just had a blow-out in me jelly shoes" I wheezed, rolling onto my back.

"You wanna stand up! If you're sick while lying down you'll choke on it!"

"In a minute, in a minute," I puffed, "How did I do, Fern?"

"Have you lost the ability to read your own watch, my friend?"

"Yep!"

"1:59:43 — you bloody did it!"

I started laughing, which turned to choking, which promptly attracted immediate attention from everyone around me. Soon I was on my feet again and breathing normally, sipping water like a man fresh in from the desert.

"How did you do, Tel?" I asked my fellow runner.

"1:15:38!"

"Bastard!" I hissed.

The next day we put to trial Terry's idea of treating the Spanish course as if it were the Wycombe route. I had to complete each mile in the exact time needed to accomplish the half-marathon in an hour and a half. Of course I was a long way off achieving those times, but if I could do just one mile in the overall average time, in this case seven minutes, then psychologically I could achieve them all.

Today our trial run would be on even ground, going from the apartments and along the beach road.

Five-Names and Tel stood beside the jeep, each with a stopwatch at the ready. They were going to start me off and then pick up the mess at the finish. "Remember, Don, you've been running it at about nine minutes per mile, but you've got to do it in seven, so we need you to speed up by roughly 15 per cent. Do you think you're up for it?" asked Terry.

"You're looking at the Wycombe Whippet, mate!"

"Ok then, but if you feel that it's too much for you, don't be too pigheaded to stop, alright?"

"Yes, Dad," I grunted.

Fernando smiled. "On your marks, set, go for it."

I was out of the traps and down on the beach road before the boys could start the Willey; oblivious to statistics and advice I just ran as fast as I could. The boys sped past me shouting words of encouragement then shrank into the foreground. It wasn't a good idea to try to sprint for a mile; after only a few hundred yards I became aware of the error of my ways. Fernando's eternal message echoed in my mind, *'tranquilo'*. I wasn't going to be able to get out of this one. The further I ran, the slower I got. I could see my two coaches waving to me at No-Cart Corner and it gave me heart; I kicked for one last time and crossed the mile marker at just past the seven-minute barrier. Five-Names stopped the watch and let out an uncharacteristic whooping noise, much to his embarrassment, then hastily regained his composure.

"See? Easy innit?" said Terry, "Just do the other 12 like that and we've got it cracked."

"When you going home?" I puffed.

CHAPTER SEVENTEEN
All round friends

I ALWAYS LOVED THIS TIME OF MORNING, downtime, a time when even ghosts slept and when darkness lost its grip on the approaching day. The silence that engulfed me possessed a texture almost as physical as the wind that teased my face, which was curling around me and threatening to rip me from my perch and propel me into another dimension. From high in my crow's nest on the corner of the *ático*, I watched the sky turn from inky black to purple-grey, then to ice-blue piercing through streaky beige clouds. The faintest hint of pink coming from the east changed to canary yellow and then to blinding tangerine as the sun decided to sweep once more over this truly majestic land.

I held a mug of black coffee in one hand and rested The History of Catalonia on my knee. I had tried to read the final chapter of my book, but thoughts of today's expectations had got the better of me. It was my last crack of the whip, my final chance to improve on my race time, and the ultimate opportunity to hone my skills as a half-marathon runner and transform myself into a winner. At 13 stone and two pounds, I had slapped the face of any doubters who had declared that this mountain of flab couldn't lose an ounce. I had put paid to those who said that I couldn't run up a hill and I had given the finger to anyone that had said I couldn't enjoy anything other than food, alcohol or a five-pound note. There remained one monster of an obstacle to conquer, however: a further seven minutes and one second from my previous best time.

We had worked feverishly on Terry's plan and achieved the correct times for each individual mile, but when the times were consolidated, I still fell short of the elusive hour-and-a-half benchmark. This was my last chance to get it right. I had the will power and I had the method, but suspected that I lacked the sheer physical ability. Even Fernando, with all his passion and enthusiasm, seemed to have resigned himself to thinking that maybe this goal was now out of reach. Thankfully, he kept his reservations strictly to himself.

At Manolo's last night we had gone over the finer points of today's run, while we ate the all important pre-race turkey pasta dinner. Five-Names had injected some faith by mentioning that the weather was in fact in our favour; it was forecast to be cloudy with a slight chance of drizzle, which was very unusual for this time of year. The most heart-warming news for me, though, was that my entire circle of friends had agreed to line the course, man the feeding stations and hurl encouragement my way. This loyal band of supporters were going to be positioned at strategic spots where I would most need them — the lonely stretches, strenuous points and at the finishing line. At these points, the belief of others in my success could prove to be vital.

I was bowled over by everyone's support. It hadn't even been necessary to prompt them to volunteer for duty; they all seemed to be wedded to my cause, even if some of them were just protecting their investments. The only downside was the pressure of having to perform well in front of a crowd, and it had already activated the bomb-bay doors quite early this morning, when I gave birth to five baby otters, and there were more on the way. At 6:30 I made my third cup of black coffee and placed two pieces of wholegrain bread under the grill. Fixing the regimental cornflakes and banana breakfast, I slipped into the utility room to sort out my trainers. The pair that I would pull on today would be crossing the finishing line in Wycombe in 11 days' time. I had kept all three pairs of Asics together even though one pair, as predicted, was now a size too big for me and another pair had burst a gel compartment but I couldn't bear to throw them away. A favourite pair, my 'lucky trainers', had risen to the fore; essentially, they were the only pair to have survived the training. I picked them up and sat them on the table with my knee supports, staring at them contentedly. My silent friends, who had put up with relentless punishment throughout the year, simply stared back, lacklustre and very morose. I didn't know what to say to them to cheer them up, so I sang, "Swing high, swing low, sweet chariot, coming forth to carry me home ..." The smell of burning toast hit my nostrils with the shockwave of a panic button, forcing me to abandon the homage to my kit and rescue my breakfast.

Flushing the loo for the third time this morning brought home to me that having a motorhome on hand for the race was imperative. I just couldn't overcome this nervous stomach business. I heard voices coming from the forecourt and glanced at the clock. 8:30 already. I rushed over to the balcony and saw Fernando and his entire crew welcoming old Josep and his wife into the fold. By the time I had dressed and made my way down to the starting line, Manolo, Christina and the *Mañana* brothers had also arrived. I welcomed them all; exchanging handshakes for piss takes about my running silks. For many of my supporters, it was the first time they had witnessed me in my training apparel, but I assured them that I was much more suited to these clothes nowadays compared with a year ago. Fernando's plan was coming nicely to fruition and the little fan club was growing by the minute, as was my celebrity status. José and Maria wandered across; Andres, his wife and his partner Pedro pulled up in a convertible Mercedes; César, Hugo, Miguel, Mila, John from Papa's and even Bernardo from the go-kart track had all turned up to offer their services.

I was busily engaged in conversation with Francisco about the massive trials that I had overcome — like his father; Francisco had a way about him that calmed the soul — when all of a sudden the side gate sprang into life again.

"Cooeee!"

Everybody jerked their heads at the sound and looked towards its shrill and unmistakable source. Through the gate swung Ronnie and Robert, outrageous and as flamboyant as ever.

"Couldn't miss a party love, even at this God-forsaken hour, I ought to be blissfully unconscious right now," said Ronnie, who proceeded to drape himself around me like a must-have accessory.

"Morning girls," I said. "Dressed for the part then?"

Everyone was grinning and commenting on the attire of the new arrivals. Ronnie was wearing a flamingo-pink running vest, skin-tight shorts and matching pink trainers, while Robert was somewhat more reserved in a bright yellow shellsuit, topped with an emerald-green sun visor. I wouldn't say that the arrival of my aerobics chums was a cure for my rumbling intestines, but they certainly took my mind off the problem for a while; they injected a spirit that set me raring to go.

"Mind if I trot along for the first mile, love? I could do with the press, my notoriety is slipping," said Ronnie.

"Not at all mate, but you'll have to keep up. I'm like a rocket these days!"

"Ooh, I always did enjoy a good solid shaft!"

"Steady!" I replied.

Five-Names handed out a photocopied course map to everybody involved, with his or her individual positions clearly defined. They also each received a coolbag containing water and an isotonic drink. Within five minutes the crowd had broken up leaving behind the usual sending-off party, plus the pink flamingo and me. José and Maria were going to stroll up to the garage to watch me pass and then wander back for my return. While I was still doing my warm-up routine by the wall with two minutes to go, Ronnie was gracing the start line, with one hand resting on his hip and enjoying the fact that I could reach down and touch my toes. He had attended many of the water aerobics classes and seemed to be agile enough in the pool, but I hadn't the foggiest idea whether or not he could run. As I stretched my tendons I wondered how he would perform. My mind drifted back to the drinking school at The George and I thought of how the lads would react if they knew that I now drank small glasses of wine, danced with ladies in a swimming pool and hung out with gay men!

Fernando checked his stopwatch and I looked at mine: ten seconds to go. I wandered over to the start line and joined my fledgling partner. Everyone here knew the importance of today's outcome. For 27 people, who a year ago I hadn't even met, to take time out of their busy lives to come and support me on a Wednesday morning, made this send-off a very special moment. I took a huge breath to quell the rising emotion and focus upon my target. "Get a grip Don." I whispered.

"Three, two, one ... go!" ordered Five-Names.

I clicked my stopwatch and pushed off, soon getting into my stride. At a quarter of a mile along the beach road I still had the 50-something drag queen by my side, but by the sound of her laboured breathing she wouldn't be there for long. Ronnie had a unique style of running that was completely unknown to the sporting fraternity: flatfooted, arms bent at the elbows jutting forward, with wrists as limp as soggy biscuits, his hands dangling lifelessly in front of him. As we hit No-Cart Corner I noticed that I was 20 seconds up on the first mile. My running partner had definitely enhanced my performance. As I neared the end of *el paseo par la sombra*, I glanced back to see that she had faded to an exhausted walk. I gave her the thumbs up to which she reciprocated with a feeble wave, before stopping completely, with her hands back on her hips.

Up ahead at the two-mile marker I could see Robert and Fernando waiting with some water. My coach had ridden the scooter down and was planning to be present at 6 of the 13 marker points. I grabbed a bottle and shouted to Robert that Ronnie was coming. "Not without my assistance these days, sweetie!" he replied. Another 20 seconds gained at this point was a direct result of this morning's mild conditions, 57° F at 9:30 a.m. was very peculiar for July, but I wasn't complaining.

I would normally have experienced an Evian shower by now, but still having water in my bottle at the steepest part of Eiger indicated unusual conditions.

Francisco and family were waiting at the top of the hill; once I had been through, the doctor would move up to another section in order to remain being close at hand. He was armed with a mobile phone just in case the unforeseen should surface. Running the Eiger for me was akin to nursing a car up a hill with a dodgy clutch; I had to keep the revs low or I would never make it.

"Looking good, Donald!" said Five-Names at the four-mile point.

"How did you get up here? I never saw you pass me!" I said, running backwards.

"You were too busy checking out a piece of tail, my friend!" shouted back Fernando.

I laughed and checked my watch again. "Shit!" I said. Somehow, I was four and a half minutes down. I needed to pick up the pace, so I turned about and changed gear simultaneously at the precise moment that my feet left the concrete surface and hit the dirt road. The combination caused me to lose my footing and I came down hard upon my right side, sliding on jagged gravel that ate into my flesh with the ferocity of a starving piranha. It only took a couple of seconds but it tore chunks out of my hip and elbow and left a nasty graze on my right thigh and ribcage. As if part of a circus routine, I was down, then up and back running again in one complete action, before Fernando could even have time to react and help me out. Although concerned at my fall, he let me carry on without intervention. Grit, sand and sweat entered fresh wounds and stung like a hundred razor cuts swabbed with lemon juice. I fought off the pain with the resilience of a tortured SAS soldier, but each step jarred my battered joints as if someone was attacking them with a cold chisel. I desperately wanted my mum. With only four miles under my belt I looked like I had been dragged through the desert behind a distressed camel — what a mess.

Without warning, somebody threw another log on the fire and the temperature suddenly rose by 15 degrees. The humidity had increased as well, which hampered my breathing. Beads of sweat broke out all over my body and exaggerated the damp spots that were already there. A nipple plaster had come away and the continuous rubbing from my running vest had caused it to bleed, adding to the claret from the accident. I was starting to look like an abattoir employee. I rounded the corner at Papa's bar to meet a celebratory scene: not only were Anna and Francisco there with bottled water, but a mini grandstand of well-wishers had crowded onto John's terrace, including waiters, the cook and half-a-dozen customers, blowing party whistles and trumpets. John had erected a long banner that read 'This way to Wycombe' with an arrow pointing north. The faces on the terrace turned from jubilant to horrified as I came into view, whistles fell silent and trumpets faded as the crowd clocked the state of its champion. I took two bottles as I passed, signalling that I was ok to Francisco, but concern was already written on his and Anna's faces. John was quick to make light of the situation, turning it to his advantage at the same time. "Mosquitoes are really bad at this time of day, you'd all better come on in and have another drink!" he declared to the crowd. The stampede was unstoppable.

I made feeble attempts to wash off the dried blood without slowing my pace. The wounds were congealing despite the constant strain of fractured skin being stretched and pounded as I ran. The blood flow was stemmed, but the stains on both cloth and skin were not a sight for the fainthearted. Conscious that I was now a greater spectacle played on my mind and sapped my fortitude. I drank a little water and then tipped the rest of the bottle over my hot head, but it did little to help. Up ahead lay my next hurdle: the underpass steps. We were at that time of the day when most holidaymakers have slept off their hangovers and start to worry that that they are missing out on some sunshine. Given that it's a commodity that doesn't exist back home and one that they had exhausted their entire savings on, they were not going to miss out on it here. They'd hauled their pasty arses out of their sweaty pits, gobbled up their ham, cheese and boiled egg breakfasts and waddled down towards the beach in oversized shorts, white socks and gleaming new trainers, each of them liberally oiled in under-strength sun block.

I caught the tail end of a dozen or so of these flabby folk corking up the walkway to the underpass and it cost me an expensive 30 seconds. They seemed oblivious to the fact that someone else had a right of passage along this path, especially someone with a more urgent agenda than theirs, or even that another human being existed outside of their rancid bio spheres. After making some breathless, anxious but polite pleas for access that fell on deaf ears, I was forced to be rude and barged my way through a couple of go-lightly Brits who seemed to be carrying the contents of a souvenir shop, beach brolly, inflatable donkey, snorkel and flippers, the lot. "Excuse me campers!" I said rather brashly, using my elbows as leverage. The female blimp slipped a step and landed on her arse in a conglomerate of plastic and pink flesh, which made her husband curse me with some colloquial expletives. I was too pressed for time to respond; five minutes were now agonisingly missing from the clock and I had to pull a miracle from out of my bag of tricks to recover.

My best shot of a revival was coming up in the form of the second-most shadiest part of the course, a welcome relief from the now-scorching sun that seemed hell bent on treating me like a hog roast and turning this day into a nightmare. "What have I done to deserve this?" I kept asking my maker. I pressed on, reaching Fernando, Andres, his wife and Pedro at the six-mile mark, but only managing to rein back one minute. I should have been grateful for that, but I realised that my best chance of recouping lost time had just passed me and it deflated my reserve. The worried looks from my supporters didn't help either. I took a bottle from Pedro who urged me on with "¡Animo!" It meant keep going — as if there were any other plan! Fernando joined in the moral support campaign by shouting out that I was doing ok, but ok wasn't good enough. From here on in I had to excel.

The next two miles took me into Malgrat. They were flat-paved sections so it was possible that I could make up decent time if I flogged myself. I passed Miguel and Mila at Mile eight; the secretary looked decidedly gorgeous today, in a flimsy, short cotton dress, with a pink and white floral pattern, that fluttered tantalizingly in the breeze. I remembered again why it was good to be alive. Mila had obviously been spending some of my cash and had apparently learnt some English along the way. "You're the bollocks!" she cried as I stomped past.

Bollocksed more like, I thought.

At the water station before the turn-off to Loret, Gina, Roberto and their children were waiting to hand me another bottle. I took a shower with it, swallowing just a little. The children were furiously chanting "Do-nald, Do-nald, Do-nald."

"Donald ducked!" I said to the smiling cherubs, who continued their chant with gusto.

Hugo, Fernando and Francisco were all waiting at Mile nine with words of encouragement to help push me up The Knackerer. I gave them the thumbs up, gritted my teeth and dropped into a lower gear. I was still down by three minutes at this point and knew that this hill was going to knock me back even further. Caked in blood, sweat, dirt and tears, I persevered until my dog-eared determination once again took a grip. I didn't give a damn what people thought of me any more, and the fanfare from passing motorists was just faint noise in the background. All that mattered now was time, and the clock was doing me no favours.

Once over the brow and heading downhill towards César's garage, the favourable gravity pull lessened the pains in my chest. I picked up speed but the pounding of my feet jarring my bruised joints and rattled my concentration. Manolo and Christina were waiting at Mile ten and I could sense their anxiety for me, even though they tried to mask it.

"¡Ya casi terminas!" shouted Manolo.

"¡Todavia no!" I panted back.

I looked at my watch and couldn't believe it. Four minutes down again! It was all going pear-shaped. César handed me an isotonic drink as I passed the garage forecourt. I drank a little but in my confused oxygen-starved state of mind, saw fit to pour the rest of the bottle over my head. "No!" I moaned out loud as the sticky fluid ran all over my face and shoulders. As if I weren't already covered in enough crap! Despairing of myself I plodded on. Still travelling downhill I passed by the fruit and vegetable fields where I was greeted by an old friend. The aroma of celery burst upon my senses and invigorated my lungs: Granddad was running with me now while giving out tips on how to plant out my allotment. Mile 11 came and went without happenstance and I rounded the bend to the beach road where I was welcomed by the *Mañana* brothers, looking like the before and after shots of a cheap makeover programme. I seized a bottle of water at full throttle and left them in the dust, speechless.

It was pointless looking at my stopwatch anymore. The last mile and a quarter could be run in eight minutes at best and I had just four minutes left to do it in. If I suddenly morphed into Steve Ovett then I might just have had a chance, but failing that unlikelihood I had to resign myself to the fact that I couldn't ever accomplish this course in an hour and a half. I was dejected. Spinning around in my head were the thought about losing the money, my pride and my sanity, but worst of all about how many people I was letting down, including myself. "Fuck it!" I said, "It's not over 'til the fat bastard sings!" I summoned up as much enthusiasm as I could muster. I thought back to football matches I had watched on television, where the underdogs were four–nil down with two minutes to go and yet they still battled hard until the final whistle, their determination carrying them through. I would join them in spirit and run it hard to the bitter end.

Leaving the coolness of the final underpass, I looked ahead and saw the apartment gates come into view. A full complement of loyal supporters waved and cheered as I appeared. For a moment I wished they were back in their homes and out of sight, so that I could just slink in through the back door without seeing their disappointed faces staring back at me. "Coward" I told myself. They had made the effort to be there for me and I had to accept their generosity with all the regal appreciation that it deserved. Anna had strung a red ribbon across the entrance way and I burst through it like a true champion, arms aloft, displaying a crooked smile and stinking like the British Lions' changing room. Instinctively stopping my watch, I staggered towards my usual drop zone on the soft grass. I should have known better, half-a-dozen red-tailed kites were circling above me and they tend to feed on carrion.

"No you don't," warned Fernando, propping me up under one armpit. "Drink!" Five-Names offered me an isotonic drink and presented me to my adoring fans. The next thing I was aware of was the sound of the elevator rushing me skyward to the haven of my penthouse. Unable to utter a word and with the adrenalin still surging through my system, I let my mentor do all the steering. Fernando looked at me and smiled. "We will soon have you in that shower, my friend, then you'll start to feel human again." The coach sat me on the toilet seat and untied my trainers. They came off with the reluctance of a pig being pulled from a quagmire. The waft was repugnant but Fernando didn't seem to mind. The soggy blood-soaked socks looked as if I had been wading in shark-infested waters rather than running a half-marathon. They landed with a splat on the tiled floor as he peeled them off. Turning on the power shower and setting it to lukewarm, Fernando said that he would be back in ten minutes to see to my wounds. The grazed one just nodded in reply.

I unveiled my torso, lifting my vest very gingerly; dried blood had stuck to the fabric and pulling it away simply ripped new tissue from raw flesh. The surviving nipple plaster came away too, yanking out several chest hairs for good measure. I didn't care; at this point, I was numb beyond the region of my brain. I discarded my skid-marked shorts and entered the cubicle. The fizzing streams of water massaged my skin, my aching muscles and my mind. The jets of bubbles stripped away the embedded grit and caked-on blood and I mindlessly watched them flow down my legs, over my feet and ebb across the tiled basin and down the drain hole. It was like a scene from a slash movie. I stood in the centre of the shower with my eyes closed, holding my face up to the water, and imagined that I were standing in an exotic waterfall with gallons of life-giving liquid pouring over me, rejuvenating my batteries. Just then the door opened; I snapped out of my reverie and flicked off the shower. Fernando had returned with a handful of medication. A year ago I wouldn't have even let Ann see me starkers in daylight — well, except for that one occasion — yet here I was naked and soaking wet in front of a man that I had only known for 12 months. This was the scale of my transformation; I was now proud of the way I looked.

"Throw us a towel mate," I said.

Five-Names obliged and while I covered my modesty and leant against the sink units, he attended to the most damaged parts of my body. He applied ointment and sprayed on germicidal second skin that stung so intensely that it felt like a burn.

"Fuck-ing hell," I shouted.

"There, right as rain," said my coach lying his arse off.

"Gimme the bad news then, chief," I said, peering at him through squinted eyes.

Fernando sighed and stood up. "You are still short by 3 minutes and 57 seconds," he said frankly.

My heart sank into a bottomless pit. "And I've only got a week left. It ain't gonna happen, is it?"

Fernando flicked his eyes at me and then stared guiltily at the floor.

"Actually, I've got a confession to make," he said coyly.

"What's that?"

"I'll get you another Lucozade. Come and join me on the terrace."

Anxious to know what the wily old bugger had been up to, I hurriedly slipped on some shorts and a top and stepped out onto the balcony.

"There you go. Good stuff this isotonic fluid; I wish that we'd had it in my day."

"Thank you," I said, waiting for him to explain.

Five-Names paused, and then looked me straight in the eye. "You know our little course that you've been pounding all year?"

"I don't like the sound of this! Yes, I know it very well!"

"Well, it's longer than the High Wycombe one!"

The full implication of his statement took a slow hold, and then I started to smile.

"You sly old bastard, you fucker, we've fucking cracked it. Fuck me, give us a kiss you fucker!" I said grinning from ear to ear.

"Hold on a moment, Don. It's only a quarter of a mile longer! But there is some more good news, the Wycombe hill is also shorter than the Eiger and you won't have the obstacle of those underpasses!"

"I knew about them, but fuck me!"

"Also, the weather today was appalling. No-one should be expected to do well under those circumstances. Given the right weather in England Don, well, I think that it is just possible!"

"Yes! Thank you, Santa Claus!" I said ecstatically.

This man had never let me down and even now, staring defeat in the face, his stoic optimism remained unbreakable. Several reasons had compelled me to take up this challenge. For one, there was my mule-like determination to beat Belington, then my vehement bitterness towards his lordship's hoity solicitors for the way they had humiliated me, and of course the money, but they were now way down the list. Next week when I stood there at the starting line, one figure would be spurring me on to victory, Fernando.

"You know that your friend Terry thinks you can do it?" he revealed. It had been an excellent tactical move to get the marathon-running panel beater to come over to Spain. What's more, he and Fernando had hit it off straightaway.

"He's as cunning and devious as you are, you old sod!"

Fernando laughed. "Come on, Quixote, there are some people waiting downstairs to congratulate you."

It had been more than an hour since I had completed the course; that's how long it had taken to make me presentable. Anna had laid on an impressive spread down by the pool area, with drinks and tapas galore. A cheer went up as I arrived. The party had swollen to about 40 people and it choked me up to receive such an accolade. Even some of my reclusive neighbours had come down to join in the celebrations. I couldn't believe that I was getting so emotional these days, I was turning into a right girl's blouse. Making a small speech in Castilian, Five-Names told them the timing I had achieved today. A huge cheer went up. Then he told them how much time I had knocked off the previous run, everyone cheered again. They all knew what time I was supposed to make today, yet they cheered even so. What a loyal band of supporters! Then, when Fernando revealed to them that the Wycombe course was shorter than this one, I got the distinct impression that most of them already knew the true facts. What a conniving load of gits! My coach proceeded to round off his speech by inviting everyone to join him in wishing me all the best for the coming week. By the time the party ended, I was heady with a cocktail of emotion, anticipation and confidence. I was also smattered in lipstick! I helped Anna and Fernando to clear up the plates and glasses and then arranged to meet my coach for a swim at 6:30 I headed off for a few hours of well-earned flop.

That evening at Manolo's the three of us enjoyed a splendid seafood *paella*. I didn't know whether Five-Names had put a word in, but I seemed to have been given larger portions than usual; perhaps I needed the protein, perhaps not, I wasn't about to start complaining. For my last week in Spain the training schedule would be drastically reduced, with just some swimming and light jogging. Fernando knew how much punishment I had taken today and my body needed rest and recuperation if it was going to be in decent shape for the big day.

We were halfway through a four-mile jog up to Malgrat and back, where the oranges were forming up nicely in their groves and the strawberries were in full production. As agreed this week's regime would be light enough just to keep me loose and supple, so the stopwatches had been retired. Just after ten o'clock Fernando's mobile phone sprang to life with a call for me about the motorhome. I had arranged for Les to drive it down for me, so that I could use it for my return journey and stay within easy reach of it before the start of the race. Fernando handed me the phone.

"Hello, Don"

"Hello, Les?"

"It's not Les, it's Ray."

"Oh, hello bruv, I was expecting Les. Where is the old bastard?"

"Right here beside me. We all felt that he was too old to go out alone now!"

I could hear Les in the background telling Ray to fuck off. "We've just gone over the border so I reckon we'll be with you in about two hours."

"Ok mate," I said. "I'll see you then."

I had no idea what kind of motorhome they had chosen for me. Although I owned a dealership, I had very little to do with the daily running of the operation, so I had left that decision to Ray. Few people could understand why, when I had an eight-bedroom house just down the road from the Wycombe Rye, I was planning to spend the night before the run in a caravanette. My reasons were sound though; I didn't want anything or anyone ruining my routine. It was a clear stratagem: to have a place for my ablutions on site and somewhere to cook my pre-race turkey supper by myself. Although I would have dearly loved to be in the arms of my wife and have my wonderful kids around me, I needed to stick to the programme; otherwise I would have no chance at all.

Returning to the apartment complex we found José out front cutting the grass, and it gave me an idea. The child inside me made an appearance now and again — well, more than now and again — and I greatly enjoyed the game when people that I had known for years no longer recognised me, so I seized a golden opportunity to play a prank on my old pals.

Anna, Five-Names and José all agreed to be in on it. When Ray and Les arrived at the front gates I would pretend to be the gardener. I borrowed José's workclothes, his hat and a stub of a cigar, which I had no intention of lighting as the taste of these things now seemed vile to me. All four of us were giggling like schoolchildren as I dressed for the ruse; my four-day growth and dark complexion aided my disguise and made me look like a true native.

"¡*Perfecto!*" said Five-Names approvingly.

It was just coming up to midday when the roof of the motorhome was spotted coming down the road above the security wall. The three Spaniards hid behind an Oleander hedge to the right of the main gate, where they could hear everything but not be seen. Les and Ray had gotten out of the cab and were peering through a crack in the gates. I had my head down in plain view and was trimming the edge of the lawn with some long-handled shears.

"Hey *amigo!*" shouted Ray.

I ignored them and carried on cutting.

"Hey!" he said again, banging the gate with his fist. I looked up and stared at the gate for a second, suppressing a snigger before slowly putting down my shears and strolling over. I had seen these two men nearly every day for the last 30 years and here I was face to face with them and neither man recognised me.

"Can I help you?" I said in Catalan.

"*Amigo* Don Simmons!" replied Ray.

"*No comprendo*," I said.

I could tell that the trio behind the bush were all splitting their sides.

"Trust us to get someone who can't speak fucking English!" piped up Les. It was good to see my old mucker after so long, and displaying the typical English attitude, expecting the locals to be fluent in the Queen's own language. I myself had been just as guilty a year ago; now it just seemed so ignorant.

I opened the electronic gates with a push of a button and stood even closer to them. Still they hadn't a clue.

"Who are you looking for?" I asked, again in Catalan.

The bushes were now visibly shaking.

"Don Simmons you deaf Dago, Does 'e live 'ere?" demanded Ray, getting annoyed.

"Don't you shout at me you fucking pig!" I said taking the hat off and hitting Ray with it. The sudden burst of English took the boys completely by surprise and they stepped back agog.

"Fuck me!" said Les. "It's fucking Don!"

"Bloody hell!" said Ray. "Bloody hell!"

Both men said no more for the next few minutes. They couldn't get to grips with the apparition. I shook them vigorously by the hand, but it was like shaking hands with limp ragdolls.

"It's good to see you both, it really is," I offered as words of welcome.

Les and Ray were now were even more confused as three laughing Spaniards emerged from behind the bushes.

"These are my friends and neighbours, Fernando and Anna. And this is the real gardener, José, who does such a splendid job here, don't you think, boys? Huh?"

No reply. They were still motionless and lost for words.

"Come on Ray, pull that beast in here and we'll go and 'ave a drink. I bet you could do with one!"

Five minutes later everyone had descended on Fernando's apartment and were enjoying tall glasses of iced tea. Les pulled out a crumpled folded envelope from the inside pocket of his jacket and handed it to me.

"'Ere mate, 'ere's a present for you."

"Nicely folded, Les, let's hope it's not photographs!"

"It ain't photos," replied Les as I tore open the folded package.

Inside were a programme, a map and my race number for the Wycombe half-marathon.

I stared at the number for a while.

"What's up bruv?" asked Ray.

"I don't believe it," I said with astonishment. "My lucky numbers have always been 8 and 23, look!" I showed them the race number: it read 238.

"It's an omen, boys. It's meant to be!" I was off on a mystical trip somewhere; running up rainbows with stardust around my heels, wearing a crown of laurel leaves and a gold winner's medallion around my neck.

Les brought me back down from the clouds. "You gotta pin it to your T-shirt or they won't let you in it."

"Very true" said Fernando. "May I suggest wrapping it in cling film first. It will protect the number from any sweating that you might do!"

"Might?" I queried, while studying the map.

We had been over it a dozen times before with Terry, but seeing it in black and white, printed and official, really brought it home to me that the culmination of a year's gargantuan effort was finally upon me. The big day was imminent.

"Where's your gaff then, Don?" asked Les.

"Upstairs mate, it's the penthouse."

"Really? What, really?"

"Yep, that's where you'll be kipping tonight. Want to get your bags and go up?"

"If you don't mind Don, I could do with getting me head down for a bit," said Ray.

"Come on then, let's go up. Thanks for the drinks, Fernando. *Graçias*, Anna.

"Yeah, thank you lady," added Les.

"Most kind," said Ray.

I walked with the boys back to the motorhome to fetch their overnight bags.

"I must get out of these clothes; it's too hot for overalls. I don't know how José does it!"

"They're not yours then?" joked Ray.

I gave him an 'as if' look and then laughed.

"D'you know, I still can't accept that it's you in there. The transformation's incredible. We can even walk at the same pace," said Ray.

"You wait till you see me run," said the Wycombe Whippet.

"I've seen you with the runs!" quipped Les.

The motorhome loomed large on the forecourt. It was a six-berth Winnebago adapted for the British market, so it drove on the left. It was luxury itself, with plush carpeting throughout, spacious beds, a generous well-fitted kitchen, satellite TV, DVD player, driver and passenger seats like armchairs, trip computer and Sat/Nav, a shower room and of course the essential piece of porcelain for my little problem.

"What a lovely bit of kit. I should have got me one of these years ago!"

"They don't make 'em in your old size," wisecracked Les.

"You keep on like that 'n' you'll be sleeping with Siete" snapped his boss.

"Who's she?"

"You'll see. Do you like big brown eyes and a sweet personality?"

"Now you're talking," said clueless.

They entered my apartment and were greeted by a gangly, overenthusiastic fluffy mutt who refused them entry unless he could bite their hands.

"Hello boy, have you missed your old dad, eh?" I said, fighting the snappy youngster off.

"Feed me!" demanded Siete.

"Who's this little fella then?" asked Ray.

"This is Siete."

"Eh?" said Les.

"I found him on the side of the road with his brothers and sisters," I continued.

Ray tussled the dog's ears between bites. "Good boy, down boy."

"Feed me!" woofed Siete again.

"Get off" said Les. "I thought Siete was an old sort you 'ad lined up for me."

"Fucking feed me!" whined Siete.

"You gotta admit mate, he is your type," I said. "You've been out with a few old dogs."

"Very funny!" snapped Les.

"Feed me now!" begged Siete.

"I better give him some grub or he'll eat another piece of furniture. Come on boy," I said shaking a packet of freeze-dried nonsense.

"Umm, lovely reconstituted cardboard again! Hasn't he heard of a butcher's shop?" muttered the hound, crunching his way through a big bowl of biscuits.

The lads got the grand tour of the *ático*. Ray adored it whereas Les thought it was too high off the ground, but they both liked the superb bedrooms. After offloading their luggage, they took to the sack until early evening, when we went to eat at Manolo's. Ray and Les were introduced to the gang, before they tucked into lobster and rump steak, while I feasted on my salad and some grilled sardines, washed down with house red. Les had a pint of lager while Ray quenched his thirst with a Guinness. Staying up until two in the morning was a rare treat for me and although I felt mighty sleepy, I enjoyed the banter with my friends. They had much to talk about, as there had been plenty of adventures played out by the members of the drinking school and a catalogue of stories that had happened in and around work. They carefully kept the business talk to a minimum though; I didn't want any of that on my mind.

The next day struck up with a ferocious heat that felt like a branding iron was being held above the land. The milky-white Brits were scorched as they sat out on the terrace eating their breakfast. "Corr, this is hot!" said Les, kitted out in jeans and a long-sleeved shirt.

"What, your coffee?" I asked.

"Nah, the weather Don!"

"Well, you are in Spain, Les! What did you expect?"

Ray laughed. He was more suitably dressed in shorts, sandals and a polo shirt.

"So you'll be home on Saturday then?" he asked.

"Yeah, I'm gonna drive straight to the Rye and kip there the night. Make sure you're there on Sunday by nine o'clock at the latest, or you'll miss the start."

"Don't worry; we'll all be there bright and early. No-one's gonna miss this one for the world."

"Unless it snows!" said Les.

Ray and I both looked at him in disbelief. Les just looked out to sea and sniffed.

By ten o'clock the boys were on their way. They took the Range Rover back to Blighty, leaving me with the Winnebago and the prospect of negotiating the tollbooths once more.

"Take care of her," said Ray. "We haven't paid for her yet."

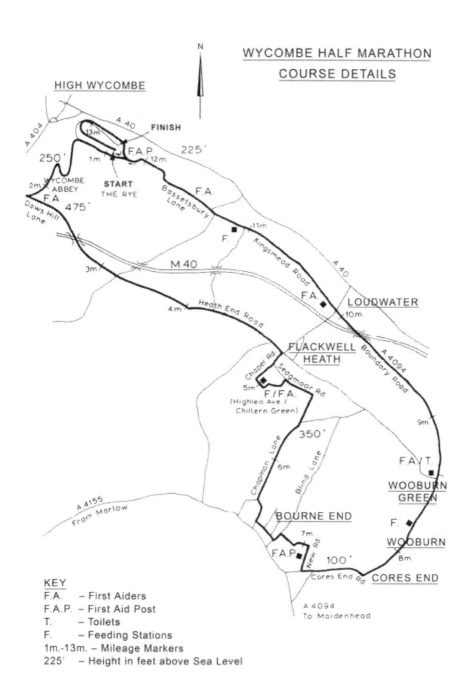

On Thursday evening, Anna joined Fernando and me again at Manolo's for what was to be my last meal there before the race on Sunday. It was a little melancholy, but also celebratory for everybody knew the obstacles I had overcome to get this far. Having myself been an impressive obstacle in the past, I thought it only right to give myself a slap on the back, now that I could reach my back that is. Andrés sent over a magnum of Moët & Chandon, tied with a red ribbon holding a gruesome picture of the night we had first met. I had forgotten that pictures were taken when I first arrived and now found myself gasping at the true horror of my former self.

"I never ever saw me as big as this, what a state, I look ridiculous!" I said to my neighbours.

"Mind you, look at the freak show that I'm standing with!" I added, pointing to the *Mañana* brothers, Andrés and Pedro.

"If the devil could have cast his net just then!" said Fernando.

"Would have been a prize catch!" I responded.

Anna heard the translation and agreed. Manolo came out with Christina carrying the main course. He suggested that it wasn't a good idea to drink the champagne while still on the diet plan and that he would keep it for me until my return. He also gave me an envelope saying that it wasn't to be opened until an hour before the race. I thanked them both profoundly and asked that my appreciation go out to all of the staff at the restaurant, for they had been the main contributors to my extraordinary weight loss. It took us longer than ever to exit the bar area that night. Hugs and kisses rained down upon their local hero from all corners of the room; even the old domino players stood up to congratulate me.

"Is it me or are there a few more people than usual in 'ere tonight?" I asked Fernando.

"They can get more people in now that there is less of you my friend!"

I laughed. "You're probably right".

We enjoyed the same scenario but on a smaller scale at Bar Hugo on the way home, but I was glad when we finally reached the apartment because I was feeling pretty tired from all the attention. Anna promised to see me in the morning and Five-Names asked if he could join me for a Tom's Special before bedtime. We leant on the balcony railings and looked out at the navy blue Mediterranean sea. The near-full moon reflected on its surface and gentle phosphorous-crested waves broke upon the darkened beach with an effervescent hush. Lights sparkled all the way up the coastline and an ocean liner sailed west on the horizon, making its routine cruise around big city ports.

"Do you hear that?" I asked. "There are no crickets singing tonight."

"That's because they too are sad that you are leaving, my friend."

"More like José has slaughtered them all with that pesticide he sprays everywhere."

Fernando nodded dolefully. "Listen my friend, whatever the outcome of the race this Sunday; I want you to know that we are all very proud of what you have achieved this year. It was an unrealistic target that you set for yourself and although I made it my vocation to see that you achieved it, I always had my reservations. But you did it Don, you did it. No-one else … and as for the race, I just have to say this. It is possible. Just put all that you have learnt into practice and it is possible!" I looked my coach in the eye. Our souls met on a par for the first time and I shivered.

"Here, I want you to have this. Open it at the same time that you open Manolo's envelope." He handed me a small gift-wrapped box and an envelope.

"I will, mate. Thank you," I said, welling up again.

The following day, after loading up the motorhome, Fernando and I walked down to Manolo's to pick up some ready meals that the chef had prepared and put in individual containers, including the all important pre-race turkey pasta.

"Refrigerate them in the motorhome, then you'll have about three days' life in them," he advised me.

"I will, and once again thank you for all your wonderful food. You alone have kept me alive."

"The pleasure was all mine, Don Quixote!"

"I'm running this race for *España* now, you understand."

"Just do your best *amigo*, just do your best."

"I'll try. *Hasta la vista chef.*"

"Bye, bye" said Manolo.

"*Luego*" added Fernando, and the two of us walked away.

It had just turned eleven o'clock when I finally pulled out of the drive. Anna had bid me a tearful farewell; she said that it had been a pleasure to have me as a friend and neighbour and assured me that Siete would be fine with them until my return. José and Maria came over for the send-off too. Maria told me to take plenty of rest stops on the way up through France and José recommended I get some *petanque* lessons while I was in England.

"Bowls!" I said in return.

I had asked if Fernando would like to come back with me to see the training programme through to fruition, but he turned down the offer, saying that the job he had set for himself last year had been completed, and besides I would have Terry on hand for any last minute coaching, together with the love and support of my friends and family. (We had already discussed the best places for them to be positioned around the course to help spur me on.)

"No Don, it's over to you!" he had said in conclusion.

It was funny to think that a year ago I viewed this place as a sort of prison sentence, but now as I looked back in my rear-view mirrors at the world disappearing in my wake, it was choking me up to leave. At the top of the road I stopped at Josep's stall and picked up some fruit for company. Choosing three bananas, three oranges and a couple of apples, I sat them on the dashboard just as I had done with their ancestors last year, and next to them I placed the two envelopes and the little gift-wrapped box.

I had made a decision that wherever I happened to be at 7:30 that night, I would pull into one of the *aire de repos* and rest there until morning. The traffic on my side of the road had been light; it seemed that the whole world and his wife were heading in the opposite direction for the start of the peak holiday season. It was still bright, warm and sunny when I reached the centre of France, at Farges Allichamps on the N71, so I pulled off the road to an almost deserted rest area. My only fellow pit-stoppers were two goods lorries, one of them a haulage company with English plates. After I had eaten and washed up the dishes, I decided to take a stroll. I had already stopped four times today but like an active dog that had been cooped up all day, my bones were aching through lack of exercise. As I passed the English artic, the driver was just getting out.

"Evening," I said.

"'Ello mate," said the driver. The man in his mid-fifties had obviously just woken up and as he reached the ground he began to stretch a rather over-indulged body. "Been on 'oliday?" he enquired, looking over at the motorhome.

It probably did look like I had, with the awning down and a plastic table and chairs out. It was the first time anyone had posed the question and I wasn't sure how to answer it. "More of a working holiday I suppose," I said. "I've been in Spain for a year."

"A year? Blimey, you 'ad a lotta work to do!"

"I 'spose I did," I replied.

"Well, a quick splash an' then I'm off," said the trucker.

"Ok then, see you," I said. Walking back to the motorhome I fancied a cup of coffee and felt that it would be rude not to ask the driver to join me. So when he came from out of the toilet block I beckoned him over by pointing at the coffee pot.

"Don't mind if I do," said the driver, on reaching the Winnebago. "The name's Dave by the way!"

"Don, pleased to meet you. Take a seat." An hour later and I had told a complete stranger all about my year in Spain, the reasons for being there and what I had achieved in that time. Dave lapped up the anecdotes and applauded me on how much weight I had managed to lose. Perhaps it was because he himself had eaten too many roadside café breakfasts and realised that he could benefit from shedding four or five stone.

"Whaddya put it all down to?" Dave asked.

"Whaddya mean?"

"What's the one thing that made it all work?"

I thought for a second. There were so many contributing factors that made it all happen, but if I hadn't taken Terry's advice about getting away from Britain, away from my surroundings then I wouldn't have had a chance. Without a doubt, it was the one, single factor, the catalyst that had created the synergy that I found in Catalonia — no distractions.

"Different surroundings mate. In Spain I had no temptations, unfamiliar routines, a new language, new friends, a new life. I'd recommend it to anyone!"

"I 'ear ya," said Dave approvingly. I could see that he was contemplating his own bloated situation.

A sudden burst from a nearby nightingale broke the silence.

"That's what make's it all worthwhile!" I announced.

"What's that then?"

"Birdsong, or the sudden appearance of a brilliant butterfly from a hedgerow bursting with wild flowers. Even if I'm really down it always brings a smile to my face, refreshes my spirit."

Dave rattled the plastic chair with an enormous fart. "That always brings a smile to my face!"

"That too!" I agreed.

Asking me to let him know how I got on in the race, Dave wrote down his telephone number and wished me all the best. We said our goodbyes and I retired for the night, contemplating my long haul up to Calais and the nightmare slog of fighting traffic on the English motorways. Overcrowded, heaving road systems were one thing that I definitely hadn't missed this past year and I dreaded the prospect.

I woke to the sound of revving diesel engines. Thoroughly annoyed at having my peace disturbed, I peeled back a corner of the curtain to find that the once-empty rest area had filled to capacity overnight and now resembled a freight yard. "Ye gods!" I said to myself. It was only seven o'clock yet the guys in the sleeper cabs were starting to rise. I couldn't go back to sleep now, so I got up and made a fresh pot of coffee. After a quick wash, I fixed my cornflakes and toast and sat down to eat while watching the lorries pull out. Pretty soon I would be passing them all somewhere up the motorway, a good hour earlier than I had planned. Sitting in the big comfy driver's seat, I peeled an orange and revelled in its flavour. I had come full circle. It was 12 months ago that I had sat in a French lay-by and tasted my first orange; I couldn't now imagine life without them.

I made good time and reached Calais by midday. Deciding to go back by boat, I caught the 12:30 p.m. catamaran and walked out on deck to get some sea air and ward off thrombosis. It was a fine clear day. The sea was like a steel-blue billiard table and no sooner had I left the French port than a dark land mass appeared on the horizon. England, free from invasion for nearly a thousand years, the crucible of democracy, a haven for free men and a stepping stone for millions of brave souls who crossed this way twice to beat off an evil tyranny. Land of opportunity, freedom of speech, birthplace of great statesmen and women such as Elizabeth I, Lord Nelson, the Duke of Wellington, Queen Victoria, Winston Churchill and Tommy Cooper. Roast beef and Yorkshire pudding, the bulldog spirit, the Mini, the Rolls Royce, cricket, The Sun newspaper, black cabs, red buses, warm beer and allotments. The home of the Spitfire, the best music in the world, scones, clotted cream and strawberry jam, football, hooligans, social-security cheats, asylum seekers, mobile-phone muggers, no-go-zone council estates, a crippling tax system, rain, ice and freezing bloody fog. I couldn't wait to go back to Spain.

The white cliffs of Dover drew ever closer and reminded me of Vera Lynn, who in turn reminded me of Marion and of what she had said upon my leaving, "I only want to see half of you this time next year!" Well, she was about to have her wish come true.

How odd, I thought, only half of me returning home!

WEIGHT CHART

Week
- 39. - 14st. 8lb
- 40. - 14st. 7lb
- 41. - 14st. 5lb
- 42. - 14st. 2lb
- 43. - 13st. 11lb 8oz
- 44. - 13st. 11lb
- 45. - 13st. 8lb
- 46. - 13st. 6lb
- 47. - 13st. 4lb
- 48. - 13st. 3lb
- 49. - 13st.
- 50. - 12st. 12lb 8oz
- 51. - 12st. 11lb 8oz

I drove off the ramp onto the quay and headed straight for the green channel. A customs official suspicious of anyone coming in from Europe alone in a large motorhome immediately stopped me.

"Anything to declare sir?" he asked hopefully.

"Yes," I said proudly through my open window, "I've lost 13 stone, quit smoking, given up binge drinking, and can now run a half-marathon in an hour and a half!"

"Very funny sir, now pull over there!" A team of customs officials went through the Winnebago with a fine toothcomb and delayed me for about an hour. Of course they found nothing and made a right mess of the place. I was seething but there was nothing that I could do about it, other than sit it out and tug my forelock.

"Thank you very much!" I said as I was handed back my keys. "I've been bored shitless back there!" I said, referring to the detention room.

"You're welcome sir," replied the smug official, self-righteous about having taught another Smart Alec a lesson. He had no idea that I had actually just been bragging.

I rolled into the Rye car park in Wycombe at around five o'clock that evening and the old familiar feeling came over me, the kind you get after a long absence, like a round peg finally fitting into a round hole. I couldn't help but smile. The Rye is the name given by the local people to Wycombe's largest playing fields because they were once the crop fields where rye was grown to make malt whisky. The irony being that malt whisky had partially led to my downfall. I loved the stuff so much that it played a major role in my obesity which, in turn, gave rise to the challenge in the first place, and now here I was, a picture of adversity over gluttony, about to start the race at the very place where the ingredients to my poison were grown.

Parking under the shade of a huge oak tree next to the old outdoor swimming pool, I got out and inhaled a lungful of Wycombe air. It smelt good, it said, "You're home whether you like it or not!" It was a warm, sticky afternoon and the park was speckled with an assortment of people all enduring the intense sunshine; one or two couples were enduring each other, sprawled out on the grass oblivious to whoever they might upset. I locked up and strolled out to the London Road to use the nearest phone box. Finding a kiosk that hadn't been vandalized was a task, but eventually I came across one that worked and called home. Ann said that she would be round with the kids within ten minutes; I then called up Les and asked him to come straight over. He had bought me the latest in mobile phone technology and although I was now quite happy to live without having one as an extension to the human form, I could very much do with one right now.

I got back to the car park just as Ann was arriving. I had so wanted to play my usual trick on the family, but she was wise to me and had reversed the tables. She had told the kids not to pay any attention to their dad. It was an extremely difficult game for Trish to play because she hadn't seen me halfway through the year like the others and was genuinely aghast when she caught sight of me. They drove past me and parked at the opposite side of the car park. Getting out and searching the immediate vicinity, they all looked straight through me. I waved but they ignored me. I got a little anxious and called Ann's name, but still they pretended not to notice. They just leant against the car with their arms crossed. Finally I could stand it no longer and raced over shouting, "It's me, I'm here!"

As planned they all saw me, screamed and ran away like a scene from a Benny Hill episode, with the whole family running in a snaking line while being chased by a giggling lunatic. I caught them in no time and we all ended up in a big bundle on the grass with Junie on top shouting "Daddy's back, Daddy's back!"

"Daddy's back's gonna break if you don't get off!" I said.

Cuddles and kisses ensued, while Trish took a long hard look at the man in front of her, hardly believing that this really was her dad. Not only had my face and body changed, but I was sporting a more conscious, positive aura.

"I'm impressed!" was all that she could manage to say.

"I'm deflated!" I mused.

June and Ann held on to me as we walked back to the motorhome.

"Look Daddy, I can get my arms around your waist now!" said the little one.

"And I can get my legs across," said the look in Ann's eyes.

I was as happy as a sandboy, and pleased to see that my two youngsters had stuck to their diet plan as well. Mathew had successfully shed a good couple of stone.

"Looks like you're on target for that moped, son," I said admiringly.

"Yep!" said Matt, clearly very pleased with himself.

"What a healthy bunch we are!" I said. "Now who's gonna help me with the awning?"

Mathew pitched in while the girls set out the table and six plastic chairs. Ann got to work in the kitchen and prepared some snacks and homemade iced tea. Les turned up a little while after and handed me the phone.

"You made it back then!"

"No Les, I'm still in Spain!"

"Sarcasm is lowest form of wos name!" he murmured.

"Yeah, but justified sometimes." I replied.

I set about calling up my nearest and dearest and pretty soon Richard, Marion, Terry, Charlie and my sisters Victoria and Jennifer and their spouses had joined us. The initial shock of seeing the transformed Don for the first time drew the same response from everyone. Utter disbelief. Most of the assembled crew had only ever seen the man-mountain version of me, and to them it was a different person that sat smiling in his tasteful plastic garden chair. Most were stunned into silence, none more so than Marion. The stern headmistress and queen of cynicism, who ruled her Weight Watchers class with a rod of iron, was melted like the Wicked Witch of the North by her own tears.

"I'm so pleased for you," she sobbed, "I had my doubts all along, but you've done wonders for the cause. Thank you so much; you're a credit to Weight Watchers. Oh I'm so proud of you!" She even found it in her heart to kiss me on the cheek.

"Thank you my dear, I shall never wash that cheek again!" I replied.

"You know that your friend Chan is on the verge of declaring bankruptcy!" she said.

I laughed. "I can believe that," I said.

"I still think that losing 13 stone in a year wasn't a wise thing to do, Don. There again, you're not the type of slimmer that I usually come across and I think that you've coped with it astonishingly well."

"I put it down to my personal trainer, Marion. He was my inspiration, my *raison d'être*."

"Is that so? Well, it's amazing what raisins can do!"

The role for my family and friends during the Wycombe Half was the same one that my Spanish friends had performed; to support me along the way and give me that marathon boost that every runner needs. Fernando had provided photocopied maps of the course and with his usual efficiency had pencilled in the strategic places where each and every one should stand. He also recommended that if the weather was not in my favour, they should act as secondary feeding stations too. By the look of things the weather was going to be my worst nightmare come true. Britain was in the grips of the hottest heatwave on record and tomorrow, according to the forecast, was expected to break all temperature records. The brown grass and dry cracked earth around us were clear evidence of the sun's heavy presence and it cast a shadow over my welcoming party. For now, though, I put it to the back of my mind. My party stayed for the best part of two hours, and then one by one made their exits, promising to return in the morning. Richard told me that he had spoken to Belington's solicitors and they would definitely be here tomorrow. As for Lord Belington we would have to wait and see.

Ann and the kids were the last to leave. They knew the situation with the race plan and understood my reason for spending the night on the Rye. Besides they only had one more night left without the old man, then I was all theirs forever.

"My husband's away, you know," Ann whispered to me sneakily on the way out, "but you can come round and see me tomorrow if you like!"

Yes, I would very much like but first, I had an important date with a start line to honour.

It was nine o'clock and still devastatingly hot when I prepared my all-important pre-race turkey pasta and salad. I sat alone at the table, sipping at a glass of Manolo's house wine, while a candle burned lemon essence to ward off mosquitoes. The green-and-white race marquees and first aid stations had been set up during the day and the start/finish line banner had been strewn across the lanes of red, white and blue bunting. A PA system hung silent from crudely erected scaffold towers; soon its country fair tones would be rallying the runners into position and announcing the various charities that were being supported. I only had one charity in mind, the Don Simmons challenge, and I aimed to bolster its funds by bagging a large cheque from that snob Lord Belington. I thought of all the other runners that would be competing tomorrow and was pleased that I could finally count myself as one of their number. "Tomorrow we will be brothers," I said "*Mañana.*"

CHAPTER EIGHTEEN
Nothing to do but run

A BLAST OF THE BEATLES' Good Day Sunshine wrenched me from a frustrating nightmare, where I was trying in vain to catch a London bus that remained frustratingly out of reach. The music jerked me into the warm reality of judgement day, a bright blue sweltering Sunday that would see me either justified or ridiculed. The clock said 6:00 a.m. Yet the sunlight that came from behind the curtains was so intense, it seemed like midday already. I lay there listening to the Fab Four on Swan FM, then to a couple more tunes about sunny days until the annoying DJ piped up with some irritating banter. "Yes folks it's Sunday the 9th of July, and today's big event of course is the Wycombe Half-Marathon, and what a lovely day we have for it. In fact it's going to be too lovely for all of you runners out there. Early predictions indicate that the temperature will be reaching well into the 90's today, which will make it one of the hottest days since records began. So plenty of fluids you guys." He then played The Spencer Davis Group's Keep on Running back-to back with Kate Bush's Running up That Hill, at which point I got up and hit the toilet.

Half an hour later I had washed, dressed and was out in front of the old swimming baths, perusing the area. The only other person to be seen was a night watchman set to guard the marquees against sabotage. He was keen to finish his shift and get off home to bed.

"Morning," I said as I passed the blurry-eyed sentry.

"Fucking hot one!" replied the guard.

"It's gonna be a scorcher, innit?"

"Yep. You 'ere for the race?"

"Competing yeah, I parked up overnight by the swimming pool. Just thought I'd 'ave a look round."

"Help y'self mate. If I were you I'd start running round now, cos there's no fucking way you're gonna make it later on. It's gonna look like a fucking war zone in 'ere I tell ya!" he said, pointing to the first aid station.

"Uh huh," I agreed, contemplating the predicted scene. I wandered off and walked up to the start line. The event seemed uneasily hollow and lifeless, right now. What a difference a field full of people would make to the atmosphere. "It's true," I said to myself, "People do make places!" My intestines gurgled as bile surged through my system, but what did I have to be nervous about? Win or lose I was a better person for getting involved with running and a damned sight healthier. The money was just a side issue now and I had met all of the other criteria, so why worry? I took a huge breath, clenched my buttocks and quickstepped back to the motorhome.

Sitting there squeezing Maltesers, I read through a letter that Richard had given me the previous night. It was from Belington's solicitors dated two weeks ago, asking whether or not Mr Simmons still intended to run the half-marathon and reminding us that any forfeit in the conditions of the contract would result in Lord Belington claiming the sum of the wager in full.

"Do I intend on running the half-marathon or not? No, you twat, I'm just gonna hand over a quarter of a million quid I had lying around because I'm sick of the sight of it!" Listen ..." I said flicking the letter to attention, "Don Simmons ain't a shitter. Well, maybe he is right now, but he don't back out of a bet no matter how fucking hard it is, got it?" With that I tossed the letter onto the floor and finished my ablutions.

Six forty-five and I was sweating already. I went to the front of the Winnebago and turned on the ignition. The outside temperature readout registered 25° C. I did a quick calculation. "Fuck me that's about 80° Fahrenheit already!" I exclaimed, slipping into the kitchen to fix my breakfast. As on all previous course days, my nervous stomach had put me off having any food in the morning, so I had often wanted to skip the most important meal of the day. Every time, Fernando had insisted that I eat breakfast and my coach's wise words continued to repeat in my head. With both sides of the awning pulled down to help ward off the sun's evil rays and shaded by two large willow trees, I sat out in the open to eat my cornflakes. I thought about Terry's warning that extreme hot weather could add between five and ten minutes to a race time. What with the minute-and-a-half deficit that I already had, it meant that a possible eleven and a half minutes had to be summoned up from somewhere. I wished Fernando were here, that old genie could turn back time. The local DJ announced that it was 7:30 in the morning and already 86° F. Although temperatures might soar into the low 100's today, the run would still go ahead.

"Fucking hell, even Fernando couldn't have predicted this!" I said aloud.

At about eight o'clock, Les rolled into the car park in the Range Rover. I watched from my shaded sanctuary as my skinny sidekick fell out of the car and sauntered over in a cloud of Old Holborn smoke carrying two bulging paper bags.

"Wotcha got there?" I asked.

"Thought you might be hungry," he said through his roll-up, plonking two egg and bacon sandwiches rammed with brown sauce on to the table. I had no idea where he had got them from on a Sunday morning and couldn't believe the ignorance of the man. Stopping short of calling him the one thing that most men adore, I simply explained to him that I didn't eat that sort of thing anymore.

"What? Food?" he replied.

I disregarded the remark, but for me its sentiment justified my year's leave of absence; my loved ones would have smothered me if I had stayed in England to train.

At five past eight, Ann and the children turned up. Trish and Matt appeared to be asleep still and could only carry out basic functions, and then only when prompted. They weren't used to getting up at such an early hour on a Sunday morning. June, on the other hand, was displaying the energy of a fuel-injected spinning top and rushed to her Daddy like a defending fly-half, grabbing me by the waist and almost knocking me to the ground. Ann was as graceful as a swan, floating into the arena and nestling against me, immune to the oppression of the day.

"And how's my worldbeater this morning? Up for it?" she enquired.

"Up for anything with you by my side!"

"I'm not coming with you, I haven't done any training!"

I laughed; I loved my wife's sense of humour.

Ten minutes later Richard breezed in. The cool dude was wearing a cream, lightweight cotton two-piece and a white shirt undone at the neck by two buttons.

It was the first time that I could remember seeing my solicitor without a tie, which proved it must be hot for him to go open-collar. Richard entered the shade of the awning and mopped his brow with a handkerchief. "Phew, I don't envy you today, Donald. You sure you can manage this?"

"You can put money on it!"

"No more bets, please, I don't think my heart could take it!"

"Or my arse!" I said.

"Don!" scolded Ann.

"Oops, sorry!" I said, suddenly remembering that June was within earshot.

"Want an egg and bacon sandwich Richard?" asked Les.

"Er, no thanks Les, I've eaten already." Turning to me he said, "I've made out the cheque for the 250,000; it's here in my briefcase, you just need to sign it."

"Ok. Where are you meeting Belington's briefs?"

"In front of the old swimming pool at nine o'clock."

"Is Belington going to be there an' all?" I enquired.

"I'm not sure. There was no mention of him over the telephone. Why's that?"

"I'd like to have a little fun. Do you want to play along?"

I explained to Richard about the joys of being unrecognisable and that I wanted to see how close I could get to the penguins before they realised who I was, if ever. Albeit reluctantly, he agreed to go along with the ruse.

The temporary car parks were filling up by the minute, as runners and supporters arrived in earnest. Terry, Phil and Steve hopped over the dyke and joined our little gathering, taking refuge under the now cramped Winnebago awning.

"Anyone fancy a cuppa?" offered Les, in his self-appointed role of catering crew. A few hands went up, but most abstained, so Mister Tea Mad went inside to put the kettle on.

"Which one of you's Don then?" asked Steve disingenuously.

Ann put up her hand. "I'm Don and so's my wife!" she said, reciting Monty Python.

Everybody laughed apart from June, who protested "No you're not, Mummy, you're Mummy!"

I stood up and gave them a twirl. "Not bad eh?" I said gloating.

The boys were impressed. They hardly knew me at all, but my previous appearance and the unimaginable notion of me running this half-marathon had stuck in their minds like a permanent fixture. While they had genuinely hoped I would succeed, they honestly didn't believe it possible, especially given the timescale.

"I'm gobsmacked!" said Phil. "Well done mate, good for you."

Steve added, "That's some achievement, Don. I wish I had your will power!"

Terry looked at me and winked. We sat around the table and talked about the weather and our tactics today. Every five minutes or so the public address system announced warnings about the extraordinary conditions and urged runners to take on extra fluids. At one point the announcer warned that there should be no heroics today and that just to get around the course would be an achievement in itself. Two extra feeding stations had been set up to cope with the anticipated demand. I couldn't help thinking that if the broadcaster had been Spanish, the word *'Tranquilo'* would have been mentioned a few times already.

Every man, woman and child would be taking heed of the words of wisdom from that Tannoy system and rightly so, all except one participant. I had set the rules for life many years ago: I always gave 100 per cent to a project and today was no exception. I was going to lay my life on the line for Fernando. Meanwhile, Les was on his third cup of tea and had descended on the two egg and bacon butties himself. Engrossed in the News of the World and encapsulated in a womb of calm contentment and tabloid fiction, he let HP sauce dribble all down his shirt without notice. His vocation for today was to act as sentinel for the motorhome and to be there as mop-up man when I finally fell through the door. This sanctuary gave me the firm foundation that I needed and with my own personal feedings stations along the route, should I need them, I had an advantage over the pit holes that I felt could bring me down. No rules were being broken here; they were just being spiced up.

It was now 8:30, Fernando and Manolo had stipulated that I was not to open the two letters until an hour before the race. Although I had checked them at regular intervals for the past 48 hours, like a child puzzling over presents under the Yuletide tree, I had every intention of respecting their instructions. Fernando had also asked me to open them in private. Everything my coach had said and done over the past year had had good reason, so making the excuse that I needed the loo, I went back inside the motorhome alone. All the blinds were down, shrouding the interior in quasi-darkness — a tip I had learnt from the Spanish for keeping places cool. I had already told the lads that my pre-race stomach nerves had made me have three turnouts so far this morning, so they must have thought that I was making a bid for the world record in bowel movements in one day. I switched on a small overhead reading lamp in the bedroom and began by opening Manolo's letter. I was never one for sending greeting cards, whatever the occasion. I viewed them as a waste of money and far too sentimental for a man to give; besides, sending cards was always Ann's department. My opinion, however, was about to change. I presumed that Manolo had been responsible, but I couldn't be sure; maybe he was just the card bearer. Somehow, somebody had managed to obtain goodwill messages from every person that I had gotten to know well during my stay in Spain. There must have been close to 50 signatures and sincere wishes on that card, written in Castilian, Catalan and English. The warmth from my Spanish friends rose from the pages and floated around my head like figures on a Victorian carrousel, making me giddy from the emotion but left me feeling fully charged. I never knew that a simple card with a pleasing picture and some kind words could mean so much. I choked back the tears, smiled and placed the card on the table beside my bed.

I wasn't getting off so lightly with Fernando's letter. His pre-race message read:

Dear Don,
When you read this letter you will have less than an hour to go before you put into practice the results that you have worked relentlessly for over the past year. I have never met a person with so much stamina and determination, and it has been my privilege to know you and my delight to have trained you.

We always said Don, that the weather would play a defining role in today's outcome, and I have to confess to you something which by now you must know all too well. I have been following the long-term weather forecast for England for the past two weeks, and I have hidden from you certain facts that you might have to face today, like the temperature being well into the 90's. I hid this from you because I didn't want to stress you out a week before race day.

I spoke to Terry at length about the Wycombe Half-Marathon while he was here, and there is one thing going in your favour: all the roads are closed off. Use this to your advantage, Don. You more than anyone know the importance of the shade. "Corra por la sombra" — run in the shade. This is the only piece of advice I have left to give you, the rest you already know.

I was going to close my letter by saying Tranquilo, but I know that this will fall on deaf ears, so I will just say this, Don. Don't kill yourself. You're worth so much more than a quarter of a million pounds, and you have a lot of friends out here who would like to see you return.

These two gifts I give to you, one you deserve and the other you may need. Remember ¡Corre por la sombra!

God bless
Fernando

My eyes were brimming over with pools of tears. Only their own surface tension held them back from spilling onto the page and ruining the most poignant letter that I had ever received. I pulled a Kleenex from its box and mopped my eyes before anyone could see me and then started on the burgundy gift-wrapped box. I had made up my mind that the box contained what seemed to be the obvious, a brand new stopwatch, as it was about the right size, shape and weight. I ripped through the wrapping and lifted the lid. Out sprang the bunny ear of a tightly compressed white, knotted, cotton handkerchief that danced and nodded with the recoil. It made me laugh aloud. It was the very same article that Fernando had tied knots in and placed on my newly shaven head to protect it from the sun when we were on Pineda beach the day after the bike accident. 'The English Sombrero' he had called it. Putting it on my head once again would make me feel like Alf Garnett. But a handkerchief couldn't be as heavy as the package suggested, so I carefully extracted the hat from its entrapment. To my utter surprise, tumbling from the cloth and falling onto the bed in dazzling splendour came a 1948, 4 x 200m freestyle relay Olympic gold medal. I caught my breath — I didn't deserve this! The true value of the Olympic champion's gesture knocked me for six. To give up such a hard-fought accolade was an act of camaraderie unparalleled by anything that I had received in my life. Tears cascaded down my cheeks like warm rivers over a dry land. I leant back against the headboard sobbing uncontrollably and clutching the medal for fear that it might melt away. Throughout my adulthood I can only remember crying a half-dozen times. There wasn't much that upset me before Spain, but my emotions were on high alert today and this had to be the kindest, most generous gift that anyone had ever given me. I was deeply touched. It seemed that as far as Fernando was concerned, I had already exceeded the merits of a deserving champion such that a half-marathon completion medal fell way too short as my prize, so he had felt compelled to award me with his own medallion!

It was a good ten minutes before I felt composed enough to face anyone, but the bloodshot eyes could not be hidden so readily. Both Terry and Richard asked me if I was alright when I emerged from the motorhome; perhaps they had heard me sobbing but I didn't really care. I decided not to mention the medal or greeting cards, instead I told them that I had just experienced a difficult birth. They looked at me somewhat incredulously.

Eight forty-five: Terry, Phil and Steve disappeared to meet with a couple of friends under one of the Rye's more familiar landmarks, an enormous ancient oak tree. They left promising to save me a place in the forward line up. I fixed Les his fifth cup of tea, poured iced tea for Richard, Ann and myself and tried to take my mind off the race by recounting the story of how I had found Siete on that rain-drenched Christmas Day. Still my butterflies continued to flutter and I dearly wished it were all over with.

At nine o'clock one of the four disabled car spaces opposite the Winnebago became occupied. A Popemobile pulled in and two rather large ladies in green two piece uniforms lumbered out and walked round to the rear of the carriage. They opened the door and started to unfasten the safety straps that held down a rather cumbersome wheelchair. I watched intrigued as the two women used the on-board hydraulics, tilting a ramp inside the car that enabled the wheelchair to be easily drawn out and brought to rest on the ground. It seemed that something had gone awry because the wheelchair was twisted at right angles and had now become jammed between the car's doorframe and the ramp. The two ladies tried in vain to right the machine, but were getting nowhere. Without hesitation Richard and I jumped out of our seats and went over to offer assistance.

The problem was clear: a safety strap had fallen between the chair's frame and its wheel and had got caught up in the spokes. We realigned the ramp and righted the chair; I leant in and freed the tangled strap so that the chair's occupant could be lowered to the floor. While we helped put things to right we got our first glimpse of its passenger. She was a very slight woman who appeared to be in her early forties, although she had actually only just turned 30. Throughout the process of her chair being extricated, she never acknowledged us once. She carried a vacant, distant stare of someone who removed herself from her pain by living in a fantasy world; besides, the chair was fitted with head and neck supports that made the slightest of head movements difficult, even if she possessed the ability to do so. Her skin was loose and insipid, almost waxy, as though it hadn't seen the light of day in years. Her hair was lank and lifeless with the heat of the day, while her arms twitched and jerked involuntarily while lying folded in her lap.

Her big brown eyes suddenly came to life as if a switch had been flicked on and I became conscious that she was silently observing my every move. I crouched in front of her to say 'Good morning' and found myself gripped by pity. For me it was like staring at an abandoned car, void of petrol, oil and water and undeniably burdened with a flat battery. The frustration and helplessness in the woman's eyes epitomised desperation; she ached to be whole again, to join in with the rest of humanity and although she didn't know where, she would rather be somewhere else right now.

"Morning love," I said, masking my thoughts. "Soon have you on your way."

My presumption that she could not reply was totally misplaced as, to my surprise and concern, a surge of turmoil began to erupt in the seat. Starting with an exaggerated arm movement, body contortions and head twisting, she worried me into thinking that she was having an attack of some sort.

"It's a fucking nuisance!" she blurted out in a tremored voice. The shock almost knocked me over and I had to regain my balance. I was both astounded and embarrassed, yet found myself laughing. The joke caught on and soon she, Richard and to some extent her carers were all chuckling. Stripped of the ability to carry out any basic functions, and with her coordination, neural network, speech and motor ability floundering, the woman remarkably still kept a sense of humour.

They can't stop you laughing, I thought, remembering a favourite line of Bernard Manning's. Richard offered to take the woman, Kirsty, over to the shade of the awning; one of the two carers who was already suffering from the effects of the day quickly followed. I put the car's ramp away and closed up the back door before joining them. Ann sorted out drinks while Les promptly bewildered everyone with an anecdote from the paper.

Kirsty had to be fed via a drinking straw, hampered by her uncontrollable shaking with every feeble attempt to get the straw in her mouth. I shuddered at the thought of having to depend on others for my basic needs. It transpired that she suffered from a disease that I had heard of but never really paid much attention to — multiple sclerosis, the bastard disease, as some people call it. Later, when I had a chance to learn more about it, the latter name seemed entirely appropriate.

Kirsty had come to watch her brother run, so I advised the two carers that the shadiest and coolest part of the course was across the other side of the dyke, where an avenue of trees cast the lane in shadow. It was also a good vantage point, as it was the first and last mile, so the runners would go past twice. They agreed that this seemed the ideal spot. Just then a guy in his early twenties and a girl around the same age turned up. It was Kirsty's brother, Rory, and his girlfriend, Lauren. The lad had his number on already, which reminded me that I'd better get ready myself. Before going into the motorhome to put on my knee supports, lucky trainers and race number, I had a quick chat with him. This was his sixth time in the Wycombe-Half; today he was going for 1:25:00, because of the weather, but his best time was 1:18:00. He looked as fit as a fiddle and his youth and enthusiasm brought out a healthy envy in me. "Which charity are you supporting?" he asked.

This was something that had not crossed my mind until now. Charities had always been a straightforward measure in the past. Unless supporting one of Terry's sponsored runs, I only ever gave to the blind or Cancer Research, both of which came out of standing orders from my bank. I hadn't even considered running for a charity, other than for my own cause until now. I supposed everyone imagined that I had enough money riding on this race as it was without worrying about raising any more cash. Yet money was no longer the issue for me; it was way down the list. What I had been privileged to experience over the past year, no amount of money could buy.

I countered the question by asking Rory which charity he was running for; it was the obvious one, the charity that would benefit his sister's illness.

"Just a minute," I said to him, and gestured to Richard to come into the motorhome with me. I asked him to write out two cheques, one for 50 grand and the other for 250, and to place them in two separate envelopes. I wrote 'Under an hour and a half on the envelope containing the 250 grand cheque and 'Over an hour and a half' on the other. Without questioning what I was doing or why, Richard carried out my request. Showing the two envelopes to Rory, I explained that I had made out two cheques for the multiple sclerosis charity. Without revealing the amounts involved, I assured him that one of the envelopes would be his, depending on how well I ran in the race.

Taken aback by the generosity of a complete stranger, Rory was at a loss what to say so he just thanked me very sincerely.

"Give them to your girlfriend until after the race," I said, "then come back here and open one of them in front of me," I said, trusting the boy's integrity.

"Ok," said Rory. "I hope that you achieve the time that you're after. I'll see you at the finish. Good luck!" With that, he said a few words to his sister and left for the start line. Kirsty contorted in her chair in the effort to muster up a sentence.

"Now I can go clubbing!" she struggled to say. I thought that she might be joking, but her face told me she was utterly serious.

Les took charge of the wheelchair and led the ladies over to the shady avenue of trees, while Ann and the children scampered off to find a good position from where they could see me off at the start of the race. After that they would be heading for the 11-and-a-half mile mark, a desperate spot where I would need them most.

"That's a mighty fine donation that you've just made, Don!" said Richard, when everyone had gone.

"Payback time mate, for all the good things that have come my way this year. Seeing that poor girl bollocksed in a wheelchair made me realise how fucking fortunate we really are. We don't appreciate the simple things in life like pouring our own drinks, or wiping our arses; we just take 'em for granted. If I can help ease the suffering with that money, then it's a small price to pay."

Quarter past nine, I went back inside the Winnebago and put on my lucky trainers. Cinderella's slippers couldn't have fitted better, and fairy dust puffed up from inside when I heeled into them. I pulled on my knee supports and pinned on my race number then went outside where I met with a short burst of applause from Richard and Les.

"This is it, mate!" Richard said.

I took a deep breath, "Yup."

Les wished me all the best. Even he had begun to realise the importance of today.

"We're late for that meeting with Belington's solicitors," said Richard.

"Let 'em sweat, mate, they've made me sweat enough!"

Richard took the lead and met with the two mouthpieces in front of the swimming pool. I walked around to the front of them and was just about to introduce myself when Belington, his grandson and a couple of others approached from the right. We all came together at once with an awkward pause. I had often rehearsed exactly what I would say when meeting up with these people again, but it all went by the by. Speaking to the grandson first, I said, "I owe you an apology, old son. Runners are definitely not wankers!"

Jaws dropped in astonishment; the look of disbelief billboarded across each and every face. Belington turned to Richard and asked if this really was Don Simmons standing in front of him. After all my race number confirmed that it was, but this man was an imposter surely?

Richard assured him that I was *the* Don Simmons. I stretched out a hand towards the grandson and it was gingerly accepted. His lordship eyed the exchange with frosty suspicion but said nothing. We three had only met once before a year ago in The George, when the old boy had been subjected to a barrage of abuse from an obese, mouthy drunkard. The contrast must have seemed enormous, but the lad and I now conversed as equals with just one topic, marathons.

Richard did the necessary with the other solicitors, while the Tannoy system announced the latest temperature reading, 93° F. I felt that I had no secrets to keep and told the grandson my best time to date which, given the heat of the day, must have assured him that his grandfather's money was in the bag. Belington and his entourage listened intently. When we had finished talking, Miss Starchy Knickers piped up, "I will, of course, be insisting on a drugs test."

"Even if I lose, Miss?"

"It's Mrs!" she replied sharply.

Poor bastard, I thought.

Belington then spoke. "That will not be necessary, Mrs Daylon."

I looked at him and nodded my appreciation. He reminded me of my new partner, Antonio López, on our first meeting in the olive grove when we had acknowledged each other with a dip of the head.

"Well, I'd better be off," I said, excusing myself.

Belington was looking straight at me; I took a couple of steps forward and put my hand out, he did likewise. Whether he meant it or not, I would never know, but he wished me good luck, nevertheless.

Nine twenty-five: I made my way to the start line where Terry had saved me a place. I passed dozens of runners, some of whom would have undoubtedly worn fancy dress costumes to promote their charitable causes if it weren't for the conditions; not today, it was way too hot, so most of them simply wore a T-shirt depicting their adopted charity. People in the crowd were fanning themselves with programmes beneath golf umbrellas or sunshades, and most were sitting on the ground. I spotted my family up near the gantry and gave them the thumbs up. Squeezing in between Steve, Phil and Terry, I considered the audacity of my position. There is no regulation about the line-up at the start, although it is recognised that one must start in order of ability. The first 200 runners should have been either seasoned athletes or under the age of 21, so I felt a little fraudulent standing this far forward. The presence of my pals eased my guilt slightly, but I still felt like a snowman in the desert. I remembered what someone had said to me in Spain, "you'll sweat buckets just standing there!" and they were right. The morning sun beat down on my head, turning my vest into a Turkish steam room. Rivulets of sweat were running over my forehead and getting into my eyes. The snowman was melting. Reaching into my shorts pocket, I pulled out the flimsy knotted handkerchief that Fernando had given to me and in true 'Brit' style moulded it to my head. Steve and Phil looked on with embarrassed amusement, but I didn't give a toss. I needed shade right now. Standing in the middle of the Rye's playing fields with no protection, waiting for that agonisingly slow clock to strike 9:30, was torturous. My English sombrero was the best shade I was going to get. I pictured Fernando, who would by now be waiting in Manolo's bar with Anna, José and Maria, and consulting his watch. They would be waiting for two phone calls from Richard: one to tell them that the race had begun and the other, of course, to tell them of its outcome. All the usual suspects would have crowded into the bar and Manolo would be doing a roaring trade.

Two thousand, five hundred runners were about to step off into the hottest day on English record, one of them with a hankie on his head, aiming to run it as fast as he possibly could and live to tell the tale! Fernando would definitely be chewing his bottom lip. Today's race was not about money or bitterness, it was about doing our best, and no-one would ask for more. Telling myself that my goal still wasn't impossible, I had an inkling that a drop of 30 degrees and a rocket up my arse might just have its advantages.

"One minute, runners." The public address system said it all; nothing to do now but run. Butterflies danced erratically as digestive acid did overtime in the pit of my stomach. All around me nervous competitors were kicking thin air to ward off anxiety and to get their blood flowing. Phil and Steve on my right both wished me the best of luck and shook my hand; Terry, on my left, did likewise. I felt that I wanted to say more but knew that it wasn't necessary. His advice and help had been invaluable, so I simply clasped his hand and thanked him for what he had done. The massive start and finish clock that was overhead said five seconds to go. I kept repeating, 'You can do it, you can do it.' Terry looked at me, nodded and then looked straight ahead.

There was complete silence.

BANG!

As Andy Warhol once said, everybody will be famous for 15 minutes; I was about to use up five seconds of mine. There were two reasons why I took off the way that I did. Terry had told me that after the first third of a mile, the course crosses the Rye road and at this point a bottleneck develops. Apparently if you're not in the first 200 or so runners at this point, it can cost you seconds, something I just couldn't afford. The second reason for this impulsive behaviour was my old speciality, stupidity. I thought that if I was in front perhaps I could stay in front and the whole throng would push me along. Incredibly, for that first five seconds Don Simmons, the 26 stone alcoholic, fast-food junkie, headed the pack of the Wycombe Half-Marathon, but when what seemed like the world and its mother overtook me shortly afterwards, I was brought straight back to reality. Phil, Steve and Terry all passed me, making gestures with their hands to calm down. Fortunately I didn't get held up as I crossed the Rye road and though position didn't matter in this race, I must have been in the first 250, at least.

The Rye had offered no shade whatsoever, so getting into the avenue of trees was sweet relief. This part I would have to run twice, and it was undoubtedly the coolest part; unfortunately, it was only a quarter of a mile long. Turning left onto Marlow Hill, I started my ascent of the Wycombe Eiger. I checked my watch. "Damn, three seconds down already!" Scores of people were passing me, which was a completely new experience and quite distressing, but I had to bite the bullet and race this my own way. I changed gear and dug in. The heat on this part of the course was intense, as it reflected back from the pavement, making me feel as though I had walked into one of my spray booths while it was baking paint dry. Fernando and Terry, with their best intentions, had deceived me about the Wycombe Hill. It was no way near as steep as its Spanish counterpart and only roughly three-quarters the length. This deception of theirs had been a good idea, but hopefully none of the gains would be spoiled by the sheer heat of the day. My vest and shorts were wringing wet by the time I reached the brow of the hill. The plasters on my nipples had slid off already. That didn't usually happen until the last few miles, if ever, and I hadn't completed Mile two yet! The important thing was to stay positive. If I let in any negative thoughts about the next 11 miles, then I might as well stop there and then.

Nobody passed me on my way up the hill; in fact it was my turn to do some overtaking and I eventually left about 30 runners in my wake, proving how essential the hill training had been in Pineda. Turning into Daws Hill Road I was relieved to see the first watering hole. The ground was strewn with spent plastic cups, which made getting to the table a hazard in itself, but I managed it without mishap. I decided to take full advantage of this feeding station, and grab two cups, even if I did have extra water stops along the way; I was determined to take on additional fluids. Checking the stopwatch again, I saw that I was 22 seconds down — not devastating but still a little disheartening.

The next three miles conveniently had some sporadic shade, but on alternate sides of the road, so I zigzagged my way along the course. It lost me a few more valuable seconds, but I was taking heed of Fernando's advice, "*Corre por la sombra* — run in the shade." Victoria and her husband Bill were waiting anxiously with their three children at Mile four, on a dry desolate spot just outside Flackwell Heath. Suddenly my white-bobbed crown could be made out among the blur of athlete's heads. "That'll be, Don" said Bill, spotting the odd one out. I stomped passed them, taking a bottle of water as I went and grinning broadly. On hearing their shouts of "Goo on Don" and "Get up there 'b'", I felt myself turn as red as a blushing raspberry. Even so, their cheers reminded me of my Spanish fan club and boosted my inner strength.

Only 20 yards on I had run up fast to the back of Terry, who was limping badly and looking over his shoulder. In all the time that I had known Terry, I had rarely heard him raise his voice or blaspheme; in fact, he was always pulling up Les and me for swearing, so what came out of his mouth next was a bit of a shocker. As I approached him, I slowed down to check he was alright.

"Run you fucker!" he blurted at me. The angry expression on his face and the tone of his voice slapped me like a teacher's ruler across an open hand. So Terry was one of the lads after all! His outburst gave a well-timed jolt to my system and I didn't need telling a second time; my lucky trainers were about to burn tarmac.

At Mile five I was parched once again. The sun was so fierce that it evaporated body fluid the moment it left my sweat glands, so it was hard to keep track of how much liquid I was actually losing. Again, I took two cups, drinking one and taking a shower with the other. By now, blood and water were blotted across my vest making it look like the trophy of a boxing match. I was glad that I had wrapped my race number in cling film; otherwise it would have been reduced to *papier maché* and illegible to the judges. Although I wasn't racing against my fellow competitors, I enjoyed the buzz of overtaking other runners. Since the bottom of the hill no-one had passed me and I was surprised to see how many athletes had slowed to a jog or were just walking this part of the course. In fairness, though, it was the sensible thing to do — I simply didn't have that luxury. My determination to run in every available piece of shade must have looked ludicrous to some, for I was running a longer course. But running in the shade kept me running, so I kept on running in the shade.

By the sixth mile I knew that I was in trouble for I was now the wrong side of my time schedule by one minute and twenty seconds. Stopping and sitting down had crossed my mind, several others had taken that option already and were swiftly tended to by the race marshals. Disobeying the council's strict hosepipe ban, a group of Wooburn Common residents lined the streets and formed water arches for the runners to pass under. It felt like I had arrived in Rivendell and flushed any thoughts of quitting from my mind. The emergency feeding station that had been set up just after the seventh mile was so crowded that I decided to pass it altogether, knowing that my own personal water supply was only a mile on. I couldn't afford to be waiting in a queue. My brother and his family were a welcome sight and, as instructed, both my nephews were waiting with outstretched arms, one with water, and the other with Lucozade, spaced roughly 25 yards apart. After I had successfully captured both drinks I continued on my way with echoes of praise ringing in my ears. I almost showered from the wrong bottle again but stopped myself just in time.

The first-aid post at the ninth mile was inundated with some 20 or so runners, whose goals and ambitions had been quashed by the scorching day, but they had nothing to be ashamed of for these were unrealistic race conditions. I now needed to make up 1 minute 38 seconds and I just couldn't see it happening. I cursed the weather over and over as I ran. Perhaps I should have cursed all the carbon dioxide that I'd put into the atmosphere over the years, then perhaps the greenhouse effect wouldn't have been so bad. The queue at the 11th Mile feeding station was worse than the one at the 7th, so it was to my advantage that I could draw from my own supply just half a mile further on. Marion and my family swung into action like a troop of cheerleaders when I came into view. Mathew and June held aloft a banner which read, 'We love you, Dad'; Trish waved two ridiculous pink pompoms that she knew would make me laugh; and they all whooped and hollered in a rather un-British manner. I sprinted towards them and successfully took water in full flight. The sight of my loved ones lifted my spirit and helped me to sail through the next half mile, gaining a precious 32 seconds to boot. With only a mile and a quarter left to go, I was still way adrift from my target.

Just after Mile 12 a small ford ran over a tributary to the river Wye. It was strongly recommended that all runners use the bridge and not get their feet wet because wet feet would raise blisters in no time. I could see a people-jam up ahead, which was forcing runners to a walking pace as they corked up tight on the narrow bridge behind an elderly couple who were either unscrupulous saboteurs or simply oblivious to the obstruction they were causing. Impulse sent me left of the bridge and splashing through the cool waters of the stream, much to the surprise of the stranded athletes. It quickly set a trend though, and a series of splashes could be heard from behind me as I sloshed down the road.

My chest pains were intense now, my laboured breaths were just short pants and my leg muscles burnt from the onslaught of lactic acid; they were no more than hot jelly propelled by kinetic energy. My knee joints felt like they had sharp blades rather than cartilage between them and my raw heels and toes were being tormented with an abrasion akin to wet sandpaper on the skin. I checked the stopwatch; it said 1:23:21. Terry had allowed me seven minutes, 40 seconds to complete the last mile and a bit of the course, which would have left me with a few seconds' leeway, but I was short on time.

"It can't be done," I despaired, "so fucking close, too!" There was nothing more that I could do, my whole body had been drained. Just to finish now was as much as I could hope for. Every competitor bar me was either jogging or walking. Listening to Fernando's advice and having the advantage of a year's training in blistering heat, though never quite as hot as this, together with my personal feeding stations, had given me an advantage. Yet even with all these resources at hand, I could not compete with Mother Nature. Many had said a year ago that what I was actually doing today would be an impossible task. I never once believed that, but reality was now biting hard. Reminding myself that 'It's never over till it's over', I realised that I owed it to too many people not to give up without a fight. Trying to conjure up that deep, locked inner strength that we all possess, the hidden adrenalin that surfaces in times of desperation, I pushed on.

I burst into the Rye again and the glorious shade of the archway of trees. I was a wobbly man, dribbling, drenched in all manner of body fluids, severely hurting and, in truth, spent. The avenue was lined with supporters, respectively applauding each competitor home and I received my full quota, as it appeared that I was the only one still running. Through blurred sepia vision, in a moment of slow motion and complete silence, I zeroed in on Kirsty, wild-eyed and contorted in her wheelchair. Her arms jerked in uncontrolled movements as she tried pathetically to raise them. Her whole body lurched as she formed a sentence from within her withered frame. Aided by her carers who helped to lift her arm, she unleashed a sentence that bore immortality. "Run for me, Don, run for me!" The torment on that once-pretty face and the anguish of being unable to use her body did an incredible thing.

••▼••

Scorched brown grass turned in kaleidoscopic motion at arm's length, two feet from my face. I was in the old Labrador pose on all fours, slowly coming back to reality. Droplets of blood fell from my vest and splashed into the dusty earth beneath me. I watched it in a dream state through the loop of a blue ribbon that hung about my neck. At the end of the silk braid, a golden glinting medallion swung to and fro, catching glints of the sun from above a steaming hunk of flesh. My heartbeat pounded in my ears like a bass drum, my jugular veins ached like they were calcified and any minute now I was going to throw up.

The Wycombe Half-Marathon completion medal, how did I get that? I strained to remember, but had no recollection and began to cry for the second time today.

The toes of a well-polished pair of old black brogue's shuffled under my nose and a white plastic cup of water was brought to my lips.

"There you go son, you'll feel better in a minute."

A reassuring hand helped me into a sitting position and administered the water.

The man from St John's Ambulance was of the old school, in his 60's and living up to his uniform, giving help, support and first aid and offering something that no manual could ever teach you, kindness.

"I'll bring you another one in a tick!" he said, and then stood up to help another casualty. "Well done, by the way, that was some spectacle," he added, looking back.

Done? What had I done? The last few minutes were a complete blank. I looked around at my surroundings; I was in the doorway of the first-aid station, a rather large marquee. It looked more like a field hospital from the Napoleonic wars. Bodies lay everywhere, and those that weren't lying or sitting down were being supported or held by friends, St John's Ambulance workers or paramedics.

Jesus! I thought, and people do this for fun!

On the menu of the High Wycombe Half-Marathon 2000 was blood, sweat and tears. They forgot to mention dehydration, sunstroke and nausea, as every man and woman who took part today would attest to. Every competitor had a right to be proud of whatever they had achieved, for today was as gruelling a challenge as they would ever have to face.

Just ask these two, I thought, looking down at a couple of wrecks who had passed out over the finish line and had to be brought in on stretchers beside me. As promised, the St John's gent returned, this time with a cup of glucose water. I thanked him for his compassion and drank the liquid in one guzzle. I then performed a large rattling burp that attracted ample attention, but made me feel a little better. I started to retrace my steps, but all that I could recollect was Kirsty's face and then being here in the recovery zone.

"Fucking incredible!" said Richard, finding me at last.

"What is?" I asked, slightly taken aback by my solicitor's sudden use of colourful metaphors.

"What you just did could entertain a nation."

"Eh?"

Richard crouched down to fill me in with the events that my mind had inconveniently erased. He had been standing in the crowd, praying for a raincloud to save him from incineration, when suddenly across from the Rye, along the avenue of trees, a lone figure burst forth from the now-pedestrian pack, at lightning speed. All eyes focused on the runner, whose performance was raising loud gasps from the spectators around him. It wasn't until I emerged from behind the boathouse that Richard realised who had caught the crowd's eye. He smiled, "Have you ever seen Forrest Gump?"

"No, why?"

"You two share the same running technique to perfection."

"Oh" I said, letting my bottom lip pout.

"You must have been doing 20 miles an hour! You flew past me and caused a breeze, but with such determination on your face that you almost looked angry. The crowd was cheering and shouting for you. When you crossed the finish line I lost sight of you."

"I don't remember a thing."

"It was fan-fucking-tastic, Don."

Forrest Gump looked at his stopwatch; it was still running.

"What time did I do?"

"What time! You did it mate, you broke an hour and a half! Look, I picked up your certificate."

I stared at the scroll in disbelief. The handwritten time read "1:29:58". I started to smile; a shiver ran up the back of my spine and the hair stood up on my scalp. I laughed and slapped a hand across the scroll.

"You sweet little bastard" I said struggling to my feet. Richard helped me to stand upright. "Does Belington know?"

"You can bet your arse on it."

"I ain't betting fuck-all any more. Come on, let's find Ann."

My solicitor put his shoulder under my arm and walked this lame warrior back to the motorhome. Just then Ann and the kids arrived with more Lucozade. I draped myself around my wife and nearly squeezed the life from her.

"I did it, I did it, I did it love," I panted.

"Told you you would!" said my cocky wife.

"'Ere give us some of that drink, Matt, your old man's dry as a bone." I drank and limped my way back to the Winnebago still puzzled by my memory loss and superhuman sprint. Panic, fear, anxiety or raging anger, all primal emotions, can induce powerful enzymes that trigger enormous strength for short periods of time, often accompanied with memory loss. It defies science, baffles those who witness it and pisses off those who lose £250,000 because of it. Belington was not amused.

Les was fast asleep in one of the garden chairs, lightly snoring with his hands locked across his belly, his legs crossed and a pee stain by his zipper. The three kids sat gently around him while Ann helped me in through the door. Richard sat down and watched the old boy in his slumber, blissfully unaware of history in the making.

"Some mop-up man he's turned out to be," said the lawyer.

Everybody laughed and Les woke with a start.

"You buggers!" he said, picking up his paper with embarrassment.

Ann disrobed her husband in the bathroom. She was upset at the sight of my flesh wounds, but I assured her they looked a whole lot worse than they felt, so she left me to shower on my own.

"Have you seen my handkerchief?" I asked as she went.

"No love, you seem to have lost it."

"Strange, I don't remember it coming off."

She shrugged and left the room.

As usual the cool water did magical things to my mind, body and soul. I stayed in there until the tank went dry, and then emerged a very stiff but contented human being. From the bedroom I could hear a party brewing outside as members of my family arrived back to hear the good news. I looked at my medallion lying on the bed next to Fernando's gold medal and thoughts turned to my pal, "Winners!" I said.

I put on a fresh pair of shorts and a polo shirt then sat down to call my coach. Richard had already let Fernando know the result, but I wouldn't be happy until I'd spoken to him myself. When Manolo answered the phone, he recognised my voice immediately and almost perforated my eardrum by shouting my name. Riotous uproar erupted in the bar at the mention of 'Quixote'. The fiesta was in full swing now that their hero had romped home and people were dancing on tables and drinking sangria straight from glass *cántaros*. Most of them were counting their money.

"You left it a bit tight!" said Fernando above the noise.

"Didn't want to break into a sweat, did I?"

"That's my boy!"

"Listen Fern, I have you to thank for that time."

"Ah, but you ran the race, my friend, the praise is all yours."

"No, but if I hadn't met you I d've given up months ago. You pulled me through."

"Maybe."

"You know I can't accept your medal, don't you?"

"Nonsense, you've done more than I could ever have achieved. You deserve ten of those, besides it only gathers dust on my shelf, Anna is always complaining about cleaning it. No, the thing is yours. You should know that in *España* it is considered an insult to return a gift. Anyway, it'll keep your medal company. I'll hear no more of it."

"That's me told then."

"It certainly is. Now, when are you coming back here? Everybody is missing you terribly."

"I don't know, mate. Maybe next week, I have to speak to Ann first."

"Ok, my friend, call me later and let me know. *Hasta pronto*."

I opened the door to the motorhome to rapturous applause and a standing ovation from the people I held most dear — even Les had stood up. I bowed in a theatrical manner and walked down the steps. The first person I approached was Terry, who was on crutches.

"How you doing, son?" I said.

"I've sprained me ankle, but I'll live."

"How did you do that?"

"Went down the kerb trying to overtake someone, totally my fault."

I winced and said I was sorry. Just then Richard caught my eye and nodded towards the car park. As they do at all the best mafia funerals, some unwanted guests had arrived. In their black suits, Belington and his briefs stood stoical and emotionless, waiting to be seen. The only fitting one among them was the grandson, still fresh as a daisy.

"I'll deal with this, Don," said Richard, but I couldn't let him steal my glory.

All went quiet at the OK Corral as Wyatt Earp and Doc Holiday approached the Clanton Gang.

"Well done!" said the grandson, offering his hand. I was taken aback by the gesture and automatically shook it in return.

"It almost killed me, to tell you the truth; I'll never set myself time limits again."

"You are going to keep on running then?"

"Absolutely, I'm a jog-junkie now!"

We both laughed.

Miss Starchy Knickers was not so amused. She clearly didn't enjoy the torturous conditions she was having to suffer and intent to close the proceedings as soon as possible. "Mr Varsley, I believe that this belongs to you," she said, handing Richard a sealed envelope, and then snapped shut her briefcase. There was no way in hell that she would have given the cheque directly to me, her misplaced ethics just wouldn't allow it. Belington looked at me with cold admiration and nodded; I nodded back acknowledging the old boy's sentiment, and then the disgruntled trio turned and left. The grandson wished me good luck, and then returned to his party. It was a strange feeling. I probably owed that man my life, but sitting down and having a drink with him and telling him what I had been through over the last 12 months was not on the agenda. So a nod of heads, out of mutual respect for each other, for now, would have to suffice.

While we were receiving my winnings, Kirsty, Rory, Lauren and the two carers had arrived. The young man approached me and spoke. "Which of these two envelopes am I supposed to open, sir?" He was such a polite and well-mannered young man.

"Give me the one that has over an hour and a half on it." I said.

He handed it to me and I tore it in half. "Give that one to Kirsty's charity, son," I continued, pointing to the one that remained in his hand. "I'm sure it will be put to good use."

"Yes thank you. I've managed to raise £855 in sponsorship myself."

"Well done, son. This'll help top it up a bit."

I had already witnessed two non-blasphemers turn potty-mouthed today but I couldn't in my wildest dreams ever have imagined the softly spoken Rory talking from the gutter. I was proved wrong. On opening the envelope and seeing the value of the cheque that had been made out to his nominated charity, he resorted to a couple of select words to express his appreciation. "Fucking hell!"

"I hope they do, I can't play the bloody harp!" I said and turned to Kirsty. I knelt down to be at her level and held her shaking hand. In her other hand, she was holding on to my knotted hankie for dear life. I saw it and gave her a smile. "It flew off when you ran past me," she managed to say.

"Then it must belong to you." I said. "You inspired me today, you know?"

"Did I?"

"Indeed you did, God bless you." I said and touched her cheek with my big hands. "You take care of yourself and come and see me race next year!"

"I will!" she said proudly. As her carers wheeled Kirsty away, she was smiling contentedly to herself, happy with her prize sombrero.

By midday a small convoy had snaked its way up through Flackwell into Daws Hill Lane and descended on my gravel drive for the biggest barbecue the Simmons family had ever laid on. Ann brought me home, back to a familiar but somehow different house. The trees had all grown and a swimming pool had been installed, but the house had an unusual feel. It seemed smaller and as if someone had stolen all the furniture and replaced it with scaled-down replicas. Still, I would address that later. There to meet us were Ann's parents who had been feverishly preparing the feast all morning.

"Good God, man, we've had all the reports but this is incredible, where did you go?" said Ann's dad.

"Down the pan I think, Jim, and splashed onto the streets of Spain of course!"

"Well it's good to see you, what's left of you that is. How do you like your tuna steak?"

"Cooked please!"

"Ooh, lot more stamina these days have we, Donald?" said Rose, with a glint in her eye.

"Mum, please!" said Ann.

"I think your daughter's gonna have to employ a few friends, just to keep up with me!" I said half-whispering.

Ann hit me.

Buck and Ben surveyed their master with cocked heads. It smelt like their dad and even sounded like him, but the shape was all wrong.

"There's something different about Dad!" woofed Buck.

"Mmm, he's had a haircut!" replied Ben.

With that, both dogs bounded over and knocked me to the floor, savagely licking me senseless. I couldn't get up through laughter and had to be rescued by Charlie and Mathew, who gave the ecstatic German Shepherds some biscuits and led them away. The kids were very excited about showing their dad the new swimming pool and dragged me round to see it. I was impressed. The builders had done a great job; it was a 14 x 7 metre kidney-shaped pool, with roman steps at one end and a diving board at the other. In no time, it was swamped with a dozen screaming bodies.

"I'll have some of that later," I said to Charlie.

"You wanna, the water's lovely 'n' hot."

We walked back round to where the food was being cooked. I had an appetite now and everything looked delicious. Naturally, it had all been personally approved by Marion.

Instead of the usual barbecue fare, Jim and Rose had laid on tuna and salmon steaks, sardines, vegetarian sausages, pasta salads, bean salads, tossed salads, jacket potatoes, fruit platters, fruit cocktail, olives, pickles, French bread and gallons of alcohol-free sangria.

We all ate our fill, and some of the party were even bold enough to comment on the fact that I only had one helping of anything; my reformed behaviour was going to take people some time to get used to. Les, who had brought back the motorhome, was now fast asleep again in a lawn chair with a roll-up hanging from his bottom lip. As in times of old, I had now taken centre stage and was entertaining everybody with my outrageous tales from Catalonia. There are some things that you just can't change in a man! Ann looked on lovingly and was clearly very pleased with her lot.

Two hours later after being dragged into the pool, thoroughly child handled and having shown off my acquired swimming skills, I took another shower and laid on my bed to call my old friend back in Spain. The party raged on downstairs but I needed a little sanctuary and a chat with my mentor to relay the events of the hardest day in my life. I told Fernando that I would be driving back to Pineda on Wednesday with Ann, and that the children would follow by air on Saturday. That way, I could show her our new home in the hills above Malgrat and have her all to myself for the first time in years. I couldn't wait.

Walking into my wardrobe to retrieve some fresh clothes I was halted in my tracks. The vastness of an old suit that was first off the rail had me staggered; I extracted the trousers and expanded the waist. "I could get three of me in there now," I murmured. "What a waste of material!"

It was eleven o'clock before the last relative finally made their way down the drive. The kids had all gone to their rooms, and we two tired people wandered out to the patio to relax on the wicker sofa and enjoy the evening lament of courteous crickets and love-struck grasshoppers. Ann curled her feet up on the sofa and laid her head on the chest of her most favourite person. The day's heat had lost its ferocity, but it was still warm enough to boil an egg in a glass of water.

"Where have you put the malt collection, love?" I asked at length.

"Oh we had great fun. Brought all the kids round, lined up the lot in the base of the empty swimming pool and smashed them to pieces with house bricks!"

I was mortified. It had taken me 20 years and more than a £100,000 to collect all those rare bottles of malt whisky and the wife had just decimated them with house bricks as though they were empty milk bottles.

"You done what?" I managed to croak, pulling away from her.

"Only kidding!" she teased, I've stored them away in a temperature-controlled storage unit. They're out of harm's way."

I breathed a sigh of relief. "You fucker, I believed you then."

"I know," said the little fox and curled even closer to me. It was then in the warm, moonlit tranquillity of an English summer night, as my heart slid back into a natural rhythm, that I told her in detail about *Finca López* and why she would love it so.

Three days later at about six o'clock in the evening, we found ourselves in the foothills of the Pyrenees, typically singing, Viva, we're off to sunny Spain … After convincing the border control guard that it really was me in my passport photograph, we journeyed on through beautiful Catalonia until we reached the coffee shop and service station at Ola Jonquera that I had used a year or so ago. It hadn't changed one iota and, of course, the barman didn't recognise me, but it still felt like yesterday. As we walked back to the motorhome we inhaled huge breaths of fresh mountain pine air.

"I've got a good feeling about Spain, Don. I think that we might be spending a little bit of time here," said Ann.

My thoughts turned to the restoration work of the old farmhouse. With the *Mañana* brothers on the team, a little bit of time might just be an understatement.

SONG CREDITS

CHAPTER ONE

If I were a rich man from Fiddler on the Roof
Words and music: Jerry Bock, Sheldon Harnick

CHAPTER TEN / CHAPTER THIRTEEN

The impossible dream
Words and music: Joe Darin and Mitch Leigh
First performed in the movie: Man of La Mancha (Don Quixote)

CHAPTER FOURTEEN

Strawberry fields forever,
Words and music by Lennon and McCartney

CHAPTER SEVENTEEN

Swing low sweet chariot
Words and music: African American Spiritual

CHAPTER EIGHTEEN

Y viva España
Words and music: Eddie Seago and Leo Caerts

If you enjoyed reading this book, would you be so kind as to write a review on either Amazon or Goodreads, or both if you have the time, oh and like our Facebook page as well, thank you so much, here's the link:
https://www.facebook.com/pages/The-English-Sombrero/555658614480373

Book two
The English Sombrero, (The Little White Ball)

Seven years on, Don Simmons finds that his beloved local football team Well Green are about to be wound up and the land developed into an exclusive housing estate. Enraged to learn that the developer is a bitter old enemy of his and saddened by the little ninth tier team's demise, he makes it his mission to buy the land embrace the club, inject into it a fortune of his own personnel wealth, and propel this rag tag crew of part time soccer players into the giant slaying arena that is the FA Cup.

This humorous, inspiring, lavish tale will have you gripped to the pages as Don prepares and supplements his boys in two contrasting landscapes, the beautiful sun drenched Spanish Catalonia, and dreary old England, towards an exciting roller coaster ride that is The Football Association Challenge Cup.

Also available on Amazon
http://www.amazon.co.uk/The-English-Sombrero-Little-White-ebook/dp/B00KC5DBWM

Made in the USA
Charleston, SC
09 April 2016